Also by W. R. Dalzell

Living Artists of the Eighteenth Century
Know the Gallery
Architecture the Indispensable Art
Architecture – A Little Colour Guide
London and its Museums

The Shell Guide to

The History of London

W. R. DALZELL

MICHAEL JOSEPH

LONDON

To
Mary Lisa,
whose parents met in London

First published in Great Britain by
MICHAEL JOSEPH LIMITED
44 Bedford Square, London WC1

© 1981 by W. R. Dalzell

ISBN 0 7181 2015 9

Filmset in Great Britain by
BAS Printers Limited,
Over Wallop, Hampshire
Printed in Singapore

Contents

Acknowledgements

Samuel Taylor Coleridge, a pupil of Christ's Hospital, which was situated during his time at the very heart of the City of London, was later to write: 'A dwarf sees farther than a giant, when he has the giant's shoulder to mount on,' and certainly no writer on the history of London can go very far without acknowledging his debt to such giants as John Stow, and to such diarists as Samuel Pepys, John Evelyn and James Boswell. From Henry Chamberlain's *A Compleat History and Survey of London* written in 1768, and from books written by two magnificent Victorians, Edward Walford and Walter Thornbury, I have not only learned a great deal but have been able to reproduce a number of engravings of London. More recent writers to whom I owe much are Walter Besant, William Kent, and, more recently, the ubiquitous and tireless Dr Nicholas Pevsner who has directed me to some of the less obvious aspects of London's architectural history. Libraries and friends on both sides of the Atlantic have contributed significantly to this book. In the USA I am indebted to the courteous and efficient staff at the Central Library on Fifth Avenue, New York; to Melvin Brod who allowed me to use his collection of difficult-to-get books; and to my oldest American friend, Dr Frederick Hartt, Professor of Fine Art at the University of Virginia, from whose advice I have benefited so much.

Nearer home, I owe a great deal to the staffs of the Guildhall and the Victoria and Albert libraries, and to the Museum of London, which is still one of the world's finest sources of information on London's history. Others who have been of immense help are Mr C. Muris and his staff at the Bedfordshire Country Library, Mr Baker and the staff of the North Bedfordshire District Library, and Mrs M. Barley of the Reader Services Department, who have never failed to produce for me even the most obscure reference book. I should also like to record my thanks to an old friend and ex-colleague, Graham Woodmansterne, not only for the use of his intimate knowledge of Westminster Abbey, but for permission to draw upon the splendid range of colour transparencies produced by his firm, and to say how much I regret that the late Kenneth Crick who assisted me in so many ways with the text died before the book was actually in print. Others to whom I owe much include Shell Petroleum who sponsored this book; Alan Brooke of Michael Joseph Ltd who accepted the brief with enthusiasm and encouragement; and latterly Miss Jennie Davies upon whom fell the difficult task of cutting and shaping a voluminous and unwieldy text to its present state – a task she performed with an efficiency and charm so that never at any time could I do other than acquiesce as she pruned to produce a far better book than it had been when it first left my hands.

Bedford, 1981

Illustrations

The author and publishers would like to thank the following for permission to reproduce their pictures in *The Shell Guide to the History of London*: Woodmansterne Publications Ltd for black and white pictures on pages 22, 27, 28, 29, 30, 35, 36, 38, 39, 40, 47, 51, 53, 54, 60, 62, 66, 69, 74, 75, 78, 79, 81, 83, 85, 87, 89, 93, 94, 97, 99, 102, 103, 127, 129, 142, 147, 153, 178, 184, 187, 189, 220, 225, 227, 231, 266, 291, 295, 315, 324, 330, 337, 364, 371, 376, 385, 426, 437, 443 and 445, and for colour pictures on pages 4, 8, 11 and 27 of the colour section; the British Tourist Authority for pictures on pages 113, 120, 260, 262, 263, 265, 267, 315 and 318; Robert Haas for pictures on pages 446, 449, 450, 456, 457, 461 and 471; John Bardsley, F.R.P.S., for pictures on pages 303, 305 and 307; the National Portrait Gallery for the pictures on page 138; and the Museum of London for their picture on page 145.

List of colour illustrations

List of black and white illustrations

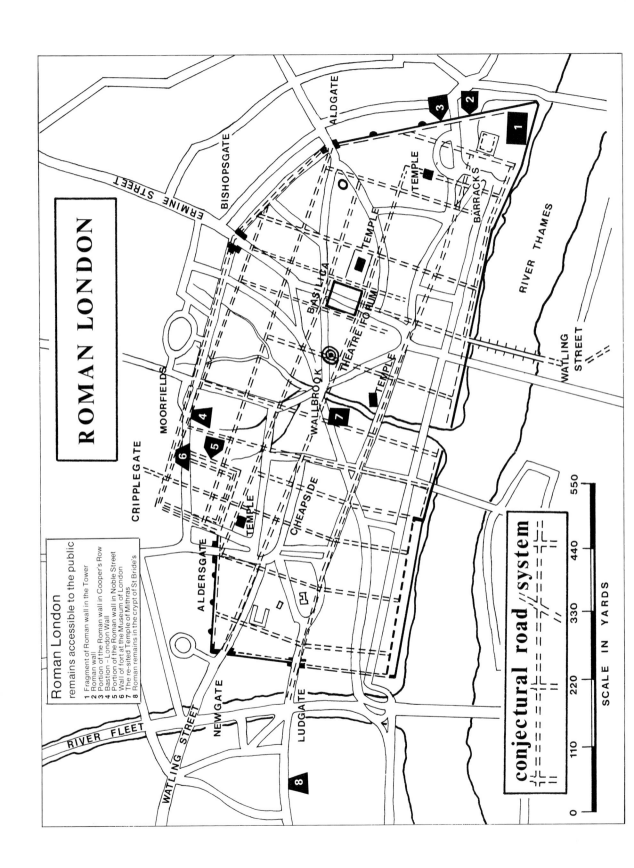

ROMAN LONDON

Roman London
remains accessible to the public

1 Fragment of Roman wall in the Tower
2 Roman wall
3 Portion of the Roman wall in Cooper's Row
4 Bastion – London Wall
5 Portion of the Roman wall in Noble Street
6 Wall of fort at the Museum of London
7 The re-sited Temple of Mithras
8 Roman remains in the crypt of St Bride's

ERMINE STREET

BISHOPSGATE

ALDGATE

TEMPLE

BARRACKS

RIVER THAMES

WATLING STREET

TEMPLE

BASILICA

FORUM

THEATRE

TEMPLE

MOORFIELDS

CRIPPLEGATE

WALLBROOK

TEMPLE

CHEAPSIDE

ALDERSGATE

TEMPLE

NEWGATE

WATLING STREET

RIVER FLEET

LUDGATE

conjectural road system

SCALE IN YARDS

0   110   220   330   440   550

I

Roman London:
the First Four Hundred Years

The excavations made in London following the savage destruction by the bombs of the Second World War brought to light extensive evidence of Roman London. The history of the city begins with the invasion of Britain AD 43 by Aulus Plautius who chose the site of London as the base from which to invade and conquer the rest of the country. By the time of the invasion by Boudicca (Boadicea) in AD 61 it had developed from a camp into a fortified town, but the legions had gone north leaving it only lightly garrisoned and vulnerable to attack.

The military capital at that time was Colchester (Camulodunum) and it was governed by Decianus Catus, a Roman Procurator whose cruelty and avarice was such that Boudicca, the Queen of the Iceni, an East Anglian tribe, was goaded into revolt. Assisted by the Trinovantes from Essex, she not only sacked and burned Colchester and St Albans (Verulamium) and put their inhabitants to death; she then swept on to raze London to the ground and to butcher all who were unsuccessful in reaching the safety of the Roman forces. Tangible evidence of this catastrophe has been found in ashes and burned reddish clay excavated in the heart of the modern City in the area of Lombard Street* and Gracechurch Street*. A more humane and tolerant Procurator, Julius Classicianus, was later to heal the wounds of the savage reprisals which followed Boudicca's rebellion, and a memorial slab to this peace-making Roman official is preserved in the British Museum.

It was a somewhat later Roman London which was to leave an indelible mark on modern London, for sometime between AD 190 and AD 210 an incredibly ambitious programme of defence was carried out, and the entire city was surrounded by a great wall some 18 to 20 feet high, and about 8 feet thick. This wall, built during the governorship of Clodius Albinus, an ambitious man who aspired to the position of emperor, was to fix the boundaries of the City of London – boundaries which are, indeed, very little different from those of the City today, although some expansion westwards was to take place later.

As London was built on clay – there was almost no stone suitable for building purposes anywhere in the area, and certainly not enough for the construction of this wall – barges were sent down the Thames and up the River Medway to be loaded with Kentish ragstone from quarries near Maidstone in the heart of Kent. One such barge, with an estimated capacity

*An asterisk in the text denotes an entry in Appendix II

A portion of the Roman wall in the Wardrobe Tower at the Tower of London

of about twenty-five cubic metres, was found buried in the river bed upstream of London Bridge, near Blackfriars; if all the barges used were of this size it has been calculated that about 1300 bargeloads of stone must have been required to build this vast encircling wall, even assuming that the efficient Roman engineers would have utilised existing fortifications and incorporated them into the new scheme of defences. The wall also incorporated and strengthened existing city gates erected to guard the exits of the important supply routes for the legions garrisoned in other parts of Britain – the broad straight roads which formed the basis for many of our modern highways.

The walls were not in fact made of solid stone. Only the outer layers were of carefully cut and squared blocks of stone, the space between being filled with rubble and irregular lumps of stone held together into a dense mass with mortar. The cut blocks were laid to the height of a yard, the in-fill was added, levels were checked and a course of red Roman bricks, each brick measuring about $1\frac{1}{2}''$ thick, 18″ wide and 12″ long was laid on top. This procedure was quite often repeated two or three times, and such brick levelling courses are clearly visible in the massive fragment of wall to the rear of Tower Hill underground station.

The wall began in the area now occupied by the Tower of London, and some of the early work can still be seen embedded in the fragment of the Wardrobe Tower just south east of the great Norman keep. The course of the Roman wall can be traced quite clearly from the Tower precincts right round

the City, despite the fact that some of it is inaccessible to visitors, having been incorporated into the cellars of factories, offices and warehouses or used as foundation stones for modern buildings. One huge piece of the wall, which rears itself up like a cliff face and which has survived wind, weather, fire and even high-explosive bombs, is to be seen to the south of Tower Hill underground station. The carefully laid ragstone courses, separated by the thin bands of levelling courses of red brick, are clearly visible here; they are also to be seen in a fragment some thirty feet long in the yard of Cooper's Row, immediately to the north of the station. There the Roman wall is topped by a substantial area of medieval wall with round-headed embrasures still intact. Inside the underground station there is another piece of Roman wall, just south of Platform 1, and another large fragment is incorporated in the wall of Roman Wall House, in Crutched Friars*, near Fenchurch Street* Station.

As our map shows, the wall of the Roman City of London continued in a north-westerly direction for about 350 yards, until it reached the old site of Aldgate*, slightly to the west of the modern Aldgate underground station. It then changed direction, running more or less parallel to modern Houndsditch*, along a track now formed by Duke's Place*, Bevis Marks*, and Camomile Street*, when it was incorporated into another Roman gatehouse, Bishopsgate*. The last gate at Bishopsgate was destroyed in the eighteenth century, but was, of course, a great deal later than the original Roman one. From Bishopsgate the course of the wall takes its rightful name, London Wall, turning due west and stretching about six or seven hundred

left, A section of the Roman wall in Tower Hill, showing the levelling course
right, A section of the Roman and medieval wall in the Coopers buildings, near Tower Hill

A section of the Roman wall near St Alphege, London Wall

yards to join the site of the Roman garrison fort of Cripplegate*. The intensive bombing of this area during 1940 revealed a great deal of the Roman fortifications, and very substantial remains are easily seen just to the north of the fragments of St Alphage, overlooking the modern street of London Wall. Here the Roman wall has been patched, repaired and heightened by medieval and Tudor builders; the small red Tudor bricks are clearly visible in parts. Still further west, separated only by a shallow moat from the churchyard of St Giles, Cripplegate, and more or less incorporated into the Museum of London in the Barbican* area, is one of the best preserved and restored of all the Roman fortifications. It can be studied from a window in the Museum of London, in conjunction with an excellent map and explanatory diagrams and text. This wall has rounded bastions and a walkway from which patrolling legionaries could have kept vigil, or, if necessary, brought the catapult-like balistae into action against any enemy forces threatening the city from the north.

From the Cripplegate Fort area, the wall turned westward, linking Aldersgate* with the fort, and then joined that gate with Newgate, the fortified exit for roads to such Roman strongholds as Silchester, Winchester and other Roman settlements still further west. The wall then turned due south, and some of this southern stretch is still to be seen near St Bartholomew's Hospital in cellars under the transport yard of the GPO on the east side of Giltspur Street. The wall is also visible in the Old Bailey area, and it was here, appropriately enough, near the modern Central Criminal Court, that the remains of a Roman counterfeit coin-maker's workshop were found

City gates before their demolition in the eighteenth century

hidden in a stairway of a Roman tower; these remains are now to be seen in the London Museum. The discovery of genuine coins, terracotta moulds and some counterfeit coins enabled archaeologists to date this part of the wall with accuracy, and it is as well that no enthusiastic amateur collector or souvenir hunter arrived first to pocket such invaluable means of identification for his own private collection.

The last exit through the wall from the Roman city was Ludgate*, which linked the western defences to those along the river bank. The Fleet river, which is now conduited under modern Farringdon Street, was not only an additional line of defence, running parallel to the north-south stretch of wall, but was at that time the western boundary to the city.

Although Aldgate and Newgate are the only two gates which are known for certain to be of Roman origin, the pattern of Roman London seems to indicate that each exit of the main roads linking the city with other Roman settlements was guarded by a well fortified gate. No record exists of the names by which they were known to the Romans; they are therefore known by their Saxon names. Watling Street* linked Canterbury and Rochester with London, entering the city over London Bridge. It appears to have crossed the city to emerge along the route now taken by Oxford Street before turning north along the modern Edgware Road towards St Albans. Another branch of Watling Street continued along the modern Bayswater Road to link London with Silchester in Hampshire. On the east side of London, Ermine Street emerged through Bishopsgate, and, turning north, led to Lincoln, then to York, and finally to Hadrian's Wall, the mighty fortification erected across the north of England to keep out the barbarian hordes from Scotland. Through Aldgate ran the main road to Colchester. It is clear from these important roads that although London was never a major Roman military base, it was clearly a nodal point of communications for Roman Britain, an important port and supply base, and a great trading centre.

While the pattern of the great wall defining the limits of the Roman city and of the City of London yet to be built can be fairly accurately established, the pattern within those walls is by no means clear. After nearly two thousand years, the arrangements of the inner streets can only be deduced by piecing together fragments of an historical jigsaw puzzle so complex that much of what has been written can only be intelligent or inspired guesswork. Nevertheless, on the evidence of Roman cities discovered elsewhere we know that the Romans, a military and engineering people, organised their settlements in a series of rectangular patterns, the temporary military camps becoming permanent cities as the country became peaceful. Thus it is reasonably certain that London too was planned with a gridiron layout. The site chosen, however, was not entirely flat, for London has two low hills – Cornhill to the east, and Ludgate Hill to the west, with the little River Walbrook forming a valley between them. The importance of traces of buildings found in different parts of the city can be deduced to some extent by the nature and the quality of things excavated in those areas, and now exhibited in the London Museum and the British Museum.

The Cornhill area, including Gracechurch Street, Lombard Street, and Leadenhall Market*, contained a large and very important building – a basilica and forum about 400 feet long. The superb mosaic pavement, discovered in Leadenhall Street in 1803 and now in the British Museum, was clearly not part of any ordinary building. Another fine specimen was discovered about two years later and is in the same museum. This complex seems to have included a City Hall, Law Courts and a commercial centre, but none of this is now visible to a visitor apart from the fragments to be seen in museums. These include remnants of a mosaic pavement and a medallion depicting Bacchus on a tiger found in Leadenhall Street in 1803.

Another important Roman building, which was almost certainly the

Governor's palace, lies buried under Cannon Street* station, just south of Walbrook*. It would appear, however, that even important buildings in London would have been inferior to those in comparable cities on the mainland of Europe, for although one almost automatically envisages a Roman building with an impressive portico and stone columns crowned with elaborately carved capitals, no single column and only one rudimentary capital have been discovered in the London area. Any such buildings must have been built of brick made from the London clay, covered with stucco, rather like those of eighteenth-century London buildings.

One very interesting relic, once believed to be of Roman London, is to be found on the north side of Cannon Street in a niche in the National Bank of China, just opposite Cannon Street station. This is the London Stone. It was formerly sited on the south side of Cannon Street, but then transferred to the north side and later, in 1798, to the wall of the Wren church, St Swithin's. When the church was destroyed by bombing in the Second World War the stone was retrieved and placed in a niche, and it is now protected by a grille. There is no documentary evidence of its Roman origin, but it is certainly of great antiquity, and it was Camden, the Elizabethan antiquary, who thought that it was a milestone from which the Romans measured distances from London to other settlements. It might alternatively be of Saxon origin.

The London Stone,
Cannon Street

21

The head of Mithras,
to be seen at the
London Museum

The whole area around this part of Cannon Street, including Walbrook and Bucklesbury*, has provided a number of important Roman relics. In 1889, a plaque dedicated to Mithras, the god around whom a rival religion to Christianity had been built, came to light in Walbrook. The most recent significant discovery, in 1954, of an almost intact pattern of foundations of a complete Mithraic temple in the same area, and a number of very fine artefacts on the same site, was of even great significance. Commercial

considerations made it impossible for the site of the temple to remain uncovered, so a compromise was arranged whereby the complete ground plan of the temple was reconstructed with the original stone on a site in Queen Victoria Street about a hundred yards west of the original temple. The artefacts are beautifully preserved and displayed in the Museum of London. There are also substantial remains of a Roman house in Lower Thames Street, discovered 1848–59, with the underfloor heating arrangement (a hypocaust) of the bath-house almost intact. At the time of writing permission to view this must be obtained through the Museum of London. So many different aspects of Roman London are so beautifully displayed in this museum (including the reconstruction of a complete room with its original mosaic floor) that visitors to London would be well advised to spend much of their time there, rather than dissipate their energies seeking out some of the less obvious and rather scattered remnants of the London of this era.

The condition of the house in Lower Thames Street has strengthened the theory that after the withdrawal of the Roman legions in AD 410, London continued much as before for some time. This withdrawal was effected by the inept Roman emperor Honorius who, appalled at the disintegration of his empire by the barbarian hordes from the east – they were even threatening Rome itself – retreated from London, the most northerly of his colonies, declaring that he could no longer be responsible for its defence. He thus abandoned Londinium, one of the wealthiest commercial centres north of the Alps – the city by this time had become a vital centre of

The temple of Mithras on its new site

communications and trade for the whole of the Roman colony. As the fertile lands of Kent and Sussex fell into the hands of invading Saxons, food supplies to the city began to dwindle, and eventually, with trade declining, it would seem that London was gradually abandoned by its Romano-British inhabitants. The house in Lower Thames Street, in fact, appears to have fallen down from neglect, and not as the result of a battle. Under the debris was found a fine circular Saxon brooch lost by some casual visitor to the ruined house.

The recent excavations at Watling Court, opposite Mansion House underground station at the junction of Bow Lane* and Cannon Street, may throw more light on this confused period of London's history.

There is a tendency for modern scholars to reject the idea of the 'Dark Ages' – that ill-defined period between the declaration of withdrawal by Honorius in AD 410 and the Norman invasion in 1066 – since so many examples of fine craftsmanship, such as jewellery and ornamental metal objects, and illuminated manuscripts, suggest the existence of a civilisation of a very superior order. Nevertheless, the inhabitants of London who replaced the Romano-British were neither builders in brick nor workers in stone, preferring the more temporary structures of wood with which they had been more familiar in their own darkly forested lands. When compared with such magnificent buildings as the churches of San Vitale or the tomb of Galla Placidia in Ravenna, both built early in the sixth century, the pathetic remnants of Saxon buildings show how inferior the new inhabitants of London were as builders and architects by comparison with their Roman predecessors and their Italian contemporaries. The troubled times which followed the withdrawal of the Roman legions were not conducive to the arts of peace, and it is significant that most of the finest objects preserved from this period are directly or indirectly connected with warfare or warriors.

Little remains of the Vikings invaders of London with whom the Saxons were continually in conflict, although a few names still to be found on the map of modern London recall the impact of the Danes on the city. St Magnus the Martyr, and St Olave are both churches whose names derive from this period, while Tooley Street in Southwark is a corruption of St Olave, too, and St Clement Danes, just outside the western boundary of the City, obviously has some connection with the Danish Christians. Among the more tangible remains, there are some ferociously beautiful axes and other weapons in the Museum of London, and a helmet of the pattern familiar to readers of popular romances of the Norsemen. There is also an intricately carved Viking tombstone, found in St Paul's Churchyard in 1852, in the Museum of London.

Of the Saxon period of London's history there is more to be seen, although there is little to compare with the splendour of the *Sutton Hoo* treasure – the Anglo-Saxon royal ship burial deposit found in Suffolk in 1939 and now in the British Museum. Again, some of the finest specimens of metalwork are weapons. There are very few architectural remains, though in the crypt of St Bride's Church in Fleet Street there is an excellent display which shows the development of one present-day City church, built on a Roman site with the foundations of a Saxon church. There is also more evidence of Roman and Saxon London in the church of All Hallows, Barking, just to the west of the Tower of London, where there are the remains of two Roman tessellated pavements in the undercroft and fragments of three Saxon crosses, the latter datable at between AD 1000 and 1060. It is, however, on the ground floor, that the most significant example of the work of a Saxon builder is to be found: a Saxon doorway, fashioned from Roman bricks – probably part of a seventh or eighth-century church on this site. Crude though it is, it is an important indication of the building methods of the early Christians in London.

To find work of a much more sophisticated kind, but of a later date, it is necessary to leave the City of London, and to go to Westminster Abbey, to parts of the original abbey built by Edward the Confessor and completed only a week before his death in 1066. One might regard this part of the building either as the very last phase of Saxon architecture, or the earliest phase of Norman architecture – or merge the two periods in the general phrase 'English Romanesque', to compare it with 'French Romanesque', 'Italian Romanesque', etc. The structural principles are the same, but their application varies from country to country, and the British, in this isolated and insular country, needed the impact of the invasion of William the Conqueror to provide access to the most modern building and engineering techniques already in use on the mainland of Europe. The first great Norman building in London was the keep or White Tower of the Tower of London.

ENTRY TO THE TRAITORS' GATE

2

The London of William the Conqueror and the early Middle Ages

W illiam the king greeteth William the bishop and Godfrey the portreeve and all burgesses within London, French and English, friendly . . .' These are the opening words of the charter which was granted to the City of London by the victorious William of Normandy when King Harold, his rival to the throne of England, had been defeated and slain at the Battle of Hastings. The charter was intended as a reward to the city for its lack of resistance; it was also a foretaste of the peculiarly independent status it enjoys even today. In spite of his grip on London, William realised that his position was still precarious, so he set to work to build a mighty castle of stone to replace the temporary wooden fort at the south-eastern end of the Roman wall.

This great Norman keep (or donjon) is the famous White Tower, which is the focal point of the Tower of London today – a 90-foot high building, roughly rectangular, measuring 107 feet from north to south and 118 feet across. It was, at that time, the biggest and most sophisticated castle ever built in this country, for the Normans brought with them a technical expertise from the mainland of Europe quite unknown to the inhabitants of this island. The walls are 15 feet thick at the base to defend the castle from being undermined, and 12 feet thick in the upper storeys. They are built from pale stone quarried in Caen, Normandy, and then ferried in a succession of rafts across the Channel and up the Thames. Neither the walls nor the columns within the castle are of solid stone. The usual practice was to build strong hollow walls of ashlar, cutting and fitting the squared blocks as precisely as possible, then filling the spaces with irregular stone well impacted, and held in place with mortar. Similarly, the columns within the castles were not usually made from drums of stone but resembled more closely a robust well, filled with rubble and capped with a solid capital. The White Tower shows all these typically Norman features, its massive walls strengthened with shallow pilaster-like buttresses of the white Caen stone from which the White Tower probably derives its name. The original entrance to the keep was at the first-floor level on the southern side, facing the river, and was reached by an outer stairway defended by a fore-building of stone, but all this has been recently replaced with a sturdy wooden staircase which is now one of the main public entrances.

Since its completion in 1097, the White Tower and its surrounding buildings have had many roles to play. Until the seventeenth century, for example, it was customary for the monarch-to-be to spend the night prior to

opposite, The Tower of London, with Traitors' Gate in the foreground

27

A model of the Tower of London as it was in the early middle ages, on view in the Museum of London

opposite: above, An engraving of the Tower of London showing the development of the outer walls, taken from Chamberlain's *History of London*; *below*, an aerial view of the Tower of London and the surrounding buildings

the coronation safely in the Tower. The Tower was always a fortress, of course, and a great armoury was essential for most of its history. It still contains a superb collection of arms and armour and is reputed to be the oldest museum in the country; there is still a team of skilled armourers on the premises who maintain the armour in its remarkably fine condition and restore pieces missing from the original suits.

The Treasury was also based in the White Tower at one time, and today the Tower of London still guards the magnificent collection of crowns, coronets, sceptres and other priceless objects which constitute the Crown Jewels. The location of the Mint was the same. In order to safeguard the country's economic stability, it was essential that the monarch should control the issue of coinage, ensure that it was of a standard weight and purity of metal, and protect the precious dies from which the coins were struck so that no unauthorised person could debase the coinage with forgeries; savage penalties were inflicted on anyone foolhardy enough to attempt this.

As Britain has been a maritime nation from the earliest days of its history, and as navigation at sea is primarily based on the stars, the all-important Royal Observatory was also located in the Tower; this occupied the north-eastern tower in the keep until Sir Christopher Wren built Flamsteed House at Greenwich in 1675. Thus, although many people regard the Tower of London only as a fortress or as a former prison and place of execution, through the centuries it has performed many varied functions. Until the opening years of the nineteenth century it was even a menagerie to which

Traitors' Gate

crowds flocked to see the lions, tigers and other exotic animals which had been acquired by the Crown. Now only the famous Tower ravens remain.

The Norman keep has always been the very core of the defences of the Tower of London, but as methods of attack became more sophisticated and more effective, successive monarchs from King Edward I onwards were obliged to increase the defences of this key fortress, encircling the whole area with a wet moat of about 120 feet wide and some 20 feet deep, fed by the Thames – a formidable obstacle to any aggressor. The moat was drained in 1843 and now acts as a parade ground, even providing space for football pitches. In addition to the moat an outer 'curtain' was built, a series of carefully sited strong points – towers which integrated the sprawling complex into one tightly locked defensive unit. Each opening in this outer wall was guarded by gatehouses equipped with portcullises – some of which can still be seen.

The effectivenes of the whole defence system can best be studied from the northern end of Tower Bridge, that Victorian pastiche of medieval architecture which contrasts so strangely with the genuine buildings of the Tower. From this site, one can more readily see how the huge White Tower dominates the outlying walls. To the north of the Tower this is less apparent, because the view from Tower Hill station is obscured by later buildings which mask the savage splendour of the Norman keep. The outer defensive wall to the south is immediately behind the wharf which borders the river and which now has a rather charming restaurant. At the eastern end of the wall, nearest to Tower Bridge, there is a minor tower called Develin Tower, and to the west of this lies the Cradle Tower, so called because it was from this tower that a cradle was suspended by which small boats could be hauled ashore, or deposited into the moat. St Thomas's Tower, clearly a most important strong point, occupies the centre of the southern or riverside wall, and guards the great arch of Traitors' Gate. During the Middle Ages, prisoners who had been condemned in the courts at Westminster were brought under escort by water to the Tower. Water was considered a safer means of conveyance than road as there were unlikely to be any desperate rescue attempts by friends of the prisoner. A number of distinguished prisoners entered the Tower by the notorious Traitors' Gate, including the young Princess Elizabeth, (later Queen Elizabeth I of England) but, unlike her, few emerged from the Tower alive. St Thomas's Tower was heavily restored in the nineteenth century, and the river now no longer flows under Traitors' Gate. Still further to the west is one of the main entrances – a guardhouse called the Byward Tower where all visitors were stopped and asked for the byword or password. The most westerly of the entrances is now the Middle Tower, but, as its name implies, there was once an outer entrance, the Lion Gate, which was destroyed when the lions were transferred to Regent's Park zoo. The site is now occupied by a modern tearoom, a tourist shop and other facilities for visitors. However, from the vantage point at the northern end of Tower Bridge, it is hardly possible to examine this side of the Tower, and visitors should walk along the eastern side, looking at the exterior walls and their defensive towers, then on westwards and southwards until they reach the Middle Tower. This walk will not only explain the geography of the Tower, but will give some idea of the complexity of the defences and of the various buildings within its walls.

Even from the pavement, despite the width of the moat, the outer curtain wall can be seen. This was largely the work of thirteenth-century masons employed by King Edward I, and it was later strengthened in the sixteenth century during the reign of the Henry VIII by the addition of two prominent bastions – one, Brass Mount, at the far end of the approach to Tower Bridge, and the other in a corresponding position on the far side, opposite Tower Hill. The Salt Tower can be seen to the north, down the gentle slope of Tower Bridge Approach. At one time it was called Julius Caesar's Tower – quite wrongly, for it is certainly not Roman work. This almost circular tower derives its name from its function during the Middle Ages, for it was there that meat was preserved in salt for the feeding of the garrison during the winter months when little fresh meat was available. It was also, of course, an essential link in the chain of watch-towers by which the Tower defences were held together. The next tower to the north is Broad Arrow Tower, but no satisfactory explanation of its name has yet been found although one reasonable one suggests that it might be connected with the custom of stamping Government property with a broad arrow mark. Still further north is Constable Tower – a strong point which was never apparently a prison, but at one time was possibly the home of the Constable of the Tower. With Martin Tower one reaches the far end of the eastern side and a tower which dates from the reign of King Henry III in the mid-thirteenth century, but nobody knows who 'Martin' was, nor why the tower is named after him. It was when the Crown Jewels were housed in this tower (they were transferred from the keep during the reign of Charles I), however, that Colonel Blood, a seventeenth-century adventurer, almost succeeded in stealing them. He was arrested and brought before Charles II, who, strangely enough, released him without further punishment and restored his Irish lands which had previously been confiscated. Immediately in front of Martin Tower is Brass Mount Battery; its gaping mouth no longer holds a cannon. Turning westwards from Martin Tower, a somewhat undistinguished building, Brick Tower, rises above a series of eighteenth-century brick houses; it was here that Sir Walter Raleigh was imprisoned and then later released by James I to undertake his unsuccessful expedition to the New World in 1615. Further to the west, standing on the remains of the old Roman wall, is Bowyer Tower, built by Edward I and formerly the headquarters of the Royal Bowmaker. This is traditionally the building in which the unfortunate Duke of Clarence drowned in a butt of Malmesey wine in 1478, having been imprisoned by his brother, Edward IV. Its companion to the west is Flint Tower, which once had the far more sinister name of Lytle Helle, although the original building was demolished and replaced by the present one in 1796. Flint Tower is joined by a secret underground passage to Devereux Tower, the most westerly fortification of the northern wall. Built during the reign of Richard II towards the end of the fourteenth century it, too, was once known as Julius Caesar's Tower. It was in this building that

Robert Devereux, the third Earl of Essex, was held after his ill-judged and ill-fated rebellion against the queen who had showed him such favours in the past. From Devereux Tower he made his last journey to the place of execution within the tower walls; he died by the headsman's axe in 1601. Legge's Mount Battery, Henry VIII's gun emplacement, is positioned in front of Devereux Tower. Turning south towards the main entrance, down the gentle slope of Tower Hill, Beauchamp Tower is the dominant central building on the western wall. It was erected by Edward I in the thirteenth century to strengthen the original fortifications and has been the prison of many distinguished people. It derives its name from the rebellious Thomas Beauchamp, Earl of Warwick, who was imprisoned there by Richard II, but restored to favour by the victorious Henry IV in 1399. From the Beauchamp Tower there is another walkway – a short passage to the Bell Tower, known as Elizabeth's Walk; it was there that the young Princess Elizabeth was held prisoner by her half-sister, Mary Tudor, in 1554. The picturesque timber walls of the yeoman gaoler's house which adjoins the Beauchamp Tower and the Queen's House beside are deceptively cosy. From the windows of this house the unhappy Lady Jane Grey was to watch her husband's headless body brought back from his execution on the following day, and the famous conspirators of the 'Gunpowder Plot', whose failure to blow up the Houses of Parliament in 1605 is still celebrated with bonfires and fireworks every 5 November, were interrogated there.

In order to examine many of the towers more closely (not all of them are open to the public) it is necessary to pause by the remains of the old causeway and foundations of the medieval drawbridge, buy tickets at the little offices by the main gate, and go to the Middle Tower, an impressive thirteenth-century gatehouse over which is carved a magnificent coat of arms of the Royal House of the eighteenth century. It is at the Middle Tower that the visitor first encounters that splendid body of men – the yeomen warders, popularly known as beefeaters. Deceived perhaps by the abundant publicity which every tourist office throughout the world carries of the yeomen warders in their magnificent scarlet and gold uniforms, it is something of an anti-climax to find them clothed more practically in their dark blue tunics with red braid and somewhat incongruous long trousers – a uniform first given to them in November 1858 to replace the ceremonial uniform. According to the *Illustrated London News* of 27 November, 'The majority of the warders approve[d] of the change. . . .' The nickname 'beefeater' should properly be applied not to the yeomen warders at the Tower of London, but to another corps dressed in almost identical uniform, the yeomen of the guard, who formerly served the buffet at St James's Palace and were therefore known as 'buffetiers'. At the Tower the yeomen warders are now used mainly as guides – and they do the job extremely well for, as their rows of medals show, they are all ex-Army men, and the experience they gained as NCOs on the parade ground has given their voices carrying power and clarity. The yeomen warders are also involved in the security of the Tower and its occupants, however temporary, although one IRA 'hero' did manage to evade their vigilance during the tourist season and planted a bomb

A picture from the *Illustrated London News* showing the new uniforms given to the yeomen warders in 1858

within the White Tower with the intention to maim and to kill innocent visitors.

If application is made in writing to the Resident Governor, it is also still possible to view one of the most ancient and most impressive ceremonies in which the yeomen warders are involved every night at ten o'clock. This is the ceremony of the keys when the chief warder of the Tower, with a guards escort, performs the ritual locking up of the Tower for the night. The history of the ceremony goes back at least seven hundred years, but as with so much of the history of the Tower, its origins have been lost.

From the entrance through the Middle Tower and its security check, one crosses the dry moat and passes under the arch of the Byward Tower, with its upper storey of timber. A high wall hides the river on the right, and on the left another equally high wall is surmounted by the thirteenth-century Bell Tower with its little cupola of wood. The next stop is obviously at Traitors' Gate, with its huge arch and St Thomas's Tower above. To the left, under a high arch with a fine vault of intricate stone, the path leads to the Wakefield Tower and ultimately to the notorious Bloody Tower. To enter the Bloody Tower and to make one's way up the narrow spiral staircase is to experience something of the difficulty which even a small, lightly armed intruder would have had in the past, particularly as there would have been an armed guard waiting at the top of the staircase. The steps are narrow even by the wall, and

above, The Byward
Tower
right, The Wakefield
Tower

34

by the central support they are so narrow that there is scarcely a toehold, let alone a foothold.

In the Bloody Tower visitors can see the cumbersome apparatus with which the portcullis was operated and, almost adjoining, the room in which Sir Walter Raleigh spent much of his imprisonment in comparative comfort – a kind of house arrest during which he fathered a son and wrote his history of the world. The furniture and fittings seen there today are of the same period, but are not claimed to be those actually used by Sir Walter. At the base of the stairs were found the skeletons of two boys, alleged to be the hidden remains of the Princes in the Tower, whose death was attributed to the villainy of Richard III by his enemy and usurper, Henry VII. The discovery of these pathetic remains during the reign of Charles II is one very good reason why this part of the Tower of London was given such a grisly name. Outside the tower is a narrow walkway from which Sir Walter Raleigh and other prisoners could gaze across the river, longing for freedom, while to the north they could see the site of the scaffold, and beyond that the chapel of St Peter ad Vincula (St Peter in chains) and its churchyard where many who died at the hands of the executioner lie buried. Here, for example, lies the body of Anne Boleyn – that body which so plagued the desire of Henry VIII, only to be flung headless into a rough wooden box which had been used for storing arrows.

There is a chapel, however, within the White Tower – the Norman chapel

Sir Walter Raleigh's bedroom in the Bloody Tower

St John's Chapel

of St John, one of the most important examples of the ecclesiastical architecture of that period in England. It has the characteristically sturdy round columns, semicircular arches, simple heavy capitals and bases, and, for so early a building, a boldly vaulted nave like a tunnel, and a gallery with the same roof construction. The bare cold stone that one sees today gives the whole building a kind of craggy dignity, but the murals on the inside walls would originally have provided a barbaric splendour of colouring. The nave has an ambulatory encircling it for processional purposes. The problem of spanning the nave with a vault has been overcome, but the problem of using only a semicircular arch throughout remains; for the semicircular end (or apse) nearest to the nave meant that to negotiate the curve, the arches had to be made smaller and the springing line raised on 'stilts' to maintain the same arch level. This was in fact an architectural problem which remained unsolved until the next century when the pointed arch replaced the semicircular arch and enabled the builders to vary the width of the arch but still to retain the same springing line and the same height.

Just south of the White Tower are the ruins of later buildings pulled down by Cromwell, including mere fragments of a great hall in which Anne Boleyn and others feasted, unmindful of the shadow of the axe. Visitors quite naturally shiver as they pass the place of execution, but are more concerned to see the magnificent display of royal regalia so splendidly set out in the vaults of the Waterloo Building – a nineteenth-century building which occupies the greater part of the northern precincts of the Tower – or the military museum to the east.

In the London of William the Conqueror, it was the huge bulk of
the White Tower which dominated one's view. To understand this mighty
fortress, it is better to visit on a bleak winter's day, when the walls and
turrets are glistening with rain, or a light fog is wreathing its towers, and not
at the height of the tourist season when the place swarms with children and
foreign visitors, for then the Tower loses much of its impact. In winter, with
the courtyards almost deserted and the very ravens taking cover from the
sleet, the Tower assumes a very different aspect.

Today the word 'graffiti' usually means the obscene scrawls on the walls
of public conveniences, or the mindless slogans squirted on the tiles of the
underground stations. The 'graffiti' incised with dreadful care and
meticulous detail so many years ago on the walls of the Beauchamp Tower
were made by men and women who, almost at the hour of death, cut or
scraped the relentless stone of their prisons to leave some permanent record
of those last despairing hours.

To find another building of comparable architectural quality belonging to
the period of William the Conqueror, it is necessary to leave the precincts of
the Tower and cross the City to Smithfield*, to visit what remains of the
great priory church of St Bartholomew the Great, founded in 1123 by
Rahere, a prebendary of St Paul's, and later an Augustinian canon. If one
walks from the Tower to Smithfield, through Mark Lane*, Fenchurch
Street, Lombard Street, Poultry (opposite the Mansion House)
Cheapside* and Newgate Street to Giltspur Street*, one is crossing the City

The font of St
Bartholomew

by highways almost as old as London itself, for the Romans knew such streets as Cheapside, even if their own highways now lie eighteen feet beneath the modern street. London was always divided into trade areas, rather like those that exist today in the Kasbah at Algiers, or the *suks* of Tunis, where one can only buy carpets, or brassware or some other craftwork in certain streets where the goods are actually being made. Some of the London trade areas persist to this day: wholesale buyers of meat go to Smithfield, the fish market is at Billingsgate*, the woodworking and wholesale furniture dealers operate round Shoreditch*, and the merchants who deal in furs are to be found in the newly named Skinner's Lane. Finance is centred round Lombard Street and Hatton Garden* is famous for diamonds. The only major change to these guild areas in recent years has been the transference of the vegetable and fruit market from Covent Garden* out to a great modern complex at Nine Elms in 1974. The names, however, remain: Bread Street, Ironmonger Row and Milk Street are all part of the oldest trade artery in London – Cheapside, the eastern end of which is still called 'Poultry' but which no longer sells anything exclusively.

The priory of St Bartholomew and its hospital, served by Augustinian monks, was founded by Rahere, who became a convert to a more serious way of life after having recovered from a serious bout of malaria during which he almost died. The church was savagely plundered during the Reformation of 1536; its great nave and much of the rest of the church were demolished, and the church lands parcelled out to followers of Henry VIII, so that only the choir of the priory church and the splendid tradition of healing still survive. The church is architecturally of the same style as the chapel of St John at the Tower of London, with massive round columns, but its semicircular arches are more lavishly decorated than those at the Tower, and despite the indignities it has suffered, it still has one of the most impressive interiors of any City church. The narrow ambulatory which links the aisles behind the high altar is roofed by a heavy Norman vault, like its counterpart at the Tower, and although at St Bartholomew's the ability to span as wide an area as the present chancel was lacking, so that a wooden roof had to be used, the arch leading into the original nave is a stupendous feat of engineering, comparable to those at Durham or Peterborough. The whole church must originally have been about 300 feet long, but there is no nave now, and even the present Lady Chapel to the rear of the altar is largely a reconstruction, for after the dismembering of the church during the Reformation this building was sold and used for all kinds of secular purposes. It was in this building that the famous American, Benjamin Franklin, worked as a printer, long before he returned to his native country to assist in the drafting of the Declaration of Independence. Later the Lady Chapel became a factory for fringes (for furniture etc.), and it was not until 1886 that it was restored as a church and reconsecrated. Benjamin Franklin's contemporary and friend, William Hogarth, the great cockney painter, engraver and social reformer was baptised in the font of St Bartholomew – a rare Pre-Reformation font of which the only other example is to be found at the Tower of London in the chapel of St Peter ad Vincula. In the southern part of the ambulatory, near

the front, is another important relic – the tomb of Sir Walter Mildmay, the founder of Emmanuel College, Cambridge, and Chancellor of the Exchequer to Elizabeth I, who told his queen, 'I have set an acorn, which, when it becomes an oak, God alone knows what will be the fruit thereof . . .' a most prophetic statement, since it was from Emmanuel College that John Harvard went to the New World and founded one of the finest universities in the United States.

St Bartholomew the Great, Smithfield

It is the tomb of Rahere, however, which attracts the attention of most visitors. This tomb, on the north side of the sanctuary, shows a lean, robed figure with two rather jolly monks kneeling beside him, heavy books in their hands, and clothed in the habit of the Augustinian order. It is obvious that this tomb is much later than the Norman church, for no sculptor of that period, not even at Canterbury, could have designed such a complicated pattern of quatrefoil and trefoil, or such delicately chiselled tracery or mouldings, so beautifully cut and fitted that they resemble some strange undulating plant petrified into its present forms. Opposite Rahere's tomb and high above the chancel is a sophisticated and modish oriel window, built there in about 1517 by Prior Bolton who was responsible for the present tomb of Rahere, according to one authority. Others suggest that it is about one hundred years earlier, i.e. *circa* 1405. Prior Bolton, an architect who also worked at Westminster Abbey early in the sixteenth century, inserted a punning device in the tracery just below his window – a 'tun' (barrel)

Rahere's tomb

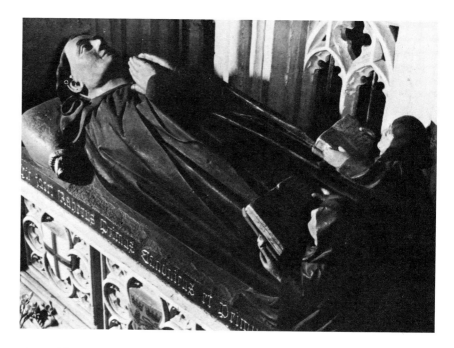

pierced by a bolt (or quarrel) from a cross-bow, spelling out his name 'Bolt-Tun'. The sophisticated workmanship of this later window is in strong contrast to the almost barbaric splendour of the Norman craftsmanship throughout the church. The stone throughout is bare and grey, bereft of its original painted decoration; the ravages of such vandals as the Reformers and the later Puritans deprived the church of almost every record of what a magnificent building it must have been when the splendour of the ritual was matched by the brilliance of the colours enriching the huge grey pillars, deeply cut mouldings and hewn capitals. Thus it is Rahere's tomb which, almost alone, recalls the original colouring of the church. Outside, the Victorian porch by Aston Webb makes a brave attempt to reproduce a suitable 'medieval' entrance, and the little sixteenth-century brick tower which now surmounts the patchwork exterior of what was once a noble building matching the size of the cathedrals of Rochester or Chester, although a little incongruous, has a charm of its own. The heavily damaged entrance to the missing nave is now surmounted by a timber-framed gatehouse.

From a room overlooking the open square in Smithfield, Queen Mary watched the burning of heretics who, at her orders, suffered an agonising death for daring to practise a different version of Christianity from the one she professed. It is perhaps some consolation to think that despite the appalling record of cruelty and bigotry of the Church since Rahere founded his priory in gentle faith 1123, the name of St Bartholomew the Great will be associated for ever with the alleviation of pain, not with the inflicting of it, and with a humanity which ignores any kind of discrimination between creed and creed, treating human beings in need as fellow creatures.

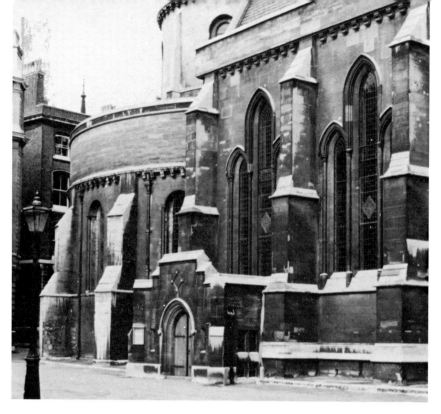

Temple Church, showing the round Norman end and the early thirteenth-century nave

From Smithfield, it is merely about a quarter of a mile to St John's Lane, to the medieval gatehouse of the Order of St John of Jerusalem in Clerkenwell, and to the remains of the Norman church. This has been damaged and rebuilt to such an extent that only the crypt might be considered to be of the same period as St Bartholomew the Great, although the introduction of ribs supporting the vaults, as distinct from the thin, sharp groin vaults of the earlier Norman churches, are an important innovation in the history of construction. However, Clerkenwell is strictly outside the City walls, and the next example of a building still surviving from the London of the Normans is the Temple Church in the area south of Fleet Street. It is quite possible to walk from St John's Gate, down Charterhouse Street* to Holborn Circus*, then down New Fetter Lane into Fetter Lane itself, across Fleet Street, and so into the Temple. The entrance to the Temple takes one under the timbered arch of Prince Henry's Room, then down the slope of Inner Temple Lane to the porch of Temple Church.

The building of Temple Church was first started in the reign of Henry II, about 1160, and the west doorway, sheltered from wind and weather by an ample porch of the Victorian period (which simulates remarkably well the style of Norman and Gothic architecture), although eroded and damaged, shows unmistakable signs of Norman craftsmanship. The carving however is not that of an early Norman axeman, no matter how deft, but a more skilled craftsman with a drill and chisel, and even partial erosion only helps to reveal the drill holes which were the starting point from which he developed with his chisel the strange half-animal, half-plant decoration with which the deeply recessed mouldings of the door are framed. The church only just escaped destruction in the great fire of 1666, but received severe

damage during the blitz of 1940–41 and had to be largely rebuilt. The main
entrance was originally the west door, but today the usual entry is by the south
door.

The Temple Church was built on a circular plan in imitation of the Holy
Sepulchre in the Holy Land and was only one of the churches built in this
form; of the others, perhaps the best-known one is in Cambridge. It derives
its name from the legendary temple of King Solomon, and was originally the
church of the Knights Templar, a body of Christians who created a new
Church Militant in order to wrest the Holy Land from the Lands of the
infidel and safeguard the pilgrimage routes. However, having fought
valiantly through a whole succession of Crusades, the Order deteriorated
and the strict discipline flagged so badly that Pope Clement V was forced to
disband it in 1312. Meanwhile, the little circular church in London had been
enlarged by the addition of a new rectangular chancel, between 1220 and
1240, built in the latest architectural style – that of the Early English period.
Described by Professor Niklaus Pevsner as 'one of the most perfectly and
classically proportioned buildings of the thirteenth century in England . . .',
the chancel displays the daring advances in roofing techniques which had
superseded those of the early Norman builders. The new airy vault, some
thirty-six feet high, make Norman work such as that in St Bartholomew's,

Smithfield, look ponderous, and the heavy marble pillars which support the roof built to replace the original one that had been destroyed in the Second World War seem almost clumsy by comparison with the slender pillars and deeply undercut mouldings of the Early English nave. Despite the extensive restoration which has taken place, in 1825, in 1842, and after the war, the development of the characteristics of the new Early English style of the thirteenth century is very obvious. Nevertheless, so sensitively has the restoration work been carried out – particularly to the roof destroyed in the 1940s – that the whole building retains a remarkably beautiful unity, and the airy quality of the later nave enobles and enhances the massive quality of the earlier church.

It is the impressive array of effigies on the floor of the circular church, however, which attracts and holds the attention of visitors, for although the figures have been sadly defaced, the knights of stone lie there still, their accoutrements eroded and chipped, and their features blurred, but still displaying a remarkable sense of power and martial strength. Some of them have still not been identified – others are the figures of such notable warriors as William Marshall, Earl of Pembroke, and his two sons, William and Gilbert. William Marshall (or 'le Mareschal') died in 1219. His son, William, was one of the Barons who enforced the signing of Magna Carta, a copy of which is to be seen in the Public Record Office not more than a hundred yards from his grave, although this is the final version as issued by Henry III in 1225. Although these effigies are still in the Temple Church, their positions have been rearranged, and in fact none of them were true Knights Templar, but were 'Associates of the Temple'. Where a knight is portrayed with his hand on the hilt of his sword, with the blade partially

Effigies in the Temple Church

withdrawn, he is actually shown at prayer, dedicating his sword to the service of Christ, and the sword is then thrust back into its scabbard at the word 'Amen'. It is not necessarily true that knights who died in battle or at the Crusades were shown in effigy with their legs crossed: this may have been a sign of the cross, just as it is usual to cross the hands over the breast of a corpse today. Examination of the earlier effigies – particularly that of a knight wearing a heavy flat-topped helmet, and thought to be that of Sir Geoffrey de Mandeville who died in 1144 – shows that at that time 'banded' mail, not chain-mail, was worn. This consisted of a number of flat metal rings (rather like washers) which were threaded on to leather thongs and then sewn in closely packed rows on to a leather garment. It is also quite likely that the protecting caps at knees and elbows, known as 'knee-cops' and 'elbow-cops' were not made of metal, but from specially hardened boiled leather. The sculptors who carved these figures have shown quite clearly which knights were wearing banded mail, and which chain-mail. Some have been restored – particularly where the face has been destroyed – but it is fairly easy to distinguish the original sculpture from a modern restoration.

One studies sculptured bosses – for example those which decorate a number of the intersecting arches built into the circular wall of this part of the church, the differences between the original work and the restoration are very apparent. The original heads have an intensity of expression – a sort of 'bite' which is usually absent from a later imitation. There are others, dating back to later periods in this church, but as we are dealing here primarily with Norman and early Medieval London these must be left until later. One feature of the Temple Church must still be indicated – a narrow slit window over a later tomb on the north side of the church at the intersection of the circular Norman church and the Early English nave. This is the window of a tiny penitential cell – a room so small that no normal man could sit or stand in it with any degree of comfort. The Knights Templar had an extremely harsh regime, and any knight who failed to observe its rules could expect the most rigorous punishment. In this cell, overlooking the church, it is said that one disobedient knight, Brother Walter le Bacheler, Knight and Grand Preceptor of Ireland, was walled up alive and starved to death. With the dissolution of the Order, the lands belonging to the Knights were confiscated and taken over, initially by the Knights of the Order of St John of Jerusalem. They were later leased to professors of common law who, together with their students, formed a little legal enclave in this part of London. Once this had been formed into a properly constituted body, it became part of our legal organisation and was first recognised as an Inn of Court by 1449.

There are now four surviving Inns of Court: the Inner and Middle Temples; Lincoln's Inn, which moved to its present site between 1412 and 1422; and Gray's Inn, which is known to have had a school of law in the fourteenth century. The buildings of the Middle Temple bear the device of the Lamb and Flag – the *Agnus Dei*. Those of the Inner Temple may be distinguished by their badge of the winged horse.*

*　　*　　*

Some other remnants of Norman London survive as parts of other historic buildings, and can often be distinguished by their massive round columns, round-headed windows, thick walls strengthened by shallow buttresses which support simple groined or coarsely ribbed vaults, and flat wooden roofs. The Wren church of St Mary-le-Bow in Cheapside, for example, has characteristic Norman work in the crypt, with groined vaults and single scalloped capitals surmounting heavy columns, and there are other Norman features in the crypt of St Bride's in Fleet Street.

The latest and most advanced developments in Norman architecture are to be seen at the great Abbey of St Peter in Westminster. The transition from the more massive, if limited architectural forms that characterise the Norman period to the brilliantly original work of medieval builders was marked by the introduction of the pointed arch. More complex vaults were developed by means of which a multiplicity of cunningly fitted ribs could convey the thrust of the roof to selected areas of the walls which had been strengthened by widely projecting buttresses. These in their turn permitted thinner walls and far greater windows. The development of such techniques, however, was gradual, so that several styles of architecture often exist in one building, each interlocking into the other to form an organic whole; it is therefore very difficult to show a building which is *wholly* Norman.

This complexity of building styles is, of course, merely a symptom of the complicated history of the city itself. It is convenient to try to deal with the story of London in some sort of chronological sequence, as long as one is prepared to accept that such a system must be sufficiently flexible to take into account the complex nature of even one ancient building. The present cathedral of Southwark, for example, at the southern end of London Bridge, underwent so many changes and was subject to such damage and indignities before it emerged as a cathedral in 1905 that even the most ardent architectural historian would be hard put to enumerate all the changes which have taken place in various parts of the present church; but fragments of Norman work can be found, even if, as in the case of a Norman portal, they have been moved from their original positions. With this complexity in mind, we leave the major monuments of the London of William the Conqueror and his immediate successors to visit the London of the Middle Ages . . . a London with which Geoffrey Chaucer would have been familiar.

3

Chaucer's London

Geoffrey Chaucer, the poet, son of a vintner, was born in Upper Thames Street around 1342 (the exact date is not certain), and the London he knew occupied the same site and the same area as the city that had been built by the Romans more than a thousand years before his birth. Successive rulers had strengthened the encircling Roman walls and rebuilt the city gates in approximately the same positions, but they had not altered the original Roman boundaries. Nevertheless, medieval London looked entirely different from both Roman and Norman London. Ludgate Hill was now dominated by the great medieval cathedral of St Paul's (begun in 1090 although not finally completed until 1387), its five hundred-foot spire dwarfing the other eighty or so church spires and towers piercing the city smoke. The eastern approaches to the city were still guarded by the Tower of London, with the great Norman keep now the core of a series of interlocking defences [and] surrounded by a wet moat. Just south of St Paul's and to the west of the Tower of London, the river bank was strengthened by a castle erected by Ralph Baynard, one of the followers of William the Conqueror, around 1100. Baynard's Castle no longer exists, and the only reminders of it now are The Baynard Castle Tavern on the corner of Queen Victoria Street, a wharf nearby known as Castle Baynard Wharf, and Castle Baynard Street. Baynard Castle was itself destroyed in the great fire of 1666. There was also one other defensive tower to be seen in Chaucer's lifetime – Montfichet Tower, which occupied a site just south of Ludgate Hill, but of this no trace remains. Although the most westerly gate of the city wall was still Ludgate, London was spreading slowly westwards along Fleet Street, and as early as 1293 a new gate known as Temple Bar was built by the Temple – a substantial gatehouse of stone which, like Newgate, appears to have been used as a gaol.

The City of London has always enjoyed a considerable measure of governmental independence – a fact admitted by William the Conqueror and acknowledged by later kings, or ignored at their peril. But no matter how powerful a ruler, he could not *create* wealth – that could only be done by craftsmen, traders, or financiers who provided the capital for him, and this placed the City Guilds in a position of great influence. Originally social and religious fraternities, formed mainly to promote and safeguard the interests of their members, by Chaucer's lifetime they were powerful organisations in the promotion of trade. They were wooed by successive monarchs by

opposite, Southwark Cathedral

above, 'Old' St Paul's,
showing the 500-foot
spire
right, The interior of
'Old' St Paul's, looking
east

the granting of certain privileges confirmed by royal charters, in exchange for financial backing for various enterprises, such as foreign wars. The guilds maintained connections with their churches, and with the patron saints associated with their crafts or trades, but usually built guildhalls in the areas in which their trades were carried on. These areas can still be identified by name, even if the practice of the crafts associated with them has long since ceased. Threadneedle Street, for example, is now concerned with finance and the Bank of England – 'The Old Lady of Threadneedle Street' – and not with the tailors who originally worked there in the Middle Ages. As self-governing bodies, the guilds (later to be known as the City Companies) preserved their own traditions and ceremonies, and on occasion wore a distinctive dress peculiar to their craft – hence the term 'livery' company. They controlled the numbers and the quality of craftsmen practising their trade, insisting that their members undergo seven-year apprenticeships at the end of which they had to pass a rigorous examination before being admitted as full members of the guild. This tradition still persists in some professions, and certificates issued to successful candidates in the City and Guilds examinations are still a guarantee of excellence in those subjects.

The City was divided into twenty-five districts, or wards, some of which still retain the names of the trades originally practised there. Thus we have Candlewick* ward, Cordwainers* ward, and Vintry* ward, where Chaucer was born.

By 1376, the guilds had all earned the right to elect members to the Common Council governing the City, and with over seventy different guilds their influence was formidable. The election of the Mayor of London (the term 'Lord Mayor' did not come into use until 1414) and of the Sheriffs and City Chamberlain is still in the hands of the City Companies, the modern successors to the guilds, although a great many members of the companies no longer have any association with the trades with which they were originally connected. It is significant that the Guildhall is still the administrative centre of the City, and that the Lord Mayor is the Chief Magistrate. Below his official residence, the Mansion House, is a Court of Justice, with cells beneath which are still in use. Perhaps the most famous Mayor of London, and one who was almost certainly known to Chaucer was Richard Whittington, a member of the Guild of Mercers. He was Mayor in 1397–8 and 1406–7, and Lord Mayor in 1419–20. Dismissing the legends told in various pantomimes bearing his name, he was undoubtedly a wealthy man, and when he died in 1423, he left substantial sums of money to be devoted to projects for the benefit of the City. He paid for the marble floor of the Great Hall of the Guildhall, completed about seventeen years after his death; he endowed the Guildhall Library, and the Greyfriars Library; and he left sums of money to repair the Hospital of St Bartholomew and to found almshouses.

The medieval walls of the Guildhall survived two major fires – the first in 1666, and the second in 1940, and the only remaining original window is to be seen in the south wall. Under this window are marked the standard measurements of the yard, feet, and inch. The hall is over 150 feet long and

49

nearly 50 feet wide, and from its splendid roof hang the banners of the twelve major City Companies. Starting in the eastern corner by the dais, they are as follows ... the Mercers, the Drapers, the Goldsmiths, the Merchant Taylors and the Salters. On the opposite cornice hang those of the Grocers, the Fishmongers, the Skinners (over the porch), the Haberdashers, the Ironmongers (over the fifteenth-century window), and finally the Clothworkers. It is also possible to view the medieval crypt – the largest in London – by application to the beadle on duty. On the balcony at the west end of the hall are two gigantic figures, carved in wood, of Gog and Magog. The original figures, which were paraded in the civic pageants of the fifteenth and sixteenth centuries, were replaced during the eighteenth century, but these too perished in 1940, and the daunting figures that stand there now are the work of a modern wood carver, David Evans, FRBS.

At intervals round the walls are various memorials to famous warriors and statesmen – William Beckford, Lord Mayor in 1772; the great statesman, William Pitt, the Earl of Chatham, whose statue was placed in the Guildhall in 1782; the statue of his son, William Pitt the Younger, stands on the opposite side of the Hall. Beside Pitt the Elder is a memorial to the Duke of Wellington. At the far end of the hall is a sculptural group in commemoration of the achievements of Admiral Viscount Nelson, and next to him there is a seated figure of that grand old warrior, Sir Winston Churchill. However, it is with medieval London that this chapter is mainly concerned, and the place of the guilds in its development.

Of the twelve greater companies and the twelve minor companies which are the successors of the medieval guilds, some no longer have any connection with their original crafts or trades, while some, such as the Fishmongers, the Brewers, the Goldsmiths and the Apothecaries are very actively concerned with the modern versions of the original crafts, ensuring that the high standards of workmanship and conduct are maintained. The Goldsmiths, for example, still superintend 'The Trial of the Pyx' every year in March to determine the quality of the coins made in the Royal Mint. All the City Companies are very active philanthropists, maintaining schools, endowing scholarships to universities and other important educational institutions, financing research, and giving valuable assistance in the maintenance of almshouses and hospitals. It would be difficult to overestimate the influence exerted for good by these City Companies, far beyond the limits of the City itself. Nevertheless, all too often they are associated only with such charming but quaint ceremonies as 'swan-upping', when members of the Dyers and Vintners share with the Crown the overseeing of the annual marking of swans on the Thames.

The façade of the Guildhall is a strange mixture of classical motifs and eighteenth-century 'Gothick' – spelt thus to distinguish it from the original Gothic architecture of the Middle Ages. The interior of the porch is the original Gothic workmanship, and the ribbed vaulting is typical of the architecture with which Chaucer would have been concerned as Clerk of the Works at St George's Chapel, Windsor. When George Dance the Younger restored the Guildhall in 1788–9, he probably thought that 'Gothick' was in

left, Interior of the Guildhall, much restored
right, Exterior of the Guildhall, also restored

keeping with the antiquity of the building, but to Chaucer, to whom Gothic meant 'modern' architecture, it would have seemed a bizarre hotch-potch. It was probably this which prompted the modern architectural firm, Sir Giles Scott, Son and Partners, to build the western extension to the Guildhall in a modern idiom, and to make no attempt to mimic the much-restored front of Dance's Guildhall.

None of the original guildhalls survive, and those of the City Companies, which are well worth a visit to see some of the splendour of the plate etc., which has been so beautifully cared for over the centuries, can only be visited by special permission from the individual company. None of these buildings were built earlier than the sixteenth or seventeenth centuries, and most had to be entirely rebuilt after the Second World War.

The guilds, however, were not the only important body in the City – the churches and other religious houses were also very powerful, although if one is to judge by the mockery to which some representatives of the Church are subjected in Chaucer's famous *Canterbury Tales*, their influence was on the wane. Yet it must be remembered that what we now call the Social Services – hospitals, schools, the care of the old and of the destitute – was entirely the concern of the Church before the Reformation of 1535–6. In spite of all its faults, it was not the parasitic growth 'grinding down the faces of the poor' that is so often portrayed by modern writers. Today, perhaps, the greatest scourge of the modern world, with its demoralising and dehumanising effect, is unemployment. In Chaucer's day, when the population of the City of London was about forty thousand, the building and equipping of one great cathedral church such as St Paul's would have ensured employment for hundreds of workmen, quite apart from the building and maintenance work in over a hundred City churches and the extensive buildings of the religious orders such as those of the Franciscans in the Newgate area.

Of 'Old' St Paul's, the predecessor of Wren's noble building, almost nothing remains, although it covered a greater area than that of the present building. The most obvious remains of the medieval cathedral are the foundations of the chapter house with its pattern of buttresses which, shadowed by a mulberry tree, are to be seen on the south side of the present building, by Watling Street. Of the huge establishment that belonged to the Franciscans, known as the Greyfriars by the colour of their robes, only the name still survives near Newgate. Nothing now remains of the Dominican community buildings, except the name by which they were known – Blackfriars – nor of the Carmelites other than their name of Whitefriars. Something of the old part of the Cistercian priory of Charterhouse is to found in Washhouse Court, but the priory buildings were thoroughly looted by Henry VIII and the monks there were treated with appalling cruelty before being executed. Thus, of all the multiplicity of church buildings fully operational in Chaucer's life, there are now only a mere handful in the City.

Not normally included among the nine Pre-Reformation churches which escaped the disastrous fire of 1666 is the little chapel of St Peter ad Vincula (St Peter in Chains) within the precincts of the Tower of London which was nevertheless a medieval church and appears in records as early as 1210. The present building, however, was built a good deal later, being largely early sixteenth-century work. Its most beautiful medieval monument was not originally situated in this church, but was transferred from the church of St Katherine on the eastern side of the Tower Bridge, when the area was cleared during the nineteenth century to make room for St Katherine Docks. This is the tomb of John Holland, Duke of Exeter, who died in 1447, and it is one of the most impressive tombs in this part of the City, with an elaborately carved canopy and a dignified recumbent figure of the knight below. The little chapel is in any case well worth a visit, with its flat timber roof supported on slender pillars, its wide windows and its original font. It is perhaps more notable for the list of victims who lost their lives at the hands of the executioner of the Tower, than for its architectural beauty. Many of them lie in the little churchyard so movingly described by Lord Macaulay: 'In truth there is no sadder on earth than that little cemetery. Death is there associated, not . . . with public veneration and with imperishable renown; not . . . with everything that is most endearing in social and domestic charities; but with whatever is darkest in human nature . . . with the savage triumph of implacable enemies . . . with . . . the cowardice of friends. . . .' The memorial tablet near the entrance of the chapel lists a terrible number of men and women who lie buried there, including St Thomas More, Queen Anne Boleyn, Queen Catherine Howard, and many others too numerous to mention, some who were, no doubt, innocent victims of a harsh regime, and

The nave of St Peter ad Vincula at the Tower of London

others who probably played for high stakes and paid their losses with their lives. Visitors are only admitted in special parties, but no such restriction is placed on those who wish to visit another medieval church, beautifully restored, just outside the Tower – that of All Hallows, Barking*.

All Hallows sustained heavy damage during the Second World War, such that the roof and much of the interior is entirely new and the medieval columns which support the roof have been restored. The blitz however, was responsible for the discovery of certain Saxon remains including a substantial archway which had been hidden hitherto. (Of the close connection of this church with William Penn, the Quaker founder of Philadelphia, and with Christ Church in that city, more will be said later in the chapter on the London of Samuel Pepys.) Much of the chancel of All Hallows was fourteenth-century work, and there is a chapel of the same date in the crypt beneath. The tower is seventeenth century. A number of medieval brasses and a tomb dated 1477 of Alderman John Croke are also to be seen there.

The next medieval church in this area is that of St Olave, a tiny church in Hart Street*, a turning just off Tower Hill or Great Tower Street. This, too, escaped the great fire, only to be heavily damaged during the blitz, and again restoration has been carried out so well that the church seems surprisingly undamaged. The roof, of course, is modern, and the windows have been re-glazed with some fine modern glass, but the simple vaulted crypt below is original, and the tomb and memorial of the church's most

above, All Hallows,
Barking
right, The interior of St
Olave's Church,
showing the memorial
to Mrs Samuel Pepys
in the top right-hand
corner

54

famous parishioners – Samuel Pepys and his unfortunate wife Elizabeth – are intact. A number of brasses, some of them sixteenth century, the others somewhat later, also remain. The little nave is fifteenth-century work, but the crypt is much earlier – some authorities date it as thirteenth century. Although from time to time there are lunchtime concerts, this is usually a little haven of quiet away from the traffic of Tower Hill, or the bustle of Fenchurch Street station just to the north. The church is reached through a gate topped by a seventeenth-century carving featuring skulls and other reminders of our mortality – this prompted Charles Dickens, to write in *The Uncommercial Traveller*: 'One of my best beloved churchyards I call the churchyard of Saint Ghastly Grim.' From St Olave, Hart Street, it is only a short walk northwards up Mark ('market') Lane and Billiter Street* to Leadenhall Street, to another medieval church. This one would not have been known by Chaucer, for it was built after his death, but he would have known one in the same area, (although not on the same site) with the somewhat sinister name of St Mary Axe, the name by which the street where it used to stand is now known. The one that stands there today is St Andrew Undershaft, a church which, according to John Stow, one of the first historians of London, was 'new built by the parishioners there since the year 1520; every man putting to his helping hand, some with their purses, other [*sic*] with their bodies. . . .' As a matter of fact it was more a case of everyone rebuilding and repairing an existing church, but nevertheless, the whole parish rallied round and did the work. The more recent custom of using a church only for worship, and often only for Sunday services, would have been incomprehensible to Geoffrey Chaucer and to the good people who laboured on this church. In the Middle Ages, the church building was the focal point of the life of the parish, and today, St Andrew Undershaft is only one of the many hundreds of parish churches to revive this medieval tradition. Every day of the week St Andrew Undershaft is buzzing with activity. Here may be found art exhibitions, often of the work of young artists who could not possibly afford the extortionate charges made by some professional art galleries, and concerts by young musicians struggling to be heard. To some it may seem unusual to find refreshments available on tables in the nave, and modern art in the aisles, but this is in many ways a return to the medieval tradition of the church as the social centre of the parish and not a wildly revolutionary idea born of the twentieth century. John Stow, a parishioner in the reign of James I, called this building 'the fair and beautiful parish church of St Andrew the Apostle', and certainly, if one does not allow oneself to be distracted by the unfamiliar appearance of the church on a weekday, it is easy to appreciate his pride in his parish church. This building belongs to the architectural period known as 'the Perpendicular period' – a phase in which emphasis was on the vertical lines of the structure. Whereas in such churches as St Bartholomew the Great, the sturdy columns and heavy capitals were structural necessities, by the time St Andrew Undershaft was built, building technology had advanced so much that walls were no longer required to bear the thrust of the vaults or of the roof. These could be supported at certain selected points by buttressing the walls, leaving the intervening spaces free for the insertion of wide windows, rich with stained and painted glass. St Andrew Undershaft is particularly well endowed with heraldic glass, a fact noted in the report of the Royal Commission on Historical Monuments which says: 'It is considered that perhaps the largest amount of pre-Reformation material (*c.* 1530) is in St Andrew Undershaft.' The shafts of the slender columns which support the roof are enriched with shallow chamfered mouldings, and the capitals which surmount them are deliberately unobtrusive so that the eye, and the spirit, are drawn irresistibly upwards to the timber roof with its 125 carved and gilded bosses.

The church also has a number of historic tombs – two of former Lord Mayors of London and others of important members of the City Companies and their wives by whose bequests Londoners – and particularly the schoolchildren of London – still benefit. But the most important tomb of all is undoubtedly in the north-eastern corner – that of John Stow, one of the first, and certainly one of the most important chroniclers of the history of London. A tailor by trade, he had a passion for history, and his antiquarian researches on London occupied the greatest part of his life, although he did edit Chaucer's works (1561) and four years later wrote *A Summarie of Englyshe Chronicles*. But his most important work was his *Survey of the Cities of London and Westminster*, published in 1598. After the production of this monumental work, Stow found himself so poor that he petitioned James I for help, and the munificent monarch, straining his generosity to its utmost, granted Stow letters patent permitting him 'to gather the benevolence of well-disposed people within this realm of England; to ask, gather and take alms of all our loving subjects'. Such was the reward of this great man – a licence to beg! The tomb in St Andrew Undershaft shows a half-length figure of Stow writing a book, with other books beside him – but the quill with which the effigy appears to be writing is not a sculptured one but a real one. Every year a competition is held in London schools for the best essay on London, and around the anniversary of John Stow's death, 5 April 1605, a memorial service attended by the Lord Mayor and Sheriffs is held in the church, after which a copy of Stow's famous book is awarded to the school from which the winning essay has been submitted. The quill in Stow's hand is replaced by a fresh one, the old one being given to the headmaster or headmistress of the successful school in a presentation case.

Although the tower of St Andrew Undershaft is mainly of fifteenth-century workmanship – somewhat older than the body of the church – the upper storey was added by a Victorian architect, Chatfield Clarke, in the 1880s.

A little to the north-west of St Andrew Undershaft, partly hidden by modern office buildings and the Leathersellers Hall, reached by a short cut across a neatly paved bombed site, is another medieval church which escaped the great fire of 1666 – that of St Helen's, Bishopsgate. Neither the history nor the plan of the present church is as straightforward as that of St Andrew Undershaft, for it is clear, from the main entrance in Bishopsgate, that this is not one church but two, side by side. The chancel

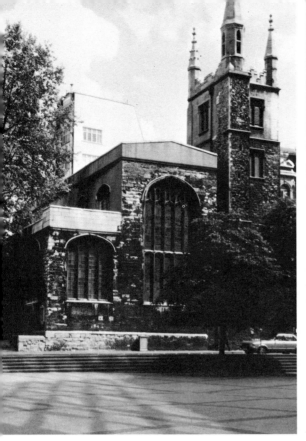

on the north side is all that remains of the priory of St Helen* for nuns of the Benedictine Order, which was founded by William, the son of William the Goldsmith, in about 1212. The second chancel to the south is that of the early parish church to which the nun's choir was joined. The present church is also the more remarkable because, in addition to an extremely fine collection of tombs and memorials of its own, it gave sanctuary to eighteen equally impressive ones from St Martin Outwich, Bishopsgate, when that church was demolished in 1874. It is this dual collection which is responsible for St Helen's being referred to as 'the Westminster Abbey of the City', since no other City church can rival the rich display of tombs to be seen here.

The original convent very soon became one of the wealthiest religious houses in the City, owning a great deal of valuable land in different parts of the City, the gifts of City merchants and their wives, and Queen Isabella, the wife of Edward II, hired a house in Lombard Street from the convent. It was on land leased from the prioress that Sir John Crosby, whose tomb is in the church, built Crosby Hall, a magnificent medieval mansion, originally located in Bishopsgate on the site now covered by Crosby Square, but taken down and rebuilt in Chelsea in 1910. With such wealth, it was perhaps inevitable that the strict rules of the Benedictine Order began to be ignored, and towards the end of the fourteenth century, following investigations into the conduct of the nunnery, the prioress was reprimanded and the nuns told, 'it is to be enjoined on them that henceforth they abstain from kissing secular persons, a custom to which they have hitherto been too prone.'

(There was presumably no objection to their kissing ecclesiastical persons.) Later, the prioress, who surely must have been the original of the lady so wickedly described by Chaucer in his famous *Prologue*, was ordered to get rid of her collection of 'smale houndes' and to be content with one or two, as they were consuming food which should have been distributed to the poor. By 1432, however, the nunnery was in trouble again, complaints having been made that the services at Easter and at Christmas had been hurried in order that the nuns might take part in dancing. At the dissolution of the convent in 1538, the lands were given at first to one of Henry VIII's followers, who later sold them to the Leathersellers Company; they used the nuns' refectory as their hall until the late eighteenth century when all the remaining buildings of the priory except the church were demolished. The screen separating the nuns' choir from the parish church was taken down immediately after the dissolution, but the doorway by which the nuns entered the church from their dormitory for the services at night is to be seen in the north wall of the nuns' choir, as well as a squint by which nuns who were not taking part in the service being conducted in that part of the church could see the elevation of the host. Although the timber roofs have been repaired, the structure is essentially original. It is not possible to describe all the tombs to be seen in this church, but mention must be made of three of the original ones – that of Sir John Crosby, who died in 1476, and his wife, to be found immediately to the south of the main altar in what was originally the parish church; that of Sir William Pickering on the opposite side of the altar from Sir John Crosby's; and that of Sir John Spencer, which is now near the south door in the chancel of the parish church.

The tomb of Sir John Crosby shows the knight in full armour, wearing his aldermanic cloak, and lying beside his wife who died in 1460, fifteen years before her husband. A Member of Parliament for London, warden of the Grocers Company, and a great benefactor of the Benedictine nunnery, Sir John was apparently knighted by Edward IV for his resistance to the Lancastrian cause in the Wars of the Roses, and the tomb effigy wears the Yorkist collar of suns and roses on its breast. The tomb of Sir William Pickering shows the effigy of a soldier and a scholar, who was Ambassador in Spain during the first dangerous years of the reign of the young untried Elizabeth I. Sir William died in 1574, and his tomb was described by William Kent, a great authority on London's history, as 'as handsome a one as can be found in a City church'.

Both these tomb figures are magnificent examples of the sculpture of their time, and each 'building', as it were, in which the figures are enclosed, shows in miniature the architectural forms in use during that particular period. The architecture of the tomb of Sir John Crosby is medieval, but by the time that Sir William Pickering's tomb was built, medieval forms had been superseded by ones derived, somewhat loosely, from those normally found in the buildings of ancient Rome – an uneasy union, for they were often derived from Flemish or German pattern books. By the time the tomb of Sir John Spencer was designed, there had been a clearer understanding of the relative proportions of the classical columns, capitals and the upper structure consisting of the architrave, frieze and cornice, and it was only about twenty years after his death in 1609 that Inigo Jones, the Jacobean architect, designed the first truly classically proportioned building in this country – the Queen's House at Greenwich.

Apart from the intrinsic beauty of these and of other monuments in this church, the tombs are also remarkable records of the costume, armour and personal appearance of the Londoners of their time, although it would not be wise to assume that they are intended as accurate portraits of the people who lie in them. The tomb of Sir John Spencer, his wife and his daughter is now on the south side of the chancel of the parish church, near a very fine doorway of a much later date – a carved doorcase which displays the taste and skill of the craftsmen of the first third of the sixteenth century, derived perhaps from the work of Inigo Jones who repaired St Paul's Cathedral at about this time, or of his master-mason, Nicholas Stone. Of a slightly later date still is another beautiful doorway in the west wall, leading out into Bishopsgate. This church is one of the most fascinating in the whole City, and fortunately one of the most loved, for it is beautifully maintained – the lovely woodwork is free from dust, the marble of the tombs is smooth and clean, and the brasses are protected, usually under rugs. Here, too, the main body of the church is used as a great social centre, with regular concerts, debates and lectures going on while the traffic grinds past in busy Bishopsgate, only fifty yards away.

St Ethelburga the Virgin, Bishopsgate

A little further north, in Bishopsgate itself, is a tiny church, so unobtrusive that its little door can easily be missed. This is another medieval church – St Ethelburga the Virgin. It is the smallest church in the City – only 60 feet long, 30 feet wide, and about 30 feet high to the centre of the building, and it has suffered sadly during its long history, which probably dates back as least as far as the thirteenth century, when it was the property of its larger sister church, St Helen's. Its main claim to fame is that Henry Hudson, the famous explorer and navigator, took his last communion in this church before setting out for the New World in 1607, to seek the North Polar route to China and Japan. He never returned, perishing with his son and with seven other seamen who had been turned adrift in an open boat by mutineers.

From this tiny, charming church in Bishopsgate to the largest parish church in the City – that of the Church of the Holy Sepulchre near Newgate, better known as St Sepulchre. It stands on the corner of Giltspur Street and Holborn Viaduct, just south of Smithfield. The original church was a Norman building and the document by which Rahere, the prior of St Bartholomew the Great, granted the living (or benefice) of the new church to Hagno the Clerk in 1137, is still preserved in the British Museum. Nothing of the Norman church now survives for in 1450, Sir John Popham, the Treasurer of the Household to the monkish Henry VI, rebuilt the church entirely. The exterior of this church shows all the characteristics of Gothic architecture, but Victorian restorers have heavily over-Gothicised the tower, the nineteenth-century pinnacles are ridiculously out of proportion, and some of the windows look mechanical and dead in

Church of the Holy
Sepulchre, Newgate

workmanship. The south porch by which the church is entered is a very fine example of mid–fifteenth-century work, with beautifully fashioned vaults fanning out to be secured at certain points by seventeen carved bosses. The interior of the church comes as a surprise, for although its spacious nave and high roof might be expected, it is actually a seventeenth-century interior – a rebuilding after the great fire of London on exactly the same scale and proportion as the burnt-out medieval church. This church is the largest parish church in the City and it looks it, particularly as the rood screen which originally divided the nave from the chancel has not been replaced. The doorway by which the priest used to climb to the balcony of the rood screen (known as the rood loft) is still visible in the north aisle, near the organ. There are also remnants of a medieval tomb in the chapel on the north side – now known as the Musicians' Chapel – and on the opposite side of the church, by the most easterly of the Tuscan columns built in the seventeenth century, one can see a melancholy reminder of the association which this church had with nearby Newgate Gaol and with its condemned cell. This is a handbell, which was taken on the eve of an execution through a tunnel (traces of which can be seen in the south wall) leading from the church to a passage outside the condemned cell, to be rung at midnight to persuade the unfortunate wretch within to repent of his sins and prepare to meet his Maker the next day. When the execution was about to take place, the great bell in the tower of St Sepulchre announced the fact to listening London. More happily, it is this peal of bells which is referred to in the old nursery rhyme, 'Oranges and Lemons', in the phrase, 'When will you pay me? say the bells of Old Bailey'.

The church is not only associated with those whose lives ended in a dishonourable grave: it contains somewhere (the exact site is not known) the body of the famous Elizabethan adventurer, John Smith, who after many adventures sailed to the New World in the *Susan Constant* and with his companions in *Discovery* and *Godspeed* established the base of Jamestown. Captured by Red Indians, his life was spared through the intervention of the famous Princess Pocohontas, and he later became President of the Council of the newly acclaimed Virginia, and Admiral of New England. He returned to this country to spend his last years drawing maps and writing books, particularly on the New World. He died in this parish near the church in 1631, and his career is described on a brass plate just south of the choir, and commemorated in a modern memorial window in the south wall.

The church of St Sepulchre is associated with a number of City Companies, so it is fitting that it has a very fine seat for the Lord Mayor, and a sword-rest for the ceremonial sword which is carried in procession before him and his retinue of Sheriffs, Aldermen, etc. on civic occasions. The kneelers embroidered by members of the parish show the crests and armorial bearings of the City Companies connected with the church, including those of the Worshipful Company of Cordwainers who hold an annual service there, and the Worshipful Company of Cutlers, whose hall is in the parish and who attend a special service there in June when a new Master of the Company has been elected.

But the City Company which is undoubtedly most in evidence in this church is that of the Worshipful Company of Musicians. Through its long history, the Christian Church has been an enthusiastic patron of music and of the arts, and all the City churches, from time to time, provide facilities and support for musical recitals of every kind. At St Sepulchre the strength of the tradition is such that it is known as the Musicians' Church and has one chapel set aside as the Musicians' Chapel. Throughout the church embroidered kneelers embody musical motifs in their decoration, or commemorate such famous musicians as Dennis Brain, Harriet Cohen, Dame Myra Hess, Kathleen Ferrier, Eugene Goossens and Sir Edward Elgar. Stained glass windows commemorate the conductor Sir Malcolm Sargent, the composer John Ireland, and the eminent Australian singer Dame Nellie Melba. The church possesses an organ built during the seventeenth century by the great Renatus Harris – an instrument which was very probably played by George Frederick Handel during the eighteenth century, and by this famous fellow-countryman, Felix Mendelssohn, in the nineteenth century. The instrument, carefully restored and adapted for modern church use has retained its beautiful seventeenth-century casing, on which, beneath the crown, can be seen the initials C.R., the cypher of Charles II (Carolus Rex). There are also two mahogany pulpits of the same period, in the style of, if not actually by, Grinling Gibbons – best known perhaps for his carving in St Paul's Cathedral.

One of the most significant events in the musical history of this church, and one of considerable importance to the whole country, was the appointment in 1882 of a boy of fourteen named Henry Wood as assistant

The Musicians' Chapel, Church of the Holy Sepulchre, where Sir Henry Wood lies buried

organist. It is fitting, therefore, after a brilliant career during which he brought fine music to millions of ordinary people, that the ashes of Sir Henry Wood, C.H., should be interred near the very organ on which he learned to play, and in the very church of which he was such a devoted member. It was in this church that the School of English Church Music, now The Royal School of Church Music, was first formed, as well as the City of London Choir. The festival of St Cecilia, in November, is celebrated here annually by the combined choirs of St Paul's Cathedral, Westminster Abbey, Canterbury Cathedral and the Chapel Royal.

At this point a visit might well be made to the Roman Catholic church of St Etheldreda, just north of St Sepulchre, where a ground check has yet to be made to see how much of the original medieval building survives. One might then proceed to the other side of the Thames, just by the southern end of London Bridge, to examine Southwark Cathedral. To reach Southwark, it is necessary to return to the Vintry, the district in which Chaucer was born, and which he visited periodically from his office in Aldgate to carry out his duties as a customs official. The whole area is now completely different from the one he knew, but many of the names of the streets, lanes and churches would have been familiar to him, even if he could not now recognise a single building. From the Church of the Holy Sepulchre he would probably have walked southwards, just inside the City walls, where the Old Bailey now stands, crossed Ludgate Hill, under the shadow of the steeple of Old St Paul's, and then threaded his way past the complex of Blackfriars, either down Blackfriars Lane, or more probably down Creed Lane and St Andrew's Hill to Thames Street, (now Upper Thames Street) to St Andrew's-by-the-Wardrobe. From this point the river would easily have been seen, as the bulk of Baynard's Castle occupied most of the north bank there. The church of St Andrew's-by-the-Wardrobe known to Chaucer perished in the Great Fire of 1666, and was rebuilt by Sir Christopher Wren, only to be gutted again in the Second World War and then skilfully rebuilt afterwards. Queen Victoria Street is of course modern, and did not exist in Chaucer's lifetime, but most of his route from St Andrew's-by-the-Wardrobe to London Bridge can be followed by a modern visitor. He would have gone eastwards along Thames Street, past the twelfth-century church of St Benedict by the Thames (now Wren's delightful little St Benet's on St Paul's Wharf), into the ward of Queenhithe*, where the natural inlet which forms Queenhithe Dock is still visible, and so into the Vintry, where he could see Vintners Hall, the City Company Hall to which his father belonged. This has been rebuilt, it is true, but it still stands on approximately the same site, now somewhat overshadowed by Southwark Bridge, a modern intruder. On the opposite side was St Michael Paternoster Royal, and no doubt here he would have encountered the swarthy merchants from Reole, the wine-growing district near Bordeaux from which the church derives its name, 'La Reole' having been corrupted into 'Royal'. Chaucer, too, would have known the famous Dick Whittington – Sir Richard Whittington, four times Lord Mayor of London, who was laid to rest in this church some time after Chaucer's death. College Street is the only surviving part of the College of Priests founded by Whittington in this area. Nearby was the church of St James Garlickhithe – in an area where garlic was sold for use in cooking to mask some of the less pleasant aspects of an age when refrigeration was unknown. On the site which is now occupied by Cannon Street station was the Steelyard – an enclave of foreign merchants of the Hanseatic League on an area granted to them by Henry III, and in the possession of the League or its successors until the middle of the last century.

By now Chaucer would have been very near to London Bridge, which was a little further to the east than the present one, and was flanked, as today, by Fishmongers Hall to the west, and the church of St Magnus the Martyr to the east. The only bridge spanning the Thames for many miles – the next one was at Kingston, on the upper reaches of the Thames – it had been erected by Peter of Colechurch in 1176, but had been patched and repaired many times by Chaucer's time. It was about thirty-five feet wide, with nearly a hundred houses and shops on either side – not unlike the Ponte Vecchio in present-day Florence, or the Pultenay Bridge at Bath – and with

A medieval statue in Trinity Square, off Borough High Street

a two-storeyed chapel over thirty feet high about one third of the way along the bridge from the north bank. The chapel was dedicated to St Thomas Becket who, like Chaucer, was also born in London, and the original architect of the bridge, Peter of Colechurch, was buried in the crypt. The bridge had nineteen or twenty broad pointed arches of various widths, and the highway was supported by massive piers with thicknesses ranging from twenty to thirty-four feet. These in turn were protected at the base by immense shoe-shaped starlings (or sterlings) of wood, which unfortunately restricted the channels so that of the total waterway of about 900 feet, a width of only about 194 feet was available for navigation; during high tides these channels were turned into raging torrents, dangerous for small boats. It was the accumulation of floating rubbish which collected round the starlings and the fact that the undredged river was shallower than it is now that caused it to freeze over regularly if exceptionally severe weather occurred in the winter.

As he crossed London Bridge, Chaucer might well have been tempted by the Glovers, the Pouch-makers, the Goldsmiths, the Bowyers and others who, according to the Bridge Records, all had their workshops there. Having passed the Chapel of St Thomas which stood on the east side of the bridge, Chaucer would have walked under a fortified gatehouse, and from there on to the drawbridge and so through the heavily guarded bridge gate into the Borough High Street of Southwark – a district well known for the eating houses and inns which lined the approaches to the City. It was natural, therefore, that in describing the assembly of pilgrims portrayed so vividly in his *Prologue* in 1386–89, Chaucer had them start from The Tabard in the Borough High Street. The inn was eventually demolished in 1875–6, and a modern tavern now occupies the site, although a yard alongside is still called Talbot Yard. A little nearer the bridge is The George, a famous inn first recorded in 1554, but this appears to have suffered from 'the inconvenience' described by William Fitzstephen, the medieval chronicler who wrote: 'The only inconveniences of London are the immoderate drinking of foolish persons and the frequent fires.' The George was burned down in 1676, but was apparently back in business by 1677 and still offers excellent food, drink and entertainment to modern visitors to London.

It was one of the fires mentioned by William Fitzstephen which was responsible for the founding of the second oldest hospital to survive – St Thomas's Hospital, found in 1212 by the Canons of St Mary Overie, in order to alleviate the distress inflicted by a fire which had caused much damage and injury to the inhabitants of Southwark. (Perhaps the 'inconveniences' of 'immoderate drinking of foolish persons' and 'frequent fires' were not unconnected.) Other medieval hospitals which no longer survive were as follows: St Giles-in-the-Fields, for Lepers; St James's Hospital for Leprous Maids (destroyed by Henry VIII to build St James's Palace); Elsing Spital by Cripplegate, for the sustentation of one hundred blind men; the Lock Hospital for the reception of lepers; and the Hospital of St Mary of Rouncevalles near Charing Cross.

All religious communities were expected to care for the sick and destitute,

Two views of the Roman wall: at St Alphege Church (*above*) and near the Museum of London (*right*)

above and left, Two views of the Tower of London
opposite, St Andrew Undershaft

left, St Helen's Bishopsgate
below, The College of Arms

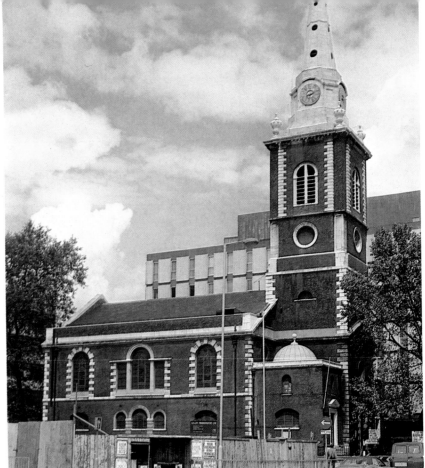

right, St Benet's
below, An aerial view of
St Paul's Cathedral and
the surrounding
churches

so that some proportion of the vast wealth bequeathed to them by penitents was used for the maintenance of infirmaries and hospitals. The estates surrounding the conventual buildings were not only used to grow food for the inmates, but also provided a surplus to be distributed to the poor and needy at the gates. (The fruit and vegetable market which was located until recently in Covent Garden developed from this practice.) Herb gardens provided medicinal plants, and many of those appearing in the *materia medica* of the monks have since been proved to have healing properties and are used in modern medicine. The clergy were in fact forbidden to practise surgery by the Council of Tours of 1163, so that this was taken over by he barber-surgeons at a fairly early date. But not all the medical skill of the clergy or the barber-surgeons was of much use against the terrible visitation of the Black Death which struck London early in November 1348, and by the end of the following May had killed about thirty thousand people – rather more than half the population of Chaucer's London. Chaucer, fortunately, was spared, but fourteen London rectors died, as well as the Abbot of Westminster and twenty-six of his monks. St Thomas's Hospital continued, however, and it was not until 1829–31 that part of it was demolished to make room for the new London Bridge; in 1871 it moved to its present site on the Albert Embankment, opposite the Houses of Parliament, most of its Southwark site having been acquired by the South Eastern Railway Company.

In 1905 St Mary Overie became Southwark Cathedral and was renamed St Saviour and St Peter. The church had endured all kinds of desecration, damage and neglect until the nineteenth century, and the nave has been rebuilt and restored twice – the first time in 1828, after which it stood roofless for nine years, and the second by Sir Arthur Blomfield in 1890–7, so that today the church has a Victorian nave, but work of the Middle Ages elsewhere. The lower part of the tower was probably the work of the great fourteenth-century architect, Henry Yevele, with whom Chaucer, in his capacity as Clerk of the Works, was to work briefly at Westminster Abbey. Yevele's west front was destroyed, however. Nevertheless, so much of the original medieval building has survived that Sir Niklaus Pevsner has described Southwark Cathedral as '. . . apart from Lambeth Palace the most important medieval monument in South London'. Fragments of Norman work are to be seen in the north transept, but most of the choir, retro-choir and transepts is thirteenth-century work, although alterations were made to the south transept at the beginning of the fifteenth century. The reredos behind the altar was originally built shortly before the Reformation, (*c.* 1520) although it, too, had to be heavily restored, and the sculptures were not placed in the niches until the nineteenth century.

Visitors enter by the south door and are usually attracted by the array of carved wooden bosses on the far side of the nave, against the wall on the left. These bosses are from the fifteenth-century roof of the nave of the old priory church and are really very much larger than they must have appeared in their former position, some fifty or sixty feet from the ground. Despite the passage of time, the carvings still look surprisingly crisp; they embody the

somewhat mischievous humour encountered in most medieval art and, of course, in Chaucer's own work. It is strange how being near enough to touch them somehow brings the whole period into focus; it makes one realise the essential humanity of the craftsmen. Each boss is about the size of a beer barrel. One carving has a typically religious motif – that of a pelican vulning – that is, pecking her breast to provide nourishment from her blood for her brood, symbolising Christ's own sacrifice. Another has a grimacing head with a gaping mouth into which is disappearing the lower half of a kilted body; this is a mythical monster of the Middle Ages, known as Bigorne, who waxed fat as he fed exclusively on a diet of obedient husbands.

The cathedral possesses a number of tombs of various dates, from that of a knight, dated about 1275, carved from oak, and with the same characteristics as those of the effigies in the Temple Church, to a somewhat sentimental one dating from the middle of the last century. Near to the thirteenth-century knight, in the north side of the church, there is a very important tomb – that of John Gower, who died in 1408. A lawyer, writer poet and courtier, John Gower was a personal friend of Chaucer and deputised for him as Comptroller of Customs when Chaucer was sent abroad on a secret diplomatic mission for the king in 1374. The stone effigy on John Gower's tomb shows him clad in a long robe, his head resting, somewhat uncomfortably, on three of his own books, and his feet resting on a crouching lion. His figure is picked out now with bright colour, and round his neck he wears a sculptured version of the coveted decoration – the SS collar. Gower was highly esteemed at Court and served under three kings, Edward III, the unfortunate Richard II and Henry IV. The inscription on his tomb describes him as 'J. Gower Armiger' – a rank of esquire, which, while it did not equal the status of a knight, entitled him to bear arms.

On the north side of the choir there is a much later and somewhat ornate tomb belonging to Alderman Richard Humble, who died in 1616; he is shown with his two wives. The tomb is sited in the most conspicuous part of the church, between the chancel and the north chancel aisle. His name may have been Humble, but one feels that he was determined that his tomb should stand proudly in his fine parish church. Still moving eastwards towards the Lady Chapel or retro-choir, the visitor will enter the Harvard Chapel, which contains some of the early Norman work. It is beautifully restored after damage inflicted during the Second World War, and is the gift of many Americans who wished to see that the founder of one of their greatest universities, who lies buried here, should be commemorated with dignity and honour.

The choir and the Lady Chapel are beautiful examples of Early English architecture. If the craggy Norman columns and semicircular arches are reminiscent of an oak tree, the slender grace and delicate proportions of Early English work are almost feminine – like a silver birch or a larch tree. The mouldings are deeply undercut, so that there are emphatic lines of deep shadow, and the capitals are generously rounded, surmounting a bell-like necking. The Lady Chapel has had an eventful, and at times unhappy history. During the brief but disastrous reign of Mary I (known as Bloody Mary), a number of protestants were brought before a court in the Lady Chapel, tried for heresy, and condemned to an agonising death at the stake, in the belief that it was better that their bodies should suffer thus, than that their souls should be subjected to the fires of Hell for eternity. Some of these martyrs are commemorated in stained glass windows in various parts of the church. The stone reredos which separates the Lady Chapel from the chancel was concealed by an eighteenth-century wooden screen until the restoration work of the last century, and the empty niches thus revealed were then furnished with statues. At the top of the reredos, in the central niche, is a statue of Christ enthroned in majesty, with little angels adoring Him on either side. In the niche immediately beneath is the Virgin Mary and the Christ Child. A double row of statues on either side portray the Apostles, a number of saints connected with the diocese, and various dignitaries, bishops, etc., who were involved with the churches on this site. The figure by the south door of the reredos is not an imaginary one, but that of Edward VII who, as Head of the Church of England, visited the church twice, the second time when it was made a cathedral in 1905. To the rear of the screen, and so high up that they are visible from the body of the church, are three sharply pointed windows – the 'lancet' windows which are so characteristic of the Early English period of the thirteenth century. The arches and walls which enclose the chancel are of roughly the same date and show the magnificently incisive quality of the carving at this time. Medieval stone carving has a kind of 'bite' which is absent from imitative work such as that on the figures of the reredos. A comparison of the carving on the tomb of John Gower, for example (although this is by no means the best of medieval sculpture), with the twentieth-century figures shows that these are flabby and sentimental, and lack the tautness and control of the earlier work. Although the figures, drapery and other details on the reredos and on some of the later tombs may seem to be more realistic, the discipline which should be exercised by the materials is often ignored, and their essential qualities are therefore lost. Medieval sculptors fashioned symbols of the human figure from their materials, interpreting its forms in terms of hard stone or grained wood. Later sculptors tended to make imitation people in wood or stone, sometimes with far too little respect for the natural qualities of the material they were using.

A number of fine fifteenth- and sixteenth-century tombs are to be found in different parts of the cathedral. One outstanding example is the tomb of Lady Clarke – a huge allegorical composition erected in the north transept near the Harvard Chapel in 1633. Another is the tomb of Lancelot Andrewes, Bishop of Winchester, whose recumbent effigy is to be seen on the opposite side of the church between the south chancel and the south chancel aisle. He was the last bishop to occupy the great palace just to the west of the church, and died there in 1626. In the choir is recorded the burial of Edmund Shakespeare who, like his famous brother, was also a player; the cathedral also has an alabaster statue of William Shakespeare although, apart from the fact that the Globe theatre was once in the vicinity of the cathedral, the poet had no sure connection with this church.

This delightful little cathedral, half hidden by far less beautiful buildings, and overshadowed by the railway arches, attracts a large number of visitors, who still find it a church with an intimacy and a quiet charm quite unspoiled by its unhappy surroundings, unlike some of the other tourist-haunted buildings in London. Perhaps its very size – for it is only 262 feet long, 130 feet wide and its vault 55 feet high – contributes to its attractions, for it has none of the awe-inspiring quality of some of the better known cathedrals. Nearby sprawls the Borough Market, teeming with an earthy activity which is not entirely connected with the vegetables and fruit being distributed there. An ancient pub, The Anchor, built on an even more ancient site, not only offers excellent food and drink, but one of the finest London views of St Paul's, across the river, from its upper dining-room. But in the main this is a sadly neglected part of London's waterfront, with derelict warehouses and quays, and the flotsam and jetsam on the muddy foreshore. Yet it was here that the bishops of Winchester and Rochester had magnificent town houses, with gardens and shaded walks. Now all that remains of these is one bricked-up rose window with eroded stone tracery, which was the window of the banqueting hall of the Bishop of Winchester's palace, and the name Winchester Walk. Among the other remnants of this medieval district there is Clink Street* – a reminder of the prison in this area in which heretics were confined until the sentence was carried out on them. The rest of the district

The Harvard Chapel

The window of the
Banqueting Hall of the
Bishop of Winchester's
Palace

owes much more to Shakespeare and the players than to Chaucer, and the Bear Garden Museum is making a brave show to bring life back into a sadly run-down part of Southwark.

Chaucer must have taken a boat from London Bridge many times – either downstream to the Palace of Placentia at Greenwich, or upstream to the Palace of Westminster. Downstream he would have started his journey from Customs House quay, but if he had intended to go to Westminster he would have been wise to walk to Swan Stairs, just west of the bridge, to avoid having to shoot the rapids which swirled through the narrow and dangerous channels under the bridge. Most of the city lay along the north bank – a city with over eighty church spires piercing the smoke from a thousand fires; a manufacturing and trading city, with quays a hive of activity as ships from all parts of Europe passed under the drawbridge to anchor, discharged their cargoes into lighters which lay alongside, or took on board cargoes of woollen cloth, leather and other goods for which medieval London was famous. At the Steelyard Chaucer would have watched ships from Lübeck, Hamburg, Bremen and the other Hanseatic ports unloading their cargoes of wheat, flax, hemp, ropes and cables, wood for ships' masts and, of course steel. Further west was Dowgate*, and Dowgate Laystall – a repository of human and animal refuse awaiting transport to Pimlico to fertilise the fields of vegetables which grew there.

The disposal of refuse and sewage is a problem even today, but it was far more difficult for medieval Londoners, for with the daily traffic of pigs, horses, cattle, sheep, the non-existent sanitation was a perpetual source of annoyance and disease. Added to all this was the organic waste from the slaughter-houses and the butchers, and from such trades as leather-tanning and candle-making. So acute was the problem of the disposal of such waste that heaps of the stinking material had to be organised at certain points along the river bank in the hope that it would not be dumped indiscriminately in the street, nor in the river, which was the only source of drinking water for most of the inhabitants of London. Further west at the Vintry, ships from France discharged the wines they exported to London. Baynard's Castle, with its turreted walls, guarded the most western limit of the city's riverside, and there, at Puddle Dock, was another huge dung wharf – a wharf so objectionable that the brewers protested that the water they needed was polluted by the effluent. It was probably for his personal comfort, however, that one of the inhabitants of Baynard's Castle, the Earl of Pembroke, prepared another laystall further west and away from his own grounds.

The river Fleet flowed into the Thames just to the west of Baynard Castle and the Dominican monastery of Blackfriars. Rising in Highgate and Hampstead near Highgate and Hampstead ponds, it flowed on a winding course through modern King's Cross and Clerkenwell and was quite a considerable river by the time it reached Holborn. From the point where the modern Holborn Viaduct now stands, it broadened until it occupied the whole width of modern Farringdon Street, with a bridge (Holeburne Bridge) crossing it at modern Holborn Viaduct, and another one, the Fleet Bridge, joining modern Fleet Street to Ludgate Hill. Barges laden with coal from Newcastle made their way up the Thames and into the mouth of the Fleet, discharging their cargoes just west of medieval St Paul's Cathedral. There is still a Seacoal Lane and a Newcastle Street in this area. But the river became choked with filth of all kinds and the stench was so strong that the Carmelite monks in their buildings at Whitefriars complained bitterly that it was powerful enough to be smelt above the incense which they used in their services. It is not surprising, therefore, that as soon as they could, nobles of both Church and State moved away from the perpetual noise and stink of the city and built great mansions for themselves farther up river. Thus, from Whitefriars to Westminster, the north bank of the river was lined with splendid mansions with their backs to the Strand and their fruit and rose gardens stretching down to the banks of the Thames. The Bishop of Ely was one of the few whose lands were to the north of the city, surrounding modern Ely Place.* Immediately adjoining Whitefriars were the tree-studded grounds of the Temple, with its ancient church and halls of residence. There, no doubt, the counterpart of Chaucer's Sergeant at Law would have been seen scurrying from court to court in his 'budge'-trimmed robe but, as Chaucer observes,

> *Though there was nowhere one so busy as he*
> *He was less busy than he seemed to be . . .*

There, too, moved the sly manciple, who, while buying provisions for the kitchens and wine-cellars of his legal masters, also made provision for himself.

And so Chaucer's boat would have glided on, with the appalling city noise growing fainter and fainter. Modern towns may seem noisy to us, but medieval London must have been considerably noisier. From the time that the cockerels in every little city garden heralded the dawn, and the city gates were opened, the streets would have been clamorous with the clatter of horses, the rumble of farm carts, the lowing of cattle, the bleating of sheep, and the squealing of pigs on their way to the slaughter-houses in Butcher's Row and the Shambles. Mingled with the cries of the animals and the shouts of their drovers would have been the noises of the trades practised in the open street, as ironsmiths and metalworkers hammered out their wares, and hawkers bawled out the virtues of the goods they were peddling. Add to this the clangour of the church bells and the incessant call to prayer of the monastery and convent belfries, which started about two o'clock in the morning (and still does in countries such as Malta and Italy), and a modern visitor might find the London of today a haven of peace, by comparison.

Immediately west of the Temple was the town house of the Bishop of Exeter, then that of the Bishop of Bath, then the one belonging to the Bishop of Lichfield and Coventry (for Coventry did not become a cathedral in its own right until 1918), followed to the west by mansions built for the Bishop of Worcester, and the Welsh bishopric of Llandaff. All these houses were to change hands later, but there are still a number of street names which are a reminder of these noble estates.

Between modern Waterloo Bridge and Hungerford Railway Bridge, the north bank of the river was occupied by a palace with which Chaucer was very familiar – the Savoy. The Palace of the Savoy derived its name from one of the counts of Savoy to whom Henry III granted the land in 1241, but in the middle of the fourteenth century it passed into the hands of the Dukes of Lancaster, and John of Gaunt, Chaucer's friend and patron, acquired it from them through a legacy bequeathed to his wife. It is possible that Chaucer was married in the chapel of the Palace of the Savoy, and it is certain that a pension of £10 p.a., which was granted to him by John of Gaunt, was derived from revenues from this estate. In the fourteenth century the river was much wider and shallower than it is today, and it would have lapped the very edge of Savoy Place (by Shell-Mex House), covering the present Victoria Embankment and the Victoria Embankment Gardens. It was this greater width and reduced depth which was largely responsible for the ease with which the entire river froze during any harsh winter.

Although the north bank was almost continuously lined with these noble houses, the south bank had far less to offer. Apart from the Bishop of Winchester's estates, which extended approximately from Southwark Bridge to just west of the modern Blackfriars Bridge, there was little to be seen but marshland and open country, with an occasional inn or a small hamlet among the reed beds, and it was not until the Elizabethan period, nearly two hundred years after Chaucer's death, that this area became the centre of theatrical and other entertainment. South of the Savoy were two more residences – those of the bishops of Carlisle and the bishops of Durham. The site where the statue of Charles I now stands on Northumberland Avenue was occupied by the Hospital of St Mary of Rouncevalles, a priory of the Abbey of Rouncevalles in Navarre, with the beautiful Charing Cross just to the west. And so to the richest and most impressive of all the residences erected by ambitious and wealthy prelates – the residence of the Archbishop of York which occupied most of that area by the river now thickly covered by the offices of the civil servants of Whitehall. York House was indeed a palace, and long after Chaucer's death, at the downfall of Cardinal Wolsey, it indeed became a royal palace for Henry VIII.

The next landmark was the Palace of Westminster, and the magnificent abbey adjoining it. Westminster Hall changed considerably during Chaucer's lifetime. When he slept in it as a young yeoman of the king in 1367, it was a rugged Norman building still, having been erected from 1097–99 during the reign of William Rufus from stone quarried in Caen in Normandy and in Reigate. The floor area was the same as it is today – an enormous space measuring 240 feet by 69 feet, but until 1394 it was covered by a flat timber roof, supported on a double row of columns (it is not known whether they were of wood or of stone). It had semicircular-topped windows, deeply splayed in a six-foot thick wall, which was strengthened with typically flat Norman buttresses. In the reign of Richard II, however, the king called upon his architect, Henry Yevele, with whom Chaucer had served as Clerk of the Works from 1389–1391, to redesign the building, and

in particular to devise a roof which would permit the removal of the double Westminster Hall row of columns dividing the hall into inconvenient nave and aisles. John Gedney, Chaucer's successor, organised the supply of materials and men, and the superb ninety-foot high double-hammerbeam roof of oak which spans the hall today was then designed by Henry Yevele and the royal carpenter, Hugh Herland. Oak was selected from different woodlands – from the king's park at Odiham, in Hampshire; from a wood belonging to the Abbot of St Albans, at Bernan; and from another wood in Stoke Park, near Kingston upon Thames. Much of the wood was sent to Farnham in Surrey, where the roof was prefabricated, then taken to pieces, and finally reassembled in Westminster on the site. To the sculptor, Robert Grassington, fell the task of fashioning the huge angels which form the horizontal supports of this, the biggest and the finest hammerbeam roof in the world. Deep medieval buttresses replaced the shallow Norman ones, allowing Yevele to open up wide window areas without endangering the strength of the walls supporting the roof. Stone carvers Walter Walton, Thomas Canon and William Chuddere provided a number of statues of kings, many of which still survive, although not all are in their original places. As William Rufus had extended the original palace built by Edward the Confessor, the main courtyard became known as Old Palace Yard, while the Courtyard in front of Westminster Hall, separated from the river

by the royal palace, to the east, became New Palace Yard, a name still in use. Just south of Westminster Hall was Lesser Whitehall – later the House of Lords – and by the river, St Stephen's Chapel.

The illustration showing the abbey as it was before the Reformation – reveals that in Chaucer's day, the whole abbey stood on an island – Thorney Island – with an encircling moat and a high wall. It was a most intelligently planned complex of buildings, designed to fulfil the spiritual and physical needs of the community living within its precincts. The abbey was founded by Edward the Confessor, who died in 1066 shortly after its dedication and was buried in the centre of the great church. His intention in founding such a community in this particular area was clearly set forth by a medieval chronicler: 'The devout king destined to God that place, both for that it was near unto the famous and wealthy city of London, and also had a pleasant situation amongst the fruitful fields lying about it, with the principal river running hard by, bringing in from all parts of the world great variety of wares and merchandise of all sorts to the city adjoining, but chiefly for the love of the Chief Apostle, whom he reverenced with a special and singular affection.' However, very little of the great Saxon church has survived.

Edward the Confessor was interred in the very heart of the church – the first of many British kings to be buried in the abbey – and his successors not only laboured to make it a worthy resting place for the saintly founder, but the scene of every coronation ceremony from 1066 onwards. Only two monarchs – Edward V (one of the little 'Princes in the Tower'), and Edward VIII, who abdicated – have not been crowned in this church, and many of them are buried here, too.

Before examining the church and the surrounding buildings, it would be as well to study the nature of the life which went on within its walls when it was a monastery. Where the rules were strictly kept, the life of a monk was one of almost incessant prayer, work and worship. The first service, Matins, was held just after midnight, and one must imagine the sleepy monks, who had been awakened by the bell after only about four hours' sleep, making their way down the night stairs, into the east cloister, past the chapter house and into the dark, lofty church. There they intoned a series of psalms and other sacred texts from memory, for the only light in the church, apart from the light at the altar, were the candles by which the cantors read at the lectern. The monks then returned through the dark, draughty cloisters and up the night stairs to their dormitory, to sleep for another four hours before being aroused and returning to the church for another service. This took place at about six-thirty or seven a.m., and from then on the day was a round of alternating periods of worship and work. The pattern of the day varied somewhat from Order to Order, and according to the time of the year and the work to be done, but an Order which kept to its rules would pray seven times a day and once at night as they were instructed to do by the Psalmist.

The tomb of Edward the Confessor

75

Only those monks whose duty it was to offer prayers for the souls of benefactors of the monastery were exempt from these services: Matins, Lauds, Prime and Terse. The first major Mass of the day followed Terse, after which the monks went to the chapter house, filing in and taking their seats in order of seniority. Here the duties of the day were allocated, sins or deviations from the monastic rules confessed, and penance or even corporal punishment meted out before the community dispersed for the day's work. Sext and High Mass followed at midday, then None, and the main meal was afterwards served in the Refectory. This was followed by two hours of work or study, with Vespers at five o'clock, a reading in the chapter house (known as a collation), and then, after Compline at seven, the whole community retired for the night. The work undertaken at such a monastery as Westminster Abbey varied considerably, for in addition to the need to feed and care for the monks, there were always visitors, some distinguished, others destitute, who had also to be looked after, and nursed in the infirmary if need be. There were the gardens to be tended, beasts to be looked after, and fishponds and beehives to be maintained, in addition to the complicated administration of the community. Those monks who had special skills would be working in the scriptoria, copying documents and books, often for other less fortunate monasteries, working on the lovely embroidered vestments, fashioning artefacts in wood and metal, and contributing their talents to the enrichment of this or other houses of God. All the buildings were integrated and planned beautifully to make the monastery an efficient combination of spiritual and creative activity. The abbey church, of course, dominated the whole area.

As Westminster Abbey was designed as an abbey, and not as a cathedral church (like York Minster or Wells Cathedral), visitors who start their tour in Dean's Yard, rather than by the West door which leads directly into the nave, have a better opportunity of understanding the whole complex of buildings designed to suit the monastic life. Dean's Yard, a charming tree-lined grassy area where Westminster schoolboys can sometimes be seen playing croquet, was originally the abbey's home farm. The range of buildings which forms its eastern side was the cellerar's range, and most of the stonework is medieval, although the buildings now have quite different uses. In the far north-eastern corner is an archway and enclosed room leading directly to the cloisters on the south side of the abbey. Built during the abbacy of Abbot Nicholas Litlyngton, (1362–86) this would have been a new building when Chaucer became Clerk of the Works. On one side of the arch is a little sculptured head representing Richard II, the king on the throne during its erection, and on the other side there is one representing Abbot Litlyngton himself. The gloomy little room in the corner was the medieval parlour where it was possible for monks to receive guests from the world outside; these were then conducted to a room next to the refectory, or to the locutorium* (or common room, now the abbey museum) where speech was allowed.

Chaucer would also have recognised the little courtyard to the left that is now part of the deanery, but it was then the Abbot's Courtyard, with a little covered staircase of timber leading to his dining hall on the left. The stone stair in the right-hand corner leads to the Jericho Parlour, built by another abbot in 1520, and then into the famous Jerusalem Chamber, with its fourteenth-century timber roof. The chamber probably derived its name from the tapestries with which it was hung, and it was here that Henry IV died, an event dramatised by Shakespeare in his play *Henry IV*. The king had been planning an expedition to the Holy Land in 1413, visiting the abbey before his departure, but he was taken ill and died happy in the knowledge that a prophesy that he would die in Jerusalem had apparently been fulfilled.

The cobbled courtyard from the deanery – the Abbot's Courtyard – is now private, but it must have been used many times by Chaucer during his long association with the abbey. From the Abbot's Courtyard a visitor must enter the south walk of the cloisters which surround the grassy cloister garth. The south walk has a doorway on the right at its western end which originally led into the monk's dining-room or refectory, but now leads to the abbey song school where the thirty-six choirboys are trained, with twelve men, for the many daily services held at the abbey. The Norman cloisters were badly damaged by fire, and the south walk was largely vaulted during the abbacies of Abbot Langham and Abbot Litlyngton, but it was again largely rebuilt by the Victorian architect, Edward Blore. During Holy Week, the Maundy ceremonies entailed the washing of the feet of thirteen

The cloisters, Westminster Abbey

old men by the abbot in the east walk, and the washing of the feet of children by the monks in the south walk. The 'faire, long bench of stone' on which the monks sat while performing this act of humility is still there. One can also see several graves of early abbots of the monastery there, as well as a large gravestone which is believed to cover a communal grave of the twenty-six monks who died of the Black Death in the middle of the fourteenth century.

Before leaving the south walk, however, one should really turn to the right to a much earlier part of the abbey, to the Dark Cloister – one of the few remnants of the abbey built by Edward the Confessor. Here there are only the most primitive architectural forms, with a barrel vault rather like the tunnels through which the modern underground trains run – Norman work earlier and far less sophisticated than that at the chapel of St John at the Tower of London, for example. At the far end of the Dark Cloister is a delightful little courtyard with a tinkling fountain, the site of the Norman abbey's infirmary. Returning from this courtyard, the visitor can see on the left the entrance to Little Dean's Yard – now part of the complex of Westminster School – and to the right, in the direction of the east walk again, the entrance to a very excellent museum of the treasures of Westminster Abbey, which now occupies another building that has survived from the early Norman abbey. Under a simple vaulted roof supported by massive cylindrical Norman columns there are exhibits which trace much of the history of the abbey and of Great Britain, too. Beautifully displayed and well documented are many important relics of the abbey's great past, not only as a monastery in one of the greatest medieval cities of Europe, but as the burial place of the monarchs of this country. As Francis Beaumont, the sixteenth-century playwright wrote, 'Here's an acre sown

The monks' dormitory, Westminster Abbey, now the library and archives

indeed, With the richest royallest seed . . .' There are many lovely objects to be seen there – a magnificent display of the abbey plate, a superb helmet and other weapons, and a fascinating selection of documents from the abbey archives, although the latter are usually kept in the muniment room, formerly the dormitory of the monks.

But of all the exhibits none is so impressive or demands so much attention as the collection of effigies which were carried on the bier through the streets of London at royal funerals. Of these, one of the most intimate is that of Edward III. The head was carved in wood shortly after his death and shows not the regal splendour of his tomb figure in the abbey, but the pathetically warped face of a man who died of a stroke; the drooping mouth of his facial paralysis somehow gives a much more human glimpse of this warrior king. As Edward III died in 1377, Chaucer served under him and was probably present at the obsequies in the abbey. He probably also attended the funeral of Anne of Bohemia, who was the first wife of Richard II and died of the plague in 1394; her wooden effigy is also on exhibition in the museum. Many of the later effigies are of wax, and are fully costumed with jewels and other enrichments, and bright glass eyes staring into the distance. One of the finest is that of Queen Elizabeth I, and another which attracts a lot of attention is that of that royal rascal, Charles II. Among those not of royal blood, there is an effigy of William Pitt, the Earl of Chatham, who died in 1788 shortly after an impassioned speech of protest against the recognition of the American Colonies. There is also one of Admiral, Viscount Nelson which his contemporaries declared to be uncanny in its accuracy.

Back into the medieval cloisters, at the junction of the south walk and the east walk, there is another door on the same side as that which leads into the Norman undercroft museum. This is the entrance to the Chapel of the Pyx* – another remnant of the Norman abbey. The Chapel of the Pyx is not normally open to the public, but as it is the same age as the undercroft which houses the abbey museum it presents much the same appearance architecturally, with its massive cylindrical columns, groined vaults, and deeply splayed windows inset in thick walls. The oak 'pyxes' or chests from which the chapel derives its name are still there – indeed some are so large that it seems likely that they were actually made on the spot, for they could not now be taken out of the door. Some of the smaller ones have been removed, however, and are in the record office in Chancery Lane. Despite the heavy chests, ponderous door and thick walls, thieves actually ransacked the royal wardrobe and the coronation regalia kept there in 1303, with the connivance of the sacrist and sub-prior of the abbey, while the king was fighting a campaign in the north against the Scots. They were eventually arrested and the ring-leader, an unsuccessful merchant named Richard Podelicote, was hanged, although the monks concerned seem to have escaped punishment.

Immediately north of the Chapel of the Pyx is the double entrance into the chapter house, and it is clear that this building is extremely important, for the decoration of the vault of the east walk and the enrichment of the mouldings rises to a kind of crescendo as the chapter house is reached.

the head of the effigy of Edward III

Immediately inside the vestibule the visitor is equipped with a pair of soft sandals which are worn over the shoes to save the medieval tiles with which the chapter house is paved from damage. Having negotiated the flight of stairs with shuffling steps, one is then able to stand just inside the door and gaze upwards to the magnificent vault which opens like a great stone flower from the clustered columns of the central pillar. It is almost an organic growth, like the ribs by which the structure of a leaf is held rigid yet is pliant in the wind, and as the eye travels up the slender columns it goes inevitably along the branching vaults to the walls where, from the outside, buttresses are meeting thrust with thrust. The windows are wide, with geometric patterns in the upper tracery, but the stained glass, alas, is modern, for almost no medieval glass has survived in the abbey. The room is octagonal, and is sixty feet in diameter, with niches in which the monks sat in order of seniority; the most elaborately decorated and beautiful one, placed on the far side of the chapter house from the entrance, belonged to the abbot.

The chapter house was to prove an important building, not just for the abbey, but for the whole country, for it was here, away from the presence of the king in the Palace of Westminster (where free speech was to some extent inhibited), that the first House of Commons was gathered, and the idea of a parliament emerged in 1282. It is not known exactly when the House of Lords and the House of Commons, who formerly met together in Westminster Hall, actually separated, but the Commons seem to have sat somewhere in the precincts of the abbey during the reign of Edward I – that is, in the latter half of the thirteenth century. The chapter house was also the very centre of the administration of this great Benedictine Abbey, and as such the abbot could order punishments to suit the severity of the sins committed by the inmates. Writing of another Benedictine monastery, the medieval writer, William Langland, who was brought up in Great Malvern Priory, makes one of his characters complain:

They have too many fierce fellows watching out for men like me, Priors, and Sub-Priors and Father Abbots. If I tell any tales there, they hold a special meeting and make me fast every Friday on bread and water. Then they give me a telling-off in the Chapter House, as though I were a child, and have me whacked with my trousers down. . . . There's nothing to eat there but stinking fish and watery ale.

This seems all very remote when standing in the midst of this superb building, which despite some dreadful maltreatment after the Reformation was beautifully restored by Sir George Gilbert Scott in the middle of the nineteenth century; the shelves, gallery and bookcases with which it was cluttered as a repository for public records were removed. It was the removal of the wooden floor of the record office which revealed the unique medieval tiles with which it is now paved. The more curious visitor might like to study the subject of these, for a number of them have allusions to legends connected with the abbey. The capitals which crown the cusped arches round the niches are much more elaborate than those of the same

period – the Early English period – in the nave at Temple Church, and in the
eastern end of Southwark Cathedral. In the chapter house the mouldings are
still deeply undercut, but crisply carved leaves spring from the necking of
the column, and although they are in no way of a copy of real, recognisable
plants, these decorative leaves have a wonderful vitality and growth. It is as
though, had the Creator decided to fashion his leaves of stone, instead of
living tissue, he would have evolved just such forms, for they have an
appearance of a life of their own despite the hard material from which they
are cut. They would, of course, have been even more splendid had the paint
with which they were decorated, survived. Indeed, the whole chapter house,
and the rest of the abbey, would have been a blaze of colour in the Middle
Ages. Some of the paintings with which the chapter house was enriched are
still to be seen, but they are sadly diminished in brilliance and sometimes
difficult to understand despite the excellent texts provided by the archivist.

Nevertheless, one can understand the abbot who wrote of this magnificent building: 'It is the workshop of the Holy Spirit, in which the sons of God are gathered together. It is the house of confession, the house of obedience, mercy, forgiveness, the house of unity, peace and tranquillity, where the brethren make satisfaction for their faults.'

Immediately outside the chapter house, and once again in the east walk, it is best to stand for a moment and look at the intricate tracery of the windows of the cloister immediately opposite the entrance. This tracery, which resembles somewhat a mesh or the pattern of a lady's reticule, is in fact known as reticulated tracery, and shows how competent in handling stone shapes the medieval mason had become by the middle of the fourteenth century. There is some geometric arcading at the northern end of the east walk, but the blank wall surface shows where the abbot had his bookcases. Under the bench opposite this arcading are to be found some metal rings. These were used as fastenings for carpeting laid there for the abbot to kneel on when he was performing his Maundy ceremony of the washing of the feet of thirteen old men. Today, the Queen goes to the abbey every year to perform her own Maundy ceremony – the presentation of specially minted coins to a number of old people on Maundy Thursday. The number of old people thus honoured is determined by the number of years the monarch has reigned, and the ceremony is attended by the Dean of Westminster and other dignitaries, with a royal escort of the Yeomen of the Guard in their scarlet and gold liveries with their ceremonial weapons.

There is a door into the nave of the abbey at the north end of the east walk, but this is deep in the shadow of a large souvenir stall, and at present is used only to shepherd visitors out of the abbey church. To go into the church, it is necessary to walk to the far end of the north walk and to enter by the door there. One passes a number of visitors busily making rubbings from plastic replicas of medieval memorial brasses from churches all over the country. Some visitors object to the commercialisation of this part of the abbey as being unworthy of a great national shrine, but the hard fact is that the mounting expense of heating and lighting this huge lofty building, and the drain on its financial resources exercised by the need for skilled restoration and repair, makes it absolutely essential for the abbey to increase its income, for voluntary contributions are not enough.

This part of the cloisters, facing south and therefore receiving a good deal of light and warmth from the sun, was equipped with little cubicles or carrels for private study, but the scriptoria where the beautiful manuscripts were actually written appears to have been sited elsewhere. Some recreation must have been allowed, however, for in the far north-western corner of the cloister, just beside the door into the abbey church, the upper surface of the stone bench has a pattern of shallow holes drilled in it. These are for the smooth pebbles used in a game called Nine Holes or Nine Men's Morris, which is not unlike the modern game of Chinese Chequers or the Victorian parlour game of Solitaire. The holes are usually hidden by the brass-rubbers' impedimenta, but they are still there. Nine Holes must have been an innocent enough diversion for the novices and young monks who

received their instruction in the west walk. There they learned the rules of the Order of St Benedict, were taught to read and write, and to memorise not only the seven daily services but the special ones for the many feast days. It was an arduous life when the rules were enforced, and it is perhaps significant that the most common ailment appearing in the infirmary records is 'housemaid's knee', a painful condition of the knee-joints brought about by prolonged kneeling on cold stone.

The entrance to the nave of the abbey is now through the door in the far north-western corner of the cloisters, and there, for the first time, the full splendour of the medieval vaulting spanning the main body of the abbey church makes its impact. The vaulting in the cloisters is comparatively low – almost within range of a tall man's outstretched hand – but that which spans the nave is just over a hundred feet high, and is immeasurably more impressive. It is largely the work of Chaucer's friend and colleague, the royal architect, Henry Yevele, through whose gate the cloisters are entered from Dean's Yard, and who built the Abbot's Hall which occupies most of one side of Dean's Court. But these are minor works by comparison with the nave which, built from 1362 onwards, was therefore much later than the eastern part of the abbey, erected by builders working for Henry III in the thirteenth century. Nevertheless, Henry Yevele continued his building westwards in much the same style, so that his more modern work would

left, The vaulting of the nave in Westminster Abbey
right, A drawing by Drake Brookshaw showing the construction of a medieval vault

83

harmonise with the earlier east end and chancel. With the cream of medieval craftsmen at his command and with experience in building which later enabled him to create not only this, the loftiest vault in England, but the splendour of the nave at Canterbury Cathedral, Yevele produced one of the most perfectly proportioned medieval abbey naves in Europe. The ribbed tracery of the vault roofing this nave seems to grow as inevitably and as naturally from the clustered columns as do the upper branches of a forest tree from its sinewy trunk, but this is an illusion. The vault is, in fact, a remarkable example of the most brilliant engineering skill of a medieval architect, with the thrust and counter-thrust of the ribs held securely, or transferred down the columns safely to the ground, or directed through the flying buttresses outside to selected points outside the great church. Later generations have allowed the walls of the nave to be cluttered with memorials and tombs – some of famous people, others of non-entities who, by political adroitness, social status, or bribery, contrived to procure for themselves a resting place in this superb building. Nevertheless, despite much which is trivial and unworthy in the nave, the vault remains serene, noble and aloof.

Most visitors see the vault for the first time from the main West door, however, and then quite naturally cluster round the memorial slab to Sir Winston Churchill, which is very close to the West door, before moving on to the grave of the Unknown Warrior of the Second World War a little further to the east. They then break off into little wandering groups to look at the memorials on the walls of the nave. The stone screen to the east, which divides the choir from the nave and acts as a reredos for the nave altar, is largely the work of a Victorian architect, Edward Blore, although it is built on to thirteenth-century stonework, visible only from the choir. The presence of this solidly built screen, acting as a permanent barrier between the worshippers in the nave and the choir, emphasises one of the essential differences between the nature of church services before the Reformation of 1535 and the Protestant services which were designed after this important event. Before the Reformation, the congregation were little more than passive attendants at a celebration of holy mysteries performed by professional worshippers, and any kind of what would today be called audience participation was not expected, especially as the services were conducted in Latin and were unintelligible to many. Apart from the climax of the service – the elevation of the host – those in the nave would see little as the service was conducted on the other side of the screen.

Even today, long after the Reformation, the retention of this screen, a relic of Pre-Reformation England, still exerts a certain divisive influence. Each day, when the abbey is hushed for Evensong, and small parties of overawed visitors are permitted to occupy seats in the choir stalls, they take very little part in the ritual. Clergy conduct the whole service, and the choristers perform the choral parts of the service with great professional expertise; the worshippers in the nave hear only the disembodied voices of the participants over the loudspeakers. On Sundays, however, when the great church reverts to its proper role as a building for Christian worship,

the transepts are filled and the whole service becomes a great act of communal worship.

It is significant of the Pre-Reformation church that the tombs and shrines of the kings, queens and powerful nobles were all near the high altar and in the eastern half of the church, well to the east of the stone screen dividing the chancel from the nave. Visitors are therefore now shepherded through the opening to the north of the screen to cross the transepts and the chancel, where the full splendour of the medieval vaults causes all eyes to be lifted to the roof. The north transept was restored during the nineteenth century, and the wheel or rose window over the north porch is not really medieval at all, but the work of John Loughborough Pearson, one of the surveyors of the abbey during the reign of Queen Victoria, who worked there partly on the designs of the more famous Victorian architect, Sir George Gilbert Scott. With the insertion of the tombs of notable statesmen, the first of which was that of William Pitt, who died in 1778, the north transept became a repository for the tombs of other statesmen and is now known as the Statesmen's Aisle. The south transept later came to contain memorials and tombs of poets, and is now known as Poets' Corner. Some visitors have commented on the incongruity of finding, in a medieval building, a number of statesmen, apparently petrified in the act of declaiming their political beliefs, clad in bathrobes, their features idealised almost beyond recognition, ranged alongside the aisle; but this is a problem which is inevitable when a building has to play a part for which it was not originally designed.

It would be almost impossible even to catalogue, and certainly to describe the many hundreds of memorials which are now housed by the abbey, and one can do little more than comment on those which are more obviously related to the development of the great medieval building, or those which seem to be particularly relevant to the twentieth-century visitor. Many – particularly those of the Middle Ages – are among the most beautiful of their kind in the world; they are worthy of respect and excite our appreciative delight as works of art, irrespective of the person for whom they were executed. Most of the finest of the medieval examples are to be found in the eastern part of the abbey church to the rear of the high altar, and are to be reached by the ambulatory which encircles this area and includes the Lady Chapel, better known as Henry VII's Chapel. This area, however, is reserved for visitors who are willing and able to pay a fixed entrance fee; the rest of the abbey, apart from the chapter house and the museum, is subject only to a voluntary subscription.

It is noteworthy that all the figures on medieval tombs lie on their backs, gazing heavenwards, with their hands clasped in an attitude of supplication and devotion – a sculptural convention which was not accepted by all those buried after the Reformation. These express a somewhat different attitude by lying not on their backs, but propped up in a reclining position of some nonchalance – a chance observed by the seventeenth-century playwright Beaumont, who wrote in the *Duchess of Malfi*:

Princes' effigies on their tombs
Do not lie as they were wont, gazing on Heaven,
But with their hands under their heads, as if
They died of the toothache . . .

Later, especially in the eighteenth century, the tomb became a kind of platform for a tableau, with an idealised version of the occupant of the tomb represented in a dramatic scene, with weeping cupids fluttering among the agitated marble draperies, and flanked by such symbolic figures as Britannia, Victory, etc., while a suitably emaciated figure with scythe and hourglass demanded tribute. The inscriptions are also highly imaginative – indeed, if they are to be believed literally, it is a matter for some surprise that the subject could bear to inhabit this sinful world at all. Among the medieval tombs there are, of course, a number of beautifully engraved memorial brasses – real ones, not polyester resin duplicates.

The apse

The superbly ribbed vault from the east, Henry Yevele's vault from
the western nave, and those which span both transepts, meet in a
triumphant climax with the carved, gilded and painted ceiling of the central
tower – a magnificent focal point at the heart of the church. The whole area
beneath is the setting for the rare but wonderfully impressive coronation
ceremony. William the Conqueror was the first monarch we can be certain
was crowned in an abbey on this very spot, but Edward I was the first to
institute the coronation ceremony in this great medieval church in 1272.
Since then, nearly every monarch of England, has been crowned here.
Thanks to the miracle of television at the coronation of our own Queen
Elizabeth II, millions all over the world were able to share the splendour of
the ritual which is an integral part of the centuries-old ceremony, and to
wonder at the beauty of the architectural setting which the abbey provided.

The chancel, crossing and choir have undergone some alterations during the past few hundred years, but the abbey is nevertheless still very much as Chaucer must have known it when he attended the coronation of his royal patron, Richard II, in 1377, or as he busied himself about the building as Clerk of the Works in 1389, although at that time work was still being carried out on the nave roof which was in some disrepair. The three tombs in the north of the sanctuary between the altar steps and the reredos might well still have been resplendent with gold leaf and bright paint, for the little one which contains the body of Aveline, Countess of Lancaster, and the larger one adjoining it of Aylmer de Valence, Earl of Pembroke and cousin of Edward I, were built between 1300 and 1326. The larger and more impressive one nearest to the reredos is that of Edmund, Earl of Lancaster, surnamed Crouchback, the youngest son of Henry III, a warrior who dealt with the insurrection in Wales in 1282 by capturing and beheading the rebel leader, Llewellyn ap Gruffydd, and who died at Bayonne in 1296 while besieging Bordeaux. His effigy in which he is portrayed in full armour is not only a splendid example of medieval sculpture, but a remarkable record of arms and armour of the period. His tomb, in common with a great many others in the abbey, reflects the style of architecture of his period, and indeed in some ways anticipates, in miniature, the period of architecture in which complete buildings were to appear later. It is as though builders used the architectural elements of the tombs as a proving ground for new ideas, supporting the canopies which roofed the effigies with tiny vaults which later appeared as full-sized vaults spanning aisles or cloisters. Even if the architectural elements were not used practically, the experimental nature of those details is particularly apparent in the decorative schemes with which the tombs were enriched. In medieval tombs, particularly, the colours used were not wholly for decorative purposes; they were an integral part of coats of arms depicted.

In the Middle Ages, disease, war, or even political assassination sometimes wiped out a whole family, leaving huge estates without a direct heir, and the one certain method by which a claimant could establish his right to the vacant title was his ability to trace his lineage through the various devices borne on his shield. Through these, the College of Arms (which still holds all records of all coats of arms legally used) could confirm or refute the claimant's right to inherit. It was not enough that he could show that his shield bore, for example, a lion rampant or an eagle displayed – the colour of the device and its background could be crucial evidence in such a lawsuit. The devices worn on the shields of early knights were fairly simple, so that they could be readily identified in battle, but later the multiplicity of quarterings – especially in the Elizabethan period – became so involved that heraldry was no longer of any practical use in battle, although the statement of the ancestry of the wearer was still announced in the coats of arms. Thus, whether the occupant of the tomb was famous or not, the tombs themselves are a never-failing source of historical reference as well as beautiful examples of the craftsmen's skill of the period in which they were fashioned. Carved figures of the earlier periods, up to about the fourteenth century, tended to be symbols of the nobleman or royal personage within the tomb, and were not very often regarded as portraits of the deceased; and although today some visitors feel that stone has such a natural beauty that it should never be painted, in the Middle Ages colour was always applied to the figure and to the surrounding architectural framework. Figures carved in wood were often used as a kind of form on which to shape a copper or 'latoun' figure, the metal being applied in thin sheets and hammered until it assumed the shape of the wooden effigy beneath; it was then decorated with beautifully executed enamels before being fastened back on to the figure permanently. Such an effigy is that of William de Valence, Lord of Pembroke and Wexford, the half-brother of Henry III and father of Aylmer de Valence. He died in 1296, and his tomb figure, which is to be seen in the Chapel of St Edmund on the south side of the ambulatory, was executed in this way. In one area near the left elbow the wood has crumbled away, and the resultant dent in the copper sheath shows by which method this figure was made. Many of the memorial brasses were originally enriched with enamels, but they were destroyed at some point during their long history and only the rough cross hatching and the little metal walls which contained them remain to show where they formerly provided decorations.

Since the abbey had access to the best craftsmen in the country, it is not surprising that there emerged there some of the most important technical advances in various crafts as well as in architectural design. The tomb figures of Henry III and Eleanor of Castile, for example, executed towards the end of the thirteenth century, were the first examples in this country of life-sized figures made in the *cire-perdue* or 'lost-wax' process of metal casting. This basically consisted of modelling the entire figure in high relief, in clay, and then encasing it with a skin of melted beeswax to the depth of

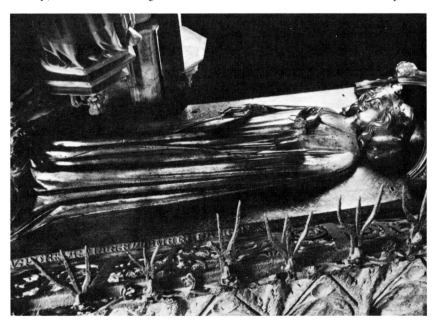

The tomb of Eleanor of Castile

about a quarter of an inch. A further coating of coarse clay then enveloped the whole figure and a number of little tunnels were drilled in this outer coating, down to the wax surface. Molten metal was then poured through some of these tunnels, the wax being vaporised and escaping through some of the other holes, its place being taken by the molten metal which encased the original figure to the thickness of the former wax sheath. The outer casing of clay was removed, and the clay within the metal (probably disintegrated with the heat) taken out. Naturally the whole process required a great deal more skill than this oversimplified account would suggest, and the craftsmen spent many weeks working over the rough casting with tiny chisels and punches before the final work was ready for installation in the abbey.

The tombs which form such a fascinating aspect of a visit to the abbey thus fall into fairly simple technical categories. Of the two-dimensional monuments, some are incised slabs of stone, others beautiful line engravings in metal in which the artists defined the features – the robes, and the fiery animals on which the subjects rest their feet – with a wonderful economy and freedom. These were usually enriched with enamels, but only the empty cross-hatched areas now remain where formerly the coloured panels shone like stained glass. Of the three-dimensional ones, there are early ones in alabaster or local stone, originally coloured and gilded, enclosed by an elaborate architectural framework. A few from this early period may be of wood, but if this is the case, they are forms which were at one time encased in metal; and if it happened to be a semi-precious metal, such as silver gilt, as on the tomb of Henry V, this was later plundered leaving only the wooden core. Of the three-dimensional effigies in bronze or some similar alloy, some were cast by the *cire-perdue* process, which later gave way to more efficient if more monotonous industrially produced figures. By the sixteenth century local or native stones were being replaced by a variety of marbles and other more exotic stones imported from overseas, and the ability of a carver was judged not by the way he accepted and respected the discipline of his material, but by the degree of his skill at deceiving the visitor into believing that what he saw was not the interpretation of a human form, in stone, but a live person, in a state of temporary rigidity, frozen to the plinth.

The development of the architecture of the abbey is less complicated. As we have seen, the earliest part is a crude cloister of the very early Norman period, but most of the building is of one of the forms of English Gothic, culminating in that style of architecture only to be found in England – the Perpendicular period. It is significant that while Michelangelo was working on the ceiling of the Sistine Chapel in Rome during the first decade of the sixteenth century, we in this insular country were still developing our own peculiar form of Gothic – one of the most striking examples of which is Henry VII's Chapel at the far eastern end of the abbey. Thus, while the mainland of Europe was already being heavily influenced by the Renaissance, in England at this time neither craftsmen nor architects had much knowledge of this movement.

The visitor entering the ambulatory from the north transept is immediately surrounded by a bewildering collection of memorials executed during almost every period of English art. Immediately to the right is a finely engraved monumental brass of Sir John Harpedon, showing a knight of about 1438 in full armour, but this, like so many other early tombs, has been moved from its original position. (Its former site in the wall of the Chapel of St John on the north side of the ambulatory is now very fully occupied by a much later and somewhat ostentatious monument to the great eighteenth-century soldier, General Wolfe, who was killed at the moment of victory, in Canada, as his adversaries, the French, fled the field.) The wall of the sanctuary on the right carries three royal tombs – that of Edward I; the second – more elaborate and still bearing some of its original mosaic decoration – that of Henry III; and the most easterly one, that of Eleanor of Castile, the wife of Edward I, with its original protective iron grille. These can be seen much more readily from the inside of the sanctuary, however. On the left there is a succession of chapels, each with a selection of tombs of various periods. The first on the left, the Islip Chapel, has been altered a great deal so that the tomb of Abbot Islip, whose chantry chapel it was, has been moved to the far end and other tombs inserted. It is still possible to see his punning device, 'I-slip', consisting of the carving of an eye, within a 'slip' or branch of a tree grasped by a hand, and man slipping from the branch; this is carved in the frieze both within the chapel and outside. (This type of visual pun is by no means uncommon – Prior Bolton's Run, 'Bolt-Tun', in St Bartholomew the Great, has already been mentioned. Other examples outside London are those of Sir Roger de Trumpington and Sir John de Swynborne – the first knight bore the device of trumpets on his shield, the second, three wild boars' heads.) A chantry chapel was, of course, normally reserved for its donor; it is here that at certain times of the day prayers would be said, interceding for the soul of the person to whom the chapel was dedicated, and who had sometimes left considerable sums of money for this purpose in the hope that such prayers might mitigate the torments which sinners less well endowed, or perhaps less prudent, might expect to suffer for eternity.

The quaintly named Chapel of Our Lady of the Pew, the next chapel to the east, has also been altered considerably in the course of time, and the stone statue of the Madonna and Child just within the doorway is one of the more recent additions. This little chapel now adjoins the larger Chapel of St John the Baptist which, like so many others in the abbey, is little more than a receptacle for tombs and memorials. It is dominated by the huge tomb of Thomas Cecil, Earl of Exeter, occupying nearly all the central floor space. On the lid of the sarcophagus are two beautifully carved recumbent figures of the Earl and his first wife, Dorothy Nevill, each dressed in the most splendid costume of the Jacobean period. The highest tomb in the whole abbey is that of Henry Carey, 1st Baron Hunsdon, on the east wall, occupying the space that was formerly the site of the altar. He was a valiant and able courtier whose task it was to guard Queen Elizabeth during the dark and dangerous years which preceded the Spanish Armada. The tomb, erected by his son, is thirty-six feet high.

The last chapel to the east in this ambulatory is that of St Paul, again so full of monuments that even the site of the altar was taken over for the tomb of Frances Sidney, Countess of Sussex. Her most important memorial is not here in the abbey, but in Cambridge where she founded Sidney Sussex College. The same chapel contains the tomb of the Nottingham engineer, James Watt, who developed the steam engine, and the somewhat later tomb of Rowland Hill, the inventor of penny postage and the forerunner of the Post Office. None of these tombs would have been known to Chaucer, nor would he have known the wonderful Lady Chapel at the eastern end of the abbey, built over a hundred years after his death and occupying the site of tenements where he had rooms as an abbey servant. This is also known as Henry VII's Chapel and it is a truly remarkable addition to the abbey – the triumphant vindication of the continuation in England of the Gothic style long after it had been abandoned on the mainland of Europe. Once again one can witness the use of heraldry for the purposes of establishing claims and legal rights: the superb bronze entrance gates to the chapel show by their heraldic symbols the noble and royal families to whom Henry Tudor was related. These are not only extremely decorative, but also emphasise visually his legal right to the throne after his defeat of Richard III at the Battle of Bosworth. Thus, among the heraldic devices on the bronze doors there are the portcullis of the Beaufort family; the marguerite or daisy which was Henry VII's mother's personal badge; the leopards of England and the fleurs-de-lis of France; and a falcon with an open fetterlock, derived from the coat of arms of his maternal grandfather, Edward IV. This part of the abbey is particularly rich in heraldry, for it contains the banners of the Knights Grand Cross of the Most Honourable Order of the Bath, an order of chivalry instituted by Henry IV, the king who had deposed Chaucer's royal patron, Richard II, in 1399. Apart from this superb display of banners, their devices are also to be found in the richly carved woodwork of the seats (or stalls) allocated to each member of the Order; at one time medieval stained glass added further to the heraldic splendour in the wide windows above, but much of this has been destroyed.

However, as with the nave of the abbey, in this chapel it is the magnificent roof which commands attention – a perfect example of English Perpendicular Gothic which has no counterpart on the mainland of Europe, unique as it is to England. The fan-vault, which made its first appearance in the cloisters of Gloucester cathedral at the end of the fourteenth century, has matured and developed into this exuberant display of the genius of the medieval stonemason. There will always be some disagreement about which is the most beautiful example in the country – some declare that by comparison with the purity of the fan-vaulting which spans King's College Chapel, Cambridge, this vault, with its great roof bosses extended into pendants that hang down like man-made stalactites, is over-decorated. Yet it was a breathtaking achievement, and to stand beneath this magnificent roof and to wonder at the engineering skill by which the craftsmen serving this first Tudor monarch could produce such a work of art provides an unforgettable experience. Many writers have tried to express its impact on

Henry VII's Chapel showing the fan-vaulting and pendentives, with Henry VII's tomb on the right

them: John Leland, the Tudor antiquary, himself a Londoner, called it *'orbis miraculum'* – 'the wonder of the world' – while the American writer, Washington Irving, who was by no means favourably impressed with everything he saw in this country, wrote an ecstatic account of his first glimpse of the chapel. 'On entering, the eye is astonished by the pomp of architecture and elaborate beauty of sculptured detail . . . Stone seems, by the cunning labour of the chisel, to have been robbed of its weight and density, suspended aloft as if by magic, and the fretted roof achieved with the wonderful minuteness and airy security of a cobweb.' But if the roof is a supreme example of the last phase of English Gothic, the tomb of Henry VII is neither English nor Gothic, but the finest example of Italian Renaissance sculpture to be found anywhere in England, apart from those examples specially acquired for museums much later. The grille which

The tomb of Henry VII and Elizabeth of York

surrounds it is indeed Gothic workmanship, probably by the same man who executed the bronze gates – Thomas Ducheman (although there is some doubt about this) – but the recumbent figures on the tomb, those of the founder of the chapel and of his queen, Elizabeth of York, together with the low reliefs which decorate the panels on the sarcophagus and the enchanting little angels which are perched on it, are all pure Italian Renaissance. These are all by Pietro Torrigiano (or Torrigiani), a fellow student of the great Michaelangelo, who achieved the somewhat dubious distinction of quarrelling with Michelangelo, knocking him senseless, breaking his nose and scarring him for life. Under the impression that he had killed him, Torrigiano fled the country, and after a spell as a mercenary soldier in Switzerland, he came to England and was commissioned by Henry VIII to execute this magnificent tomb. Henry VII had left orders that he should be represented in a kneeling figure with wood, covered with plates of fine gold and in full armour, but his son disregarded these instructions and ordered the tomb as it is seen today. By the time that Torrigiano arrived in England Henry VII had been dead for two years (Elizabeth of York had died six years before her husband), but the artist made careful studies from the death masks of the king and his wife, idealising the somewhat mean features of the king, and concealing his rather crafty and avaricious character under a bland and enobled portrait. Henry VII's death mask is still on view in the abbey museum. Nothing quite like this tomb had been seen in the country before. The rigidity of the folded robes and pleated garments, the carefully ordered pattern of hair and beard, the elimination of personal characteristics in favour of a royal image of kingship – all features which were typical of medieval sculpture – were discarded. In their place, the Italian introduced a freedom of interpretation and a contrived natural appearance; the robes were draped in accidental folds, and there was a convincing likeness in the faces of the recumbent figures. This was a very different approach from the earlier medieval conventions governing the presentation of a royal personage in the Middle Ages. It is likely that Torrigiano also executed the terracotta bust of Henry VII now in the Victoria and Albert Museum in South Kensington, and the portrait bust of the young Henry VIII in the Metropolitan Museum in New York. He also designed a sumptuous altar for the Lady Chapel, but this was later destroyed and the present one is modern, although it incorporates fragments of the earlier one in its construction. The painting of the Virgin and Child, executed by Bartolommeo Vivarini, a Venetian painter, in about 1480, is also a twentieth-century addition, having been presented by Lord Lee of Fareham in about 1935.

The magnificently carved stalls which flank the chapel have also undergone considerable rearrangement and reconstruction, but those which form the front row are nearly all from the original monastic chapel and have that strange and endearing blend of religious subjects and earthy Chaucerian humour which is characteristic of medieval art, even in churches. On the south side, for example, there is a beautifully carved misericord, the subject of which, far from portraying connubial bliss, shows instead an irate housewife belabouring her husband, pulling back his doublet in order to get a clearer view of her target. The visitor with time to spare will find it rewarding to examine the carvings with which these stalls are decorated. The chapels, too, house an outstanding display of intact medieval sculpture, a sad reminder of how much must have enriched the churches in the rest of England before the Reformation and the later vandalism of the Puritans. Many of the statues are of saints, each with the typical symbols, yet often in the contemporary costume of the period in which they were executed; the medieval worshipper would have seen nothing incongruous or amusing in a statue of St Matthew with a pair of spectacles perched on the end of his nose, or of Mary Magdalene in 'modern' dress. The rounded end of a medieval church is normally known as an apse, but the eastern end of the abbey formed by Henry VII's Chapel – with smaller chapels inserted between the flying buttresses supporting this superb roof – is called a chevet, a common enough feature in French architecture, but rare in Great Britain. Immediately to the rear of Henry VII's tomb and altar is the former Jesus Chapel, now re-dedicated as The Battle of Britain Chapel, a memorial to the 1495 aircrew who lost their lives during that crucial period in 1940. The modern stained glass windows show the badges of the squadrons who took part in the Battle of Britain, and a Roll of Honour records the names of these gallant youngsters from Great Britain, the Colonies and the Dominions, from Belgium, Czechoslovakia and Poland, and one lone volunteer from the U.S.A. It is fitting that these men should be remembered in the abbey among so many illustrious dead, and Lord Trenchard, Marshal of the Royal Air Force, by whose efforts the Royal Air Force was formed and developed, is buried in the same chapel. A plaque in the floor on the outer border of this chapel records the former burial place of Oliver Cromwell and his associates. After the Restoration of the monarchy in 1660, many felt it unseemly that the regicides should be interred in the burial place of kings, and the bodies were removed, hung like those of any common felon on the gallows at Tyburn, and then disposed of dishonourably.

Of the other tombs in this part of the abbey, none is more worthy of attention than that of Elizabeth I in the north aisle. When she succeeded to the throne as a young woman of twenty-five, few would have expected her to survive for very long. The remarkable achievements of her reign can perhaps be detected in the splendidly carved features of the marble effigy by Maximilian Colt (also known as Poultrain) lying on the great marble sarcophagus, showing the queen in her full regalia. The head was carved from a death mask and is surely one of the most penetrating portraits of this superb and indomitable woman ever produced. Her half-sister (known to some as 'Bloody Mary') is buried in a grave beneath this tomb, but with neither memorial nor headstone. In the same chapel is the double grave of two young children whose death, after five hundred years, is still a complete mystery. This is the grave of the young Edward V and his brother, Richard – the famous Princes in the Tower. Two other children are buried near to the tomb of Queen Elizabeth at the eastern end of the aisle. In what has now become known as Innocents' Corner there are two tiny figures over the graves of the two youngest children of James I, also the work of Maximilian Colt – one in a cradle of stone, the other, only two years of age when she died, represented reclining on one elbow.

On the other side of Henry VII's Chapel in the south aisle, there are two more important tombs, both containing the remains of women who had considerable influence on this country during their lifetimes. The earlier one is that of the mother of Henry VII, who died a few weeks after her son at the age of sixty-nine, and whose tomb was also the work of Torrigiano. Margaret Beaufort, Countess of Richmond, was indeed a remarkable woman. Henry was born in Pembroke Castle when she was already a widow, aged thirteen, but she survived this traumatic experience to become one of the most brilliant women of her time. Highly intelligent and widely read, she was Instructress-General to the Royal Princes, and she founded not only the Chair of Divinity at both Oxford and Cambridge but was also foundress of two Cambridge colleges – Christ's and St John's. Realising the importance of the newly invented craft of printing, she was the protector and patron of William Caxton, and arranged for him to set up his workshop in the almonry just west of Abbey Green. At her funeral Bishop Fisher declared: 'Everyone that knew her, loved her, and everything she said or did, became her.' Her tomb figure shows the same psychological insight and beauty of execution as the other portrait figures carried out by Torrigiano, and since the grille which surrounds the tomb is not as high nor as close, the figure can be more easily studied and enjoyed.

The second tomb, further from the altar, is that of a much more controversial woman – Mary, Queen of Scots, who would certainly not have merited the eulogy given by Bishop Fisher. Beheaded in Fotheringhay Castle, she was buried in Peterborough Cathedral, but her son, James I, on succeeding to the thrones of England and Scotland, had his mother's body disinterred and re-buried in Westminster Abbey. The tomb is the work of Maximilian Colt and John de Critz.

With a building which is as complex historically as Westminster Abbey, it is clearly impossible to keep to one period of architectural style; Tudor London has already been mentioned, and after leaving the south aisle of Henry VII's Chapel, one returns to the Middle Ages, passing the wooden effigy of Henry V. This was fashioned about 1422, but is now little more than a man-shaped block of wood, for the fine metalwork with which it was originally encased has long since been plundered. His chantry chapel, however, is still remarkably intact, with a fine array of medieval sculpture and, on a rod above, the saddle and the shield made especially for his funeral which took place with great ceremony in November 1422. The tradition that the tilting helmet on display is one that the warrior king wore at Agincourt is nonsense. The helm for a tournament had a very restricted area of vision – all that the knight had to see was his oncoming adversary. To wear a helm such as the one shown in battle would have meant that the knight could have been attacked on all sides before becoming aware of his danger.

From the chantry chapel of Henry V, one comes to the very heart of the medieval abbey, and the most sacred part of the whole complex of buildings – the sanctuary, which contains the shrine of Edward the Confessor, the founder of the abbey. In the Middle Ages, the pilgrims who thronged to Westminster went there to pray to the saint, and sometimes to leave a sick relative for the night in one of the little niches in the side of the shrine, in the hope that they might be made well by the morning. Only the lower part of the shrine erected by Henry III as a fitting resting place for the remains and the relics of the saint now survives, and this is sadly defaced, for at the time of the dissolution of the monasteries in 1540 the tomb was ruthlessly plundered. Nevertheless there are still pilgrims who come to this shrine, not as tourists but as supplicants and worshippers. Despite the mutilation it has undergone, and the modern casket above, sufficient of the mosaic decoration remains to indicate what a splendid sight the shrine must once have been. Until the reign of Richard II the sanctuary was reserved for royal burials only, but despite protests Richard insisted that John of Waltham (the Bishop of Salisbury), his Keeper of the Privy Seal, should be buried there and his damaged brass is in the south-western corner. The sanctuary has one of the finest collections of medieval tomb figures to be found anywhere in England. The jewels and enamels with which the figures were once ornamented have gone, as well as the crown, sceptre and orb with which some were represented, but despite this loss, the figures are of great beauty and provide wonderful examples of medieval craftsmanship. Immediately inside the sanctuary, to the right, is the tomb of Eleanor of Castile, the first wife of Edward I. The mother of Edward II, she was very dear to Edward I, although the legend that she once saved the king's life at grave risk to her own by sucking the poison out of a wound he had sustained from an attempted assassination is not now thought to be true. She died at Harby in Nottinghamshire in 1290, and when her body was brought to London for burial, each place that the cortège rested at night was later marked by a splendid cross, of which only three remain today – Waltham Cross in Essex, and Geddington and Northampton Crosses in Northamptonshire. Charing Cross was destroyed during the Reformation; the cross now standing outside Charing Cross station in the Strand is an earnest Victorian reconstruction of the one which used to stand at the head of Whitehall on the site now occupied by the equestrian statue of Charles I. The grille which protects the tomb of Eleanor of Castile was fashioned by a Bedfordshire ironsmith, Thomas of Leighton. Her effigy, as well as that of her father-in-law, Henry III, which lies a little to the west, were both carried out by the same craftsman, William Torel, Citizen of London and Goldsmith, who cast both figures in 1291, using the lost-wax process. The bronze figures were then gilded with the gold from 476 Flemish crown pieces; the cost of both figures came to a total of £113 6s. 8d. (It would be quite impossible to estimate their worth today.) Both figures show that remarkable discipline of design which is so characteristic of the best medieval sculpture, and the faces of the subjects are enobled and restrained. The tomb of Henry III must have been particularly magnificent, with the elaborate plinth and casket which were wrought by Italian workmen brought specially to this country to carry out the carving and to insert the mosaics, and it is still a very striking exhibit whether it is seen from ground level in the sanctuary, or from below, from the ambulatory. The tomb of Edward I has no effigy, but his great seven-foot sword and his shield are nearby, and give some idea of the stature of this martial king whose height earned him the surname of Longshanks.

The Coronation Chair stands against the westward wall of the sanctuary, and battered and scarred as it is, it is still one of the most revered objects in the abbey, and will have been seen by millions of people all over the world during the televising of the last coronation. Edward I, known also as the 'Hammer of the Scots' once he had subjugated that proud and independent people, removed the ancient Stone of Scone upon which their kings had been crowned since it was taken to Scotland from Ireland in the ninth century AD, and took it to Westminster. He had the Coronation Chair made to contain it, and in that chair and above that stone every British monarch – apart from two notable exceptions – has been crowned. Later generations treated it with less than the reverence with which it is regarded today: a number of eighteenth-century vandals sought a brief notoriety by carving their names or initials on it, and eighteenth-century guides extracted a fee from visitors to the abbey who wished to be able to say that they had sat in the chair themselves.

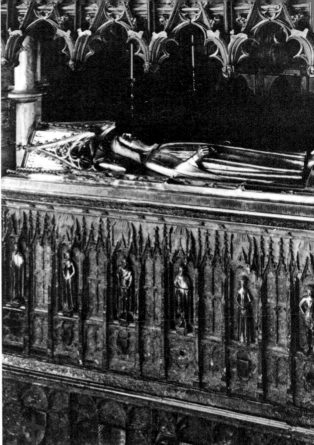

One of the most sumptuous tombs is on the south side of the sanctuary overlooking the south ambulatory. This contains the bodies of the murdered Richard II (who was supplanted by Henry IV) and his first wife, Anne of Bohemia. Richard II, a great patron of the arts, was devoted to the abbey and was responsible not only for the rebuilding of Westminster Hall, but for Henry Yevele's work in part of the nave. His tomb was designed by the same architect, and the figures of Richard and his wife are almost certainly portraits. (Some comparison can be made with the painting of Richard II which hangs from a pillar just inside the west door of the abbey, to the right.) The elegant clothing which they both wear is most beautifully formalised, as is his curling hair and thin wispy beard. The tomb was completed in Richard's lifetime and cost £670, of which £279 was for the marble only.

The most splendid tomb figure of all in the sanctuary is perhaps that which is just to the east of the tomb of Richard II and Anne of Bohemia. This is the effigy of Edward III, and although it could, of course, be a likeness, the nobility of the treatment of the flowing beard and stylised hair, and the dignified folds of the royal robes, present the king in a very different guise from the pathetic, doll-like figure to be seen in the abbey museum. There, the 'image of the likeness of a king', made for the funeral procession by a craftsman named Stephen Hadley at the cost of just over £22, shows the distorted death-mask of a man who died from a stroke, and the blankly staring face has a drooping mouth and all the signs of facial paralysis. The figure formerly wore a wig, and the eyebrows were simulated with dog hairs.

left, The Coronation Chair
right, The tomb of Edward III, showing the weepers

99

The image in the sanctuary is rather that of an immortal, and was very probably the inspiration for some of William Blake's drawings of God the Father, or some of his patriarchal figures from the Old Testament. There is no doubt, however, that the marble effigy of Philippa of Hainault, Edward III's queen, is a portrait, for there is an authenticity about her rather homely features which can hardly be mistaken for an idealised version. The king arranged for it to be executed by a famous French sculptor named Hennequin de Liège, and spent a very considerable sum of money on the tomb – about £3000 – but this tomb, too, has been most savagely despoiled and is a ruin, apart from the scanty fragments which were reassembled during the last century.

From the sanctuary, the visitor should turn westwards along the south ambulatory, where there are yet three more chapels containing marvellous examples of the mason's and sculptor's craftsmanship from various periods. The first, the Chapel of St Nicholas, contains few medieval monuments, and indeed, had probably scarcely been built by the time of Chaucer's death, but it does contain some fine Elizabethan work. The eldest son of Anne, Duchess of Somerset, who died in 1587, erected a monument to his mother, saying 'in this dolefull dutie carefull and diligent, doth consecrate this monument to his deere parent'. This rather fulsome epitaph is contradicted by Sir John Hayward, who owed no allegiance to the widow of the Protector Somerset and described her as 'a mannish or rather a devilish woman, for any . . . imperfectibilities intolerable, but for pride monstrous, exceeding subtle and violent'. The most impressive monument is the one erected in the late 1580s by Lord Burghley to his second wife, who died in 1589, and his daughter Anne, who died in 1588. The whole monument, twenty-four feet high, is lavishly decorated with multi-coloured marble, and heavily gilded, and it occupied the space where the altar stood before the Reformation.

Much finer medieval tomb figures are to be found in the next chapel to the west which is dedicated to St Edmund and reserved as a burial place for the relations of the sovereigns. The tomb figure of William de Valence, Lord of Pembroke and Wexford, with its wooden core encased in plates of beaten copper and its rich decoration of enamels from Limoges, has already been referred to as being typical of the process by which early effigies were often produced. On the opposite side of the entrance is an equally fine medieval tomb figure, but this time wholly carved from a block of creamy white alabaster. This is the tomb of John of Eltham, Earl of Cornwall, who died in 1337, and it displays the medieval sculptor's mastery of the chisel. The Earl's surcoat bears the royal leopards of England, and it is a delight to see how the sculptor has managed to preserve the fiery stance and the lashing tail of the royal beasts. It seems probable that it was the same hand which carved the superb figure of the Earl's father, Edward II, which now lies in Gloucester Cathedral.

The chapel leading into the south transept is St Benedict's Chapel, and as the abbey was served by the Benedictine monks, it is reasonable that this chapel tended to be reserved for those who were connected in some way with the abbey. When the time came for Geoffrey Chaucer, a faithful servant of

The Jewel Tower

the abbey, to be laid to rest, it was natural that the site chosen should be one near the entrance to St Benedict's Chapel. He passed his last years in the tenement leased to him by the keeper of the Lady Chapel of the abbey – the document is still preserved. From there he must have watched the feverish comings and goings from the Palace of Westminster, and heard all the rumours about the fate of his royal patron, Richard II, during those last fateful days before Henry Bolingbroke claimed the throne. From his tenement he could also see the monks' graveyard just to the east of the chapter house; this is now a lawn at the head of which is a white stone statue of the late George V. Opposite Chaucer would have been able to see the whole complex of the Palace of Westminster, dominated by the magnificent hall still to be seen there today, and beyond that shimmered the Thames. To the south was the ancient Jewel Tower, which was built in the middle of the fourteenth century by Chaucer's colleague, Henry Yevele, and has since been restored and converted into a museum, which contains some of the sculpture from the Norman Westminster Hall which the same architect rebuilt. To the north, literally and metaphorically in the shadow of the abbey, was the early parish church of St Margaret, but the present building is considerably later – probably sixteenth-century – and has been extensively restored during the past two hundred years. Building was still in progress on the abbey when Chaucer died, and the western towers, in fact, were not completed until the middle of the eighteenth century.

Chaucer died on 25 October 1400, and was buried under a plain stone slab near the entrance to St Benedict's Chapel. It was not until 1551 that Nicholas Brigham, a Tudor poet, felt that such a tomb was wholly unworthy

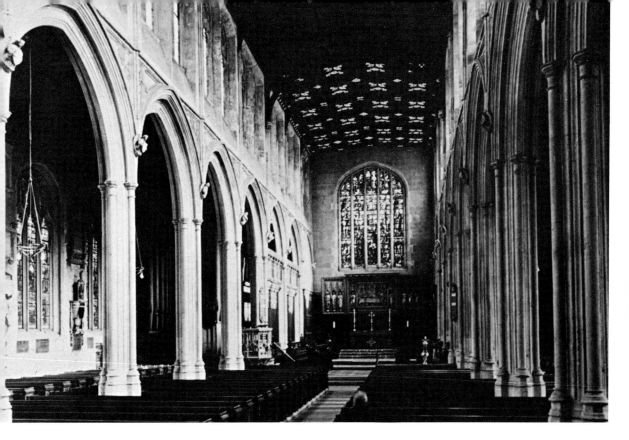

St Margaret's,
Westminster

of the first great poet of the English language, and he had the remains moved
to their present resting place, and the new tomb built. The south transept
was at that time just another arm of the great church, but it gradually
accepted the remains of more and more writers and poets until it became
known as Poets' Corner, and contains many more memorials to poets than
are actually interred there. On the south wall of the transept there is a
medieval mural painting which was concealed until recently by later
monuments. It is painted with the same formalised grace and sweeping lines
which can be found in most of the medieval figures, and is but a fragmentary
reminder of how richly painted the whole abbey would have been before the
Reformation. Still further to the south is the tiny Chapel of St Faith,
reserved for private prayer – a salutary reminder that, however
overwhelming the pressures exerted by the thousands of visitors to the
abbey, it must still provide a haven of peace for quiet reflection and private
prayer, if it is to fulfil the role for which it was originally built.

In Chaucer's lifetime and for a century afterwards at least, Westminster
Abbey would have been brilliant with colour – not only in the stained
glass windows, but on the walls and arches. Of such a church, in about 1100,
Rugenus of Helmershausen commented:

> Thou hast approached God's house in all faith, and adorned it with
> abundent comeliness, and having illuminated the vaults of the walls with
> divers works and divers colours, thou hast in a manner shown forth to the
> beholders a vision of God's paradise ... For man's eyes knoweth not
> whereon first to gaze; if he looks up at the vaults, they are as mantles

embroidered with spring flowers; if he consider the light streaming through the windows, he marvelleth at the priceless beauty of the glass and the variety of this most precious work . . .

Westminster Abbey from the west

This is how the abbey church would have appeared to Chaucer, and although one can perhaps regard his gentle mockery of the Church in his famous *Canterbury Tales* as a symbol of the growing dissatisfaction with the way it was being corrupted, he would have been sick at heart to see what was to happen to so many of these noble buildings and their contents during the Reformation, and later. Until as late as the first quarter of the sixteenth century, when Henry VII's wonderful Lady Chapel was being built, the abbey was intact and apparently safe, but when the King challenged and defeated the power of the Church in England, the way lay open for the most ruthless plunder and destruction of all church buildings. Not even the abbey was immune, even if Henry VIII later made it a cathedral church (although this status lasted only ten years from 1540 to 1550) and his son, Edward VI, tried to make it a cathedral 'in the Diocese of London', and not in a separate Diocese of Westminster. One of the most significant preludes to the coming catastrophe was the confiscation of lands owned by the abbey upon which stood St James's Hospital – a charitable church organisation for the curing or nursing of 'leprous maids'. The hospital was destroyed, and the lands taken over as a hunting park for Henry VIII; his hunting lodge was the new red brick palace of St James. With the erection of St James's Palace a new era, unlike any which had previously been seen in London, was to emerge, and the London Chaucer had known was gone for ever.

4

Shakespeare's London – Tudor and Elizabethan Times

Visitors to London, deceived perhaps by brochures showing the much photographed group of timber-framed houses in Holborn, and therefore hoping to find areas of Shakespeare's London as jealously preserved as those in Stratford-upon-Avon, are liable to be acutely disappointed when they realise how little of Elizabethan London is still to be seen. Most if it was burned to the ground in the Great Fire of 1666, or fell victim to the air-raids of the Second World War. Of the remainder, only those buildings which were under the protection of the Crown, or belonged to bodies sufficiently powerful to withstand the ruthless onslaught of the property developers, managed to survive.

St James's Palace was preserved, and Lambeth Palace, the town house of the Archbishops of Canterbury since the twelfth century, despite bomb damage, is still an outstanding example of Tudor architecture. In the City, the lawyers held on to most of their Inns of Court, and Lincoln's Inn, also a legal preserve, was able to resist drastic modernisation and commercial vandalism. Yet the number of Tudor buildings accessible to the general public is very limited, and although they can usually be inspected from the outside without too much difficulty, it is by no means easy for visitors to enter them without special permission which sometimes has to be obtained in advance.

Outside London, about ten miles upstream from Westminster, Hampton Court, which became a royal palace in 1526, gives some idea of the splendour of the mansions which lined the north bank of the river from the Temple to Westminster, but which have long since disappeared. None of them equalled the grandeur of Hampton Court, it is true, but they must have been a splendid sight when seen from one of the many boats darting over the glittering surface of the Thames, with formal gardens, studded with trees, stretching down to the riverside, each with its own little jetty. They were still somewhat medieval in general appearance, but many were built of brick – a fairly recent innovation as brick hadn't been used since Roman times – with flat-arched doorways and windows framed in stone, or with cut and moulded brick rendered with a thin coat of plaster made from lime and sand to simulate stone. Tudor bricks were smaller than those in use today – indeed, it is often possible to distinguish the original work in Tudor buildings from modern restoration by the sizes of the bricks. Mortar joints tended to be wider, and the surfaces of the brick were more irregular. If there was any danger of an extensive wall surface becoming monotonous in

opposite, The gatehouse, St James's Palace

appearance, the Tudor builder introduced simple geometric patterns by using a coloured brick which, having been fired for a longer period, or in a hotter kiln, had a vitrified bluish-black surface, with considerable variety of colour and tint. In the early Middle Ages, some of the bricks were actually imported from Flanders, or were made by Flemish refugees who had fled from the religious persecution they suffered from their Spanish rulers and settled in East Anglia, but by the sixteenth century many of the bricks used in London would have been made from local clays. One major difference to the skyline of medieval London was the multiplicity of chimneys, filling the air with dense black smoke from the coal brought from the mines in the north-east of England and unloaded at the jetties on the River Fleet, near Ludgate Hill, where Seacoal Lane still stands. The change from the log-burning open fires occupying the centre of the great hall, to the coal-burning fireplaces built in the thickness of the side walls and requiring a cluster of beautifully fashioned chimney stacks, was noted, with some disapproval, by William Harrison, Rector of Radwinter and Canon of Windsor, who saw the demand for fireplaces and chimneys as yet another symptom of the degeneracy of the age. Writing about 1577 he complained: 'Now we have manie chimneys and yet our tenderlings complain of rheumes, catarhs and poses. Then we had none but reredosses and our heads did never ache . . .' and he goes on to suggest that, ' . . . as the smoke in those daies was supposed to be a sufficient hardening for the timber of the house . . .' it was also a valuable feature in the toughening of the inhabitants as well. Some of the finest of these chimneys are to be seen at Hampton Court.

As the chapter about medieval London ended with a survey of the abbey and included references to the Renaissance in England and to its influence on many of the later tombs in Henry VII's Chapel, it seems logical to cross St James's Park from the abbey to examine St James's Palace, which, despite the additions, alterations and restorations which have taken place since it was first built as a hunting lodge for Henry VIII in 1532–33, is still a recognisably Tudor building. The main gatehouse was repaired extensively around 1832, but it is still typical of much Tudor architecture, with vestigial battlements – a remnant of the architectural style of the Middle ages – and, just to the rear of the modern sentry boxes, Tudor doorways with flattened arches, chamfered mouldings, and stiffly carved foliage clamped into the corners of each doorway arch. The windows of the Chapel Royal, slightly to the west of the gatehouse, are also typical of the architecture of the Perpendicular period – the last phase of English Gothic. In some parts of the building, the original Tudor work can be distinguished from later repairs and restoration by a comparison of the size and arrangement of the bricks used. This is particularly clear on the first archway in Marlborough Road, the short street which leads down to the Mall to the east of the palace. Tudor bricks are not only much thinner than modern bricks – looking more like thick tiles – but they are laid so that alternate courses on the face of the wall are composed of 'headers' and 'stretchers' – a method of bricklaying called the English bond. (The 'stretcher' is the brick as seen lengthwise, and the 'header' shows only the end of the brick.) Later bricklayers at St James's

Palace used the so-called Flemish bond in which 'headers' and 'stretchers' appear alternately *in the same course*, and the modern bricks are to be distinguished by their larger size. This comparison of old and new is quite apparent in several parts of the palace, although on the eastern wall of the Ambassadors' Court, a later architect appears to have built an extension to the Chapel Royal wall with smaller bricks to harmonise this with the existing building.

Very little of the palace is accessible to the public, although it is possible to walk about Friary Court, opposite the Queen's Chapel in Marlborough Road, and to watch the ceremonial Changing of the Guard, performed by the St James's Palace detachment of the particular Guards regiment on duty.

The reason for the existence of a St James's Palace detachment, as well as a Buckingham Palace detachment, should perhaps be clarified. In 1698, when Whitehall Palace was gutted by a fire, which destroyed every building apart from the Banqueting House on Whitehall, St James's Palace became the official residence of the sovereign. Although the monarch now lives in Buckingham Palace when in London, it is St James's Palace which is still the official Court, and it is to the Court of St James's that every foreign ambassador is accredited. After a ceremony in Friary Court at about 11.20 a.m., the St James's detachment of Guards, resplendent in scarlet and gold, swings left along Cleveland Street, past the gatehouse, and eventually joins the Buckingham Palace detachment in the forecourt of Buckingham Palace for the main ceremony, returning afterwards to Ambassadors' Court for dismissal. The guardhouse is in Engine Court, but neither this nor Colour Court to the rear of the gatehouse is accessible to the public. At one time the announcement of the accession of the monarch used to take place in Colour Court, but since 1862 this has been in Friary Court, a far more public place. Admittance to the historic Chapel Royal, the ceiling of which was, it is believed, designed for Henry VIII by Hans Holbein, is also restricted, although services are held there every Sunday throughout the year except for a short period between Easter Day and the end of July, when the services are held in the Queen's Chapel, to the east of St James's Palace in Marlborough Road. Thus, although the visitor is allowed to look at a good deal of the outside of the building, it is still a very private place, with private apartments and offices – including those of the Lord Chamberlain, housed in some delightful buildings on the north side of Ambassadors' Court, built in the first half of the eighteenth century and at one time the State Kitchen.

The next major example of sixteenth-century architecture is on the other side of the river from Westminster – Lambeth Palace, which has been the town residence of the Archbishops of Canterbury since *c.* 1495. It can be reached by crossing the river either at Westminster Bridge or by Lambeth Bridge.

Whichever route is chosen from St James's Palace to Westminster, one has to cross St James's Park. The charmingly irregular lake which is now such an attractive feature was a long thin rectangular canal during the Tudor period, with bird decoys and nets at the Whitehall end. The site now occupied by the Horse Guards and the Treasury was then covered by a conglomeration of buildings, including the tiltyard where the young athletic Henry VIII jousted, the royal cockpit, the tennis court and other additions made by Henry VIII to Wolsey's confiscated palace, when it was renamed Whitehall Palace in 1530. Downing Street had yet to be built – it was a seventeenth-century creation – but a sloping court on the north side of the street, just past the famous No. 10, leads to quite substantial fragments of some of the buildings erected by Henry VIII at this time where it is possible for the serious student to examine much more closely the construction and arrangement of Tudor brickwork. The street joining Trafalgar Square to Parliament Square (both comparatively recent additions to London) which we now know as Whitehall was then divided by two large gatehouses erected by Henry VIII. The one immediately south of the Banqueting House, later known (quite wrongly) as the Holbein Gate, resembled the gatehouse at St James's Palace; it was, however, not built of brick, but of two different types of stone, arranged to form a checkerboard pattern – a device often found in medieval architecture. It was also adorned with terracotta roundels from which projected sculptured heads of classical celebrities – gods and goddesses, and Roman emperors, which were dispersed when the gate was demolished in 1759, some of them being added to Hampton Court while others, it is believed, were taken to various country estates.

The second gatehouse, which was nearer to Parliament Square on a site about fifty yards south of the present Cenotaph, was called the King's Gate, but this too was destroyed in 1759.

Once at the western end of Westminster Bridge, the visitor seeking Lambeth Palace has a choice of routes – he may either cross the river there, or walk along Abingdon Street and Millbank and cross the river by Lambeth Bridge. The route over Westminster Bridge and along Lambeth Palace Road gives a magnificent panoramic view of the whole riverfront of the Houses of Parliament and of Westminster beyond, but the approach to Lambeth Palace is less impressive than by the second route. But both routes give the visitor an opportunity to see how cleverly the Victorian designers of the Houses of Parliament, Sir Charles Barry and Augustus W. N. Pugin, used a form of Gothic for the general appearance, but incorporated recognisably Tudor motifs in the extensive decoration of the building. The route along Abingdon Street and through the very pleasantly ordered Victoria Tower Gardens by the river leads to the western end of Lambeth Bridge, and by crossing this bridge provides a far better approach to Lambeth Palace than the one by the east bank. As London Bridge was the only bridge spanning the Thames until the middle of the eighteenth century (apart from the one at Kingston, many miles upstream), the palace of the Archbishops of Canterbury must normally have been reached by boat, and the view from Lambeth Bridge with the jetty in the foreground is very much as it must have appeared in Tudor times.

Lambeth Palace has another imposing Tudor gatehouse, with polygonal towers flanking the central entrance, but it is still a private residence, and although parties are sometimes taken round by special invitation, tourists

must usually be content to look only at the exterior of the fine gatehouse, built in about 1485 by Cardinal John Morton, the Archbishop of Canterbury at that time. The walls of red Tudor brick are enlivened with a diapering of darker, more densely burned brick, and the main entrance has a flattened arch, with Perpendicular windows above, and with battlements – ineffectual but decorative – on the turrets. The window over the arch was probably that of the cardinal's audience chamber; the gatehouse also used to have a more sinister function, for it was in this building that a certain Friar Peto was imprisoned for having dared to criticise the marriage of Henry VIII to Anne Boleyn. A room in the left-hand tower might well have been used as a prison, for it still has iron rings fastened to the wall. The so-called Lollards Tower was in fact a water tower built by Archbishop Chichele in 1435 at a cost of £291 19s. 4½d. There is no foundation to the belief that the Lollards, followers of John Wycliffe, who were labelled and punished as heretics because they wished to reform the Church in the fourteenth century, were ever connected, even by chains, with this building. The great hall at Lambeth Palace was rebuilt after the Civil War by Archbishop Juxon in 1660–3, but it suffered heavy damage again during the Second World War. It is the gatehouse, therefore, which is the most characteristic and the most accessible of the buildings erected during the Tudor period at Lambeth Palace. The church of St Mary, just beside the gatehouse, has retained its medieval tower, but the rest of the church is skilfully added Victorian 'Gothic' built in 1851–2 by Philip Hardwick.

Fulham Palace, the official residence of the Bishops of London, upstream from Lambeth Palace, is also largely of the Tudor period, with small Tudor

View of St James's Palace before the great fire, from Chamberlain's *History of London* bricks enriched with a darker diapered pattern, and a gatehouse with a flattened sixteenth-century archway leading into the courtyard. However, it is not open to the public and little can be seen but the gatehouse, the outer walls, and the upper part of a building which resembles a sixteenth-century manor house. The most conspicuous feature – the Lodge – is nineteenth-century, and there have been many alterations to the main building over the centuries.

Major buildings from this period are difficult to find and not always easily accessible, and from Lambeth it is necessary to return to the City of London, and particularly to the Inns of Court, to see more of Tudor London.

About half-way along the Strand, on the south side, is Savoy Hill, the site of the Chapel of the Palace of the Savoy, built originally as part of the Hospital of St John which was founded by Henry VII from 1510–16. This was certainly a sixteenth-century building, but this has been almost entirely rebuilt and hence hardly qualifies as an example of Tudor building. Nearby in Strand Lane is another somewhat strange relic – a bath, which was for many years called the Roman Bath, but which has since been established as seventeenth-century work. It was known to Charles Dickens, who mentions it in *David Copperfield*, and both the bath and Savoy Chapel can be visited quite easily. Once in Fleet Street, however, there are more important and more imposing relics of Tudor London to be seen. Middle Temple Lane, on the left of Fleet Street, leads down towards the river and to Middle Temple Hall, a most impressive building on the right, built of brick, but with stone facing and widely projecting buttresses. Begun in about 1562, it was known to Queen Elizabeth, although there seems to be some difference of opinion as to whether she actually opened it in 1576. It is a noble building: the Great Hall is over 100 feet in length, 40 feet wide, and 50 feet high, and is spanned by one of the finest double-hammerbeam timber roofs in Europe, with the walls panelled up to the window-sills, and a sumptuously carved screen at the eastern end, decorated with that strange mixture of motifs – drawn from textbook patterns of Renaissance details and the old-fashioned medieval elements – which is a characteristic of Elizabethan art. The bay windows have some early stained and painted glass dated 1540. The walls are hung with impressive portraits, including some of the kings and queens of England: Queen Elizabeth; Charles I (a replica of the one at Windsor Castle); James II as Duke of York; his brother, Charles II; William III; Queen Anne, and George I. At one time it was claimed that Queen Elizabeth attended the first performance of Shakespeare's *Twelfth Night* in this very hall, but this has now been disproved, although it is certain that the play was performed here at a feast in February 1602 – a magnificent setting it must have been for the players from across the Thames. When the superb collection of plate is displayed on the Grand Night of the members of the Middle Temple, it stands on a table which it is said was presented to them by Queen Elizabeth I, and which was made from oak supplied from the royal forest at Windsor. A serving table (or cup-board) in the middle of the hall is believed to have been made from the timbers of Drake's great ship, the *Golden Hinde*, with which he circumnavigated the world. Both the Middle Temple and the Inner Temple claim Sir Francis Drake as a member. Sir Walter Raleigh also resided there in his early twenties, although this did not protect him later from being prosecuted by the first Chief Justice of England, Edward Coke, who also prosecuted the foolish and rebellious Earl of Essex, and the conspirators of the Gunpowder Plot. It is not difficult to imagine these great Elizabethans dining in this historic hall, especially as two tombs in the Temple church a hundred yards away – one of Edmund Plowden, Treasurer of the Middle Temple, who died in 1584, and a later dignitary, Richard Martin, Recorder of London – show the costumes these individuals wore when they were in office. Their tombs display the same strange architectural mixture of an imperfectly understood system of classical columns, capitals and entablatures, with decorative strapwork derived from the woodcuts in Flemish pattern books, and relics of the outworn medievalism. It is only by studying such motifs on tombs such as that of Elizabeth herself and other noble tombs in Westminster Abbey, or those in the City churches of the same period, that we can glean some idea of what Elizabethan architecture was really like, for many major buildings, such as the first Royal Exchange, built around 1565 and visited by the Queen in 1570, perished in the fire of 1666. Contemporary paintings of this building show that Sir Thomas Gresham, a mercer who was also financial adviser to the Queen, went to the bourse in Antwerp for his inspiration, and even used Flemish materials and Flemish workmen to build it. Only a few paving stones remain today.

Elizabethans seem to have been notoriously liable to borrow all sorts of ideas from various European countries, and to combine them in a very individual way. These borrowings, not only in architecture and the arts, but in costume and habits as well, are commented upon by Shakespeare in *The Merchant of Venice* when Portia, talking about her English suitor, young Falconbridge, says: 'How oddly he is suited! I think he bought his doublet in Italy, his round hose in France, his bonnet in Germany, and his behaviour everywhere!' Away from London, buildings such as Wollaton Hall, just outside Nottingham, are good examples of this Elizabethan weakness for assembling details from all over Europe. It is difficult to assess the extent of this early cosmopolitanism in London as so few major buildings from this period have survived.

The tomb of Edmund Plowden in the Temple church is a reminder that he was the treasurer of the Middle Temple when this remarkable building was being erected, and although the exterior of Middle Temple Hall is more reminiscent of the great hall of a medieval country house, the interior is certainly Elizabethan. From Fountain Court, in which Middle Temple Hall stands, one can look out over the Temple Gardens – these are traditionally the gardens in which the Yorkists and Lancastrians, shortly to be locked in the deadly civil war known as the Wars of the Roses, chose the red and white roses which are still the symbols of those counties.

Before moving to the next important building of this period in Chancery

left, The statue of
Queen Elizabeth at St
Dunstan's-in-the-West
right, The entrance to
Lincoln's Inn

Lane, it is worth visiting the church of St Dunstan's-in-the-West, about fifty yards or so to the east along Fleet Street, for on the outside of this church there is a contemporary statue of Queen Elizabeth, looking very much as she must have appeared when feasting with the members of the legal profession in their great halls. The statue, which used to stand in a niche on the old City gate, Ludgate, shows the Queen wearing an elaborate costume with a great ruff framing her face.

On the left-hand side of Chancery Lane (looking northwards) is Lincoln's Inn, with its historic entrance of small red bricks and flattened Tudor arch surmounted by three coats of arms, picked out in colour. (It is said that Ben Jonson, the playwright, worked on this very building as a bricklayer in his less prosperous days. If this is true, perhaps he was responsible for the rather charming diaper pattern with which the wall is decorated.) The first coat of arms is that of Henry Lacy, Earl of Lincoln, on whose property the Inn was built, and who may well have been its founder. The royal coat of arms is that of Henry VIII, in the centre, and the one on the right is that of Sir Thomas Lovell, a benefactor of Lincoln's Inn. The door is of weathered oak, so seasoned since it was built in 1564 that the wood is as hard as the ironwork which binds it, but the postern on the north side is nineteenth-century work. Immediately opposite this entrance is Old Hall, built 1489–90, on the site of an earlier building which, by the look of traces embedded in the modern archway linking Old Hall with the chapel, must have been of the thirteenth century. The much eroded Early English capital with its dog's tooth moulding beneath is a clue to the age of the earlier hall.

Old Hall is not normally open to the public, but a serious student can always apply to the Porter's Lodge and is not likely to be refused permission to view the building if it is a convenient time of day. The screen at the south end of the hall is not nearly as elaborate as the one in Middle Temple Hall, but it bears the same strange mixture of motifs, with carved half-figures called terms blending into an odd anatomical combination with scrollwork and architectural pilasters. The roof is a simpler but fine example of the timber work of the period. Quite out of period, but far too important to be omitted here, is the huge painting on the north wall by the great cockney artist, William Hogarth. The biblical subject – St Paul being brought before Felix, the Roman procurator of Judea, for judgement – is unusual for Hogarth, and the scale of the painting is far bigger than one might expect, for it is 14 feet wide, and just over 10 feet high. It was originally commissioned for the chapel, but it eventually transpired that there was no place suitable for it there, and it was thus hung in its present position opposite the great carved screen in 1748. The chapel just north of the hall has a strangely open undercroft through which barristers walk in their wigs and gowns, under a late medieval-type vault, with later nineteenth-century additions. Although the chapel – which is open to visitors during the lunch hour – has a superb painted roof, and is richly furnished with high carved pews, the altar is a bare, austere table, and the pulpit a beautifully restrained early eighteenth-century example. The wide windows, filled with painted glass, record the names and the coats of arms of distinguished members of Lincoln's Inn, and are only occasionally related to religious matters. From the lists of the

The inside of Lincoln's Inn, showing the early seventeenth-century chapel by Inigo Jones

113

preachers shown at the west end of the chapel, it seems that this appointment, until the late nineteenth century, was clearly a valuable stepping-stone to bishoprics and even higher office, for a number of archbishops appear to have started their career as the preacher attached to this building. The best known name there is probably that of John Donne, poet and priest, who later became Dean of St Paul's Cathedral; he was the preacher at Lincoln's Inn Chapel from 1616–1622.

The next Elizabethan buildings that have survived are to the north of Chancery Lane, very near to where it emerges into Holborn. These are the famous timber-framed houses of Staple Inn, opposite the end of Gray's Inn Road; their upper storeys are 'jetted out', lurching heavily over the pavement, giving protection (from the weather, and the contents of chamberpots!) to the passers-by, and providing an early example of rooms cantilevered out to provide progressively larger floor areas than those below.

The broad archway from Holborn leads into one of the most charming of all City courtyards – an oasis of quiet trees which Nathaniel Hawthorne, the great American writer, came upon quite by accident, and described in his work, *Our Old Home*, published in 1863.

> There was not a quieter spot in England than this, and it was very strange to have drifted into it so suddenly out of the bustle and rumble of Holborn; and to lose all this repose as suddenly on passing through the arch of the outer court. In all the hundreds of years since London was built it has not been able to sweep its roaring tide over this little island of quiet.

Even in the twentieth century, Staple Inn still retains much of the quality of peace which endeared it to Nathaniel Hawthorne. A plaque just inside the Holborn archway has an intriguing inscription which records that Staple Inn was originally built between 1545 and 1589 by 'Vincent Enghame and Another'. The timber-framed inner walls were replaced by brick ones in 1826, some time before Hawthorne came upon it, and the whole building was heavily restored in 1886 by Alfred Waterhouse, who also built for its owners the Prudential Assurance Company – that incredibly raw red brick and granite 'Gothic' suite of offices which dominates the opposite side of Holborn. During the Second World War a flying bomb destroyed the hall of Staple Inn and heavily damaged the surrounding buildings, but it has all been most beautifull repaired; the hall was rebuilt with a good deal of the old material such that the little courtyard looks very much as it did when Charles Dickens wrote *Edwin Drood* and made the Inn the scene of the office of Mr Grewgious, the lawyer. The hall (which is not open to the public) bears the symbol of the Merchants of the Staple – the guild of dealers in wool during the Middle Ages – on the rainwater pipe. It may well be that the name, Staple Inn, was derived from the temporary occupation of the Inn by the wool merchants towards the end of the fourteenth century.

An even quieter and more secluded Inn of Court, which was also well known to Charles Dickens as he was a clerk there, is on the opposite side of

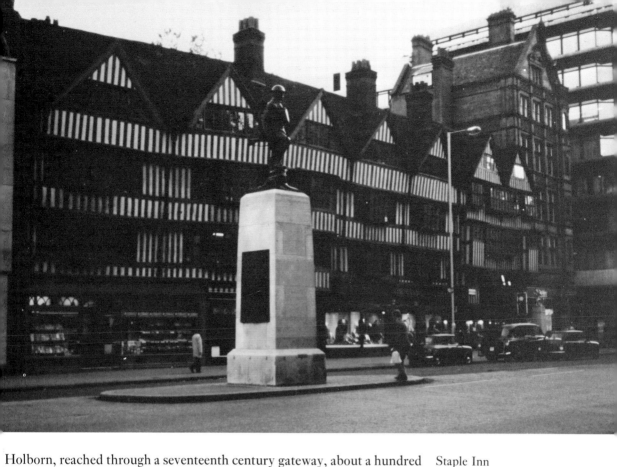

Holborn, reached through a seventeenth century gateway, about a hundred yards to the west of Gray's Inn Road. The visitor enters a small courtyard through the gatehouse in Holborn where there is a little sentry box to the left; the porter inside wears a maroon-coloured uniform with a peaked cap bearing the badge of Gray's Inn – a golden griffin on a black background. He is there to answer enquiries but it would be as well to point out that although the Inns of Court all seem to be used as thoroughfares by visitors who have no business there, they are in fact private premises; although tourists are always treated with the utmost courtesy, they are intruders. The historic halls, attractive as they are to visitors to London, are still in daily use by the people for whom they were originally designed, and can usually only be seen if special application to view them has been made and permission granted.

Despite severe damage inflicted on it during the Second World War, the hall of Gray's Inn, now restored, is still one of the finest examples of Elizabethan architecture in the country. The great hammerbeam roof within has been so skilfully repaired that it seems apparently untouched since 1556–8 when it was pre-fabricated in the fields outside, and then erected to span the hall. Strangely enough, the damage which necessitated the repair and cleaning of the magnificent screen at the end of the hall also provided confirmation of an old tradition that the wood from which it was made was provided by timber from Spanish ships which were part of the Armada. At that time the hall had no screen, but in 1950, when the damaged screen was being examined, it was found that it was made not from oak, but from Spanish chestnut. An expert from the Maritime Museum was called

Staple Inn

in, and he discovered that the pillars which are part of the main structure correspond almost exactly to the measurements of the timbers which supported the decks of the kind of Spanish galleon which was captured intact and sailed up the Thames to Chatham by an English crew. This, together with the fact that Lord Howard of Effingham, the Lord High Admiral of the victorious English fleet, was also a member of Gray's Inn, makes it extremely likely that the tradition was a true one. The carving on the screen is far more restrained than that found on similar screens of this period, and the Flemish strapwork in low relief is to be seen not only on the mouldings, but on the Ionic columns which are part of the main structure. The little carved nymphs bearing wreaths of victory and palm branches (an allusion, perhaps, to the defeat of the Armada in 1588), tucked into the upper angles or spandrels of the arches, are much closer to their classical originals than those usually found in Elizabethan sculpture. On the wall, at the far end behind the dais and the high table, there are a number of portraits, including a rare example of a portrait of Queen Elizabeth I at the age of twenty-six, painted a year after she succeeded to the throne. On the same wall one can see portraits of two very important members of her Council of State who were also members of Gray's Inn: William Cecil Lord Burghley, her First Minister, and Sir Francis Walsingham, the founder of a Secret Service which thwarted all the plots made to assassinate the Queen. There is also a portrait of Thomas Cromwell, Earl of Essex, who served her father, Henry VIII, but was later executed, and one of Sir Francis Bacon, who served her successor, James I. The oriel window on the north side of the hall is original. The one on the south side is modern, having been most generously donated by the American Bar Association. In this hall, members of the Inn entertained Queen Elizabeth with masques and shows, and there seems little doubt that among the players was a young actor named William Shakespeare. In 1594 the hall staged a performance of his play *A Comedy of Errors*. The tradition of entertainment still persists, and no matter how grave the legal issues dealt with during the week, Friday night at Gray's Inn Hall is still Music night. The library which adjoins the hall is entirely modern – a seemly, if a little unimaginative twentieth-century 'Georgian' building replacing the one destroyed by enemy bombs. The chapel has also been entirely rebuilt, and there is now a modern statue of Sir Francis Bacon (Baron Verulam and Viscount St Albans) in South Square. Bacon not only wrote that delightful essay 'Of Gardens' beginning, 'God Almighty first planted a garden. And indeed it is the purest of human pleasures . . .' but was actually responsible for the layout of Gray's Inn Gardens, which are known as The Walks, and are open to the public in the lunch hour, proving in twentieth-century London that the garden is indeed '. . . the greatest refreshment to the spirits of man'. These gardens form a haven of quiet between the traffic of Gray's Inn Road to the east, the noise of Theobald's Road to the north, and the bustle of Holborn to the south.

The next important area in Tudor history is to the east of Gray's Inn, but little but the place names – Hatton Garden, named after Sir Christopher Hatton, a favourite of Queen Elizabeth, and Saffron Hill and Herb Hill – are

St John's Gate,
Clerkenwell

there to remind us of the rural past of this somewhat sad area of Clerkenwell. From Gray's Inn, it is best to walk northwards within the precincts which are bordered by Jockey's Fields to emerge in Theobald's Road which, as soon as it crosses Gray's Inn Road to the east, changes its name to Clerkenwell Road. On past Clerkenwell Green, either on foot or by bus, a visitor will find Jerusalem Lane on the right, a small road furnished with small shops and cheap van-driver's cafés which leads into St John's Square, and straight to a Tudor gate – that of the Priory of St John of Jerusalem.

The whole area is so built over and intersected that it requires a considerable effort to imagine it as a placid priory, with its own church and ancillary buildings. Nevertheless, the splendid gatehouse of brick with stone facings, erected by Sir Thomas Docwra in the opening years of the sixteenth century to replace one badly damaged during the rebellion of Wat Tyler in 1381, has been beautifully restored and bears proudly the coat of arms and the flag of the Order of St John of Jerusalem. The twelfth-century crypt of the priory church has been carefully preserved and maintained, but the church above was almost entirely destroyed in the Second World War. The crypt, the church, the gatehouse and a delightful museum are open to the public on three days of the week, and there one can see many lovely objects connected with the long history of this noble order – of which the tradition of service and of healing is still very active in twentieth-century England. The crypt of the church contains a magnificent alabaster effigy of Spanish workmanship. This is the figure of Don Juan Ruiz de Vergara, the Proctor of the Langue of Castile of the Order of St John, who died in 1567. The effigy, showing him in full Elizabethan armour, was originally in Valladolid Cathedral, but was removed during the rebuilding of the cathedral in the last century. Nearby is the lower part of a tomb of William Weston, the last Grand Prior of the Order in England before its dissolution by Henry VIII. The figure is of an emaciated body – originally there would have been a figure above showing the prior in his ceremonial robes, reminder that no matter how powerful a man he had been, he was only mortal, and to dust he must return. It was that same prior, William Weston, who gave to the priory church the lovely painting, possibly by the Flemish artist Rogier van der Weyden, which now forms the reredos to the altar in the restored church. Originally consisting of three panels – hence the term triptych – its main central panel disappeared during the Reformation and only the side panels, painted on both sides, have survived. It is rare to find a painting of this date and of this quality outside a great national collection.

The following centuries dealt harshly with the priory church and its buildings. A semicircle in brick in the square outside shows the extent of the original apsed church, but the church was converted into a Presbyterian meeting house early in the eighteenth century, then burned by rioters in 1710, restored again, used as a parish church for two hundred years, returned to the Order in 1931, and then burned out by incendiary bombs in 1941. The gatehouse has been rather more fortunate. It was used at one time as the office for the Master of Revels to the Court of Elizabeth I, and much later, in the eighteenth century, it housed the editorial offices of the *Gentleman's Magazine* for which Dr Johnson was a hack writer; it was to the workmen in the office that the famous David Garrick gave his first performance in London. Much of the original building has survived, although the delightful coats of arms of the Order and of Sir Thomas Docwra are carefully designed modern work.

The last and perhaps the finest complex of buildings of Tudor and Elizabethan times is that at Charterhouse, south of Clerkenwell, and only about three hundred yards from St John's Gate. It was originally a monastery of Carthusians, the name Charterhouse being a corruption of Chartreuse, the town in France where the order was founded in 1084. Remnants of the original monastic buildings can still be found, but as members of this order spent most of their lives in separate cells, the pattern of the buildings differed quite considerably from that of Westminster Abbey, for example. However, it is the later history of the site and its buildings with which we are concerned, after the monastery had been dissolved, and the whole site passed into entirely different hands, although it is strange to reflect that the quiet, private square near to Smithfield meat market is actually part of the thirteen acres bought by Sir Walter de Manny to provide room for a common grave for the thousands of victims of the

Charterhouse

Black Death in the middle of the fourteenth century. It was he who erected a small chapel on the site. The Carthusian monks arrived there in 1371; Sir Walter de Manny died the next year and was buried at the foot of the high altar. Historians later confused the chapter house, which had been converted into a church, with the original priory church, and it was not until the bombing of the Second World War revealed new facts that their mistake was discovered, and the tomb of Sir Walter de Manny found. The site is now marked by a modern stone. The Carthusians, who defied Henry VIII and refused to acknowledge him as head of the Church, were treated with the utmost cruelty, and after their prior, Houghton, had been hung, drawn and quartered, his limbs were nailed to the very oak door which hangs in the entrance today. The looted and desecrated buildings passed through a number of hands, but some of the most important of the buildings which now survive were adapted or built by Sir Edward North, who entertained Princess Elizabeth at his home in the Charterhouse when she was on her way from Hatfield Palace to London for her coronation. The house was later owned by the treacherous Duke of Norfolk, and the infamous Ridolfi, the agent of the King of Spain and the notorious Duke of Alva, actually went there to discuss their plan to land an invading force from Flanders, to arrest the Queen and put Mary, Queen of Scots, on the throne. The plot was discovered, and Norfolk executed on Tower Green in 1572. The property eventually became the London home of another member of the Howard family – Lord Howard of Effingham, the famous and loyal Admiral of the

The tudor and medieval courtyard, Charterhouse

Fleet who commanded the *Golden Lion* against the Armada, and was honoured by a visit from the Queen shortly before her death in 1603. Her successor, James I, was also a guest there very early in his reign; he held a council in the Great Chamber on 11 May 1603, creating 133 knights and making Norfolk, Earl of Suffolk.

The new Earl of Suffolk sold Charterhouse for £13,000 to a Lincolnshire man, Thomas Sutton, a successful businessman who had at one time been Master of the Ordnance in the north of England. Sutton bought the premises not to live in, but to found a hospital and a school. The inhabitants of the hospital were to be 'decrepit or old Captaynes either at Sea or Land, Souldiers maymed or ympotent, decayed Merchaunts, men fallen into decaye through Shipwrecke, Casualtie or Fyer or such evill Accident; those that have been Captives under the Turkes etc. . . . .' From the first, the hospital was designed as an almshouse for impoverished gentlemen who had fallen on bad times through no fault of their own. It is still a home for elderly single men or widowers, although the number housed there has now been reduced to forty – half the number of the original pensioners. Sutton's little charity school for forty poor boys eventually developed into the famous public school, and moved out to more spacious, modern premises in Godalming in 1872.

Thus, the visitor to Charterhouse is confronted by a series of buildings with a complex history, and it is perhaps the presence of the pensioners there today which makes it so different from Elizabethan houses elsewhere. This is no mere historical relic, preserved as a museum, or lived in partly by an impoverished noble family trying to raise death duties. The whole complex has a warmth of feeling, of being lived in and loved. The grounds are beautifully tended, the great Elizabethan hall is dined in every day, the fireplaces filled with freshly sawn logs. As it is fully occupied, it is not open to the public very often – but occasionally guided tours are conducted through some of the finest Elizabethan and Jacobean rooms in the country, each in a wonderful state of preservation and maintained with great care. A charter granted by Queen Elizabeth with a magnificently preserved great seal of the Queen on horseback hangs in the entrance hall, but the stair is a modern replacement of one burned in the blitz. The great hall, now the dining hall, has a carved oak screen, embellished with all the familiar motifs of this period – Flemish strapwork, little classical details, and some medieval hints from the past. It is pierced by three archways which originally led to the buttery, the pantry and the kitchen, which, although it is modernised to provide food for the present inhabitants of Charterhouse, stands on the site of the kitchen built for the monastery. The hammerbeam roof was altered somewhat by Edward Blore, the Victorian architect, in 1841, but the bomb damage inflicted a century later enabled the restorers to rebuild the damaged roof in such a way that it now corresponds much more closely to the original one. The gallery on the north wall was probably built by Thomas Sutton around 1614 at the same time as he inserted the fireplace which bears his coat of arms, and carved groups at either end of the entablature containing cannon, cannon-balls, and a gunpowder keg – an allusion to his former post of Master of the Ordnance. The fireplace has been skilfully cleaned, and the carving is apparently as crisp and as sharp as it was in Sutton's day. By this time, heraldry had lost most of its importance in battle – a development which caused much greater emphasis to be placed on the enlargement of the shield, and the diminution of the helm (one of the signs of decadent, i.e., non-functional, heraldry). It is thought that Francis Carter designed not only this fireplace, but the one in the newly formed Brothers' Library – fashioned from the monastic refectory or dining-room – as well as the arcade along one side of the cloisters and the door at the end, leading into the chapel. The chapel was actually the chapter house of the original monastery, the priory church having been destroyed by Sir Edward North after he had acquired the buildings in 1545; but the building was not large enough to accommodate the eighty pensioners, the forty boys, and the officers and staff for worship, so an extra aisle was built for Sutton on the north side, and the three arches have his armorial bearings on their keystones. The chapel contains an elaborate monument to Thomas Sutton, embellished with various symbolic figures, a low relief representing a gathering of the community, mostly in alabaster, and a life-sized figure of the founder, recumbent, his hands clasped in prayer. This is the work of Nicholas Johnson, one of a family of masons, whose brother, Gerard, was responsible for the famous monument to Shakespeare in the church at Stratford-upon-Avon. The whole Sutton monument appears to have been the result of collaboration between Nicholas Johnson and a much more famous mason, Nicholas Stone, who was master mason to Inigo Jones, England's first Renaissance architect, who built the Banqueting House in Whitehall and the Queen's House at Greenwich. The woodwork in the chapel – the pews, the pulpit and the screen and organ gallery – is some of the finest early seventeenth-century work in the country, and it is fortunate that so much survived the bombing which destroyed some of the complex of buildings in 1941. Strangely enough, some of the damage inflicted on the cloisters actually revealed substantial remains of a Carthusian monk's cell containing a little serving hatch through which he would have been given food by a lay brother, built about 1371. There is more medieval work to be seen in the tower, once the treasury of the monastery, where bombing revealed a squint at third-floor level. It was the position of this squint which led to the discovery of the tomb of Sir Walter de Manny, which was known to have been placed in front of the high altar, and which therefore gave the exact position of the site of the monastic church.

One other seventeenth-century room has yet to be mentioned – the Great Chamber – a noble room with an extremely impressive fireplace, delicately painted in black and gold, more beautifully proportioned and more restrained in decoration than most fireplaces of this period. The Elizabethan and Jacobean gentlemen, knowing that the fireplace would be the focal point of any state room, lavished much of their wealth on it, making it imposing and suggestive of their money and prestige, sometimes with unfortunate results. The fireplaces at Charterhouse, however elaborate, are never ostentantious or vulgar in their use of ornament, and the workmanship is superb.

So many buildings of this period of London's history were consumed during the great fire of 1666, and it is fortunate that it was eventually checked at Pie Corner, about 150 yards east of Charterhouse, near to St Bartholomew's Hospital. Two important buildings of the Tudor period have yet to be mentioned – one well to the north of the City, and the other on the western boundary, very near to the old site of Temple Bar in Fleet Street. The first of these Tudor buildings is Canonbury Tower in Islington, formerly the country residence of the canons of the Priory of St Bartholomew, Smithfield. A short walk from Highbury and Islington station, it is a tall red-brick tower which is now looked after by a theatrical repertory company in Canonbury Place, and in order to see the very fine Elizabethan interiors application has to be made to the Warden, although the rooms may also be seen by members of the Theatre Club and their friends after the last performance on Saturday nights. The other building – Elizabethan in feeling, if built just a little later – is the gateway to the Inner Temple which leads from Fleet Street into Inner Temple Lane. Pronounced by Professor Pevsner to be 'one of the best pieces of half-timber work in London', it was built around 1610–11, and restored in 1906, but the timber has weathered so beautifully that only an expert could distinguish the restored parts from the original. The archway is of stone, with a

The gateway to the Inner Temple, 'Prince Henry's Room'

semicircular arch, and the storeys above overhang in the familiar Elizabethan fashion. Inside is Prince Henry's Room, a fine late Elizabethan room with a plaster ceiling embellished with the badge of the Prince – the eldest son of James I – and his initials, P.H. The gateway is open to the public, and normally contains an exhibition of books and papers associated somewhat loosely with Samuel Pepys, the diarist.

Of the many artefacts of Elizabethan and Tudor London, the finest collection is in the Museum of London on London Wall, just east of St Bart's. There, for example, they have, most beautifully set out and displayed, the 'Cheapside Hoard' – the stock-in-trade of an Elizabethan jeweller's shop in Cheapside which, having been buried, was lost until it was dug up in 1912. The rings, necklaces, fine chains with pendants, earrings and brooches are displayed in the Museum of London with the finesse of a Bond Street shop window. There are also excellent models of Elizabethan London – the Royal Exchange as it was when first designed by Sir Thomas Gresham in 1568, London Bridge, Cheapside and so on.

Visible from the windows of the museum, in a paved area bordered by the restored bastions of the Roman walls of the City, is the church of St Giles, Cripplegate, formerly a Perpendicular period church built around 1546 on the site of earlier churches; although it survived the great fire, it was almost entirely destroyed in the Second World War, but has since been rebuilt. Two notable seventeenth-century people are associated with it (Oliver Cromwell was married there in 1620, and John Milton, the poet, buried there in 1674), but it still bears a close resemblance to the original church of the Tudor period and therefore finds a place in this chapter. It has a light, airy and peaceful interior, and as such is much enjoyed by the people from the offices around during their lunch hours.

Other museums containing examples of Elizabethan arts and crafts, although not necessarily of Elizabethan London, are the Geffrye Museum in Kingsland Road, Shoreditch, well to the east of the Museum of London; the Wallace Collection in Manchester Square, just off Oxford Street; and the Victoria and Albert Museum in South Kensington; but only the Museum of London specialises exclusively in this period of London's history. Nothing remains of the Elizabethan theatres which made Shakespeare famous in his own lifetime, but on the south bank of the river, in the shadow of the power station opposite St Paul's Cathedral and to the west of Southwark Bridge is the Bear Garden art gallery and museum, devoted largely to the Elizabethan and Restoration theatre, enterprise of enormous imagination and courage. It is the creation of Sam Wanamaker, the American actor – it was he who had the vision to plan it there among derelict and ruined warehouses, and it is now one of the most exciting museums in London. It has assembled a display of prints and reproductions of documents recording the history of this area from the Middle Ages to the end of the seventeenth century. The south bank of the river between modern London Bridge and westwards to Blackfriars Bridge Road was notorious for the type of entertainment which flourished there in the Middle Ages, largely outside the jurisdiction of the City. It was one of the 'red-light' quarters of medieval London, some of the brothels being built on land owned by the Bishop of Winchester (a fragment of whose palace can still be seen there), and the ladies who provided the entertainment were therefore sometimes known as Winchester geese. The first theatre in London, however, was The Curtain, built in Shoreditch in 1577 by the actor-manager, James Burbage, but the first theatre to appear on the south bank was The Rose, built in 1587. Of these theatres nothing remains apart from their names – there is a Curtain Road just north of Liverpool Street Station, and Rose Alley between Bear Garden and Southwark Bridge Road. The famous Shakespearean theatre, The Globe, was built in this area in 1599, made from materials from the Curtain theatre in Shoreditch which had been demolished after objections by the Puritans. With their close proximity to the bear-baiting, bull-baiting, and stews of Bankside, and often with the same audiences, it is not surprising that theatres and the actors were a target for the most vigorous attack by Puritans. The plays were described as 'a special cause of corrupting their youth, containing nothing but unchaste matters and lascivious devices . . .', and the theatres were defined as 'ordinary places for vagrant persons, masterless men, whoremongers . . .'. Nevertheless, theatres and other entertainments survived until the Commonwealth, and were temporarily revived there after the Restoration, but the main centres of entertainment shifted westwards, the whole area fell on evil days, and if it were not for the Bear Garden Museum, there would be little there to attract a visitor today.

By the end of the Elizabethan era, the city was so hopelessly overcrowded that expansion was essential. The estimated population in 1563 was about 93,000. By 1605, it had increased to 250,000, so that overcrowding was bound to drive some of the population away to seek better living conditions. The increased use of coal, and the prevailing south-westerly winds which blew the sulphurous fumes eastwards across the city, meant that more and more people who could afford to went westwards towards Westminster and the Court of St James. It was therefore in the Whitehall area that the most important development of London took place, with the erection of the new Banqueting House 1619–22 for James I by a revolutionary architect – a cockney born in Smithfield – Inigo Jones, whose visits to Italy had not only taught him much about theatrical innovations abroad, but about the new architecture of the Renaissance of which the average Englishman knew very little. The work of Inigo Jones, cruelly cut short by the Civil War, was nevertheless to be crucial in the development of the London of the Stuart dynasty, and laid the foundation for the building of a London which was the envy of seventeenth-century Europe.

5

Seventeenth-Century London

The history of seventeenth-century London divides itself into four distinct phases. The first, which began with great promise in the opening years of the reign of James I, continued into the reign of his son, Charles I, and up to the outbreak of the disastrous Civil War in 1642. It was a period in which certain theories of proportion and harmony, already being practised in Italy, began to influence not only individual buildings in London, but the layout of squares.

The Civil War and the Commonwealth which followed was an almost completely non-productive period of some eighteen years during which many fine buildings were destroyed, although the city had in fact supported the Cromwellian cause, having been soured by what it had regarded as unwarranted interference in its affairs and undue taxation by the Stuart kings. It was a decision it learned to regret, for it found in due course that the monarchy had been replaced by a regime which, while thinly disguised as a parliament, became a dictatorship even more repressive than that of the king it had executed.

The third phase began in 1660, when London welcomed the Restoration of Charles II, the son of the martyred king. All kinds of development were underway when the city was decimated by the Plague of 1665, and almost entirely destroyed by the great fire of the following year.

The last phase – which might be called the London of Samuel Pepys, since it was during the period that the great diarist recorded much of its history, and one through which he lived for the remainder of his life – was one of the most creative and important periods in the history of London, and one which, thanks to the genius of Sir Christopher Wren, has left an indelible impression on the London of today.

The *mélange* of architectural motifs which was characteristic of Elizabethan building was due largely to the lack of understanding of the code of architectural proportions known as the Orders of Architecture – a system of column and entablature of different, clearly recognisable characteristics originally evolved by the ancient Greeks, adapted and enlarged by the Romans, and then revived in Italy by such architects and writers as Alberti, Serlio and Andrea Palladio in an attempt to find a formula for perfect beauty in architectural form. Alberti, for example, defined beauty as 'the harmony and concord of all parts achieved in such a manner that nothing could be added or taken away except for the worse'. Palladio, in his most important

opposite, St Paul's Cathedral, the west front, on the occasion of Winston Churchill's funeral book, *The Four Books of Architecture*, published in 1570, explained the theory by which the proportions of a bulding were determined by a series of mathematical formulae, and its parts related to each other as the notes in music were grouped to provide harmony. One of Palladio's own buildings had its rooms arranged in the proportions 2:3, 1:1, 3:5, and 1:3. These correspond to the musical harmonies measured in distances on a monochord, i.e., a fifth, unison, a major sixth, and two octaves. Thus, the new Renaissance buildings, unlike the traditional English houses which tended to grow naturally or organically, were consciously designed with the precise geometry of a snow crystal. There had been a tendency to symmetry in English buildings ever since the beginning of the sixteenth century, but this was far less rigid in approach than that in the new European theories of architecture. As the cult of mathematical proportion began to grow, those thinking about and planning the design of a building began to find certain shapes for rooms more correct than others. It eventually resolved itself more simply into a series of precepts such as: 'The most beautiful shapes for a room are round, square, diagonal proportions, a square and a half, a square and two thirds or two thirds' (Inigo Jones). Jones studied Palladio's book with great care, and his own copy, now preserved in the library of Worcester College, Oxford, shows his notes in the margin, and little pin-pricks where he checked the accuracy of the diagrams with dividers. His first commissions for James I and his queen, Anne of Denmark, however, were not strictly architectural, but were theatrical designs for the masques and entertainments held in Whitehall Palace in which members of the court (including the queen) took part. In his capacity as theatrical designer he incorporated ideas he had learned by studying Palladio's *Teatro Olympico* in Vicenza, although Palladio was in fact dead by the time Jones visited Italy and he had to rely somewhat on his own investigation and a conversation with Scamozzi, Palladio's former pupil.

The first architectural commission was for Jones, as the royal Surveyor General, to design a hunting lodge for the queen on the outskirts of Greenwich Park – the Queen's House, now part of the Maritime Museum. Building began in 1616, but ceased at the death of the queen in 1619, and the house remained unfinished until the reign of Charles I. The core of the house is a perfect cube, 40 feet high, 40 feet wide and 40 feet deep, and its disciplined classical proportions and untroubled skyline must have seemed revolutionary indeed to a court used to Hatfield House and Blickling Hall – houses which had been built in the established tradition. Named, most aptly, the House of Delight, it will be examined more closely later in the chapter along with other buildings of this era at Greenwich.

The most important building designed by Inigo Jones was the Banqueting House in Whitehall, completed around 1622 – it is now the sole survivor of a number of new buildings erected on the site of the old, out-of-date Whitehall Palace. Despite alterations made to it later, after Jones's death, when it lost an apse at one end, it is still one of the most strikingly beautiful interiors open regularly to the public in the whole London area. Jones used a double cube for the main room, which measures 55 feet high,

left, The Banqueting
House, Whitehall
below, Interior of the
Banqueting House

55 feet wide, and 110 feet long, and which has a gallery supported on classical brackets, with wide windows on either side – the westerly range looking out over Whitehall, and the opposite one towards the river. The sash windows which are there now are, of course, later additions, for Jones designed casement windows with mullions and transoms dividing the window areas into smaller rectangles carefully proportioned to take their place in the geometrically calculated façades. (Sash windows did not appear in England until the 1690s). The ceiling is divided into deeply recessed panels, and these are filled with a quite remarkable series of pictures painted for Charles I by Peter Paul Rubens in 1632, the great Flemish painter and diplomat. He came to London on a diplomatic mission in 1629, and stayed until the next year, when he returned to his great picture factory in Antwerp to produce these mighty decorations for the Banqueting House. The theme is the Apotheosis of James I – a diplomatic charade which, if the work of art itself were not so splendid, would be almost nauseating in its glorification of a monarch quite unworthy of such a tribute. It is, however, a masterpiece of Baroque painting, and shows the king, idealised almost beyond recognition, surrounded by Justice, Zeal, Religion, Honour and Victory, with such symbolic figures as Minerva, the goddess of Wisdom, driving Rebellion into Hell (no doubt an allusion to the unsuccessful Gunpowder Plot of 1605), and the rapturous Union of Scotland with England. Oval panels carry the same theme of the benefits bestowed by the reign of James I, with Bounty trampling on Avarice (this must have evoked a wry smile from those who knew of the treatment of John Stow, the historian) and Minerva spearing Lust, which Rubens must surely have inserted tongue in cheek in the light of James's notorious homosexuality. But it is a superb decoration and enhances an already lovely room. Rubens was paid £3000 and given a knighthood by Charles I, who received, in return, not only this series of panels, but a famous painting, now in the National Gallery, of the benefits which accrue when Wisdom protects Peace from the horrors of War, and a rare landscape, now in the Royal Collection. The Banqueting House was later converted into a royal chapel, and still later, in 1890, into a Services Museum, when its lovely spaces became cluttered up with tattered banners, cannon-balls and assegais. It has now been very well restored by the Ministry of Works, and banquets are still held in it from time to time. It is a melancholy thought that this is the last room which Charles I saw in his life, for it was outside this building that the regicides erected the scaffold on which the king was beheaded, after having been brought under heavy escort across the Park from St James's Palace where he had been held prisoner.

Across the Park, beside St James's Palace, there is a chapel built by Inigo Jones for the reception of the Spanish Infanta to whom the young Prince Charles (later Charles I) was to be married. These diplomatic arrangements came to nothing, however, and the chapel was completed in time for the new bride, Henrietta Maria, in May 1625. This building is not accessible to the public, except for worship on most Sundays in the year. It stands on the north side of Marlborough Road, facing Friary Court, its clean stuccoed facade and delicately proportioned windows a contrast to the older red brick

The statue of King Charles I which stands on the site of Old Charing Cross

palace opposite. This building, too, has a lofty, deeply coffered ceiling, enriched not with paintings but with exquisite plaster decoration. The Queen's Chapel is flooded with light, especially from the triple window over the altar, the central light being arched, and those on either side narrower, with square heads. This particular type of window, introduced into England by Inigo Jones, should strictly be called a Serlian window after the sixteenth-century architect, Sebastiano Serlio, who illustrated it in his book published in 1537. It is much more commonly known, however, as a Venetian or Palladian window, and was widely used during the eighteenth century in houses as well as churches by the followers of the Palladian revival. The beauty of this chapel, of the Banqueting House in Whitehall, and of the Queen's House in Greenwich makes one realise how tragic was the Civil War and the Commonwealth which followed, for these three examples of English Renaissance are representative of the magnificent buildings that might have been built in London if the country had not been plunged into the Civil War. For all his faults, Charles I was a discriminating patron of the arts, and had the Royal Collection been kept intact instead of being sold off by the Cromwellians, there is no collection in the world which could have rivalled it today. As it is, one is forced to go to Paris, Vienna or Madrid to see some of the finest paintings which should rightfully be housed in Windsor Castle or Buckingham Palace.

From the Queen's Chapel it is only a short walk along Pall Mall to the head of Whitehall, where the equestrian statue of Charles I stands, on the site of medieval Charing Cross, looking down Whitehall. Modelled by a French sculptor, Hubert Le Sueur, about 1630, the statue was ordered to be destroyed for the value of the metal it contained, but a brazier named Rivett bought it from Cromwell's representatives, buried it, and sold souvenirs of

York Water Gate,
Embankment Gardens

knife-handles, candlesticks, thimbles, spoons etc., pretending that they had been made from the king's statue. After the Restoration it re-emerged, and was finally set up in its present position.

Of the rest of the seventeenth-century buildings in this area, very little remains, although York Water Gate, at the bottom of Buckingham Street just west of Shell Mex House and on the edge of Victoria Embankment Gardens, is still to be seen. This was built in 1626 by Nicholas Stone, to the design of his master, Inigo Jones, and at one time marked the edge of the Thames – a private jetty by which the occupants of York House would be able to embark. One of the owners of York House was the second Duke of Buckingham, and when the whole site was sold by him, he insisted that the purchasers should record his name in those of the streets they were building. As his name was George Villiers, Duke of Buckingham, it was used for George Court, Villiers Street, Duke Street, Of Alley(!) and Buckingham Street. Duke Street no longer exists, and Of Alley has now been renamed York Place.

Speculative building was unknown until the opening years of the seventeenth century. A nobleman might buy land in London in order to provide a site for his town house, or even to ensure that nobody else could acquire it and spoil his view, but it was not until about 1609 that Robert Cecil, Earl of Salisbury, was given permission by James I to buy land for development on the east side of Leicester Square, along the line of St Martin's Lane. Charles I was later to regret this decision; in 1630 he complained bitterly that the drainage from this area was damaging his palace at Whitehall. In 1631 Francis Russell, 4th Earl of Bedford, whose ancestors had acquired Covent (or 'convent') Garden from the Abbey of Westminster, obtained permission to develop the area, and Inigo Jones was commissioned to design a piazza with arcades and a church as a complete unit. Of this project, only the church of St Paul's, Covent Garden, has survived, and that has been rebuilt, but in the same form. So impressive was the original design for this area that, but for the Civil War, there is no doubt that a great deal more of London would have been developed in the same way.

This development between the City of London and the City of Westminster along the Strand was echoed a little further to the north, with the laying-out of Lincoln's Inn Fields to the design of Inigo Jones in 1638. This area of open fields, known as Purse Field and Cup Field, was used as an open space for the recreation of Londoners, and strong objections to its being used for building were made by the Benchers of Lincoln's Inn whose property bordered the site. Nevertheless, in 1638 a speculative builder named William Newton obtained permission to built thirty-two houses there, and before his death in 1643, part of the south side of the square had been built, and the whole of the western side, including one magnificent house designed possibly by Inigo Jones. Now called Lindsey House, after Robert Bertie, 4th Earl of Lindsey, who owned it in 1703, it was divided into two houses about 1752. Despite the alteration to the façade which was necessitated by the building of two new doorways to replace the central one, the concealment of Inigo Jones's brickwork behind stucco, and a certain amount of visual litter on the roofline, it is still a noble building. Although it was built about 1643, it is so classical in detail that it looks more like a house of the next century.

A somewhat more typical house of this period, dated 1631, is to be found in Kew Gardens, and is known as the Dutch House. Built by a merchant of Dutch descent named Samuel Fortrey, it is of red brick and laid in a Flemish

St Paul's, Covent Garden, the western end

Lindsey House,
Lincoln's Inn Fields,
by Inigo Jones

bond; it was later taken over by the Royal Family and is now known as Kew Palace. Cromwell House on Highgate Hill is yet another brick house of this period; none remain in the City. The handsome façade of a house built in Bishopsgate about 1624 was removed from the squalor of that district towards the end of the last century to be preserved in the Victoria and Albert Museum. This was originally the front of the house belonging to Sir Paul Pindar, a wealthy seventeenth-century merchant who traded extensively and profitably in the Levant, and who contributed £10,000 towards the repair of Old St Paul's, which had suffered neglect and desecration during the troubled times following the Reformation.

Little church building took place during the century after the Reformation of 1535, and although it is true that Inigo Jones built the chapel in Lincoln's Inn, and the church of St Paul's, Covent Garden at that time, the cathedral was still in a lamentable condition. For years, the nave had been used as a rendezvous for businessmen, and by the reign of James I it had deteriorated into a kind of covered market, notorious for the swindlers, confidence men and pickpockets who preyed upon gullible visitors to the cathedral. Money for the repair and restoration was not forthcoming, however, and it was not until the reign of Charles I that work could actually begin. Some of the stone acquired for repairs had even been removed by the Duke of Buckingham and was used to build his York Water Gate!

The whole situation changed with the appointment of William Laud as Bishop of London in 1628. He not only contributed over £1000 towards the restoration of the cathedral, but exerted his very powerful influence in obtaining both funds and backing for the task. A rigorous and bigotted persecutor of all dissenters from the Anglican church, he sent some Nonconformists into exile, imprisoned others and exacted heavy fines, which were then channelled into the restoration funds for St Paul's. By 1642 (by which time Laud was even more powerful, having become Archbishop of Canterbury), a new west front had been built to Inigo Jones's designs – a great portico supported by eight round Corinthian columns and two Corinthian pilasters, topped by a tall gable supported by large scroll-like buttresses, and flanked by twin towers. The whole of the exterior was in the process of renewal, and the tower scaffolded in readiness for rebuilding, when the Civil War broke out, and all building ceased. None of Inigo Jones's work now remains, although the one effigy to be rescued intact from this church after the great fire was that of John Donne, the poet who was the Dean of St Paul's during Laud's administration. Of the original medieval cathedral there is nothing to be seen today, apart from the foundations of the chapter house on the south side, opposite the modern information centre on Watling Street. Of the other chapels and churches built or restored under Laud's influence, one remains in the City – the church of St Katherine Creechurch (a corruption of Christchurch) on the north side of Leandenhall Street in the east end of London, about two hundred yards west of the Aldgate underground station, in the shadow of the tall Cunard Building. Consecrated by William Laud in 1631, it occupies the site of an earlier church of which the tower, built about 1500, still stands, but with the later addition of a cupola. The church is not very lofty, for the strangely ribbed vault, supported on walls carried by Corinthian columns, is only 37 feet high; but it gives an impression of much greater height, as it is only 51 feet wide and seems even narrower because the aisles are both boxed in and used as parochial offices. Only the nave and the far end of each aisle are actually available for worship, and the light from the windows is also reduced to some extent by the walls of these internal buildings. The roof has Gothic-looking ribs superimposed on it, with a pattern of gaily painted bosses, but as the ribs have no constructional role to play, there is no real flow from the walls to the roof as there would be in a medieval church, and the junction between roof and walls is unhappily like that of an ill-fitting lid on a long narrow box. Yet there is a light, airy feel about the church, and the pulpit is finely proportioned and delicately carved, the ornament being much more restrained than is usual in this period. The sounding-board over the pulpit is decorated with a pattern of fine inlay, and it is interesting to find that early guide books of the nineteenth century comment on the beautifully inlaid work on the *table top* in the vestry. The so-called table top was, in fact, this sounding board, now restored to its proper position and use. The reredos is another example of fine craftsmanship in wood, but this originally belonged to the church of St James, Duke Street, Aldgate, and was installed in its present position when the other church was pulled down in 1874.

Immediately beneath the reredos, and discreetly covered with a rug, is a memorial brass – that of an Elizabethan gentleman – but engraved by order of one of his descendants in the last century. This nobleman, Sir John Gayer, was an intrepid traveller, and one night, while on an expedition in Asia, encountered a mountain lion. To his immense relief, the lion did not attack him, and as an offering of thanks for what seemed to Sir John to be a miraculous escape, he bequeathed to the parish of St Katherine Cree (or Creechurch) the sum of £200, partly for charitable purpose, but also for the establishment of an annual sermon, now called the Lion Sermon. It is still preached every year on 16 October by a guest priest such as the Dean of St Paul's. Above the altar the east window is in the shape of a Catherine wheel – an allusion to the saint to whom the church is dedicated – and it is filled with stained glass of various periods. The modern stained glass window on the south wall commemorates those who lost their lives when the troopship *Lancastria* was sunk with heavy loss of life in the Second World War. In the south-eastern corner there is an impressive Elizabethan tomb which was saved when the earlier church was pulled down in 1628. This commemorates Sir Nicholas Throckmorton (or Throgmorton), one of the chamberlains of Queen Elizabeth and her ambassador to France, whose daughter, one of the Queen's maids-of-honour married Sir Walter Raleigh secretly and without the Queen's consent, and spent a few months in the Tower of London with her husband for her temerity. This tiny corner of the church is also devoted to the memory of Charles I. There are still a number

The tomb of Sir Nicholas Throckmorton

of English people who regard him as a martyr, and the sensitively carved statue in wood of the king – his crown, sceptre and orb gilded – and the embroidered banner opposite, turn this part of the church into a small shrine to his memory. On the opposite wall is a portrait of Archbishop Laud, who was another victim of the Cromwellian executioner's axe because of the over-elaborate ritual he practised at the consecration service of St Katherine Creechurch, laying him open to a charge of Popery.

There is an alabaster font with an extraordinarily carved pedestal of the seventeenth century on the opposite side of the church, to the rear of the pulpit, and a carved organ case, with much of its original seventeenth-century carving intact, stands at the west end of the church. This instrument was built in 1686 by the master organ builder, Father Smith or Schmidt.

The Civil War was responsible for extensive destruction to churches and cathedrals throughout the county as triumphant Cromwellians engaged in an orgy of plunder. The east end of St Paul's Cathedral was divided by a wall, and a Puritan chapel installed there, but the remainder of the church was used as a barracks for 800 dragoons. (By 1651 the citizens of London in this area were petitioning successfully for a ban to be put on the playing of skittles in the cathedral after eleven o'clock at night!) The silver vessels of the cathedral were sold to finance Cromwell's artillery, and the vestments melted down for the gold which could be extracted from them. With much of his army demanding their arrears of pay, Cromwell ordered that the

left, Portrait of Samuel Pepys by John Hales

right, Portrait of Sir Christopher Wren by Sir Godfrey Kneller

scaffolding round St Paul's be disposed of to provide wages for his troopers; its removal caused further damage to the cathedral, and part of the transept fell down. Inigo Jones was captured at the siege of Basing House in 1645, and although he was a sick man, was carried out naked, wrapped only in a blanket, and imprisoned. His estates were sequestrated, and he was fined.

The year after the king was beheaded outside his own Banqueting House, Samuel Pepys, a former pupil of the grammar school in Huntingdon where Oliver Cromwell had been educated, entered Magdalene College, Cambridge, where he graduated in 1653. In the same year Christopher Wren graduated from Wadham College, Oxford. No one could possibly have foreseen the impact which these two young men were to have on the history of London. But for the time being, at least, the short-lived English Renaissance which had emerged in the reign of James I with so much promise was at an end, and it was not until the Restoration of the monarchy in 1660 that the cultural life of London could awake from its Puritan coma, and the long task of rehabilitation begin. An examination of the maps of London for 1643 and 1660 shows that very little change occurred during those years, but the next forty years were to show incredible and far-reaching developments, the results of which are still very much in evidence in London today.

No writer on the history of London can possibly repay the debt we owe to the seventeenth-century diarists who recorded the social, political and cultural developments with such fidelity and wit. Of these writers, the two most outstanding and the most readable were Samuel Pepys and John Evelyn. Pepys was born in Salisbury Court, just west of the church of St

Bride's, Fleet Street, the son of a tailor, in 1633; he was a short vigorous cockney who kept his diary for ten vital years before failing eyesight forced him to give it up in 1669. John Evelyn was born in 1620 in rather more comfortable circumstances in the village of Wotton, near Dorking in Surrey, some twenty-five miles south of London. His diary spans a greater period than that of Pepys, for he started it in 1641 and continued it until within three weeks of his death in 1706. Both men were intimately involved in the affairs of state and with the court, although in somewhat different spheres, and their diaries give us a vivid picture of seventeenth-century London and the remarkable changes which took place in the city during this period. Samuel Pepys, at one time a staunch Cromwellian with a strong Puritan upbringing, was later to change his mind and, as clerk to Lord Montague, was actually part of the delegation which went to Holland to invite the exiled Charles II to return to reclaim his throne. John Evelyn was a Royalist all his life, but spent a great deal of the Commonwealth away from England, travelling on the Continent, and was apparently much respected as a man of integrity by both factions. Apart from the writers of the period, there was also an outstanding artist – Wenceslas Hollar, from Bohemia – whose landscape portraits of London before the great fire provide an invaluable record of the city and its inhabitants. He was in Basing House with Inigo Jones when it was captured by the Cromwellian forces in 1645, but was allowed to make his way to Antwerp, and after the Restoration was appointed H. M. Scenographer and Designer of Prospects and produced many etchings and engravings which form a unique record of the appearance of seventeenth-century London.

It was John Evelyn who was to give a vivid description of the ecstatic welcome which London gave to Charles II when he returned from exile in 1660. Landing at Dover, the king and his retinue were greeted by General Monck with various civic dignitaries; the procession then moved on to Canterbury where it took the road to London along the old pilgrimage route used by Chaucer's famous pilgrims. Passing over London Bridge, the king was welcomed with great solemnity by the Lord Mayor, the aldermen, and members of the City Companies in full regalia, and from there moved on to the great sprawling palace of Whitehall. Evelyn noted in his diary that the king was accompanied 'with a triumph of above 20,000 horse and foot . . . the ways strewed with flowers, the bells ringing, the streets hung with tapestry, the fountains running with wine . . .' and that the procession which tailed back as far as Rochester, some thirty miles away, took seven hours to pass into the city, 'even from two in the afternoon until nine at night. I stood in the Strand and beheld it, and Blessed God. And all this was done without one drop of blood shed . . .'

The king was showered with gifts, and poets strove to outdo each other by producing the most extravagant verses in his praise. And indeed, during those first halcyon months it would seem that the king did his best to justify the good opinions and high hopes of the writers. The spring of 1660 seemed to hold out promise of a fairer summer than London had enjoyed for years. The king encouraged dramatists and writers, and licensed two theatres – the

King's Theatre in Drury Lane and the Duke of York's in Lincoln's Inn Fields. The small circle of scientists and mathematicians, which included such illustrious men as Christopher Wren, Robert Boyle, Robert Hooke, Isaac Newton, John Locke, John Evelyn and Samuel Pepys, was not only granted a royal charter to become the Royal Society of London for Improving Natural Knowledge (the oldest scientific society in Great Britain, and one of the oldest in Europe), but was joined by the king himself who took the liveliest interest in some of the experiments being conducted by its members. He was an immensely energetic man, and a keen sailor, and as Bishop Burnet, who had been in exile with the king, observed: 'His compass of knowledge was very considerable, for he understood physics and chemistry, mechanics and navigation well, and the architecture of a ship a little more exactly than what became a prince. . . .' But the good bishop was under no illusion about the new king's character, for he wrote:

> The King was then thirty years of age, and past, one would think, the levities of youth and the extravagances of pleasure. . . . He had a good understanding, was well acquainted with the state of affairs both at home and abroad, and had an easy affability and softness of temper that charmed all who came near him, until they were made sensible how little his good looks, and kind words, and fair promises, wherein he was liberal to excess, were to be depended upon. . . . He thought no man sincere, nor woman honest, out of principle. . . . No one, he fancied, served him out of love, and he therefore endeavoured to be quits with the world by loving others as little as he thought they loved him. . . .

The noblemen who thronged his court in Whitehall Palace certainly did little to alter these opinions. The infamous secret council, called the Cabal – a title derived from the initial letters of the names of the men who formed this group, Clarendon, Ashley, Buckingham, Arlington and Lauderdale – was made up of cynical men of affairs, concerned only with feathering their own nests. Ham House, the home of Lauderdale near Richmond, where the Cabal sometimes met, is now open to the public, and many of the furnished interiors are remarkably fine examples of the architecture and fittings of this period. Of the king's many mistresses, only Nell Gwynne, perhaps, did not try to manipulate him for political ends, and Lady Castlemaine, whose beauty so dazzled Pepys from his little rooms over a gatehouse in Whitehall Palace, was a vicious and promiscuous woman who weilded considerable political power.

Some of the noblemen who had returned from the lean years of exile now began to recoup their losses by acquiring land and building on it to their own profit – a new development of speculative building which was practically unknown until the seventeenth century. The westward development of London, which had started before the Commonwealth when Inigo Jones planned the Covent Garden area for the Earl of Bedford, began anew after the Restoration. Thomas Wriothesley, Earl of Southampton, had wished to develop the district we now know as Bloomsbury during the reign of Charles

I, but did not in fact receive permission to build until Charles II was on the throne. It was the Earl of Southampton who built the first of the squares for which London is justly famous – Bloomsbury Square. This was planned like a modern neighbourhood unit, with houses for the wealthier occupants, shops, and smaller, more humble houses for tradesmen and 'mechanics'. John Evelyn commented favourably upon the project; his diary records that he 'Dined at my Lord Treasurer's the Earl of Southampton, in Bloomsbury, where he is building a noble square or piazza, a little town. . . .' The great house and the rest of the property was later to be absorbed into the Bedford estate to the north, for William Russell, heir to the Duke of Bedford, married Rachel, the heiress to the Southampton estate, in 1669. The original builder's name is still preserved in the street name Southampton Row. Bloomsbury Square still exists, but has been entirely rebuilt.

Another noble speculator was Henry Jermyn, Earl of St Albans, who leased forty-five acres of St James's Fields with his friends, John Harvey and Sir Thomas Clarges, buying it outright later, as the area attracted a great many more tenants, who sought to escape from the smoke and filth of the city, and thought it prudent also to be within easy reach of the Court of St James and the Houses of Parliament. It was for this area that Sir Christopher Wren was to build a magnificent parish church – St James's, Piccadilly. It was the success of such ventures as St James's Square that encouraged others to indulge in speculative building, this time in the fields in the area of Soho and St Giles-in-the-Fields. The new streets included Wardour Street (named after Sir Edward Wardour), Frith Street (after Richard Fryth), Compton Street (after Sir Francis Compton) and, just north of Covent Garden, Neale Square, which has now been changed to Neal's Yard and Neal Street. Nothing remains of the original seventeenth-century development.

The king, meanwhile, was often to be seen riding or walking in St James's Park or in the Privy Garden in Whitehall Palace. His stallion's name, Rowley, was the basis of the nickname that he earned by his renowned sexual prowess – 'Old Rowley'! His interest in science prompted him to cultivate herbs and rare plants for his laboratory, and to introduce new and exotic birds into the Park, as well as maintaining the stocks of waterfowl which came to the canal. In February 1665 John Evelyn's diary recorded the arrival of the first pelican in St James's Park, 'a melancholy waterfowl, brought from Astracan by the Russian ambassador . . .' and his delight in observing the dexterity of the bird as it caught a fish thrown to it, and then turned it round in its bag-like throat.

At other times the king could be seen playing tennis, or a game brought from France in the seventeenth century known as *paille-maille*. This was played on a long narrow court and entailed hitting a ball through an iron hoop suspended from a pole eight feet above the ground with a wooden mallet. The name was derived from the French *paille-maille* – a ball and hammer – but soon became anglicised into Pall Mall, and gave its name to the narrow processional way which was built on the site of the original court.

A contemporary picture of St James's Park, showing the Regency layout

Once firmly established on the throne, the king's easy nature allowed him to forget those who had executed his father and sent him into exile, but there were many at the Court who did not share John Evelyn's jubilation at the Restoration having been accomplished 'without one drop of blood shed', and were determined to have revenge on those at whose hands they had suffered. By October 1660, not only had a number of regicides been tried and condemned to death, but had suffered publicly the dreadful fate of being hanged, then cut down before they died of strangulation, disembowelled while still conscious, their limbs and head hacked off; these reeking members were then exhibited in such places as Charing Cross, where some of the executions took place, outside Westminster Hall, and on the City gates. Not content with their revenge on the living, some courtiers, on the anniversary of the execution of Charles I, disinterred the bodies of Oliver Cromwell, Henry Ireton and John Bradshaw from their tombs in Westminster Abbey, and had the corpses dragged through the street on hurdles before hanging them on the gibbet at Tyburn, like common felons. The bodies were then buried beneath the gallows, although there is a widely held belief that the head of Oliver Cromwell was rescued and is now immured in the walls of his old college, Sidney Sussex, in Cambridge. Despite the king's distaste for the settling of old scores, as late as March 1662, three regicides who had sought sanctuary in Holland were brought back to England, tried, condemned and suffered the same dreadful death as the others.

Throughout its long history London, as a great seaport, has received many immigrants – some welcome, others less desirable. Among the latter, one of the least acceptable was the black rat, host to the fleas which carried the virus of the bubonic plague which ravaged London from time to time, but never as disastrously as in 1665. It claimed its first victim in the parish of St Giles-in-the-Fields near Soho, and then swept with increasing virulence through the whole London area. Yet despite its appalling effect on seventeenth-century London, there is little for a modern visitor to see but a few well-exhibited relics – syringes, pipes smoked by those who buried the dead etc. – in museums such as that of the City of London, and the records of the burials in some of the surviving registers of the City churches.

The main sources of information are still the diaries of Samuel Pepys and John Evelyn. Pepys, who by this time had moved to a house in Seething Lane to be near to the Navy offices just north of the tower, remained at his post when many of his colleagues had contrived to join the Court away in Salisbury, or the Parliament in Oxford. John Evelyn, too, involved in the difficult task of feeding and keeping secure the many thousands of prisoners of war captured during the battles at sea, also stayed in and around London, despite the constant danger of infection. No one knows quite how many people died during that dreadful year, but it is estimated that roughly 110,000 people were victims of the plague – about one third of the population of London at the time. During that hot rainless summer, the death rate rose so high that corpses were tipped into common graves

Engraving by Grignon of a mass burial

143

wherever an open space could be found, as the churchyards became choked with the mass of bodies. There was one huge graveyard in the Aldgate area, and another as far west as Tothill Fields, near to the present St James's Park underground station. (Bunhill – or 'Bone-hill' – Fields, just north of Moorfields, is often associated with these mass burials, but it was in fact used for burial much earlier than the seventeenth century, and until 1665 was kept almost exclusively as a cemetery for Dissenters.) No scars from the disastrous year of the plague are visible on twentieth-century London, and neither the house of Samuel Pepys in Seething Lane, nor that of John Evelyn in Sayes Court, Deptford, has survived.

The king returned to London early in the spring of 1666, and although work had been temporarily halted, it was begun again on the fine new palace at Greenwich, designed by John Webb, the faithful Royalist who had been the assistant of Inigo Jones earlier in the century. The condition of St Paul's Cathedral was also deplorable, and somewhat surprisingly it was not Webb, but Christopher Wren, known to the king through his activities with the Royal Society, who was asked to survey the damaged cathedral and to suggest what might be done to repair it. During the plague Wren has spent a few fruitful months in France, seeking out all the important architects in Paris and studying with great care not only the historic buildings, but 'modern' ones in the course of construction. He would obviously have been interested in the new buildings being added to the Palais du Louvre, and he even had a short interview with the great architect, Bernini, who had come from Rome to present his own designs for the Louvre (but which were rejected). Wren's own experience as an architect was really very limited – he had built the Chapel of Pembroke College, Cambridge, and had already began to plan the Sheldonian Theatre, Oxford – and he was eager for any information and advice which would further his career. His short visit to Paris was significant in that it provided him with ideas and inspiration for some of the buildings he was to design for London during the next few years. François Mansart's new Church of the Val de Grâce, and Jacques Lemarcier's Church of the Sorbonne, still under construction, were two very important examples studied by Wren; for it must be remembered that apart from St Paul's Church, Covent Garden, and the chapel opposite St James's Palace, both built by Inigo Jones, there were almost no contemporary churches on which Wren could base his ideas. In the light of what was to follow, it is the more astonishing to realise that Wren was virtually self-taught.

Wren produced a beautiful drawing (now in All Souls College, Oxford) for a tower and dome to replace the ruined central tower of Old St Paul's – a design which clearly shows the influence of his visit to Paris, but sadly it was never carried out. On the night of 2 September 1666, Thomas Farrinor, the king's baker in Pudding Lane, just north of Billingsgate Fish Market, omitted to quench a few smouldering faggots under his oven and before that night was out, a great fire, fanned by a high easterly wind, was raging through the sleeping city, leaping across the narrow streets, showering areas

as yet untouched with flaming embers to start a new outbreak there, so that
the fire spread rapidly across the tinder-dry roofs, devouring everything in
its path. Thomas Farrinor and his family awoke to find their house ablaze,
but crawled to safety along the roof, thus escaping with their lives, but little
else. Surprisingly few people lost their lives in the fire, although no one will
ever know how many died at the hands of criminals released from the jails
and ripe for loot, and there were appalling material losses. Once the fire
reached the warehouses which lined the river, it found ample fuel there
among the stocks of pitch, oil, cordage and other inflammable materials, and
many wealthy merchants were penniless and homeless bankrupts by the end
of the week. The famous account to be found in the diary of Samuel Pepys is
certainly one of the most dramatic and factual descriptions of this dreadful
episode in London's history, for he saw the fire, first from the Tower, and
then later from the tower of All Hallows, Barking. It is this account which is
used as a commentary to the excellent diorama of the great fire in the
Museum of London. But it is from the diary of another eye-witness, John
Evelyn, that one can more readily trace the path of the fire, for he saw it from
Bankside, near Southwark, and from there could see the development of the
whole conflagration as it raced across the City. He described how he saw 'the
whole south part of the City burning from Cheapside to the Thames, and all
along Cornhill ... Tower Street, Fenchurch Street, Gracious-street,
(modern Gracechurch street) and so along to Baynard's Castle, and was now
taking hold of St Paul's Church (Cathedral) to which the scaffolds
contributed greatly. . . .' He returned the following day to see that by then
the fire had reached the Inner Temple. 'All Fleet-street, the Old Bailey,
Ludgate-hill, Warwick-lane, Newgate, Paul's-chain, Watling-street, now
flaming, and most of it reduced to ashes; the stones of St Paul's flew like

The Fire of London,
1666, Dutch school

grenados, the melting lead running down the streets in a stream, so as no horse, nor man, was able to tread on them. . . .' Both Pepys and Evelyn comment on the lack of anyone willing or able to organise efforts to fight the fire; people concentrated on salvaging their individual possessions and carried them away to safety as best they could, leaving what remained to the fire. It was not until Samuel Pepys had gone to Whitehall and alerted the king and his brother, the Duke of York, that any co-ordinated plans were made to fight the fire. The king then not only gave orders that streets which lay in the path of the fire should be blown up to act as fire-breaks, but actually rode out to supervise the campaign himself, rewarding the exhausted fire-fighters with handfuls of coins to persuade them to redouble their efforts. John Evelyn was put in charge of one party selected to save the western end of Holborn, by Fetter Lane, and it was undoubtedly through their efforts that the fine row of timber-framed houses of Staple Inn has survived to this day. As more and more people were rendered homeless, huge camps of refugees gathered in any open space that was safe from the fire: there were many thousands in tents and other temporary accommodation on Moorfields, just north of London Wall, and Evelyn calculated that some 200,000 were encamped in the Islington and Highgate areas, while others were billeted on friends and relatives in safe parts of the suburbs. The king organised relief funds, and contributions poured in from every part of the country – even poverty-stricken Ireland offered both cash and cattle. After four or five days the fire burnt itself out, although sporadic outbreaks from smouldering debris in cellars continued to give trouble long after the main areas of fire had been quenched; the Temple was once threatened with a fresh outbreak, which was fortunately dealt with immediately. Evelyn was concerned for the wounded prisoners of war being tended in the hospital of St Bartholomew, but the fire died out in the Cock Lane area, in Smithfield, the limit being marked to this day by a little gilded cherub high up on a modern building at the north end of the lane. But the city had suffered grievously. As John Evelyn wrote in his diary on 10 September 1666: 'I went again to the ruins; for it was no longer a city.'

When seventeenth-century Londoners came to count the cost it was found that about 87 parish churches, 13,200 houses, 44 of the Halls of the Livery Companies, the Royal Exchange and the Customs House had been destroyed completely, with extensive damage inflicted on many more important buildings, including the great cathedral of St Paul's. The area of devastation extended over 373 acres within the City itself, and 63 acres outside the City walls. About four-fifths of London lay in ruins. The advantage was that a clean sweep had been made of much that was unworthy and ignoble, and offered a fresh start – an opportunity to build the finest city in Europe. Plans for the rebuilding were produced in a surprisingly short time. Hardly had the embers chilled when Christopher Wren, who arrived in London very shortly after the fire, presented his master plan to the king. He was soon followed by John Evelyn with an alternative, but somewhat similar plan; indeed Evelyn noted, 'Dr Wren got the start of me, but both of us did coincide so frequently that his Majesty was not displeased.'

Unfortunately the decision did not rest entirely with the king; the citizens of London, led by the Lord Mayor and the Aldermen, were traditionally an independent body, and for them it was imperative that business be resumed as soon as possible. Some of the suggested rebuilding would have taken years to accomplish, and many of London's traditional trade areas and thoroughfares would have disappeared if either plan had been adopted. Nevertheless, the regulations concerning the density and the height of the new buildings, as well as the materials from which they were to be built, were so obviously in the City's interests that they were accepted without demur. The new building code insisted that the houses should be built of brick or stone, and ordained that they should be of four basic types: two, three or four storeys high, excluding basements and garrets, and some of four storeys, clearly for the more wealthy merchants, would be set back from the road. The first problem was the financing of this gigantic building project. Much of the initial cost, especially for the building of wharves, warehouses and markets, and the City prisons, was met by levying a shilling on every ton of coal brought into the City. This was later raised to three shillings per ton, and a great deal of the additional income was set aside to finance the rebuilding of the City churches, and the great new cathedral of St Paul's.

A special court occupied the relatively undamaged hall of Clifford's Inn, off Fleet Street, to settle the multitude of lawsuits which inevitably resulted from the claims and counter-claims of tenants who had lost all in the fire, and of the landlords whose livelihood had disappeared. Laws against craftsmen from outside the City, which had been jealously maintained by the City Companies in the interests of their members, had to be waived for several years, so great was the demand for bricklayers, stonemasons and all the other building trades, and so too were the regulations which controlled the imports of tiles, bricks etc. One new set of regulations ordered the rationing of Portland stone, and others made striking or the 'withdrawal of labour' illegal.

The Monument, designed by Wren's colleague and friend, Robert Hooke, stands 202 feet above the Fish Street area, and the same distance from the site of the baker's house where the fire started in Pudding Lane, and it has an inscription on its south face which declares: 'London rises again, whether with greater speed or greater magnificence is doubtful, three short years complete that which was considered the work of an age.' It once bore an even more inaccurate inscription than the one quoted, for as a result of the perjury of Titus Oates, another one appeared, attributing the blame for the great fire to the Roman Catholics who had apparently started it 'in order for carrying on their horrid plott [*sic*] for the extirpating the Protestant and old English liberty, and introducing Popery and slavery'. This inscription was removed in 1685 during the reign of James II, reinstated in 1689 during the reign of William and Mary, and finally removed in 1830.

The estimate of three years given on the Monument's inscription for the rebuilding of the City of London was optimistic, to say the least – it took nearer twenty-five years for the City to be entirely rebuilt, for despite the

The Monument

superior quality of the houses and the streets in which they stood, many of the former residents of London, having moved out to the suburbs, were most reluctant to return to live in the City again, and the poorer people who had remained behind could not afford the increased rents demanded for the improved houses. Indeed, the suburbs had become so attractive that it was necessary to fine heavily any Alderman who declined to return to live in the City. Another inducement was to offer, gratis, the freedom of the City to any man of substance who took up residence there – a privilege for which most men had paid heavily in the past.

The harbour designed by Wren at the bottom of Ludgate Hill and Fleet Street, with its broad wharves and more liberal spaces by Seacoal Lane, did not prove the attraction it was hoped; the wharves eventually became cluttered with all sorts of merchandise and were used as a highway, so that the river itself deteriorated and soon became a refuse tip for all sorts of garbage, a scandal which the City authorities could not afford. The first public building to be erected was the new Customs House – a splendid example of Wren's design, but, alas, burnt down early in the nineteenth century. A new Royal Exchange suffered the same fate at about the same time. The first City Company to build its new hall was that of the Fishmongers, but this has also been rebuilt, and in fact almost nothing remains of the seventeenth-century architecture which has not been either rebuilt or so entirely altered that only small parts of the original buildings remain. The most substantial survivors of this great rebuilding process are to be found in the areas round the Inns of Court, and among the City churches. These City churches are all well worth a visit: in any one of them a visitor may enjoy the atmosphere of calm and tranquillity, often surrounded by craftsmanship in wood and in metal of the most splendid quality. Sometimes there is even the opportunity of hearing a concert, a mannerly discussion of a short sermon during the lunch hour.

None of these seventeenth-century churches, whether they were designed by Wren or by his assistant, Nicholas Hawksmoor, are exactly as they were originally built. Many of them were grievously damaged during the second fire of London in the 1940s, although, oddly enough, even if the body of a church was gutted by fire or destroyed by high explosive, the towers have often survived – indeed, in some of them, only the tower and spire remain to be preserved as a reminder of a noble church that once stood on that site. Others have had to be rebuilt, and the modern architect has taken great pains to restore them as closely as possible to the original, modifying the plan from time to time so that the new building is more suitable for the use of a society far different from that for which it was originally designed.

Wren's declaration of the principles on which he designed this remarkable range of City churches – about fifty in all – is still valid. He said:

... but still, in our Reformed Religion, it should seem vain to make a Parish church larger than that all can both see and hear. The Romanists, indeed, may build larger Churches, it is enough if they hear the murmur

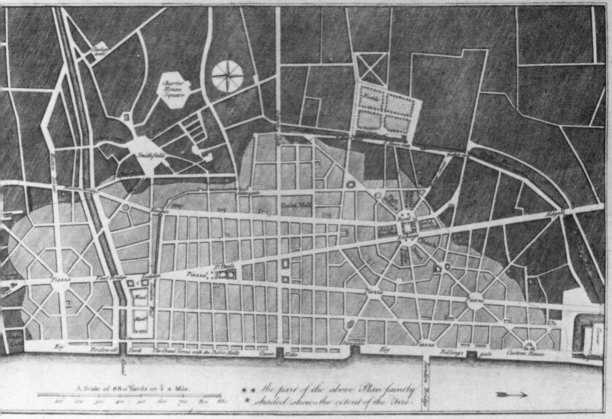

of the Mass, and see the Elevation of the Host, but ours are fitted for
Auditories. I can hardly think it practicable to make a single room so
capacious, with Pews and Galleries, as to hold above 2000 Persons, and all
to hear the Service, and both to hear distinctly and see the Preacher . . .

Thus, the City churches are all fairly small and intimate – occasionally
lofty, but no member of the congregation is ever very far from the pulpit,
nor from the altar. Wren was obliged to build many of his new churches on
the irregular sites previously occupied by a medieval church and
churchyard, although some of the earlier parishes were combined and the
overall number of churches reduced. The fashion of the period, however,
demanded classical symmetry or apparent symmetry and so Wren rarely
built in the medieval style except for St Mary Aldermary, and there were
probably special reasons for this departure from his normal procedure. The
visitor to the City will find it worthwhile to note that clusters of seventeenth-
century churches can often be found within a hundred yards or less of some of
the modern underground stations. The most obvious of these groups is that
which encircles St Paul's Cathedral, which has it own underground station,
named after it, just to the north of St Paul's churchyard. Immediately across
the road from the underground is St Vedast, Foster Lane, while a little to the
west stands the superb tower of Christ Church, Newgate Street – all that
remains of a Wren church which, in any case, had been somewhat altered in
1834. By the east end of the cathedral is the tower of St Augustine's, Watling

Street, now incorporated into the choir school, its tower bearing a fibreglass replica of the original Wren steeple. Much more beautiful, and in an open courtyard just north of Queen Victoria Street, is St Nicholas, Cole Abbey, which was largely rebuilt after the Second World War, and well south of the cathedral, at the junction of Queen Victoria Street and Upper Thames Street, is the enchanting little brick church of St Benet's, St Paul's Wharf, which has been the church of London's Welsh community since 1867. A little to the north-west of St Benet's, by St Andrew's Hill, is the church of St Andrew-by-the-Wardrobe, another Wren church so badly damaged during the blitz that it had to be almost entirely rebuilt. To complete this group of churches which almost encircles the cathedral one must return to Ludgate Hill, the western approach to St Paul's, where the sharp, black spire of St Martin's, Ludgate, acts as a magnificent foil to the rounded amplitude of the great dome of the cathedral. There is one more Wren church within easy walking distance of St Martin's, Ludgate, also possessed of a superb spire – St Bride's, Fleet Street, about 200 yards to the west of Ludgate Hill.

Two other groups of seventeenth-century churches, so close that they form almost one, are to be found to the east of St Paul's, in the very heart of the City. The more westerly of the group, for which the underground station is Mansion House, includes the famous church of St Mary Le Bow, on Cheapside, between St Paul's and the Mansion House. St Mary Le Bow, famous for the association of its bells with the cockney probably has the most beautiful spire of all Wren's churches, but the nave has been almost entirely rebuilt. To the north of Mansion House underground is one of the few churches which Wren designed in the Gothic style – St Mary Aldermary – but the group is otherwise strung out on either side of the thoroughfare which runs due south from the Guildhall to the river, starting as King Street, and then changing its name to Queen Street as soon as it crosses Cheapside. Very near to the Guildhall is the church of St Lawrence Jewry, a Wren church heavily damaged during the blitz, but beautifully and sensitively reconstructed. Much further south are two more Wren churches – St James, Garlickhythe, on the western side of Queen Street and St Michael, Paternoster Royal, on the eastern side, just north of Upper Thames Street.

The second group, a little further east, for which the Bank underground is probably the most convenient station, begins with a church built by Wren's brilliant assistant, Nicholas Hawksmoor – St Mary Woolnoth – a craggy west front with twin towers, built at the junction of Lombard Street and King William Street. To the north, behind the Bank of England, but still within easy walking distance, is another Wren church, St Margaret Lothbury, while to the rear of the Mansion House stands one of Wren's masterpieces, the domed St Stephen, Walbrook, now closed for extensive repairs. Tucked in a little courtyard between Cannon Street and King William Street, up Abchurch Lane, is one of the most intimate and delightful of all the Wren churches – St Mary Abchurch, which is almost hidden away from the passers-by. St Clement, Eastcheap, just off King William Street, and St Edmund, King and Martyr, in Lombard Street, east of St Mary Woolnoth, are both Wren churches, while an alley up the side of St Edmund leads past the famous inn, The George and Vulture (where Mr Pickwick stayed), and so into Cornhill to two more Wren churches – St Michael, and St Peter, Cornhill, both considerably altered since Wren designed them. From the Monument underground station it is easy to walk to three more outstanding churches by this most creative of amateur architects. The first is in Lower Thames Street, at the bottom of Fish Street Hill – St Magnus the Martyr, with its arched porch still spanning the flagstones of one of the early London Bridges. (The present London Bridge is just to the west of the original site.) Still further east, in a turning just opposite Billingsgate Fish Market, is St Mary at Hill – one of the most secluded of all Wren's churches which is normally entered up a narrow alleyway to which a visitor can be directed. At the top of the same hill, but much more obvious from its dominant spire, is St Margaret Pattens, another Wren church which has suffered somewhat by alterations to the interior. These, then, are the most important seventeenth-century churches, although such splendid fragments as the tower of St Dunstan's in the East, just east of St Mary at Hill, are not to be missed. Many of these churches were not finished until the first decade of the eighteenth century, but it is convenient to group them as they were built as a result of the great fire. Some of their individual characteristics will be described later in the chapter. Some of Wren's churches were destroyed by the march of progress. His church of St Antholin was destroyed to make way for Queen Victoria Street, and other earlier victims of this kind of commercial vandalism were St Christopher-le-Stocks, swept away to make room for the Bank of England; St Benet Fink, demolished to provide a site for the Sun Fire Office; and St Michael, Crooked Lane, destroyed during one of the rebuildings of London Bridge. Fortunately, some of the beautiful craftsmanship with which such churches were furnished was preserved, and pulpits and screens, organ cases and reredosses were sometimes distributed to other churches – not necessarily in the City of London. The parish church of St Peter and Paul, in Blandford Forum in Dorset, for example, has a pulpit salvaged from St Antholin. When Wren's All Hallows the Great was demolished in 1894, its screen found a new home in another Wren church, St Margaret Lothbury, and after the Second World War, an altar-piece from St Olave Jewry, of which only the tower now survives, was also installed in that same Wren church. Other churches, heavily damaged by bombing, were also sometimes able to make good some of their losses by accepting artefacts from other City churches.

Some of the earlier City churches also had seventeenth-century additions. St Helen's, Bishopsgate, for example, one of the score of churches saved from the great fire by the strong easterly wind, was 'modernised' during the seventeenth century by the addition of two fine inner doorcases and a new pulpit. One doorcase, dated 1633, and the pulpit are attributed to Inigo Jones, although the second doorcase seems to have been a few years later. At this point mention must be made of two City churches which, while they were not strictly seventeenth century, have such important connections with this period, and are so conveniently placed near to the Tower Hill underground station, that they might be mentioned in this chapter. The first is All Hallows-by-the-Tower or, as it is often called, All Hallows, Barking, because of its early foundation by the monks of Barking Abbey. This is a medieval church, very heavily damaged during the blitz, but with strong seventeenth-century associations, for it was from this tower that Samuel Pepys surveyed the progress of the great fire, before making his way to alert the king at Whitehall. It also possesses one of the most beautiful examples of Grinling Gibbons' carving still in existence – a font cover, kept safely behind a gate in the north-western corner of the church. Grinling Gibbons carved this in 1682, and despite the wealth of his woodcarving to be found in St Paul's Cathedral and in many City churches, this must surely be his masterpiece. The magnificent pulpit is also his work, but was originally part of the church of St Swithun, Cannon Street, destroyed in the blitz.

A little to the north of All Hallows, in Hart Street, is another church associated with Samuel Pepys. This is the church of St Olave, and the churchyard, which is full of the victims of the plague of 1665, is entered through a gateway with a strangely macabre decoration of carved skulls. Elizabeth Pepys, the wife of Samuel Pepys was interred in the church in 1669, and is commemorated by a portrait bust set in an oval niche which was erected by her husband. Samuel Pepys also lies buried there and, as a devoted servant of the Admiralty, used to occupy a gallery reserved for members of the Navy Office. The gallery has gone, but admirers of the great diarist have erected a commemorative plaque in the area it formerly occupied. Neither the Navy Office, nor the house occupied by Samuel Pepys in Seething Lane has survived. The carved pulpit which is now to be seen in St Olave was originally in the church of St Benet, Gracechurch Street, but was saved from destruction by being stored in the crypt of St Paul's Cathedral after the sale of its former church in 1867.

Both All Hallows-by-the-Tower and St Olave are generally open to the public, but in 1954, when the number of parishes in the City was drastically reduced from 108 to 24, 15 churches were selected as Guild churches and perform special duties, which means that they are not usually open at all on Sundays, neither are all their services open to the general public. Other City churches are only kept open if volunteers can be persuaded to be on duty during the weekdays because they have neither a verger nor a permanent vicar of their own, so the casual visitor may not always be able to see the interiors of these historic churches. On Saturdays and in the afternoon they are particularly likely to be closed, but are open at lunchtime.

One particularly fine church by Wren which is nearly always open is St Magnus the Martyr, a hundred yards or so south of the Monument underground station. Its magnificent tower is somewhat dwarfed by the monstrous bulk of Adelaide House which occupies the entrance to the new London Bridge. St Magnus has a wide porch, spanning the footpath which used to be part of an earlier London Bridge, and relics of this and other parts of London's riverside are to be seen there. The main body of the church was completed by 1687 but the tower, 185 feet high, was not added until 1705.

Every church in the City has a personality of its own, although this is not entirely due to the fact that Wren never repeated a design. Some churches, if not actually neglected are nevertheless not loved, but the church of St Magnus the Martyr emits its own special kind of warmth as the heavy door closes softly, shutting out the roar of traffic along Lower Thames Street: the woodwork smells right, the flowers are fresh, the light is brisk. Nonconformists, used to the austerity of their chapels, may be taken aback by the frankly High Church tone of the fittings and by the faint resinous smell of incense which permeates the church. But it would be a pity if sectarian disapproval were an obstacle to the enjoyment of one of Wren's most lovely churches, especially in this ecumenical age. There is a stupendous reredos behind the high altar – its upper storey an addition made during the reconstruction after the Second World War – and two seventeenth-century doorcases have been converted into altars at the head of each aisle. St Magnus has a magnificent gallery and organ loft to balance the reredos, and a carved pulpit with a great sounding-board towers over the pews below. Despite some later and somewhat unfortunate stained glass which Wren would not have expected, the church is light and lofty, with elegant fluted Ionic columns supporting the airy barrel vault. The church has a very early foundation – St Magnus is a somewhat obscure saint, and a

left, The font cover by Grinling Gibbons at All Hallows
right, St Magnus the Martyr

rather spurious effigy, to be seen on the south wall, is the only jarring note in these lovely surroundings. Henry Yevele, the architect of much of Westminster Abbey and of Westminster Hall, was buried in the former church on this site, which was burned in the great fire. Miles Coverdale, who translated the scriptures into English in the reign of Henry VIII, was the rector of St Magnus for two years, and now lies buried to the south of the high altar. A framed replica of the title page of his Bible is kept on a ledge behind his gravestone. This church also has a richly ornamented sword-rest of wrought iron. These are by no means uncommon in City churches, for it was likely that one of the more important parishioners would be elected Lord Mayor and would therefore attend civic services in the full splendour of his robes, the great sword of state being borne in front of him, and then placed, blade uppermost, in one of these sword-rests specially made for that purpose. They would often be decorated with his coat of arms (if he was entitled to bear one), and also with the arms of the Livery Company of which he was a member. In 1709, the parishioner so honoured was Sir Charles Duncombe, a leading banker and a member of the Goldsmiths Company, and he not only presented this sword-rest to the church of St Magnus, but the clock which is such a prominent feature of the tower from outside. Three years later he presented the church with an organ, and although it has undergone some modification during the past 200 years, it is basically the same instrument first erected there in 1712. With such a wealth of furnishings, it is not surprising that so great an authority as Sir John Betjeman should describe this church as 'one of the top City interiors'.

From St Magnus the Martyr it is a short walk eastwards to yet another of Wren's masterpieces. The church of St Mary at Hill lies between two narrow lanes, Lovat Lane and St Mary at Hill, which rise steeply from Lower Thames Street to Eastcheap – the eastern extension of Cannon Street, *not* of Cheapside. Unlike so many Wren churches which suffered drastic alteration during the nineteenth century, the Victorian craftsman who enriched this interior with so much of his woodcarving did it with such skill and sensitivity that it is dificult to distinguish it from the carving carried out by Grinling Gibbons in the seventeenth century, and that which was added by W. Gibbs Rogers during the remodelling of the church in 1848–9. Measuring about 96 feet long and 60 feet wide, this church has almost exactly the same dimensions as St Magnus the Martyr, but with its very light ornate eighteenth-century plaster shallow dome it seems somewhat more spacious. It has a superb pulpit with a wide hexagonal sounding-board, richly inlaid with differently coloured woods; a splendidly carved seventeenth-century reredos, lectern and pulpit, the latter with some skilfully inserted nineteenth-century workmanship; and no less than four wrought iron sword-rests. The church is the only Wren church in the City to retain the high box pews, and although the rector's pew and reading desk is proudly inscribed V.R. 1848, there is nothing to choose between the craftsmanship of the seventeenth century, and that of the nineteenth century. In spite of the vulnerability of such work to woodworm, fire and so on, it is quite extraordinary what a sense of permanence it has. The men who

left, St Mary-at-Hill
right, The 'Gothick'
tower of St Dunstan's-
in-the-East

cut and chiselled those panels with their rippling arabesques, freeing the
hanging fruit and flowers from the solid wood, have long since died, yet they
left behind something which was so much a part of them that the church is
alive with their presence. And the church is wonderfully quiet, protected as
it is from the City noise by its position between two steep, narrow streets.
Yet St Mary at Hill is considerably more than a well preserved relic of a past
age: towards the end of the last century, Rev. Carlile, the rector of the
church, established the City Samaritan Office, defined as 'a free club
conducted by evangelists of the Church Army, to aid destitute but deserving
clerks, warehousemen, and hopeless, starving outcasts'.

Less than seventy yards to the east from St Mary at Hill, there is a tiny
green oasis among the ruins of another Wren church – St Dunstan's-in-the-
East – and under one of his most unusual and most beautiful spires: a
charming little garden which has been fashioned against the grey stone
backdrop of Wren's bomb-blasted church. The tower – a 'Gothic' one with
a finely designed corona of stone – was clearly visible from Lower Thames
Street until 1979, but a modern block of buildings was built during 1979 on
Lower Thames Street, isolating the little garden still more completely, and
hiding the superb Wren spire such that few people will see it unless they
seek it out. In form it resembles the coronas which crown the cathedral of St
Giles, in Edinburgh, and the great parish church of St Nicholas, Newcastle
upon Tyne.

Returning to St Mary at Hill, it is easy to see the next complete church

designed by Wren after the fire – St Margaret Pattens, which is a short walk away up Eastcheap, on the corner of Rood Lane. This church also has a 'Gothic' spire – a very high one, about 200 feet, though it is given extra height by its position at the top of the hill. It is one of Wren's most lofty spires. The church derives its name from 'pattens' – clog-like footwear with wooden soles to which were attached iron rings to raise the wearer above the thick mud of medieval London, and which were presumably made and marketed in this area. Inside the church there is a glass case containing specimens of this strange footwear. The church is painted in light airy colours, and is about 30 feet high, but although it is actually 66 feet long and 52 feet wide, its width is much reduced by the filling in of the north gallery (which in Wren's period would have been open to the chancel) and its conversion into glass-panelled offices – not a very happy alteration. There is some fine woodwork of the seventeenth century – the imposing western screen with the Royal Arms is dated 1686 and is positioned in the gallery above a great organ which reaches to the roof. There are two canopied pews, and a splendid reredos, and an altar-piece of 'Christ at Gethsemane' by the Italian Old Master, Carlo Maratti, who died in Rome in 1713.

St Margaret Pattens is a busy church, and there is nearly always an exhibition of some kind in the choir stalls on the north side of the chancel during the week.

Walking westwards from St Margaret Pattens and Rood Lane along Fenchurch Street and Lombard Street to the Royal Exchange, it is only about 350 yards to the church of St Mary Woolnoth – the craggy, fortress-like building built by Wren's assistant, Nicholas Hawksmoor, and the first of one of the groups of churches in the City. Technically this is an eighteenth-century church, built between 1716 and 1727, after the original church, which has suffered badly during the great fire of London, had been repaired extensively but ineffectively by Sir Christopher Wren. One entrance of the Bank underground station actually runs beneath the church, and this is therefore a very convenient landmark from which to start a tour ranging from St Margaret Lothbury to the north; St Mary Abchurch, just off Cannon Street, to the south; and St Peter, Cornhill, to the east.

St Mary Woolnoth apparently derives its strange name from an early twelfth-century founder named Wulfnoth, but the present church is entirely of the eighteenth century and is one of Hawksmoor's finest and most original churches. It stands at the junction of Lombard Street and King William Street, braving the traffic like a great fortress, its twin-turreted tower looking as though it has been hewn from rock, not built from blocks of stone. The church is entered by a flight of shallow stairs which seems to lift the body of the church above street level, and probably contributed to the feeling of splendid isolation from the frenetic business world outside. Despite its somewhat aggressive exterior, the church has a noble and placid interior. It is almost square in plan, with a lofty panelled ceiling supported by slender Corinthian columns, and it possesses a wealth of eighteenth-century woodwork, with communion rails of wrought iron, intricately fashioned. Despite some rearrangement of the interior fitting by Butterfield, the Victorian architect, who removed the galleries in 1875–6, much of the organ-case and gallery is intact and bears the banners of the Goldsmiths Company, with which it has been associated since the seventeenth century, on projecting brackets. The organ was built by the famous Father Smith and one vicar, at least, was a musician: John Newton, who was a close friend of the poet, William Cowper, wrote two of the best-loved hymns in use today – 'Glorious things of Thee are spoken' and 'How sweet the name of Jesus sounds'. His memorial tablet is on the north wall. Edward Lloyd, who died in 1712, the founder of the world-famous insurance firm, Lloyds of London, is also most appropriately buried in this church in the very heart of the City.

By following the western wall of the Bank of England for about 100 yards, one arrives at Lothbury and the Church of St Margaret Lothbury, built by Wren in 1686–90. Its impressive 140-foot high spire is yet another example of Wren's resourcefulness; all his spires have characters as individual as those of human beings. This church, like St Mary Woolnoth and St Mary at Hill, has a bracket clock projecting over the pavement, but there are no steps to this church, nor a concealed entrance, only a simple pedimented doorway leading directly into it. The name of the street, Lothbury, is thought to have been derived from Loteringi, the name of a family living in this area during the twelfth century. After that it became Loteringi Bury, then Loter Bury, and finally Lothbury. The church is 66 feet long and 54 feet wide, with a simple roof 36 feet high, and it has been singularly fortunate in being given several very beautiful fittings from less fortunate churches which were sold and demolished during the last century. Thus, one of the two surviving chancel screens designed by Wren was inserted in St Margaret Lothbury when its original owner, All Hallows the Great in Upper Thames Street, was demolished in 1894. It is a most sumptuous piece of carved woodwork, probably of German workmanship, with a magnificent Royal Arms set in the central pediment and a mighty carved eagle immediately above the entrance to the chancel. The screen was given to All Hallows the Great by a German, Theodore Jacobsen, between 1685 and 1690, and it is difficult to realise how bare St Margaret Lothbury might look without such a splendid addition. Its own pulpit now has an ornately carved sounding-board, also from All Hallows, with a great flutter of plump cherubs grasping wreaths and swags of great richness. The ornate altar-piece now in the south aisle originally came from St Olave, Jewry (a church of which only the tower now survives), and the wooden painted figures of Moses and Aaron which flank St Margaret Lothbury's own fine reredos came from the destroyed church of St Christopher-le-Stocks.

Having received these fittings which enrich St Margaret Lothbury so much, the church now undertakes the parochial work of six defunct parishes, including some of those from which the fittings were given. The exquisitely carved marble font is attributed to Grinling Gibbons, whose work in wood and in stone can be found in so many of these churches, and in St Paul's Cathedral. He was discovered quite by accident by John Evelyn, at work in a cottage in Deptford, and the great diarist was so impressed by him that he introduced him to Charles II who, in turn, introduced him to the Surveyor General, Sir Christopher Wren. It would naturally not have been possible for one craftsman, however hard he worked, to produce personally all the carving in St Paul's Cathedral, for example, but all the work carried out under his supervision in the City churches, in the cathedral, and elsewhere, bears the stamp of his genius. It is fitting that he should have been appointed Master Carver in Wood to the Crown, although he did not work exclusively in wood, as the marble font at St Margaret Lothbury shows. A bronze statue of James II in the guise of a Roman emperor which stands outside the National Gallery in Trafalgar Square is also his work.

Another truly magnificent pulpit by Gibbons stands in the church of St Stephen, Walbrook, to the rear of the Mansion House. To reach St Stephen, it is necessary to return along Princes Street to the crossroads by the Mansion House, but unfortunately urgent repairs have necessitated closing this church for at least two years. This is a very sad, if temporary loss, for it is generally agreed that St Stephen, Walbrook, is not only one of Wren's most exquisite interiors, but that its outstandingly beautiful dome was one of the many experiments which Wren carried out in order to create his mighty dome at St Paul's. The dome of St Stephen's, seen from within, is certainly its crowning glory, but the whole interior, so cleverly contrived to look classical and symmetrical, is built on an irregular and awkward site – a fact more apparent, perhaps, from outside than from within. The church has a charming little font and font cover, also by Grinling Gibbons, and a superbly soaring pulpit with a great sounding-board rivalling that at St Margaret Lothbury. It also possesses a huge painting, the 'Martyrdom of St Stephen' by Benjamin West, the American artist from Pennsylvania, who arrived in England in 1763 and established such a reputation that he succeeded to the Presidency of the Royal Academy on the death of Sir Joshua Reynolds in 1792.

Although St Stephen, Walbrook, is closed to the public, it will undoubtedly continue with one of the activities for which it is justly famous: the Samaritans. It was in this church in the summer of 1953 that the newly appointed vicar, Chad Varra, started a voluntary movement of Christian aid which now has branches in every major city and town in the British Isles. Although it was started in a Christian church it is in no sense selective in the people to whom it extends its help. Thus, although the church itself may have closed its doors temporarily, the door at the side which leads down to the main offices of the Samaritans will never close down.

From Walbrook it is a short walk southward to Cannon Street, and then eastwards to Abchurch Lane, a narrow rising alley on the north side, leading to a little paved court in which stands yet another of Wren's beautiful little brick churches – St Mary Abchurch. The name has been variously described as a corruption of Up-church as the church stands on a slight rise, or of Abba's church, the church having been founded by an entirely unknown man named Abba. Like St Stephen, Walbrook, St Mary Abchurch has a dome, but St Mary is almost square, and its dome, unlike that at St Stephen's, which is decorated with light rococo plasterwork, is covered with a rather dark painting, pierced a little above the base of the cupola with four circular windows. The painting, by a local man named William Snow, depicts a heavenly scene, the focal point of which are Hebrew characters for Jehovah or God, and various allegorical figures and angels are grouped around the inscription to pay tribute. There is a lavishly carved reredos and an equally impressive pulpit with a carved and inlaid sounding-board which has definitely been established as the work of Grinling Gibbons, as documents recording his request for payment for the work done here still exist. The richly carved reredos which is such an important feature of this church was badly damaged during the blitz, but thanks to the devotion and the courage of one old lady – a kind of verger in the church during those terrible years – who salvaged many of the fragments of the carving at great risk to herself, it was possible to restore it so completely after the war that it is virtually impossible now to detect any signs of the reconstruction. The font, however, is not the work of Grinling Gibbons, but was carved by a master mason, Christopher Kempster, in 1686; the year after he completed it, he joined the select team working for Wren on St Paul's Cathedral. There are familiar fretted and carved arabesques on the panels behind the pews and in the front of the benches on the north side, just under the superbly carved pulpit. The church also contains two wrought iron sword-rests, and a most elegant staircase at the west end leads up to the organ gallery. The organ-case was originally in the church of All Hallows the Great.

This little brick church by Wren has an intimacy which one misses in some of the more ostentatious City churches, although its dim light, caused partly by later stained glass, would hardly have been approved of by its

The pulpit in St Mary Abchurch

architect, whose churches must all have been much lighter when the windows were filled with light tinted glass, and were not shut in behind great office blocks.

The next church, St Clement Eastcheap, in St Clement's Lane just off Cannon Street, about 100 yards to the east of St Mary Abchurch, is also of brick. Built 1683–7, St Clement was probably built of brick as the demands on the quarries for Portland stone were proving enormous, and Wren had already started on the building of his great cathedral by June of 1675. There had also been some difficulty with supplies of stone, one shipload having been intercepted and carried off by French privateers in the English Channel. Thus, for the smaller parish churches, Wren preferred to use brick, and to reserve the stone for such churches as St Bride's, Fleet Street, and of course, St Paul's. It is probably significant that even so important a project as the Royal Military Hospital at Chelsea, the foundations of which were being inspected by Sir Stephen Fox, the Paymaster General, and John Evelyn, in 1682, was built very largely in brick, with a portico of stone and stone facings on the major buildings.

At St Clement, Eastcheap, the 88-foot high tower, as well as the main body of the church, was made of brick, with stone facings; this material was not only cheaper but more easily worked than the expensive stone. Wren was again confronted by an irregular site – a difficulty he overcame by producing an aisle on the south side of the church. But if he economised on the building materials, he exercised no such restraint on fittings: as the reredos and pulpit are quite as lavishly carved and as beautifully decorated as those in some of the larger churches. St Clement suffered a certain amount of 'improvement' at the hands of the Victorian architect, William Butterfield, famous (or notorious) for his well-meant attempts to 'Gothicise' existing churches, and for the strident colour schemes in his own buildings. Much of the nineteenth-century work at St Clement, carried out about 1870, has been modified more recently, but the reredos was enriched by Sir Ninian Comper as late as 1933, and its bright colour tends to clash with the more sober tones of the older woodwork. This is the church which is often associated with the famous nursery rhyme, 'Oranges and Lemons, say the bells of St Clement's', but this line could refer equally well to the church of St Clement Danes in the Strand. Thanks to the relatively small amount of stained glass in the church and the plain wall surfaces, St Clement's is a light airy church, and although it is 64 feet long and only 40 feet across, with a comparatively low ceiling, it gives the impression of being much larger.

In Lombard Street, opposite the far end of St Clement's Lane, is another Wren church, St Edmund, King and Martyr, built between 1670 and 1679. Unlike the normal Christian church which has its altar at the east end, this church was built on an axis at right angles to the usual one, so that its altar is geographically at the north end. This could well have been due to the awkward site on which Wren had to build after the great fire, but one eighteenth-century writer thought otherwise: 'I believe it was done to save Ground whereon to build Houses fronting the Street which here fetch very great Rents', he observed. Lombard Street was named after the financiers from north Italy who replaced the Jews when they were expelled from London by Edward I in the late 13th century, so St Edmund's is in the very heart of the most finance-conscious part of the City. The 136-foot high steeple of St Edmund is over the main doorway façade at the south end of the church, and a fine bracket clock above the door projects over the pavement. The steeple has a particularly exciting silhouette, although its impact is somewhat modified now that it is no longer the tallest building in Lombard Street. It was completed about 1706. The interior of the church is a simple rectangle about 60 feet long and 40 feet wide, the fittings having been somewhat rearranged by William Butterfield during a restoration in 1864, when the high box pews were sawn up and made into panelling for the walls and the lectern. By comparison with those in some of Wren's other churches, the reredos here is a simple one, and the pulpit has lost its sounding-board which, to judge by the richness of the carving on the pulpit, would have been a very splendid one. As it is, the present pulpit is one of the most lovely things in the whole church, although some of its richness extends to the stalls. There is also a wrought iron sword-rest as fine as almost any one in the City. These five features, with the handsome font and font cover, prompted one visitor to say that, 'St Edmund's . . . resembles the private chapel of a nobleman's house.' Stained glass windows, inserted much later, tend to make the church somewhat gloomy except on the most sunlit of days, but the charming paved courtyard on the east side of the church, known as George Yard, not only reflects the sunlight back on to the stone walls of the church, but lights up the interior as well, to some extent. It is, in any case, a very pleasant place in which to sit, to study the outside of the church, or to watch the sunlight on the life-sized Neptune-like figure which presides over the fountain in the middle of the square and, trident in hand, appears to be exhorting his water-spouting companions to even greater efforts. Tucked away in the north-western corner of the yard is one of the doorways of an old inn, The George and Vulture, parts of which are claimed to be of the seventeenth and eighteenth centuries. It is probably more famous, however, for its association with Charles Dickens, for it was at The George and Vulture that the naïve Mr Pickwick and his friends stayed during the notorious breach of promise case of Bardell v. Pickwick.

From the sunlit George Yard, it is necessary to thread one's way through little courts and alleys to reach Cornhill, where there are two more of Wren's City churches – St Michael, in Cornhill, and St Peter, on the corner of Cornhill and Gracechurch Street. Both were altered during the nineteenth century, and St Michael was drastically 'Gothicised' by Sir George Gilbert Scott, better known for his 'Gothic' St Pancras Hotel and station façade. St Peter, Cornhill, managed to escape the worst excesses of this period of sweeping change.

This passion for converting any classically designed church into a more acceptable 'Gothic' one was an article of faith with some Victorian architects. To such men, it seemed outrageous that any church with Roman Corinthian columns and classical details reminiscent of a pagan temple should be used for Christian worship, and they set to work, full of religious zeal, to convert such churches into a style more like that of the medieval buildings erected to the glory of God and the Christian faith. This wholesale conversion was not approved of by all Victorian writers. Of St Michael, Cornhill, one nineteenth-century author wrote: 'At present it conveys the impression of a nineteenth-century imitation of medievalism; which is further heightened by the pretentious, but feeble, Gothic porch appended at the north-west, facing Cornhill, in 1857. . . .' But it is through that same porch that one still enters the church.

It is almost impossible to study the outside of St Michael's from Cornhill – particularly the fine tower built by Nicholas Hawksmoor between 1715 and 1722, and indeed a better idea of the exterior as a whole can be gained from the little churchyard behind the church to the south, reached by a Victorian Gothic cloister. One has to be a great deal further off to appreciate the 130-foot tower, inspired by that at Magdalen College, Oxford, and glimpsed between office buildings, particularly from the south, near Lower Thames Street. Up the short flight of steps, and through Scott's 'Gothic porch' on Cornhill, one enters the church – one of Wren's larger City

St Peter, Cornhill

churches, as it is 87 feet long, and 60 feet wide. Its vault is now supported by Victorian angels, and Wren's reredos has been replaced by one of the nineteenth century. Scott did, however, retain two seventeenth-century panels of Moses and Aaron, painted by Robert Streater (or Streeter), who was made Sergeant-Painter in 1663, and who was responsible for the magnificently painted ceiling which spans the Sheldonian Theatre, Oxford, one of Wren's very earliest buildings. Much of the Victorian carving is fortunately by W. Gibbs Rogers, who had been so conspicuously successful in matching the work of Grinling Gibbons at St Mary at Hill. The bench-ends at St Michael, Cornhill – enriched with carvings by Gibbs Rogers of the coats of arms of such Livery Companies as the Merchant Taylors, the Drapers, and the Clothworkers – are very much in the manner of Grinling Gibbons and suit the Wren church exactly. The bowl of the font is dated 1672, but its stem is Victorian. The fiercely coloured decoration so favoured by the Victorians has been toned down, and although Scott's Venetian Gothic tracery is still in the windows, much of the garishly coloured glass has gone, and that by Clayton and Bell, inserted in the Wren windows in 1858, is at least inoffensive. One prominent eighteenth-century addition to the church of St Michael is a large carving of a pelican 'in her piety', which was originally installed in the church in 1775 as part of the altar-piece but is now at the west end. The church has a number of monuments from various periods, mostly commemorating local celebrities, although Thomas Gray, the poet, world-famous for his 'Elegy Written in a Country Churchyard', was christened in this church and lies buried in the churchyard a few yards to the south of it.

It was in St Michael's Alley near the church that the very first coffee-house opened in the 1670s, but prior to this, about 1657, a tent was pitched in the churchyard to introduce the new drink to a sceptical public.

St Peter, Cornhill stands about 60 yards to the east of St Michael, on the corner of Cornhill and Gracechurch street. The whole of its east end – an impressive stucco-covered facade pierced by a meticulously symmetrical array of classical windows, with Ionic columns emphasising their pattern – is clearly visible in Gracechurch Street, and there is some faded lettering giving the name of the church. St Peter, Cornhill, has a brick tower, topped by an obelisk-shaped spire perched on a small dome. The gilded weather-vane carries the device of the great key of St Peter, some 140 feet above the south-west side of Cornhill, but probably more easily seen from the churchyard to the south.

As Wren gained more experience in church design, he developed new ways of supporting the galleries which normally occupied three sides of a church – balconies which not only increased the capacity of the church, but also encouraged audience participation. Many of the churches have now lost these galleries, apart from the western one supporting the organ. At St Peter, Cornhill, and at St Clement Danes, Wren designed high pedestals to the columns supporting the roof to carry the weight of the galleries, thus the excessively high pedestals which are still visible today look odd because they no longer support any gallery, nor are they masked by high box pews. St Peter, Cornhill, is unique in one respect at least: it is the only surviving Wren church to have retained its seventeenth-century screen in its original position. One of the most notable examples of seventeenth-century woodwork in the City, the screen is decorated with a carved Royal Arms, flanked by a lively lion and a unicorn, rampant. St Peter, Cornhill, is a large church, 80 feet long and 47 feet wide, with a lofty coved plaster ceiling which, comparatively restrained in decoration, only serves to enhance the richness of the decoration of the chancel screen, the pulpit, and other fittings such as a particularly fine doorcase. It is not difficult, even now, to imagine the church filled with a seventeenth-century congregation, the 'quality' in lace and brocade, the tradesmen and 'mechanicals' in more sober materials, while a bewigged parson with billowing sleeves thundered his sermon from that pulpit under its superbly carved sounding-board; not even the more recent stained glass can spoil this illusion. The organ, built in 1681 by the famous Father Smith, was played by Mendelssohn in September 1840 – an early example of the fine musical traditions still preserved and practised by City churches today.

Going westwards from St Peter, Cornhill, past the Royal Exchange and the Mansion House, and along Poultry into Cheapside to King Street, within sight of the Guildhall, one arrives in Gresham Street* where there is another very imposing Wren church – St Lawrence Jewry*. The church of St

Lawrence Jewry, despite its appearance, is an almost entire reconstruction, for the original Wren church was very heavily damaged during the blitz. It is difficult to believe that with its famous carved organ gallery and vestry reduced to ashes, and little but the east wall standing, it was possible for modern craftsmen to construct so beautifully and so convincingly the church which dominates the south part of the paved square in front of the Guildhall today. The font is seventeenth-century work, having been transferred from a destroyed church in the Minories on the far side of London, just north of the Tower. St Lawrence Jewry is no longer a parish church, but a Guild church, reserved for the Corporation of London. When Cecil Brown, the architect, rebuilt it, installing in it an altar-piece of his own design, he realised that the church would also be used for concerts and musical recitals, and in addition to being a church, it now functions as a most delightfully spacious and airy concert hall. The tower at the western end is also part reconstruction and part restoration.

To the north-west of St Lawrence Jewry, behind the new Guildhall Library in Aldermanbury Square, is the site of another Wren church, St Mary Aldermanbury, with its shrubbed and flowered little churchyard. This church underwent many changes before being heavily damaged in 1940, but enough of it survived to be transported across the Atlantic, where it is now an active and living church again, at Westminser College in Fulton, Missouri. Little stumps of stone mark the sites of its original columns, and a well carved plaque at the western end of the former nave tells the story of its present home in the USA, together with an engraving showing its present appearance. In the little garden to the south, formerly part of the churchyard, there is a high plinth upon which stands a bust of Shakespeare. The garden commemorates two seventeenth-century friends and actor-colleagues of the great poet, who both lie buried in this churchyard. These men, Henry Condell and John Heminge, not only preserved the original manuscripts of Shakespeare's plays after his death, but edited them and produced the first collected edition – the First Folio of 1623. The inscription on the plinth has a record of the title page which reads: 'Mr William Shakespeare's Comedies, Histories, and Tragedies. Published according to the True Originall [*sic*] Copies.'

If one walks southwards back to the paved square of the Guildhall, now with a modern administrative block, one has to walk a little to the east to see the tower of another Wren church – that of St Olave Jewry – and although it can be reached through a churchyard this tower is no longer part of any church, but is the entrance to modern offices.

Back into Cheapside, the next visible Wren church is the famous St Mary-le-Bow, but this will be described in greater detail in relation to St Paul's Cathedral. The next seventeenth-century building to be seen in this area is not a church, but was the predecessor of the Mansion House, the official residence of the Lord Mayor of London. It is now a restaurant known as Williamson's Tavern, and claims to be the oldest licensed premises in the City. Built after the great fire in Bow Lane, it was the residence of the Lord Mayor until 1753 when it was acquired by Robert

Williamson who founded the hotel. It has a notable pair of wrought iron gates at the end of a tiny alley on the west side of Bow Lane which are said to have been a gift of William and Mary.

Bow Lane leads into Watling Street and then into Queen Victoria Street (almost opposite Mansion House underground station) and on the corner of Bow Lane there is a most unusual Wren church. This is St Mary Alder*mary*, not to be confused with St Mary Alder*manbury*, the Wren church in the USA. St Mary Aldermary is so called because, as John Stow explains, it was 'elder than any church of St Marie in the City' – the oldest City church dedicated to the Virgin Mary. St Mary Aldermanbury was connected with the 'bury' or 'borough' of the 'alderman' – hence St Mary Alderman – bury. The tower of St Mary Aldermary is 135 feet high and strangely medieval in appearance, not at all unlike towers such as that on Gloucester Cathedral, for example. The lowest storey of the tower has in fact survived from the church built in 1511. The next storey was added early in the seventeenth century, and the upper part added by Wren in 1702–4, during the rebuilding of the church after the great fire. It is the interior, however, which is so strikingly unlike the normal Wren church, for there he produced a magnificent array of fan-vaulting, with a succession of saucer-shaped domes

St Mary Aldermary

supported by the vaulting in the centre of both the nave and the aisles. None of this remarkable roof is actually an integral part of the construction, as it would be in a medieval church, but it is certainly a most effective decoration in plaster, and unlike any style we associate with Wren. A substantial legacy (about £5000) was left by a parishioner, Henry Rogers, for the rebuilding of the church, and it has been claimed that Wren was obliged to build in the Gothic style under the terms of the will, but more recent research can discover no documentary evidence to support this.

The church is 100 feet long and 63 feet wide, and with this elongated proportion, together with stained glass windows added during the last century, it would have a somewhat medieval appearance if such details as the plasterwork bearing the coats of arms which are ranged along both sides of the nave had not been the work of much later craftsmen. The finely carved doorcase at the west end, however, came originally from the Wren church of St Antholin, demolished in the nineteenth century. Both the wooden sword-rest and the pulpit have been attributed to Grinling Gibbons. (Wooden sword-rests are quite rare, but there are others in the City – in the south aisle of St Helen's Bishopsgate, for example.) The whole of St Mary Aldermary is a refreshing and enjoyable departure from many seventeenth-century church interiors as the style is so uncharacteristic of Wren – another example of his astonishing versatility.

From St Mary Aldermary one can descend to Lower Thames Street either by a continuation of Bow Lane, or by Queen Street, one of the first major streets to be built after the great fire, but now containing little of historic importance other than two very fine eighteenth-century houses. These now have a preservation order on them so that they cannot be altered nor destroyed by property dealers. Upper Thames Street is so named because it is westwards above London Bridge; Lower Thames Street is that part which is down river from the bridge and hence lower than Upper Thames Street. In Upper Thames Street, shored up with gigantic baulks of timber which seem to be preventing it from slithering down into the road, there is another Wren church – St James, Garlickhythe. Its name is derived, according to John Stow, 'for that in old time, on the bank of the river of [*sic*] Thames near this church, garlick is usually sold. . . .'

To enter St James, Garlickhythe, iit is best to take a little alleyway which runs along the east and then the north of the church to a little railed-in doorway on the far west end. This church offers the most delightfully quiet haven from the feverish rush of the traffic and city life outside. Although it has a fine Baroque steeple, some 125 feet high, the church gives no hint from the outside of the beauty to be enjoyed within. This is Wren's loftiest parish church with a high nave vault lit by a succession of clerestory windows of clear glass which flood the interior on sunlit days despite the nearness of warehouses on one side. It is richly endowed with fine woodwork, not only of its own, but augmented by some from St Michael, Queenhythe, a Wren church demolished in 1876. The superb pulpit and some of the woodwork at the back of the stalls came from this church, and the whole church is most beautifully maintained. It has all the signs of a prosperous seventeenth-

left, St James
Garlickhythe in Upper
Thames Street
right, The pulpit in St
James Garlickhythe

century congregation, with sets of elaborate sword-rests bearing arms of different City Companies, two sets of carved and painted lion and unicorn devices, and iron hatpegs to the rear of the churchwardens' pews just under the impressive organ gallery. The parson would have reached his high pulpit by the lovely stairway and, standing under the ornate sounding-board, would probably have removed his wig and hung it on the wigstand – a peg in the back of the pulpit, which is still there – before warming to his work.

The original seventeenth-century reredos has gone, and been replaced by a much humbler one behind the original altar table, but this sets off to advantage a large oil painting of the Ascension by the Scots artist, Andrew Geddes, better known perhaps for his extremely fine etchings. This was installed in the church in 1815. Despite the richness of the interior, the carved lions and unicorns, the Royal Arms, and all the trappings of civic pride, this is still an intimate and restful church, beautifully restored after the damage it suffered during the blitz, and no one should be discouraged from visiting it by the huge wooden buttressing and the squalor of its immediate surroundings.

Still in Upper Thames Street, but west of Queen Street, stands St Michael Paternoster Royal, designed by Wren, but probably carried out by one of his master masons, Edward Strong, from 1686–1694. This church used to be tucked away out of sight in College Street, but for once the *Luftwaffe* performed a useful service by destroying the buildings in front, and the church now lies back behind a charming little paved open space with lawns and trees, and is easily seen and enjoyed. It is now the headquarters of the Missions to Seamen. The name Paternoster is derived from 'Our Father' and Royal is a corruption of La Riole (or Reole) – the district near Bordeaux from which came the wine merchants who lived in the Paternoster Lane area during the Middle Ages. College Street is called after Whittington College, founded by the famous Dick Whittington, and two ornate seventeenth-century doorways, which were later additions to the original college, still survive in College Hill, west of St Michael Paternoster Royal. The church was restored quite beautifully after the bombing, and its steeple, with its high, square tower, dominates this stretch of Upper Thames Street. It was fortunate to retain its seventeenth-century reredos and pulpit, both attributed to Grinling Gibbons, the font cover, and a beautifully fashioned chandelier of brass. There is at least one monument of some interest – that of a former Mayor, Sir Samuel Pennant, who died of gaol fever in 1750 during his term of office. This disease was of course an occupational hazard for anyone brought into contact with the unfortunate occupants of the eighteenth-century gaols, and although our judges today are no longer exposed to this kind of infection when they administer justice, they are nevertheless presented with a posy of fresh flowers at the opening of each

St Michael Paternoster Royal

session – a reminder of the dangers that their predecessors faced in the past.

And so to the last group of Wren churches which form a great ellipse at the centre of which is his masterpiece, St Paul's Cathedral. Nine or ten churches, some of them but ruined shells of their former splendour, form a kind of coronet at the centre of which is the most precious gem of all – the cathedral. Beginning outside St Paul's underground station, to the east down Cheapside is one of Wren's most famous churches – St Mary-le-Bow. When the buildings which surrounded St Paul's were scaled to pay homage to the cathedral, so that it could play its correct role on the skyline of London, the church steeples nearest to the great dome were designed by Wren not to compete with it, but to enhance it by their spired beauty. Today, hemmed in by monstrous office blocks, they have little relationship with the dome, and it is difficult for a visitor to manoeuvre himself into a position where a spire can be seen in its correct relationship, silhouetted against the dome. The steeple of St Mary-le-Bow is undoubtedly one of Wren's greatest creations, and he lavished £7388 on it – a very large proportion of the cost of the entire church. It is about 220 feet high, the second tallest of Wren's steeples, the highest being that of St Bride, Fleet Street, which stands on lower ground. Starting with a sturdy square tower, the steeple rises in nicely calculated stages so that the eye is drawn inevitably to the sharply pointed spire, which is topped with a great copper weather-vane – a dragon, one of the symbols of the City of London. Despite the blitz, when the nave was destroyed and the bells came crashing down through the tower, it survived. The church that is seen there today, apart from the tower and steeple, is almost entirely a skilful rebuilding by a modern architect, Laurence King. In the tower facing Cheapside there is a balconied window – Wren's architectural reminder of a viewing gallery which stood outside the medieval church and provided a grandstand from which the king and his nobles could watch processions and tournaments which were a feature of this medieval street. The doorway on the west side of the tower is one of the few examples of a detail which can be said to have resulted from Wren's brief visit to France during the plague. The elements displayed there, rearranged and adapted, resemble those of a similar door in the Hotel de Conti in Paris, built by Wren's contemporary, François Mansart and almost certainly studied, perhaps even sketched, by Wren. But Wren was no mere plagiarist – anything he observed was subjected to a process of digestion; it nourished his creative imagination and later emerged as something wholly original. Many details of his work are reminiscent of buildings in other parts of Europe, but since he can only have acquired his information from two-dimensional engravings, they can only have served to stimulate his imagination; he could not have copied something three-dimensional from them, even if he had wanted to do so. His range and versatility were never more obvious than in the study of his steeples and towers, for no design was ever repeated. It is fortunate for us that the freakish behaviour of blast from high-explosive bombs which shattered the bodies of his churches often left the towers and steeples almost intact. Wren built St Mary-le-Bow over a

left, St Mary-le-Bow
right, St Vedast

Norman crypt, strengthened to take the weight of his new building, and it is the arches of this crypt (or bows, for the church was once known as St Marie de Arcubus) which gave the church its present name. Even today, the ecclesiastical court known as The Court of Arches owes its name to this crypt where it used to sit, although it is now held more comfortably in Westminster. On a more light-hearted note, tradition declares that although one can be a citizen of London by being born in the city, only those born within the sound of Bow Bells are entitled to call themselves true cockneys.

West of St Mary-le-Bow, on the opposite side of Cheapside at the end of Foster Lane, one can see the spire of the church of St Vedast, another of Wren's churches which had to be entirely rebuilt after the war, although the steeple survived. This church lost all of its original woodwork, including a magnificent reredos by Grinling Gibbons, but it fortunately was able to secure another fine one from the church of St Christopher-le-Stocks, demolished to provide more space for the Bank of England in 1781. This reredos was found preserved in Great Burstead in Essex, and is now once again the focal point of a City church. The font and its cover came from the church of St Anne and St Agnes, a small church about 53 feet square which has now been taken over by the Lutheran Church in Aldersgate; and the pulpit came from All Hallows, Bread Street, demolished in 1876. The eighteenth-century organ-case seems to have come from a Wren church called St Bartholomew-by-the-Exchange via another church in Cripplegate which disappeared in 1904. Thus the treasures of these other churches have been transplanted to serve a living church and can now be appreciated by visitors and congregations at St Vedast, Foster Lane.

No such revival was possible, however, at Christ Church, Newgate Street, scarcely 100 yards to the west of St Vedast, for although its notable 153-foot steeple of Portland stone survived the blitz and needed repairs and strengthening, the nave was gutted, and the church has now been abandoned. The spire was one of those designed by Wren to act as a foil to the dome of St Paul's, but modern developments in the area make it almost impossible to see the spire and the dome in any sort of spatial relationship. Yet, if it is only regarded as an isolated piece of architectural form – a kind of gigantic architectural sculpture without any useful function – the spire of Christ Church, Newgate Street is so fine an object that London would be a poorer place visually if it had not been preserved.

From Newgate Street it is a short walk south to the east end of St Paul's, along New Change – a road built after the Second World War, clearing away unsuitably narrow streets to allow the traffic to pass swiftly round the end of the cathedral and providing a pleasant little enclosed square. There one can see a fibreglass replica of a Wren steeple on the original tower of St Augustine, Watling Street; this steeple was also originally designed with a spiky contour to emphasise the rotundity of the dome against which it would be seen. A new choir school has now been built against the tower, and although its design is controversial, it is apparently very successful musically.

Across the open paved space south of St Paul's there is another very individual Wren spire, that of St Nicholas, Cole Abbey. It has a square tower and a newly reconstructed replica of the original spire which, with its encircling balcony, narrows to a sharp point upon which there is a splendid weather-vane in the shape of a sailing ship, previously on the steeple of another demolished church, St Michael, Queenhythe. The church of St Nicholas, Cole Abbey, is entered from Queen Victoria Street, but it is not an easy church for the casual visitor to get into, as the gates are often padlocked. It has a fine display of seventeenth-century furnishings, including a carved pulpit, a communion rail with twisted balusters, and a sword-rest, and the clear glass on the south side facing the river ensures that it is a light and spacious-looking Wren church. It was rebuilt most ably by a modern architect, Arthur Bailey.

Still further west on the same side of Queen Victoria Street is another most delightful seventeenth-century building, this time in brick: the College of Arms, sometimes referred to, incorrectly, as the College of Heraldry. This modest red-brick building with Ionic pilasters has rather a Dutch look, although it was in fact completed in 1688, the year that Queen Mary and her Dutch husband, William of Orange, ascended the throne of England. This building was probably designed not by an architect, but by Maurice Emmett jun., master bricklayer to the Office of Works, with some advice from Francis Sandford, the Lancaster Herald. The cost of the building after the great fire was borne by public subscription, but the Earl Marshall was so tactless with would-be subscribers that much of the cost was borne by Sir William Dugdale, with a substantial subscription to help

from Sir Henry St George, King of Arms. It is certainly a suitably dignified building for such an august body as the College of Arms, although its appearance was modified somewhat when Queen Victoria Street was built. Its general appearance anticipates the style of domestic architecture that appeared during the next reign – that of Queen Anne. The building now stands behind an elegant wrought iron screen (from Goodrich Court, Herefordshire – a gift from an American donor), and is not open to the public except to those on official business.

Almost opposite the College of Arms, south of Queen Victoria Street but standing on a lower piece of ground, is one of Wren's most endearing churches, St Benet, St Paul's Wharf. Built of brick, with dapper little swags, window and door surrounds, and quoins of light Portland stone, this building also has a very Dutch appearance, although it was completed in 1685. The low site does not give a very prominent appearance to the 115-foot high steeple, but it is a most attractive church and quite unlike any other built by this most versatile of architects. The church is about 50 feet square, with one aisle, and has been reserved for the Welsh community of the City since 1879; its not an easy church to visit, for it appears to be open only on Sundays. Anyone attending a service, which is conducted in Welsh, would not only see a charming interior, but be able to enjoy the rich choral harmonies which are so much a feature of any Welsh church or chapel. Its interior is but little changed since it was completed in 1685, and it has retained its original galleries and pulpit, although the organ is Victorian. The Royal Coat of Arms of the Stuarts is to be seen on the doorcase at the west end, and altogether it is such a charming church that one can only regret that it is usually closed.

above, St Nicholas, Cole Abbey
left, St Benet, St Paul's Wharf

Further to the west, near to Blackfriars Bridge, there is yet another of Wren's brick churches – St Andrew's-by-the-Wardrobe, which benefited considerably by the building of Queen Victoria Street, for not only was the church much lighter when the surrounding buildings were pulled down, but it was invested with a new dignity as it stood poised over the new road. It is significant that this church, completed in the 1690s, was built of brick, and that the tower has only brick facings. The cost of the entire church was about £7000 – roughly the cost of the tower alone of the stone-built St Mary Le Bow; it is 75 feet long and 59 feet wide, with an 86-foot high square brick tower, without steeple or spire. The church was so badly damaged during the Second World War that it has been rebuilt by Marshall Sisson, and although its tower is original, the remainder of the church is modern. It lost all of its seventeenth-century fittings with the exception of a sword-rest and a couple of beadles' staves, and although it is elegant and airy with its new woodwork and beautifully restored roof, it does lack something of the atmosphere of some of the more fortunate City churches. The very delightful pair of eighteenth-century houses by the north porch in St Andrew's Hill are well worth seeing, particularly the one nearest to the church which is the vicarage. The Apothecaries Company holds its annual service in St Andrew's-by-the-Wardrobe. Its hall is nearby in Blackfriars Lane – much of it seventeenth-century work, built after the great fire and altered somewhat in the next century. It is not open to the public, but one and take a tantalising peep through the doorway on the right-hand side of Blackfriars Lane.

St Bride, Fleet Street, which is situated in a little court about 100 yards from Ludgate Circus, is one of Wren's major City churches, and the steeple is not only the highest of all his churches, being 226 feet high, but one of his most distinguished, despite repairs which had to be made to it when it was struck by lightning in 1764, shortening it by about eight feet. The stages of the spire with their arched spaces are so beautifully graduated that they have an almost mathematical harmony, like a Bach fugue – indeed, this is an example of a kind of architectural music.

The church was gutted during the blitz and there is now a modern interior – a compromise between a reconstruction of the church as it was originally designed by a seventeenth-century architect, and the creation of a modern architect who has done his best to provide something worthy of both periods. Thus Samuel Pepys, who was christened in the medieval church on this site before the great fire, and who watched the building of Wren's church, would recognise such features as the barrel-vaulting of the nave ceiling and the aisles, but be puzzled by the disappearance of the galleries which used to be on either side of the church, and by the rearrangement of the seating accommodation. Nevertheless, the twentieth-century architect, Godfrey Allen, has respected the earlier period, and has designed an altar-piece as near as he could to that of a genuine Wren interior; the result is a dignified and charming church. In the crypt, St Bride has one of the most interesting displays to be found in any of the City churches: it is a combination of the actual remains of Roman, Saxon and

Apothecaries Hall

medieval buildings on this site, with small objects retrieved during excavations and a well-documented history of the series of churches which have stood there and of the people who worshipped in them. There is a great deal of material relating to various events in the history of this part of London – it is almost a history of London in miniature, and includes documents and reproductions of documents illustrating vividly such dramas as the plague, the great fire, and the blitz of the Second World War. It is a fascinating exhibition, and every visitor to London would benefit from its study.

Outside the church, it is clear that at one time the churchyard would have been an excellent vantage point from which to look down on the quays on either side of the River Fleet, and that the tall steeple would have been a marvellous landmark as travellers entered through Wren's new Temple Bar, along Fleet Street, across Fleet Bridge itself, and so on up Ludgate Hill to Watling Street and the heart of the City. The River Fleet has now been conduited and flows unseen beneath Farringdon Street to the Thames, but this did not happen before it had deteriorated so badly that it was called the Fleet Ditch and had become a byword for filth and a stinking reproach to the City.

From Fleet Street, despite the atrocious iron railway bridge which slashes right across the view of the west front of St Paul's, the steeple of St Martin, Ludgate, is one of the few which can still be seen in relationship to the great dome of St Paul's. The church is built entirely of stone and was completed about 1687, just at the time when funds from the coal tax were being diverted from the City churches, which were nearing completion, to St Paul's Cathedral. (The reallocation was such that whereas in 1686–7 the cathedral received only £12,346, its share in 1687–88 was nearly £34,000.) In designing the spires of those churches nearest to the cathedral, Wren could only imagine what they would be like in relation to his dome, for it was some time after the beginning of the construction of the cathedral before he was able to decide the final shape which the dome would take. Although many of the church towers were in being by the beginning of the eighteenth century, the dome was not completed until some time in 1708. Even so, the spire of St Martin, Ludgate, 158 feet above the street, while it is unusual when seen in isolation, it is the most perfect foil for the curve of the great dome.

St Martin, Ludgate, is protected from the hideous traffic noise from Ludgate Hill by a vestibule, and the body of the church is reached up a short flight of stairs to the left. Even on the brightest summer day it is cool and very dark inside until one's eyes have adjusted from the light outside to the gloom within. This was not, of course, intended by Wren, but the church has suffered a rush of stained glass windows to the nave. It is a strange shape, too, for while it is 66 feet wide and nearly 60 feet high, it is only 57 feet from the west to the east end, and even that distance is curtailed visually by the western gallery carrying the organ. The woodwork throughout is richly carved, particularly the doorcases beneath the west gallery which supports an organ designed by Renatus Harris in the seventeenth century. Even the wooden screen on the south side of the church, inserted as a barrier against the noise from the street, has its share of chubby little cupids and swags of decorative fruit and flowers sweetly and crisply carved. Immediately in front of this screen there is usually a very broad cane-bottomed and cane-backed chair with a carved frame, made in 1690, and sufficiently wide to accommodate two churchwardens seated side by side. For a Wren church the reredos is comparatively simple, but most beautifully proportioned, and although the pulpit is by no means as flamboyant as in some City churches, it is still a predominantly fine piece of work in a church which must have as fine a display of seventeenth-century craftsmanship as any in the City: the communion table and the communion rails, the wrought iron sword-rest and the great brass chandelier are only details of an overall excellence of the most unpretentious kind. The font, typically seventeenth century, was

St Martin, Ludgate, on the left with St Paul's Cathedral in the background

presented to the church by a parishioner in 1673 and carries an inscription in Greek which reads the same backwards as forwards, a Palindrome. The translation is: 'Cleanse my transgression, not my outward part only.' St Martin, Ludgate, is now a Guild Church, with a particular interest in marriage guidance work; it also holds exhibitions, study groups and discussions for City workers during the lunch hour. It is a pity that what an eighteenth-century writer, Sir Horace Walpole, described as 'the gloomth [sic] of the abbeys' should make it somewhat difficult to see all that the church has to offer. Apart from a painting of its patron saint performing his traditional act of kindness by dividing his cloak for a beggar, American visitors in particular would be interested in the painting entitled 'The Ascension' by Benjamin West from the Wren church of St Mary Magdalene, a church seriously damaged by fire towards the end of the

The model of Wren's alternative plan for St Paul's, which was rejected

nineteenth century and subsequently demolished.

St Martin, Ludgate Hill, brings one almost to the steps of the west front of St Paul's Cathedral, and although there are yet three more Wren churches to be studied, it is appropriate at this point to examine the great cathedral which, crowned by that superb dome, is one of the greatest buildings in Christendom.

It was hoped, at first, for reasons of economy, that the old cathedral might be repaired, for much of the seventeenth-century work added to it by Inigo Jones had apparently survived; but this eventually proved impracticable, and Wren was invited to prepare plans for a new cathedral. In the meantime the long and tedious task of clearing the site of debris was carried on, the main task of demolition of the old shell being carried out by thirty labourers wielding a battering ram after gunpowder had proved dangerously unpredictable. Wren suffered many frustrations in trying to produce a design which would satisfy the caprices of a committee, and models kept in the library in the triforium of St Paul's Cathedral show at least two versions. The model of the first design is fragmentary, but that of the second is 18 feet long – a magnificent model which was worked out in great detail and cost £500. This design was rejected, however, and it was not until May 1675 that a Royal Warrant was issued for a design which, judging by the drawings of it to be seen in the library of All Souls College, Oxford, was so grotesque, with a dome surmounted by a spire somewhat like that of St Bride's, Fleet Street, that it would have been a disaster had it been carried out. Wren was able to present his plans in such a way that he was able to reserve the right to make certain adjustments, and he proceeded to build the cathedral as he wished, secure in the layman's notorious inability to read plans sufficiently well to envisage the effect of the final building. The foundation stone was laid at the south-east corner of the site on 21 June 1675, but it was not until thirty-six years later that an old and embittered architect was to see the completion of his masterpiece.

The new cathedral was to lie at a slightly different angle from that of its predecessor, and was to be slightly smaller. (The medieval building was 644 feet long and 315 feet wide, whereas the present cathedral is 510 feet long and 280 feet wide.) While the site was being cleared one incident occurred which, in a sense, symbolised the rebuilding of the cathedral – and indeed, the City of London as well. Wren required a piece of stone to mark a certain point on the plan of the building and sent a labourer to find a suitable fragment for this purpose. The man dragged out a part of a damaged tombstone which still retained intact part of the inscription, which read 'Resurgam', i.e., 'I shall arise again.' The theme of the cathedral rising phoenix-like from its own ashes was to become that of the sculpture still to be seen in the lunette over the south porch, facing the river.

The task Wren had undertaken was an immense one, for, quite apart from the workload which he was to carry for the next thirty years or so – with fifty-one churches, the cathedral, work at the Palaces of Whitehall and Winchester (both since destroyed), major additions to Hampton Court Palace and Kensington Palace, the building of the Royal Military Hospital at Chelsea, the Royal Naval Hospital at Greenwich, and work at Oxford and Cambridge – there were other non-architectural problems. There were, inevitably, financial difficulties after so great a catastrophe. The Fleet was laid up for the sake of economy, but in vain: taking advantage of England's temporary weakness, and led by mutinous English sailors who, despite the efforts of Samuel Pepys, were hopelessly in arrears with pay, the Dutch launched an attack in June 1667. They sailed up the Thames, and not only severely damaged a number of ships lying off Sheerness and the mouth of the River Medway, but actually captured and carried off 'the pride and glory of the British fleet', the *Royal Charles*. This devastating blow not only increased the financial problems, but left the Channel free for a French privateer to capture a ship carrying a load of Portland stone destined for St Paul's Cathedral, so that it had to be re-purchased from the Rotterdam merchant to whom it had been sold. A severe landslide in 1696 hampered the quarrying of Portland stone, which was apparently the only stone capable of resisting the corrosive effect of the London atmosphere, so that although others quarried in Rutland and Oxfordshire, for example, could be used inside the cathedral, only Portland stone would be suitable for the exterior. The stone was normally brought in freighters up the Thames as far as the Pool of London, but it then had to be offloaded into barges which were small enough to pass under the arches of London Bridge, and landed at St Paul's Wharf to be hauled up the steep slope to the cathedral site, some 200 yards away.

The harsh winter of 1684 had brought other difficulties. The broad shallow river froze solid, and although many Londoners turned this to good account by erecting booths and shops on the ice, arranging ox-roasting and races on the frozen surface, the intense cold hampered work on the cathedral. Time was wasted also in protecting those parts of the cathedral which were already under construction, for half-completed walls had to be thatched or somehow protected against frost and snow. But the king joined in the festivities taking place on the frozen Thames and patronised a printer named Croom who produced custom-made tickets of commemoration from his press on the ice. Preserved in the City of London Museum, the ticket produced for the king and the royal party reads as follows (the spelling is original): 'Charles, King. James Duke. Katharine, Queen. Mary Dutchess. Ann, Princesse. George, Prince. Hans in Kelder.' The last-named refers to Princess Anne's pregnancy – her usual condition. It is worth pointing out that on that one card there is a record of the reigning monarch and his queen; James II, his successor; Queen Mary, who was to succeed him; and finally, Queen Anne, who was to succeed her sister in 1702.

Despite the many unforeseen difficulties, and the malevolence of the Parliament who harassed Wren by withholding much of his salary under the mistaken impression that this would bring the cathedral to a more speedy conclusion, work continued until by December 1697, the choir could be used for the Thanksgiving Service for the Peace of Ryswick which ended the war between France and the Grand Alliance of Great Britain, Sweden and the Netherlands. The first Sunday service was held in the same week. It is clear that work was in progress on every part of the site for Wren was afraid that, had the east end only been complete and functional, the committee might have been tempted to halt the rest of the project on some excuse or another. By 1706 work was almost completed on the two magnificent western towers which frame the dome so satisfactorily from the Ludgate Hill viewpoint. The design of the dome itself, however, was probably not settled until that year; it was to be a proof of the remarkable inventiveness of Wren who, without architectural training, turned his great intellect on to architectural problems and solved them by methods which were unique, and which would probably not have occurred to a man trained in the traditional methods and ways of thought. One is now so used to the appearance of the west front, with its double tier of coupled columns, that it is difficult to imagine it designed in any other way. Yet according to drawings in the library at St Paul's, Wren intended originally to have gigantic monolithic columns rising, uninterrupted, from the steps to the pediment; this plan was apparently abandoned because the quarries at Portland could not produce stones large enough to span the huge gaps between the columns, and the present design was adopted instead. Despite a certain amount of criticism – one writer recently called it 'slightly pedestrian' – it is still one of the most satisfactory façades on any cathedral in the world, and the interplay of light and shade caused by the repetition of double columns and the subtle designed gaps between makes a marvellous contrast to the solid masses of the towers which flank the main motif. This is repeated in miniature by the columns in the drum which supports the main mass of the dome. The source of the design for the twin towers has been traced back to St Agnese in the Piazza Navona in Rome, although it should be stressed that Wren had seen only a flat two-dimensional engraving of the building, not the original in Rome.

Before entering any major building – and this is particularly true when studying any of the great English cathedrals of the Middle Ages – it is an illuminating exercise to walk right round the building first, viewing it from every angle, and deducing from such constructional details as flying buttresses what sort of a spectacle the vaults – which make such buttresses necessary – must present from within. But anyone studying St Paul's Cathedral from the outside is going to have a succession of surprises when the real nature of Wren's constructional methods becomes known, for he used devices of which almost nothing can be seen from outside, and very little from within. A walk round the outside is nevertheless most rewarding, although the beauty of the proportions of the wall surfaces cannot easily be appreciated as the lower part is, in the main, masked by a cast iron fence which was erected despite Wren's protest, and which hides the relationship of window to wall on the lower stages. One can still see the rich interplay of light and shade on the dome and its supporting drum, with the buttresses – which are an essential support for the weight – concealed as niches, and the carved enrichments over doors and windows, and in such prominent places as the lunette over the south transept porch. These enrichments were carried out by master craftsmen, and as some of them are so high above pavement level that they can scarcely be seen by the naked eye, it is a great asset to take a pair of binoculars with which to study such details during this walk. A monumental group, 'The Conversion of St Paul', in the pediment over the main west entrance, is too difficult to see without binoculars; this work by Francis Bird, an English sculptor, who trained partly in Brussels and Rome but was attached for some time to the workshop of Grinling Gibbons, has been described as 'one of the most successful examples of Baroque sculpture in England'. Grinling Gibbons, more famous for his wood-carving, contributed all the charming little panels which decorate the bottom of each of the round-headed windows, and which are therefore quite easily seen from ground level.

Wren chose his craftsmen with care and was always appreciative of exceptionally good work. The Dean's doorway at the base of the south side of the western tower has an external pediment carved not by Grinling Gibbons, but by William Kempster, a stonemason who was also responsible for the beautiful spiral staircase within. The public cannot normally see the staircase, but the doorway outside is easily studied, and was so much admired by Wren that he rewarded the mason with an extra £20 – a considerable addition to his ordinary wage – for his 'Extraordinary Diligence and Care used in the said carving and his good performance of the same'. Somewhat to the east are to be found the foundation stones of the chapter house of the old medieval cathedral, under a large mulberry tree, and in the centre, on a slab, there is a prostrate bronze figure by Bainbridge Copnall, a modern sculptor, of St Thomas Becket, the great Canterbury

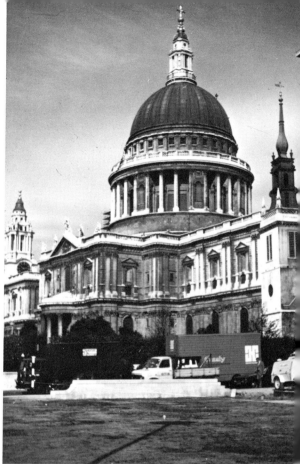

martyr. A little further to the east one comes to the semicircular south porch, and above this, the lunette carved by a Danish sculptor, Caius Gabriel Cibber, whose work can also be seen on the base of the Monument commemorating the great fire. To appreciate the whole of the south porch, it is better to cross the street and to take up a position on the south side of the paved square, from where one can see to some advantage Cibber's carving of the phoenix, the mythical bird which, like London, was reborn from its own ashes, and the superb build-up of this part of the cathedral to the triumphant climax of the dome.

One of the few places remaining from which one can see the relationship of a Wren spire to the dome of St Paul's is a little further east – a traffic island at the junction of Cannon Street and Friday Street, the short street linking Queen Victoria Street and Cannon Street. There the spiky spire of the church of St Augustine, Watling Street (even if it is a fibreglass replica put on the tower after the last war), demonstrates the way in which Wren designed such a spire to enhance the rotundity of his great dome, and the modern gardens to the east of the cathedral give light and air to the whole area which, before the war, was badly congested and cramped. From this little garden it is possible to sit quietly and survey the whole of the east end of the cathedral, and watch the perfect transition from the drum to dome to the golden cross which surmounts the cathedral, and to notice how the three tiers of nave and aisle windows are linked by tall slender pilasters, so perfectly in proportion that the vastness of the whole project is imperfectly realised until one starts to compare the height of the walls alone with the red London buses passing by, or the cluster of tour coaches parked on the south side. It is only then that the full scale of the cathedral can be appreciated.

In the shadow of the east end, but slightly to the north, stands St Paul's Cross – a column designed in 1910 by Sir Reginald Blomfield to mark the site of the medieval preaching cross; the latter became a most important place from which announcements were made and denunciatory sermons preached before crowds of curious Londoners. (Thomas Carlyle, the Victorian historian who lived a great deal of his life in London, referred to St Paul's Cross as '*The Times* newspaper of the Middle Ages'.) Seventeenth-century pictures show that by the reign of James I it was a substantially built pulpit, with a little dome above and permanent stands of wood for the accommodation of the more distinguished spectators. It was destroyed by orders of the Cromwellian Long Parliament in 1643. Stones now mark the shape of the octagonal structure upon which the pulpit stood.

The whole of the area round St Paul's was devastated during the blitz, but the cathedral itself was almost miraculously preserved from severe damage, although it did receive two high-explosive bombs and several incendiaries, which fortunately caused no major injury. But those who remember the quaint business premises, the little drapers' shops and the host of small bookstalls with which the north side was lined, will regret the brash buildings which have replaced them, even if the area to the north is now more open than it was before and affords a series of fine views of the west front with its twin towers.

The usual entry to the cathedral is by the doors in the south-western corner, under the tower wearing the clock. At first the cathedral seems dark, after the daylight outside, but very soon the aisle gives way to the nave – great airy spaces with open semicircular arches with deeply coffered surfaces, supported on mighty classical piers. Transverse arches spring from the upper end of the panelling which marks the beginning of the triforium, reaching a height of nearly 90 feet, and the nave, about 41 feet wide, is lit by a series of semicircular windows piercing the triforium, a fact not visible from outside, for the high screen wall gives the impression that nave and aisles are of the same height. A series of shallow plaster domes is held between the transverse arches, defining the bays into which the nave is divided and enhancing the light and spacious quality of the nave. The aisles are lit by huge windows with semicircular heads, except at the west end where a chapel on either side produces the impression of darkness on entry, but makes the light of the nave seem even more impressive. In Wren's day the nave would have seemed more impressive still, since there were no monotonous rows of chairs, and the way to the altar was blocked, against Wren's wishes, by a mighty carved choir screen upon which was placed the central organ. (It was not until the nineteenth century that the organ was divided in two, and the present arrangement made.)

One very tall monument on the north side of the nave blocks the whole of

one arch into the aisle. This is the monument to the Duke of Wellington, the famous statesman and soldier who lies buried in the crypt beneath. About 80 feet high, it is surmounted by an equestrian statue of the 'Iron Duke', and although there is no doubt plenty of room between his hatless head and the top of the arch, from ground level it does appear, as he said of the Battle of Waterloo: 'It has been a damned nice thing – the nearest run thing you ever saw in your life.' The monument was designed by one of the best and one of the least appreciated of English artists, Alfred Stevens, and although he entered his competition design in 1856, the equestrian figure was still only a three-dimensional sketch in 1875 when he died, and it was not until 1912 that the whole monument was completed and installed in its present position, another sculptor named John Tweed finally constructing the figure from the sketch. (One of the reasons for the delay in completing the monument was the prejudice against having the statue of a horse in a cathedral!) Some of the finest modelling by Alfred Stevens can be seen at the base of the monument in the symbolic groups of Valour defeating Cowardice and of Truth triumphing over Falsehood, and some of the mosaic work which can be seen just under the central dome was also the work of this versatile English artist.

The central dome is the climax of the interior of the cathedral, and it is not surprising that there is always a number of people seated in this area, marvelling at the splendour of the great curved shape above, and the circular oculus which, like a great round eye, lets the sunlight through. The great open space at the crossing under the dome is an excellent standpoint from which to survey the whole nave westwards, and also to examine the splendour of the chancel and altar to the east. To create a level on which to support his dome, Wren had to insert an extra arch to supplement those of the nave and the aisles – an expedient which perhaps only he would have devised. It might have been clumsy, but it is in fact very effective, and not only reinforces the support but also emphasises the weight and power of the whole of this impressive structure. About 100 feet from the cathedral floor, the Whispering Gallery, with its iron railing, prepares the eye for the dome which rises above and the *trompe l'œil* paintings by Sir James Thornhill on themes from the life of St Paul. These were inserted against the wishes of Sir Christopher Wren but are probably more impressive than the mosaics he had intended to be there. Both the mosaics and the paintings will be discussed at a later stage in the chapter.

Until about 1860 the whole chancel was enclosed in screens of wood and of metal and Wren's original pulpit stood between the altar and the chancel screen to the west, a little to one side. The present pulpit was designed by Lord Mottistone in 1964, and is much more in keeping with the Wren architecture than the one designed in 1803 (now in the Trophy Room above the north-west chapel), and certainly much happier in its present setting than the one placed there in 1860 and now to be seen in the crypt. The lectern has a noble eagle in metal, and was made by Jacob Sutton in 1720 at the cost of £241. It is, however, the organ-case and the choirstalls which compel admiration, for although the architectural structure would have been decided by Wren, it seems obvious that he allowed his craftsmen a very

The nave of St Paul's

free hand in the design of the carving which enriches it, relying entirely on their skill to produce work which was suitable for the whole architectural scheme. Fully justifying his confidence in them, they produced what Professor Pevsner has described as 'exquisite metalwork and woodwork, amongst the finest done at the time anywhere in Europe'. The carving of the choirstalls, the organ-case and the Bishop's chair is exquisite, and although it is exuberant and imaginative, Grinling Gibbons and his men were far too much in harmony with their materials to force them beyond their natural qualities, using soft woods for the more riotous decoration, and hard wood where restraint was called for. Little blind-eyed cupids abound, angels make their soundless music from celestial instruments, and cornucopias of fruit and flowers enrich the dark architectural structure. Gibbons' fecundity of invention was rivalled by his fellow craftsmen, the ironsmiths, who, under Jean Tijou, the Huguenot refugee, produced structural metalwork and decorative additions with equal facility and an almost intuitive respect for the materials in which they were working. Certain modifications had to be made when the chancel screen was removed, and the organ divided in two to flank the newly opened chancel. Some of the Grinling Gibbons woodwork was adapted to make a magnificent doorcase for the south transept, and the ironwork was adapted to form the screens which are on either side of the new high altar and shut it off from the eastern end of the aisles on either side.

St Paul's, like Westminster Abbey, abounds in monuments and memorials of varying quality and to people of differing degrees of importance in the history of England. The first statue to be erected in St Paul's, although it is not a notable example of sculpture, is dedicated to a man as worthy as any to be venerated and remembered in this splendid building. This is the statue of John Howard, a quiet hero who left the peace of his country estate in Bedfordshire to investigate the horrors of the jails in England, risking his life again and again in order to obtain the evidence he needed to promote reforms not only in the conduct of the jails, but in the penal code itself. He died, a martyr, of the dreaded jail fever, while on a visit to the jails of Russia in 1790. In the fashion of such memorial sculpture at the time his statue shows him dressed in a pseudo-Roman costume, his legs as muscular as those of any gladiator, but his most permanent memorial must be the Howard League for Penal Reform which is still active in investigating the problems of crime, its causes, and its prevention.

John Bacon the Elder, the sculptor who designed and carried out the John Howard memorial, also produced that to the famous lexicographer, Samuel Johnson, which stands on the opposite side of the crossing from that of John Howard. Dr Johnson is buried in Westminster Abbey, however. He, too, has been transformed into a kind of Roman dignitary, his obese and grotesque form idealised beyond recognition and clothed in appropriately classical dress, although the heavy features are recognisable. Standing on the north-eastern side of the crossing, he faces a statue of his old friend, Sir Joshua Reynolds, whose grave is in the crypt beneath.

Entering the northern aisle, the visitor can see the rear of the choirstalls, which are somewhat plainer than the stalls themselves but still beautiful

ball and cross, still incredibly remote and small.

It is only a short climb from the Whispering Gallery, which is about 100 feet above the floor of the cathedral, to the outer Stone Gallery, some 70 feet higher, where one emerges into the open air. There for the first time one of Wren's ingenious tricks is exposed. Each of the outer walls of the nave and the chancel carries a whole dummy storey which hides flying buttresses from the street level. These flying buttresses, which would have looked odd indeed, are concealed and stabilised by the same wall, which exerts a downward thrust to combat the outward thrust of the vaults within. Thus the dummy walls form a kind of continuous pinnacle, weighting down the real walls beneath, and at the same time acting as a screen which conceals the construction supporting the vaults.

The next climb upward towards the upper balcony of the Golden Gallery just below the lantern, ball and cross is by a series of steep steel stairways, and there the second and most daring of Wren's deceptions is revealed. The inner dome is too shallow to appear of any great importance from outside, so Wren devised a magnificently ample dome to dominate the skyline of London, and created the impression that it was the same dome as that which is seen inside. However, neither of the domes could possibly sustain the weight of the lantern, and so Wren produced a solution which is unique in the history of architecture. The whole weight is taken by a strong brick cone, concealed from the inside of the cathedral by the 18-inch thick dome of

left, The flying buttresses
right, Drawing by Drake Brookshaw showing the inner and outer domes and the brick cone

brick decorated with the Thornhill paintings, and from the outside by the superbly curved outer dome of wood and lead – neither dome being constructional to any extent. As one climbs the zig-zagging steel stairs, the brick cone is clearly visible, but once one reaches the Golden Gallery, about 275 feet above ground level, there is no trace of the construction, apart from the deeply inset upper windows in the outer dome which allow light to seep through windows in the cone and complete the illusion. To make doubly sure of his construction – for not even Wren had ever invented such a device before – he embedded an iron chain in the base of the cone to ensure that it could not slip outwards. He wrote: 'Although the dome wants no abutment, yet, for greater caution it is hooped with iron in this manner. A channel is cut in the bandage of stone, in which is laid a double chain of iron weighing 95 cwts, 3 quarters and 23lb, or five tons, [a total of about 11,100 lbs] strongly linked every ten feet and the whole channel filled with lead.' Later generations of architects to St Paul's have encircled the cone with other chains, and the one at the base is now stainless steel. The incessant vibration of traffic round the cathedral, the underground railways and sewers which undermine the structure, and the appalling strains imposed by the blast from high-explosive bombs in the Second World War have seriously impaired the stability of the whole building, so that Wren's masterpiece is ever in need of continual repair and restoration – a never-ending strain on its finances. A glimpse into the stonemason's yard at St Paul's will show work which, once it has weathered, will be undistinguishable from that of Wren's craftsmen – but such work has to be paid for, and although visitors have to be charged for entry to the Whispering Gallery, etc., much more money is required if the greatest church in the City is to be saved for generations to come.

The view of London from the Golden Gallery is breathtaking, but it is doubtful whether anyone but a Londoner will see very much more than a jumble of parti-coloured buildings with delicately poised spires over-shadowed by huge office blocks or multi-storey housing schemes. Yet there is a multiplicity of historic buildings to be seen, as well as the magical curve of the river winding upstream to Westminster, or downstream past the Tower and the Pool of London. Not many years ago, one could not see the warehouses downstream for cranes, derricks and shipping, but Tooley Street and its neighbourings areas are now ghost-haunted areas with piles of brick skeletons, and a ship of any size is a rarity. On the more optimistic side, before the Festival of Britain of 1951, there were no buildings of any quality between County Hall, Westminster, and Waterloo Bridge, an out-of-date and shabby structure, and many of the buildings in the area were shattered and derelict. Since then, starting with the erection of the Festival Hall, a complex of modern buildings has emerged, the National Theatre east of the new Waterloo Bridge being the latest achievement. The whole of this South Bank complex is a living and exciting place to visit.

Little of Wren's London can be seen from the Golden Gallery (apart from the wooded slopes of Hampstead Heath to the north) unless his spires are sufficiently well known to be recognised from this height. Walking round the Golden Gallery, there are Wren churches to be seen at every point of the compass, and also some of those built by his pupil and assistant, Nicholas Hawksmoor. One of Hawksmoor's churches is to the north-east – the façade, like a triumphal arch topped by a spire, of Christ Church, Spitalfields, dominating the mean streets around it, and now bravely struggling to restore itself to something of its former dignity after a phase of graffiti abuse, protective barbed wire, locked doors and shattered windows.

Returning to the Stone Gallery by the steel stairs supported by the brick cone, one can study the city in greater detail by means of a number of coin-operated telescopes and listen to a commercial commentary from different parts of the gallery. It is also possible to examine more closely the splendour of the western towers of the cathedral, and, to the east, to see the flying buttresses which sustain the thrust of the chancel vaults. From the Whispering Gallery, with its magnificent inner dome, it is then only a short descent to the triforium level, to the library, where fragments of the model of Wren's first design, together with the well-preserved Great Model, 18 feet long, and documents connected with the history of the cathedral can be seen; this is only possible if written application has been made, and casual visitors are not usually admitted to see the models and the archives.

The entrance to the crypt is a door in the east wall of the south transept, where again a small fee is charged. The crypt is low, and divided into small areas by the massive pillars which support the church above. The lighting is subdued, and the whole of this part of the building reverently hushed. At the east end there is the Chapel for the Order of the British Empire – a modern creation by Lord Mottistone, a beautifully discreet room far removed from the bustle of visitors in the rest of the church. The tomb which immediately attracts one's attention is that of the Duke of Wellington – a massive sarcophagus of Cornish porphyry, supported by four sulky lions reluctant to be released from their hard stone bed, and resisting, it seems, every blow of the chisel with which they were shaped. More graceful, by far, is the tomb of Admiral Lord Nelson which stands under a shallow dome in the centre of the crypt. This tomb was not the work of craftsmen of the time of the Battle of Trafalgar, but was fashioned by the Italian carver, Benedetto da Rovezzano, for Cardinal Wolsey in 1524–9. But Cardinal Wolsey died in disgrace and the tomb was confiscated by Henry VIII; it lay unfinished in Windsor and the Italian workmen returned to their own country. Charles I hoped to use it, but he also died before any more work was done upon it, and it was not until the death of Nelson in 1805 that it was brought to London in two parts and used for the reception of Nelson's body.

It should perhaps be mentioned at this point that although many of the famous people whose memorials are to be seen in the crypt are in fact buried there, a number of them are commemorated there and buried elsewhere. The crypt offers a remarkable record of funereal sculpture of the past 300 years. The earliest examples in this macabre exhibition are the blackened and mutilated remnants of Elizabethan and Jacobean tombs figures salvaged from the ruins of the burned-out medieval cathedral. There are examples of sculpture from every period of art since the great fire, including the

Relics in the crypt of St Paul's

memorial to the great English poet and writer, W. E. Henley, by France's most famous sculptor, Auguste Rodin, and a striking portrait bust of the Socialist statesman, Sir Stafford Cripps, by the modern sculptor, Jacob Epstein. The pre-fire figures are assembled on the north side of the crypt, not far from an excellent exhibition showing the deterioration of the cathedral fabric through age, industrial pollution and bomb damage, and emphasising the urgent need for funds to enable the church authorities to continue the work of restoration and repair of this noble building. There, too, are examples of some of the original craftsmanship – two carved heads by Grinling Gibbons, a fragment of wrought ironwork by Jean Tijou, and part of a tombstone with the word 'Resurgam' carved upon it, although this is not necessarily the original stone which the workman found and which was used by Sir Christopher Wren to mark the central point of his crossing.

Another extremely impressive exhibit, which occupies almost the whole of the western end of the crypt, is the ponderous 18-ton funeral carriage of gun-metal upon which the body of the Duke of Wellington was brought in solemn procession to the funeral service conducted in the cathedral by Dean Milman. There are many more memorials to men and women who have made distinguished contributions to the life of the nation: the names are too numerous to list here, but they are drawn from many professions and callings – poets and writers, soldiers and sailors, musicians, artists, engineers, surgeons, architects – the list is almost endless. There is one at least which should not be omitted: for in the south-eastern corner, under a simple marble slab, lies one of the greatest of this illustrious fellowship – Sir Christopher Wren. Above the grave his son, Christopher Wren, placed a plaque bearing an inscription in Latin, which ends: *'Lector, si monumentum requiris, circumspice'*, meaning, 'Reader, if you seek his monument, look around you.' Near to the grave of Sir Christopher Wren lies that of his only daughter, Jane, who died in 1702. They lie in noble company, for in the same area are to be found memorial tablets and gravestones to Sir Joshua Reynolds, the first President of the Royal Academy; his successor in that office, the American artist, Benjamin West (the first American artist to achieve international fame); and his two immediate successors, Sir Thomas Lawrence and Sir John Everett Millais. There are also some famous architects in the same area, although none as great as Wren himself.

So varied are the memorial tablets in the crypt that there is scarcely a visitor to the cathedral who will not have heard of some of the great names they commemorate – Savoyards will know and love Sir Arthur Sullivan, poets, William Blake, and so on. And every writer and lover of London will pay his sincere tribute to Sir Walter Besant, simply but inadequately described as 'Historian of London'.

Returning to the level of the nave, a visitor emerging from the crypt is almost certain to stop at a large painting in the south aisle by the Pre-Raphaelite artist, W. Holman-Hunt. This is 'The Light of the World', typical of the painfully sincere work of the Pre-Raphaelite Brotherhood which created such a stir in the 1840s.

The original plan of St Paul's as devised by Wren (and not as on the Warrant Design), provided a chapel at the west end of each aisle – which make the entrance to the cathedral from the west rather dark – and a chapel on the south side which was used as a Consistory Court for some time. The chapel on the north side was known as the Morning Prayer Chapel, and it was there that the services were held until the nave had been completed. The Morning Prayer Chapel is now dedicated to St Dunstan, and the Consistory Court became the Chapel of St Michael and St George about 1818, shortly after the foundation of the Most Distinguished Order of St Michael and St George as a reward for meritorious services in foreign affairs of the Empire. There is also a small subsidiary chapel dedicated to All Souls on the same side as St Dunstan's Chapel. This now contains the tomb of Lord Kitchener, better known today, perhaps, as the Field Marshal of the First World War whose stern features and whose equally stern command appears on the famous recruiting posters. Earlier generations knew him as Kitchener of Khartoum for his victories in the campaigns in the Middle East in 1898.

It was Jonathan Maine, another of Wren's master craftsmen, who produced the magnificent wooden screen for St Dunstan's Chapel on the south side of the aisle in about 1698. In this chapel lies buried another redoubtable soldier, General Charles Gordon, who lost his life at Khartoum in 1885; he should be remembered not just for his courage as a general, but as a philanthropist who founded schools for the education of the under-privileged urchins who roamed the streets in Gravesend and elsewhere. Frederick Lord Leighton, a painter and sculptor who became President of the Royal Academy, is also buried there.

Jonathan Maine was also largely responsible for the fine woodwork and screen of the Chapel of St Michael and St George, but this is furnished partly with woodwork which was removed from the choirstalls when the alterations took place in the chancel in the 1860s. This chapel also contains a number of memorials – mostly to soldiers, as one might expect in a chapel dedicated to two warrior saints – and even the memorial to the Bishop of Tasmania, the Rev. H. H. Montgomery, has military associations as he was the father of Field-Marshal Viscount Montgomery.

Despite the splendour of his buildings, Wren's last years were clouded by the injustice of his treatment at the hands of the Commissioners, who withheld half his miserable salary of £200 per annum, believing that this would expedite the completion of the cathedral. In 1718, at the age of eighty-six, Wren was dismissed from his post as Surveyor-General to be replaced by William Benson, a man described by a former librarian of St Paul's as 'a person of sublime incompetence'; he lost his position after a year in office. Wren was attacked publicly by the new group of architectural patrons who had 'rediscovered' the rules of Andrea Palladio, and found to their horror that Wren had not only ignored such pedantry if it suited him, but had dared to create something entirely original by sheer personal genius. One such attack, delivered by the Earl of Shaftesbury, read as follows:

> Through several reigns we have patiently seen the noblest buildings perish, if I may say so, under the hand of one single architect, who, if he had been able to profit by experience, would long since, at our expense, have proved the greatest master in the world. But I question whether our patience is like to hold much longer . . . Hardly as the public now stands should we bear to see Whitehall treated like a Hampton Court, or even a new cathedral like St Paul's.

Today it is inconceivable that anyone could have been so blinded by an architectural theory that they were unable to appreciate Wren's achievement. One has only to stand on St Martin's Hill and examine the great west front with its twin towers framing the dome, or look at the dome itself, still serene above the cathedral despite the way in which it is gradually being shut in by taller buildings, to realise just how much it means to London, and to the Londoner.

There are still three more of Wren's churches to be explored – one within the boundaries of the City, and two in the City of Westminster. The nearest one is St Andrew, Holborn, most easily reached by walking up Old Bailey and then turning westwards along Holborn Viaduct to Holborn Circus. Altered considerably by the Victorian architect, S. S. Teulon, it was gutted during the blitz – although its tower remained intact – and has now been rebuilt by Lord Mottistone, the architect who has contributed so much to St Paul's. Apart from the high box pews with which the original Wren church would have been equipped, the rebuilding by an architect sensitive to Wren's style produced a church which was remarkably like the original building of 1686–7, although certain eighteenth-century furnishings, such as the font, the pulpit and the organ have been brought in to replace those lost when the church was reduced to a shell during the Second World War. The Wren-like galleries are supported by square-panelled columns of wood, from which rise stone columns topped with carved Corinthian capitals to support the carved plaster roof; this is divided into panels decorated so convincingly in the style of the seventeenth century that it is difficult to believe that it is the work of twentieth-century craftsmen.

The very finely worked organ-case came from the Thomas Coram Foundling Home in Lamb's Conduit Fields, just north-east of Russell Square; it was upon this organ that Handel played regularly as he was choirmaster to the Foundling Home and a friend of William Hogarth, one of the governors. Near to the organ loft there is a modern memorial to Captain Thomas Coram, the founder of the home, who will be mentioned again in the next chapter.

The next area of seventeenth-century buildings lies some half a mile or so to the west, near Chancery Lane underground station, most conveniently reached on foot or by bus. The entrance to Gray's Inn has been considerably altered, but was probably late seventeenth- or early eighteenth-century work, and is to be found on the north side of Holborn, nearly opposite the timber-framed shop-fronts of Staple Inn. Gray's Inn suffered a great deal of damage during the blitz, but there are still a number of seventeenth-century buildings to be seen there – one in South Square (No. 1) and others of the late seventeenth century or early eighteenth century among the chambers occupied by members of the Inn. The delightful gardens are still there and are open to the public under certain conditions and at certain times – a charming oasis of trees and grass, still as peaceful as it was when Samuel Pepys enjoyed his strolls there. There he might have discussed *Fumifugium* with its author, John Evelyn – a protest against the pollution of the atmosphere of London by the smoke from sea-coal and the fumes from noxious industries, which were making London such an unpleasant city in which to live. (It is ironic to think that the funds for the rebuilding of London after the great fire should have been largely dependent on the increased use of sea-coal.)

But the quiet trees and opned fields to the west of Gray's Inn soon came under attack from an unscrupulous and determined land speculator named Dr Nicholas Barbon. The son of the notorious Roundhead, 'Praise-God' Barebones, he had studied medicine abroad and prudently decided to change his name before returning to Restoration England; but he very soon realised that there was far more money to be made from the acquisition and development of land in the London area than from practising as a doctor. Dressed in the height of fashion, a plausible and clever con man, Barbon was able to persuade his victims to part with the leases, and was not above demolishing any property which stood in his way, relying on costly and protracted lawsuits to wear down the opposition, who might be only too willing to concede defeat rather than face bankruptcy.

Much of the land on the west side of Gray's Inn is still the property of

left, Entrance to Gray's
Inn
right, Gray's Inn

Bedford Corporation, part of the gift of Sir William Harpur for Bedford
School and other charities, but Barbon obviously persuaded the Mayor of
Bedford to allow him to build on the property (as he did the governors of
Rugby School in the same area), and very soon the pleasant fields
disappeared under bricks and mortar. Bedford Row, west of Gray's Inn, is
only one of the developments which attracted the opposition of the Benchers
of Gray's Inn. Pitched battles were fought between Barbon's workmen and
the Benchers with brickbats and stones, but in vain – Barbon triumphed and
building continued. Bedford Row now has an eighteenth-century
appearance, but many of the small panes of glass of the original windows
have been replaced by large nineteenth-century sheets which ruin the façade
of a street built as a unified whole. Numbers 36–43 are still recognisably part
of Barbon's original scheme.

Despite the preventative legislation passed after the great fire, the risk of
fire was still very great, and it is Nicholas Barbon's credit that he introduced
the first system of fire insurance in the country – a project which later
developed into the Phoenix Assurance Company. This was only a means of
compensation after the house had been damaged by fire, but early in the
eighteenth century, two measures were passed to make houses less
vulnerable to fire. The first, in 1706–7, made the widely projecting wooden
cornices illegal, and houses built after this date in London, at least, have

cornices of brick or stone or parapets of either material. Sash windows had been in common use since the second half of the seventeenth century, their window frames almost on the same level as the brick surround. The second measure, passed in 1709, ensured that window frames were set back into the thickness of the wall, with a generous margin of brick separating the wooden frame from the surface of the wall. These two changes in the building of houses make it easier for visitors to London to detect houses built by Barbon or his contemporaries, even if changes have occurred to the façades more recently.

Barbon meanwhile continued to develop estates westwards towards Red Lion Square (now entirely rebuilt), and along Theobald's Road into John Street and the Great St James Street areas to the north. He also moved southwards to the area of Lincoln's Inn, where other seventeenth-century developments had been initiated by Inigo Jones before the Civil War. The finest late seventeenth-century house in this area is Powis House, on the north-western corner of Lincoln's Inn Fields. When it passed into the hands of the Duke of Newcastle, the Lord Keeper of the Privy Seal, about 1705, it was renamed Newcastle House, but after many changes of ownership, by 1930 it was in poor condition and the present house is actually a very skilful rebuilding by Sir Edwin Lutyens on the lines of the original mansion. A little to the south of Newcastle House is Lindsey House, originally built as part of a new town-planning scheme, never fully realised. Lindsey House was named after the 4th Earl of Lindsey. It was to Lindsey House that the decapitated head of Lord Russell was taken to be sewn back on to his corpse, after his execution in Lincoln's Inn Fields in 1683 for his alleged complicity in the Rye House Plot, a conspiracy to assassinate Charles II.

The most impressive array of houses of this period is to be found in Lincoln's Inn, the entrance of which is diagonally opposite Lindsey House on the eastern side of Lincoln's Inn Fields. New Square, laid out by Henry Searle, was also a private venture in 1685–97, and now occupies the whole of the southern half of Lincoln's Inn. Although some of the houses have been repaired and slightly altered since the seventeenth century, the dignified domesticity of the square has not been spoiled, and the wide green lawns, rose-beds and trees make this one of the most attractive places in London. In the south-eastern corner there is a decorative gateway dated 1697 which makes a lively and almost flamboyant contrast to the sobriety of the houses forming the square. When the Law Courts are in session, it is interesting to be in New Square at lunchtime and to watch the bewigged figures striding through to their chambers, or standing in earnest little groups with their clients. Searle Street, named after the designer of New Square, occupies the western edge behind the square, and Carey Street, named after Sir George Carey whose house once stood there, later became so intimately connected with the bankruptcy courts that to be 'in Carey Street' became a euphemism for being bankrupt.

The shops at this end of Chancery Lane are largely concerned with the supply of wares for the barristers and lawyers – horsehair wigs, gowns and the large bags in which they are carried from court to court tied with a heavy

left, The gateway to
Lincoln's Inn
right, A view from
Fountain Court in the
Inner Temple

cord, as well as all the rest of the office equipment needed for legal business.

Chancery Lane emerges into Fleet Street directly opposite Inner Temple Gateway, dated 1610–11. A little further west is Middle Temple Gateway, dated 1684, at one time attributed to Sir Christopher Wren, but now thought to have been designed by Roger North, a Bencher who dabbled in architecture, as did most cultivated men of his time. The late seventeenth-century houses on the east side of Middle Temple Lane with their overhanging fronts, plastered to conceal the wooden construction, are really very old-fashioned for 1693, but the block of New Court, reached through an archway dated 1677, was designed by Nicholas Barbon and is slightly more fashionable for the period. It looks particularly well from Fountain Court, from beside the old, but still fruit-bearing mulberry trees. The tall, single building just north of Fountain Court was part of Barbon's development which included Essex Street, built after he had demolished Essex House. There are delightful little glimpses in and out of Devereux Court, and the public house, The Devereux, is built on the site of a famous coffee house, the Grecian Coffee House, and contains a bust of Devereux, Earl of Essex, dated 1676, although this must be of doubtful authenticity, since he died in 1646. Essex Street has undergone so many changes that anything of Barbon's original scheme is difficult to find, and the strange arch at the end which leads out to the Embankment has been rebuilt.

Barbon was by no means the only speculator at work after the great fire, for apart from Henry Jermyn, Lord St Albans, and his friends, Gregory King, an engraver who was also Rouge Dragon pursuivant of the College of Arms, developed King's Square (now better known as Soho Square), in 1681. Others have already been mentioned, including Sir Thomas Bond, who invested rather unsuccessfully in the building of the Bond Street area, and more successful contemporaries, Lord Grosvenor, who started Grosvenor Square in 1695, and Lord John Berkeley, who built Berkeley Square some three years later.

By the end of the century the drive westwards had gained momentum, and while the river was still an important route to Westminster, coaches began to ply along the Strand so that it became possible for a wealthy citizen to live away from his business and to commute to the City when necessary. This caused considerable resentment among the watermen, and from time to time there would be fierce fights between the watermen and their coaching rivals. The coach became something of a status symbol, and it was a matter of deep satisfaction for Samuel Pepys when he was able to own a coach and horses with a liveried coachman to drive him, in 1668.

St Clement Danes is the first of the Wren churches to be encounterd outside the City. Its name implies the presence of a much earlier church, but little of that remains, except in the crypt. Wren started to build the church in 1680, but his tower was left unfinished and it was James Gibbs, one of the new generation of eighteenth-century architects, who added the extremely impressive Baroque storeys above the level of the clock. Unfortunately the nave of the church was blasted by high explosive and gutted by fire in the Second World War, thus the present building in the Strand is virtually a new church, apart from the tower. W. A. S. Lloyd, the modern architect who rebuilt it, used photographs and drawings of the church as a basis for his reconstruction, and it is really a very fine copy of the original. It is now the memorial church to the Royal Air Force, and the pavement of the nave is inlaid with slate carvings of the badges of all the RAF units who fought during the last war.

The last of the Wren churches was built on a new site as part of the complex round St James's Square laid out by Lord St Albans, who in fact bore a good deal of the cost of its construction himself. This is St James's, Piccadilly, which is within a hundred yards of Piccadilly Circus underground. Of the fifty-two churches designed by Wren this was his favourite; he felt that he had at last succeeded in producing a building perfectly fitted for Protestant worship. St James, Piccadilly, was in fact the church to which he was referring in the passage quoted on page 148, for the definition of his requirements for such a church ends: 'I endeavoured to effect this, in building the Parish Church of St James's, Westminster, which, I presume, is the most capacious with these Qualifications, that hath yet been built.' He was fortunate in having a site unencumbered with the remains of a burned-out medieval church and churchyard, which meant that he did not have to adapt a symmetrical plan to an irregular and cramped area between narrow alleys or winding roads. His church was somewhat modified during the nineteenth century when the proper entrance facing Jermyn Street was bricked in and a window inserted instead, but it was the extensive damage inflicted in the Second World War which necessitated so much repair that it is now virtually a new building, erected within the outer shell. The task of reconstruction was undertaken by the late Professor Sir Albert Richardson, one of the greatest experts on eighteenth-century architecture in the country, who was very sympathetic to the Wren building. It was he who designed the present spire, for the original one, destroyed during the bombing, was a clumsy and inept design by an ambitious carpenter named Wilcox. St James's, Piccadilly, is larger than most City churches, with galleries round three sides to accommodate the fashionable congregations from the newly built areas round St James's Square. Both the organ-case and the reredos (fortunately protected during the war) are decorated with carving by Grinling Gibbons of the most sumptuous kind. The organ was built by Renatus Harris for James II in 1685 for the Roman Catholic chapel in the Royal Palace in Whitehall, but after the accession of William and Mary it was transferred in 1691 to this church and installed by Father Smith. John Evelyn was delighted with this church, for an entry in his diary for December 1684 reads as follows:

> I went to see the new Church at St James's, elegantly built. The altar was especially adorned, the white marble enclosure curiously and richly carved; the flowers and the garlands about the walls by Mr Gibbons, in wood: a pelican with young at her breast; just over the altar in the carved compartment and border environing the purple velvet fringed with I.H.S. richly embroidered.'

It is perhaps strange that John Evelyn did not then go on to comment on the marble font carved by his young protégé, for it is clearly one over which Grinling Gibbons took a great deal of trouble: even to modern eyes it has a sentimental naturalism which one associates more with the ecclesiastical art of the Victorian period than with that of the seventeenth century. The bowl of the font is supported by a stem which is carved to represent the tree of knowledge in the Garden of Eden, complete with the serpent and flanked by the naked figures of Adam and Eve, the latter tempting Adam with the apple. The bowl of the font is also carved, but with three low reliefs, one inspired by the Old Testament and the other two taken from the New Testament. The first is Noah's Ark upon the waters, the second represents the baptism of Our Lord by John the Baptist, and the third, the baptism of the Treasurer of the Queen of the Ethiopians by St Philip, which is somewhat strange as the church is dedicated to St James. Among the famous people to be christened at this font were William Blake, poet, artist and mystic, and the great statesman, William Pitt the Elder, Earl of Chatham.

The high curved plaster ceiling, supported on elegant Corinthian columns with an elaborately decorated entablature of plaster, was largely reconstructed by using plaster casts taken from fragments salvaged from the ruins after the raid, and from drawings. Inset in the plaster decoration is the

Kensington Palace

coat of arms of Henry Jermyn, Lord of St Albans, on whose land the church stands, and who defrayed part of the cost of building the original building. Over the new stairway in the north vestibule, leading out into the courtyard and to Piccadilly, there is a vigorously carved coat of arms, consisting of the Royal Arms of Stuart with a small shield in the centre bearing the arms of Nassau, the complete coat of arms of William and Mary. Among the distinguished company buried in the church are the Willem van de Veldes, father and son, famous painters of seascapes, whose accurately painted pictures of seventeenth-century ships and the battles of the Dutch wars are housed in the Queen's House and the Maritime Museum at Greenwich and will be mentioned again later.

A handful of the seventeenth-century houses built in this area have survived, Schomberg House in Pall Mall, for example, built for the Duke of Schomberg in 1698, but, like many others, this was altered so much during the eighteenth century that it will be described in the next chapter.

The next major seventeenth-century building of interest is Kensington Palace, on the far western side of Hyde Park and Kensington Gardens. Unlike the European palaces which were built to house vast numbers of nobles whose attendance at court was compulsory, English palaces were designed as homes for the monarch and just a small retinue. In the seventeenth and eighteenth centuries the English nobles were far too busy administering their own estates to be persuaded to go to Court, and they would certainly not have contemplated living there, even if there had been sufficient accommodation. Kensington Palace known in the seventeenth century as Kensington House, was a country retreat for that sober domestic couple, William and Mary II, the daughter of the deposed James II. It is therefore essentially *domestic*, not 'state' architecture.

Kensington House was previously known as Nottingham House, and was bought from the Earl of Nottingham, the Secretary of State, for £18,000 in June 1689. Neither William nor Mary were comfortable in the rambling Palace at Whitehall and the foggy river air only aggravated William's asthma, so both looked forward to living on the higher, dryer ground of Kensington. Wren set out at once to convert the small Jacobean mansion into a more suitable home, and work commenced almost as soon as Nicholas Hawksmoor was appointed Clerk of the Works in July 1689. In the meantime the queen found temporary accommodation in Holland House, another Jacobean mansion less than a mile to the west; sadly, this was a ruin after the boming of the Second World War but has now been beautifully incorporated into a modern youth centre.

Despite some constructional failures, due to the queen's impatience the building of Kensington House was sufficiently advanced by Christmas 1689 for occupation, although as late as February 1690 John Evelyn noted that it 'but was as yet a patched building, but with the garden, however, it is a very sweet villa. . . .' For a great deal of the time that work was going on at Kensington, King William was away fighting in Ireland.

The whole complex of buildings at Kensington which is to be seen today has been altered and extended by a succession of monarchs – particularly George I; but since less than a quarter of the present building is open to the public (mainly the south-eastern side), it seems irrelevant to describe the many modifications to the remainder of the building, parts of which are still used from time to time by members of the Royal Family, or as Government offices. However, Wren's clock tower over the entrance to the house from Clock Court can still be seen from the outside.

The tour of the State Apartments open to the public starts by entering a most beautiful Wren doorway in the north-eastern corner. It has a curved hood protecting a delightfully carved cartouche bearing the interlaced initials of William and Mary – the work of Thomas Hill, a master mason who had worked for Wren at St Paul's. This stone doorway is one of the more restrained notes of decoration on a building which is otherwise almost entirely of red brick, another characteristic which strengthens the feeling of domesticity to this, the least palatial of all palaces. Built towards the end of the seventeenth century, the door forms an interesting contrast to the Georgian doorway on the north side of the same corner, with its more elaborate classical structure of a pedimented entrance supported by Corinthian columns of stone.

Immediately inside the Wren door the visitor is confronted by a simple well-proportioned staircase, made by a carpenter named John Hayward, whose more elaborate doorway into the Queen's Gallery at the top of the three flights of stairs shows that he would also have been capable of carving a deeply moulded pediment to the door at the foot of the staircase.

At one time the Queen's Gallery, a spacious room over 80 feet long, contained a rich collection of Chinese and Japanese artefacts collected by Queen Mary on the Continent, but this has now been dispersed, and many of the fittings which used to enrich it have gone, too, so that it looks a little barren. Fortunately two of the mirrors with surrounds carved by Grinling Gibbons have remained in place, and the carved doorheads and cornices by other craftsmen are also still to be seen. It is rather more a portrait gallery: there is a good dual portrait of King William and Queen Mary by the Dutch artist, William Wissing, painted in 1685 at the request of James II, and a portrait of Anne Hyde, the Duchess of York, his first wife and the mother of Queen Mary, painted by Sir Peter Lely about 1662. The most striking portrait, however, is the one at the far end of Peter the Great, The Tsar of Russia, which was painted in Kensington Palace by Sir Godfrey Kneller during the visit of the Tsar in 1698. As John Evelyn writes: 'The Tsar of Muscovy being come to England, and having a mind to see the building of ships, hired my house at Sayes Court, and made it his court and palace. . . .' It was a decision John Evelyn was to regret, as a note from his servant might have warned him: 'There is a house full of people and right nasty.' The Tsar was an unruly house guest, and by the time he left not only did 300 panes of glass have to be replaced, but John Evelyn found his beautiful grounds in ruins, as one of the Tsar's less endearing relaxations when drunk, was to be trundled through the neatly tended hedges at high speed in a wheelbarrow. Among the other paintings in the Queen's Gallery is a portrait of the future William III as Prince of Orange at the age of fourteen, clad in full armour; it is by the Dutch artist, Adrieen Hanneman, who worked in England during the reign of Charles I and modelled his style on that of Van Dyck. This particular picture was executed for Charles II and used to hang in his bedchamber in Whitehall Palace.

Leading off Queen Mary's Gallery there is a little room known as Queen Mary's Closet – a small private apartment associated with Queen Anne, where, as 'Mrs Freeman' (for her Royal titles irked her sometimes) she enjoyed the company and sometimes the advice of 'Mrs Morley', the redoubtable Duchess of Marlborough. Appropriately it is in this room that one can see not only the profile portrait of Queen Anne by Sir Godfrey Kneller, which was used for the face on the coinage of the realm, but also a copy of a portrait of Sarah, Duchess of Marlborough, by the same artist. The room was denuded of its original panelling in the nineteenth century.

Next to Queen Mary's Closet is Queen Mary's Dining-Room, which has been altered, but still has the original marble fireplace and wooden panelling. Hanging over the fireplace there is a portrait of Queen Mary as a child of ten in a kind of fancy dress, as Diana the Huntress and Goddess of the Moon, carrying a little bow and arrow and wearing a tiny crescent moon on her forehead. Painted by Sir Peter Lely in 1672, this is certainly the most important painting in the room, and hangs in pride of place.

Queen Mary's Drawing-Room, next to her Dining-Room, was heavily damaged by fire during the blitz of 1940, so that none of the panelling now survives, although enough of the magnificently carved cornice with its ebullient acanthus leaves curling round the crown ·and monograph of William and Mary remains to give some idea of the richness of the decoration of the room before this catastrophe. The curtains, which are modern, are copied from designs by Daniel Marot, a French artist-craftsman who fled from France in 1685 after Louix XIV had revoked the Edict of Nantes and who worked for William of Orange at Kensington Palace and Hampton Court. Most of the paintings in this room are by foreign artists, for English painters had received very little royal patronage and the prestige which accompanied it since the reign of Elizabeth I; it was not until the reign of George I that an English artist, James Thornhill, was appointed Seargeant Painter to the King.

Queen Mary's Drawing-Room houses some of her original collection of Oriental porcelain, exhibited in a most beautifully inlaid cabinet made by a Dutch cabinet-maker and 'glasse-seller' named Gerrit or Gerreit Jansen, and later anglicised into Garret Johnson.

Both Queen Mary's Drawing-Room and her Bedchamber were badly damaged by incendiary bombs in 1940; it was during this air-raid that some of the notable carving in this room by Grinling Gibbons was reduced to ashes. The wide floorboards made of elm planks were the only ones to survive in any of the state apartments. Some of the furniture is also original.

The Privy Chamber, next to Queen Mary's Dressing-Room, is a larger and grander state room. The panelling is now concealed by three tapestries woven in the royal factory at Mortlake for Charles I when he was Prince of Wales. It was he who acquired the famous Raphael cartoons for use in the royal tapestry works, apparently on the advice of Peter Paul Rubens. They are now on permanent loan by Her Majesty to the Victoria and Albert Museum and are one of the greatest treasures to be found in that precious collection. The black marble mantelpiece is part of the original seventeenth-century room, but most of the décor is clearly of a much later date and was carried out under the direction of William Kent. An indifferent painter, Kent was studying in Rome early in the eighteenth century when he was fortunate enough to attract the patronage of the rich and influential Lord Burlington, one of the noblemen who attacked Wren for his deviation from the rules of established by Andrea Palladio. Once attached to Burlington's entourage, Kent became a furniture designer and interior decorator, a designer of landscape gardens, and eventually an architect. The ceiling of the Privy Chamber is his work and is partly derived from examples by Raphael and his pupils which Kent had studied in Rome. The theme is of Mars, the God of War, and his consort, Minerva, the Goddess of Wisdom, who is attended by various mythical characters representing the arts and sciences. The whole ceiling is actually an obsequious compliment to the martial prowess of George I, and George was sufficiently impressed by Kent's accomplishments to pay him £300 on the completion of the paintings in 1723.

Although Clock Court is not open to the public, it is possible to get an excellent view of it from the windows on the west side of the Privy Chamber, and to compare Wren's work with that of later architects who worked at Kensington Palace. The royal arms of William and Mary can just be seen in the pediment over the entrance, and their monogram is to be seen on the weather-vane over the neat little cupola which crowns the clock tower. The present clock came from Carlton House which once stood on the north side of the Mall, but was pulled down in 1828 to make way for Carlton Terrace.

The next room, the Presence Chamber, is one of the original rooms built by Wren during his alterations to the old Jacobean mansion, Nottingham House, and very little of his work remains unchanged; even the magnificent overmantel decorated with some of Grinling Gibbons' most lively and inventive carving which probably came from another part of the building is of the same period. Once again the ceiling by William Kent attracts one's attention – nothing quite like it had been seen in London before. The style is known as Etruscan or Pompeian and was quite outrageously inaccurate historically. The style found little favour in England.

By this time Wren's popularity was waning and his interiors must have seemed very old-fashioned to the newly-arrived Hanoverian king who proceeded to turn Kensington House into Kensington Palace. The room is therefore richly furnished with eighteenth-century painting and sculpture.

From immediately outside the Presence Chamber the visitor has a very fine view of the king's staircase, which was originally built by Wren as a counterpart to the queen's staircase, but was later converted into a much more splendid stairway with a balustrade of wrought iron by Jean Tijou replacing the more humble one of wood. Jean Tijou surpassed himself with this ironwork, for the metal has been coaxed and disciplined into a series of panels of graceful and virile curves, work carried out in 1692–3 when he must have been at the peak of his craft. Wren redesigned the whole staircase in 1692–3, inserting three flights of stairs of black Irish marble, setting out the landings with squares of black and white marble, and replacing the wooden balustrade with the superb Tijou one now in position. The stairway originally led down to a new Guard Chamber which has now disappeared, but if it resembled the King's Guard Room he designed at Hampton Court Palace, it must indeed have been a magnificent room.

During the reign of George I, major alterations were made to this area. Wren's panelling was ripped out, windows were filled in, and other alterations made, the most sweeping change being the insertion of *trompe l'œil* paintings on canvas by William Kent. Kent had already superseded Sir James Thornhill as chief mural painter when his design for the painted ceiling in the Cupola Room in this building was selected in preference to the one submitted by Sir James Thornhill.

Kent's work round the staircase was his most ambitious effort at that time, and was somewhat imitative of the work of his French contemporary, Louis Laguerre, who had replaced Sir James Thornhill at Blenheim Palace after the Duchess of Marlborough had found that the Frenchman was prepared to work more cheaply than his English rival. Wren himself said in 1692, in a speech to Christ's Hospital: 'It was observed by somebody that our English artists are dull enough at invention, but when once a foreign pattern is set, they imitate it so well, that commonly they exceed the original.' This was certainly true of the work of Sir James Thornhill, but less obvious with Kent's work – this type of illusionist painting was done so much better by Paolo Veronese, for example, in Palladian villas in Italy. Kent's staircase, with its dummy columns, false niches carrying mock statues, shadows looking as though they are cast by the light from the windows, and highlights giving the effect of projection could be carried out today by any good professional scene-painter working in the West End theatres. Nevertheless, it produced the effect of classical sculpture and clearly pleased Kent's royal clients.

Kent's paintings on the upper floor of the King's Staircase are even more derivative, for there he resorted to the trick of inserting recognisable people, including his own self-portrait, as part of the decoration, a convention which had already been used by the Italian painter, Paolo Veronese, in some of the Palladian villas in Northern Italy, by Sir James Thornhill at Greenwich, and by Laguerre at Blenheim.

The rooms below the King's Staircase are not open to the public so the Visitor is next shown into the King's Gallery, reached through a narrow passage, in which various orders of chivalry, medals from Windsor Castle, are exhibited from time to time. The King's Gallery, 90 feet long, has a selection of paintings from the Royal Collection, although they are not necessarily the paintings which King William would have enjoyed when he lived there; Buckingham Palace had not yet been built, so that some of the fine collection of paintings acquired by Charles I, then sold off by the Cromwellians and bought in again after May 1660 by a special commission would have been there. It was in Kensington Palace, for example, that Queen Caroline, the widow of George II, quite by accident found the priceless collection of drawings by Leonardo da Vinci which is now one of the treasures of Windsor Castle. There are a few outstanding pictures still to be seen in the gallery, although it must be stressed that they are rearranged or reallocated from time to time, and sometimes loaned to international exhibitions including works by Rubens and Van Dyck.

The King's Gallery must also be remembered as the room in which William III was walking when he felt the first signs of an illness which was to prove fatal. He was recuperating from a heavy fall from his horse when he fractured his collarbone, bruising him badly, an accident which gave some satisfaction to his Jacobite enemies abroad who drank toasts to 'the little gentleman in black velvet' (a mole) which had caused it. Complications set in, and before very long the king died of pleurisy in Kensington Palace. It was in the same room that Queen Mary wrote to her husband when he was on active service in Ireland: 'My poor heart is ready to break every time I think in what perpetual danger you are . . .' And as she later lay dying, William wrote to a friend: 'You can imagine what a state I am in, loving her as I do. You know what it is to have a good wife. . . .'

The next suite of rooms in the palace was converted by the Duchess of Kent and her daughter, Princess Victoria, in 1834–6, despite objections by an outraged William IV, and rearranged and redecorated again in 1932–3 under the personal direction of Queen Mary, the wife of George V, who was born there in 1867. Thus for the remainder of the public tour it is necessary to digress into the nineteenth century.

The Duchess of Kent's Dressing-Room was once part of the private apartments of William III, but considerable alterations were made in 1835, and the heavy black marble fireplace installed there. The room is furnished in the style of the 1840s and 1850s and gives the visitor an admirable idea of the furniture, the paintings and the various *objets d'art* to be found in the royal apartments at that time. Only the carved cradle is seventeenth-century workmanship, and this was made in Germany and only acquired by Queen Victoria in 1843. The piano and the large ornate cabinet against the wall are both veneered with tulipwood and embellished with a great many little porcelain plaques and other somewhat lavish decorations very characteristic of the taste of the period. The cabinet was a birthday present from Queen Victoria to her husband in 1856.

The Ante-Room adjoining the Duchess of Kent's Dressing-Room was originally part of King William's Great Closet, but the present south wall was inserted early in the nineteenth century. The showcase contains a delightful little doll's house with which Princess Victoria used to play, and a selection of her other toys.

Queen Victoria's Bedroom, next to the Ante-Room, was originally the State Bedchamber of William III, but the William Kent painting with which its ceiling was once decorated had long since gone and the room now appears to be entirely Victorian. This is the room in which Queen Mary, who arranged the decoration, was born in 1867, and where the young Princess Victoria slept with her mother; she was awakened there to be told in the sitting-room beneath that she had become Queen of England. The furnishings of the room were gathered from other royal residences.

The next room – the King's Drawing-Room – has a much earlier style of decoration and was clearly a more official room, for the ceiling decoration by William Kent is one of the best of his paintings, and the room lacks the intimacy of Queen Victoria's Bedroom. The huge central oval panel of the ceiling is decorated with a scene from classical mythology. It is certainly one of William Kent's best paintings, and he received £500 for it in May 1723. He was also responsible for the arabesques and the figures supporting the medallions with which the coving is so lavishly decorated.

The Council Chamber, adjoining the King's Drawing-Room to the north, was rebuilt entirely in about 1836. It is now furnished as an exhibition room and contains a great many works of art and craft characteristic of the Victorian period, some made specially for the Great Exhibition at the Crystal Palace which was originally erected on the south side of Hyde Park, within view of Kensington Palace.

The whole room is a remarkable record of the taste of the period, led by the queen and her consort and followed by most people wealthy enough to afford such craftsmanship. One of the most significant objects is the throne and footstool of ivory which occupies the centre of the room. This is Oriental craftsmanship and was presented to Queen Victoria by the Maharaja of Travencore in 1851, a tribute to the pervasive influence of the British queen in the Far East, although it was to be another twenty-five years before she was declared Empress of India at the opening of Parliament in 1876.

The Cupola Room was the first of the schemes in Kensington Palace to be carried out by William Kent, whose designs were preferred to those submitted by Sir James Thornhill in 1722 and established the ascendency of the younger man in the royal favour. The room is an eighteenth-century exercise in Roman grandeur, no doubt a flattering suggestion that the first of the Hanoverian kings had much in common with the victorious Roman emperors.

It was in the Cupola Room that Princess Victoria was christened by the Archbishop of Canterbury on 14 June 1819, and in the room beneath, the Red Saloon, that, as the new Queen of England, she held her first privy council on the morning of her accession, 20 June 1837.

The way out of the State Apartments open to the public lies back through the Privy Chamber and the rooms linking it to Queen Mary's Gallery, so that a visitor has another opportunity to have a last look at many of the remarkable *objets d'art* on show. It should be emphasised, however, that all of them may be moved from place to place, so that it cannot be guaranteed that they will be found as described in this chapter.

It remains to describe two other places connected with the palace: the Orangery built for Queen Anne, one of the most charming buildings in this part of London, and a sunken garden surrounded by a pleached hedge of lime trees which, although it was actually installed early this century, was designed with a formal layout and with eighteenth-century lead cisterns in order to harmonise with the Orangery. The Orangery is an excellent example of how skilfully related proportions of mass and window areas, with a gentle emphasis on a central feature and fine craftsmanship throughout, can produce in a building an unobtrusive beauty which seems to grow with renewed acquaintance. It is a pity that it is closed at the time of writing – for many years it has been a quiet haven for students, nannies and many other regular visitors.

The central entrance is flanked by pairs of double columns of beautifully cut and moulded brick, for the stone dressings are used very sparingly indeed, with great effect. There are four tall windows on either side of the entrance stretching from within a foot or so of the paved terrace to just below the cornice, and these, with the round-headed ones at either end, ensure that the maximum amount of sunlight penetrates the interior. Wall surfaces which might have been uneasy blank spaces are filled with gauged and rubbed brick niches which, although uninhabited by statues, cast deep shadows enriching the surface. There is no building by Wren or his contemporaries in which the brick craftsmanship can be seen to better advantage than in this building.

The inside of the Orangery is almost austere in the severity of its decoration, although a pair of swags and a tumble of carved flowers and fruit by Grinling Gibbons is to be seen on the inner side of the walls which separate the main hall from the little circular rooms at either end. A few good copies of classical sculpture used to enrich the north wall, and at one time a real classical vase about eight feet high occupied the central space immediately inside the door.

above, The Orangery, Kensington Palace
left, Interior of the Orangery

A formal procession of trees from the steps in the centre of the Orangery terrace leads down to the sunken garden to the south – a garden which is partly concealed by the shaped and pleached lime trees which border the walk surrounding it and could easily be missed. It is always colourful and it is difficult to say when it looks at its best – early in the year, when its beds contain battalions of beautifully marshalled tulips and other spring flowers, or on high summer days when it is a controlled riot of herbaceous plants too numerous to mention.

Immediately to the east of the garden is the Round Pond, one of the few reminders of the grand design produced by Henry Wise. It is not easy to pick out the main avenues as they are intersected by a number of later paths, but the vigorously modelled 'Physical Energy' – a statue by G. F. Watts – marks a point through which the main drive was established in the earlier pattern. The so-called 'New River' had to wait a few more years before the present Serpentine was developed by linking a number of pools and cleansing the boggy area from which it eventually emerged to form the present arrangement.

Leaving Kensington Palace, the next major seventeenth-century building – one of Wren's masterpieces – lies southwards in Chelsea. From Sloane Square underground station it is only about ten minutes' walk down Lower Sloane Street to Royal Hospital Road, which runs westwards to the rear of the Royal Military Hospital. This was founded in 1682 by Charles II, influenced by the enthusiastic description given to him by the Duke of Monmouth who had visited the *Hôtel des Invalides*, established by Louis XIV in Paris in 1670 for the relief of the maimed and elderly veterans of his army. The Royal Military Hospital was also heavily subsidised by Sir Stephen Fox who had been Paymaster-General to the Forces. Its inception was recorded by John Evelyn on 27 January 1682:

> This evening, Sir Stephen Fox acquainted me again with His Majesty's resolution of proceeding in the erection of a Royal Hospital for emerited soldiers on that spot of land which the Royal Society had sold to his Majesty for £1,300, and that he would settle £5,000 per annum on it, and build to the value of £20,000 for the relief and reception of four companies, namely 400 men to be as a college or monastery.

The pensioners who live there number about 500 and are called in-pensioners, but there are a great many out-pensioners who also benefit from the foundation, and it is from them that the selection of the in-pensioners is made. They must be of good character, unable to earn their own living and, unless disabled in military service, over fifty-five years of age. When he enters the hospital to live there permanently, an old soldier surrenders his out-pension, but he is then provided with his food and a room of his own, his clothing, a pint of beer daily, or tobacco in lieu, and usually a small allowance. The pensioners are administratively organised on military lines, with a governor and officers, consisting of a lieutenant-governor, two

medical officers, a chaplain, adjutant, quartermaster and six retired officers, called captains of invalids, who command the six companies into which the pensioners are divided.

The Royal Military Hospital, Chelsea

The Royal Hospital chapel and dining hall are normally open daily during the week for a couple of hours, mornings and afternoons, and on Sunday afternoons, but it would obviously be a courtesy to write to inform the authorities if a party visit is contemplated. The Council Chamber is also on view on Sundays and in the summer on Saturday afternoons.

The oldest part of the hospital is the Figure Court, named after the statue of Charles II in the centre by Grinling Gibbons. The Figure Court has an imposing central portico – an announcement of its importance as the main entrance to the dining hall and the chapel where the in-pensioners eat and worship communally. Wren reduced the size of the columns for the colonnade to a human scale, and this is where the veterans can sit in the sun, sheltered from the wind, passing the time of day.

The massive wooden doors to the Octagon Porch in the centre are original, and the entrance to the dining hall is to the left. There are staves of nearly a hundred trophies captured from former enemies – Americans, Dutch, French, Prussians and Russians, as well as some from the Far East – but the original colours have been removed in order to preserve them and those now on show are replicas. The guns which stand on either side of the porch were captured from the Dutch, dated 1623, and from the French, dated 1706.

The dining hall has had its share of history, for it has also been used for courts martial, Army entrance examinations and even concerts, and it was

211

there that the body of the Duke of Wellington lay in state before being interred in St Paul's Cathedral. It is an impressive room, with a huge mural painting at the far end over the dais showing its founder, Charles II, on horseback, and the usual seventeenth-century charade of gods and goddesses strongly approving his action in founding the Royal Military Hospital. It was begun by Antonio Verrio, who came to England in 1671 and was appointed Chief and First Painter to the King in 1684, having worked at Hampton Court, Windsor Castle and Whitehall Palace. It seems likely, however, that the mural at Chelsea was completed by an English painter, Henry Cooke. There is also a selection of royal portraits by various painters, but the portrait which probably attracts the most attention is that of an in-pensioner named William Hiseland, who married for the third time at the age of 100 and eventually died at the age of 112. He is shown in full uniform, with a cocked hat and a drawn sword.

The chapel is on the opposite side of the Octagon Porch and, as in most college chapels, the pews face each other across the central aisle. Here there are more trophies and flags on display. The reredos is comparatively restrained with some carving by William Emmett, Master Carver before he was replaced by Grinling Gibbons, and some by Gibbons himself. The painting on the apse is somewhat later and was painted by Sebastiano Ricci, who was in England in 1712 with his nephew, another Venetian artist, competing, unsuccessfully, for the commission to paint the inside of the inner dome of St Paul's.

The hospital possesses some superb seventeenth-century altar plate and a very fine modern altar cross by Leslie Durban, one of the best of the twentieth-century silversmiths. The chapel was consecrated in August 1691, and today the pensioners parade for church in the Figure Court (near the statue of Charles II in his Roman attire) at 10.50 a.m., when visitors are welcome to join in the service.

Only the eastern part of Light Horse Court, which was added by Wren in 1687–88, now survives, and the court was laid out in its present form by Sir John Soane in 1819. Before that it was a plain gravelled courtyard, and the wrought iron cage and lamp-post in the centre formerly protected a well from which the horses used to be watered. The Infirmary Court is the counterpart of the Light Horse Court on the west of the Figure Court; only the central part of the north and south wings are by Wren, and these were added in 1687–88. Some of the remainder of the buildings of the hospital are eighteenth-century work, and other parts are mostly modern.

Unlike the designer of the *Hôtel des Invalides* in Paris, Wren had great consideration for the well-being of the inmates of his military hospital and arranged that the living quarters in the wings of Figure Court should be open to the light and air, with windows lighting the main corridors, off which were built series of private cubicles. It says much for Wren's intuitive understanding that as early as the late seventeenth century, he rejected the idea of an all-pervasive institution and divided his building in such a way that although eating was more conveniently catered for in the dining hall and worship was communal, he allowed for each individual to have a little place

Marlborough House
Chapel by Inigo Jones

he could call his own. Thus, although this is an institution housing about 400 old people, it retains a humanity and an intimacy so often lacking in more recent buildings designed for the same purpose. It could well be that the very extensive use of a warm red brick adds to the domestic feeling of the whole complex. It was the first time that Wren had used brick quite so extensively, but he used it with great sensitivity, and the general effect of this beautiful building was admirably summed up by Thomas Carlyle, the Scots writer who spent a great deal of his life in Chelsea in Cheyne Row. Of the Royal Military Hospital, he wrote:

> I had passed daily for many years without thinking much about it, and one day I began to reflect that it had always been a pleasure to me to see it, and I looked more attentively and saw that it was quiet and dignified and the work of a gentleman.

From Sloane Square it is a very short ride to St James's Park underground station to what is the next important seventeenth-century building – Marlborough House. Access to this is not always possible, for it is also used as the Commonwealth Information Centre and can only be visited if conferences are not in session, and by special written arrangement with the Administration Officer. To reach it from St James's Park underground one must cross St James's Park northwards from Birdcage Walk, over the little bridge which spans the lake to Marlborough Road, past the Queen's Chapel and St James's Palace to Pall Mall.

Marlborough House, built by Wren while Vanbrugh was at work on Blenheim Palace, was completed in two years, 1709–11. A charming red-brick house, it was enlarged by Sir William Chambers in 1771, and added to still further in the nineteenth century when it was the home of the Prince of Wales (later Edward VII). Despite a great deal of internal rearrangement one can still see some of the mural paintings by Louis Laguerre of the Battle of Blenheim, as well as others by the same artist of Marlborough's victories at Ramillies and Malplaquet.

The mention of two more buildings by Wren and his contemporaries will bring the seventeenth century to a close and lead almost imperceptibly into eighteenth-century London. The first of these, Hampton Court Palace, is about twenty miles from the City as the crow flies and so will not be described in detail here, but it is well worth a visit. Almost the whole of the eastern half of the Tudor palace, commissioned by Wolsey and offered as a gift to Henry VIII, was entirely reconstructed by Wren in the seventeenth century and it represents some of his best work.

The second of the buildings was also once a palace, but it was later entirely rebuilt to become first the Naval Hospital, then the Royal Naval College at Greenwich. In the seventeenth century, the journey by boat from Westminster Bridge down river to Greenwich – whether by royal barge or waterman's skiff – would have been on a river which was broader and shallower than the Thames today. Great stretches on the Lambeth side would have been little more than water-meadows, and London Bridge was the only bridge to span the river east of Kingston upon Thames. At that time it had many narrow arches and the tide racing through the constricted channels was so dangerous that many passengers preferred to disembark, to walk round, and then to board the boat again when London Bridge had been passed. The journey by boat to Greenwich today is particularly recommended because although much has changed since the seventeenth century, it is the only way to appreciate fully the splendid panorama with which the journey ends. Although some mention will be made of the many exciting buildings of all periods to be seen during this journey, the emphasis will still be on the seventeenth century.

It is convenient to divide the journey into seven sections, the length of each section being determined by the distances between the bridges which now span the Thames. As the river sometimes follows an east-west course rather than a north-south course, it is occasionally more appropriate to refer to the banks of the river as the left and the right, the left being as the boat travels downstream from Westminster to Greenwich.

Immediately north of Westminster Bridge on the left is the Ministry of Defence, which must be one of the ugliest buildings in this gracious part of London. In the vaults beneath it are Henry VIII's wine cellars, which can still be visited by written application to the Department of the Environment. The eagle with outspread wings tops a memorial to the Royal Air Force and is clearly visible from the river; in front of this is Whitehall Stairs, the site where seventeenth-century travellers would have embarked.

A tall, many-spired building behind the green lawns and trees of the Victoria Embankment Gardens houses a whole succession of clubs. On the right-hand side of the river is County Hall, the headquarters of the Greater London Council, and a little further down, a new complex which includes Shell Centre, with its viewing tower 317 feet high above the river.

On the left, the wide area of the Embankment Gardens shows how much of the original river was taken when the Embankment was built in the middle of the last century, and although it is not visible from the river, the York Water Gate at the bottom of Buckingham Street, built in 1626, was only a short distance from the house where Pepys lived from 1679–88, and was probably used by him when he took a boat to his Admiralty office in Seething Lane or to the shipyards at Greenwich. A prominent landmark on the Embankment which would have been unknown to Pepys is Cleopatra's Needle, an Egyptian obelisk which was taken there and eventually erected in its present position in 1878. To the rear, high above the Embankment gardens, is Shell-Mex House, with the largest clock-face in London – a craggy modern building of the 'modernistic' era between the wars, built on the site of Cecil House, the town residence of Lord Salisbury. Beside it is the Savoy Hotel, one of London's most famous hotels, and Savoy Hill where the famous BBC studios of the days of 2-LO used to be housed.

The right-hand bank, known quite properly at this part of the river as the South Bank, is a remarkable example of what can be done with a derelict and run-down area if there is the will and the inspiration to make it work. The Royal Festival Hall is the one permanent building from the famous Festival of Britain of 1951, and it was the beginning of a quite remarkable transformation of a dreadful area. Those who can remember this area after the last war must surely rejoice at its condition now, especially since the addition of such buildings as the Queen Elizabeth Hall and the Hayward Gallery. The National Theatre is the latest building in this complex and will be described later in detail – for many, it constitutes the best contribution made to London's life in the twentieth century. Waterloo Bridge is also modern, having been built in 1945 by Sir Giles Gilbert Scott to replace the much earlier bridge of 1811–17.

On the left bank of the river (now the north bank), there is a much older building, Somerset House, an eighteenth-century design by Sir William Chambers erected on the site of the house of the Protector, Edward Seymour, Duke of Somerset, who was executed in the Tower of London in 1552. The present building has bold semicircular archways which used to be right by the water's edge, and one can still see the metal rings by which boats were tethered. Joined to Somerset House further downstream is King's College, a somewhat later addition to the whole very dignified façade. On the river at this point there are four ships – H.M.S. *Discovery*, H.Q. *Wellington* (the headquarters of the Honourable Company of Master Mariners), H.M.S. *Chrysanthemum* and H.M.S. *President*. The *Discovery* was the ship used by Captain Falcon Scott for his first expedition to the Antarctic, and it is possible to go on board and to see his cabin. H.M.S. *Chrysanthemum* and H.M.S. *President* are both training ships belonging to the Royal Navy's London Division of the Royal Naval Reserve. Behind the ships, beyond the Embankment, the quiet gardens with flowering shrubs have a sinister history, for in the seventeenth century, owing to some unrepealed right of sanctuary left over from the Middle Ages, they were the refuge of every criminal of both sexes and were called 'Alsatia'. The Temple is a little further downstream, and the Temple Gardens lie just across the road which forms the Embankment.

The right bank of the river has at present little to offer, for it is in scarcely better condition than the South Bank was before the rebuilding programme transformed the area. Blackfriars Bridge is the widest bridge over the river – an iron and stone structure with some remarkable Victorian decoration which can just be seen as the boat glides beneath. Just beside the bridge on the left bank, an iron pipe marks the exit of the River Fleet which was once part of a fine harbour, built by Wren; the harbour fell on evil days and the river was eventually confined into a conduit and disappeared from view. Farringdon Street now covers the route that the Fleet used to take.

Between Blackfriars Bridge and Southwark Bridge stand some of the most beautiful of all London's seventeenth-century buildings, even if they can only be glimpsed from time to time between some of the more modern buildings. Puddle Dock, in the shadow of Blackfriars Bridge, was once the harbour for Baynard's Castle which was destroyed in the great fire of 1666. The site is now partly occupied by the Mermaid Theatre, although there are still a number of buildings in course of construction and roads being widened, giving the area a somewhat chaotic appearance at the time of writing. Behind the more recent buildings there are still tantalising glimpses of the little Wren church of St Benet, the glorious dome of St Paul's or the spire and tower of St Nicholas Cole Abbey, but it is difficult to be certain of seeing many of Wren's spires, some of which appear only momentarily between the tall modern office blocks as the boat glides past.

The right bank has little to offer on this stretch of the river. One is very conscious of the huge mass of the South Bank power station, which dwarfs every building in the area. A little further downstream there are a couple of interesting houses – one is the Provost's house, the other, somewhat earlier in date, by Cardinal Cap Alley, is a seventeenth-century house in which it is alleged that Sir Christopher Wren lived while building St Paul's. This part of Bankside is in a dreadful state of neglect, although it has partly been improved by the temporary theatre and museum opened there by Sam Wanamaker, next to Bear Gardens. The next turning is Rose Alley, named after the Rose theatre opened there in 1587. The whole area is badly in need of the kind of enterprise which could revive and transform it into something like the South Bank-complex. The Bear Garden Museum has shown that given the money and the will, it could again become the centre of entertainment it once was. The range of entertainment need not of course be so wide – nobody would welcome the reintroduction of the baiting of the bulls and bears which suffered such agonising deaths there in the seventeenth century.

Few of the halls of the City Companies are visible from the river, but it is just possible to glimpse the one belonging to the Vintners on the north bank, shortly before the boat passes under Southwark Bridge. From Southwark Bridge to London Bridge, there is little of note on the south bank other than The Anchor, a charming little inn with a garden tucked away beside the railway bridge linking Cannon Street station to London Bridge and Waterloo. The date of the building is open to question, as is the somewhat extravagant claim that it was once patronised by Shakespeare, but it is generally agreed that the date of the present building is probably early eighteenth century. A plaque of Barclay Perkins Brewery on the wall beside it records that the famous Elizabethan theatre, the Globe, was opened on this site in 1599.

On the north bank most of the landmarks on Upper Thames Street are concealed by modern buildings, but on the riverside one can still see Old Swan Pier, a much altered jetty which was once an important part of the medieval waterfront. There is little hope of identifying such important Wren churches at St James Garlickhythe or St Michael Paternoster Royal, both on Upper Thames Street, but just before passing under the new London Bridge, Fishmongers Hall becomes clearly visible. This clear-cut classical building was built in 1834 by Henry Roberts, an architect whose pupil was the much more famous George Gilbert Scott, but the bombing of the Second World War inflicted severe damage on the original building and extensive restoration was carried out most successfully after the war by Mr Austen Hall. The only building of outstanding merit at this point on the south bank is Southwark Cathedral which, despite its awkward position below the approaches to the new London Bridge, is still a noble Gothic church and holds its place on the skyline of this part of London.

Once under London Bridge there is a great deal to be enjoyed, especially on the left-hand side, the north bank of the river. Immediately east of the bridge is the church of St Magnus the Martyr, one of Wren's outstanding buildings, and behind that, up Fish Street Hill, appears the gilded top of the Monument. To the east of St Magnus the Martyr is Billingsgate fish market, one of London's oldest and best-known markets, now entirely devoted to the sale and distribution of fish, but originally a general produce market. Next to Billingsgate is the Custom House, which was built after the one designed by Sir Christopher Wren had been burned down. The central part visible from the river was built by Sir Robert Smirke, the more famous of a pair of architect brothers, who added this section to the earlier part by D. Laing (1812–17) in 1825. It is an impressive façade, after which there is little else to see until one reaches the Tower of London.

The Upper Pool of London was at one time one of the busiest parts of London's river but is now almost deserted of shipping, and the cranes and the derricks on the south side stand virtually still. Hay's Wharf, which was once a textbook example of the brave new modern architecture of the 1930s, is almost as run down as its companions. The anchoring of the 11,500-ton cruiser, H.M.S. *Belfast*, just off the south shore has provided some interest to this part of London and it attracts a great many visitors, but Tilbury now handles the traffic which used to make it so exciting, and a new role must be thought out if it is not to deteriorate still further.

There is no need to enter into further detail about the splendours of the Tower of London, except perhaps to point out Traitor's Gate, labelled and clearly visible from the river, and the remarkable bridge ahead, Tower Bridge, will be described more fully in a later chapter. It is indeed a notable Victorian engineering feat, with its bascules each weighing 1100 tons, but it may be a very long time before a ship sufficiently large to oblige them to be raised finds its way to this part of the river. Once under Tower Bridge, the boat enters the Pool of London proper, and on the left-hand side there is a most delightful and enterprising redesigning of an obsolete part of the waterway. This is the redevelopment of St Katharine's Dock, which has now become a lively and exciting rendezvous for people who like boats of any kind, and a museum preserving many types of craft which might otherwise have been destroyed. A new life now flows through the whole area, and it is the north bank's answer to the challenge of the South Bank scheme. One has by now reached the heart of London's dockland area; the north bank is occupied by Wapping, with Wapping High Street following the bank of the river like a giant towpath, and Rotherhithe Street following the shape of the land on the right-hand side. The river takes a southward curve at this point, so that left side and right side are essential directions in this section of the journey. The Thames Tunnel, which links Wapping on the left with Rotherhithe on the right, was begun in 1825 by Marcel Brunel, but it took many years and cost many lives before it was opened to traffic in 1843. It is now used by the underground. A tall Victorian wharf, Oliver's Wharf, on the left side still looks very much like a wharf, but it has in fact been very skilfully converted into flats. A little further downstream on the site of the old Morocco Wharf there is now a repair yard for the launches of the Thames river police – a modern boatyard in which glass reinforced plastic has been used extensively such that the building tends to stand out among the earlier buildings in this area. A little further on is an ancient inn called The Town of Ramsgate (the fishermen from Ramsgate used to land their catches there at one time, thereby bypassing Billingsgate), and then Wapping Old Stairs – no longer the haunt of smugglers, crimps out to shanghai seamen, or pressgangs eager to recruit, forcibly, men for the navy of Samuel Pepys and his royal master. Nearby there is a warehouse painted with a huge letter 'E' for Execution: this is Execution Dock where felons were hanged, the bodies being left on the gibbet until three tides had passed over them. The oldest riverside inn in London is in Wapping: The Prospect of Whitby at the east end of Wapping Wall, now beautifully restored and a popular resort for visitors to London. The origin of the name is lost – one explanation is that a ship from the Yorkshire town used to anchor at the quay, but there does not seem to be any substantial evidence for the explanation and the inn is so old that nobody really knows.

The patch of grass and trees which seems so conspicuous in this built-up area is the King Edward Memorial Park; the area is one which was used extensively by various writers as settings for their novels, usually for the more sinister scenes. Shadwell was named after a medieval well dedicated to

St Chad, and Limehouse, which featured in so many lurid episodes as the Chinatown of Sax Rohmer's novels was so called because of the lime kilns which used to be a feature of this area. Charles Dickens knew the area well and used it as the setting for some of the scenes in *Our Mutual Friend*, although there is some doubt as to whether the seventeenth-century inn called The Bunch of Grapes which can be seen from the river is actually the original of The Six Jolly Fellowship Porters mentioned in that same novel.

Just before the river turns southwards, to the left-hand side is the entrance to the Grand Union Canal, for many people the place from which to start a memorable holiday by barge or longboat along the inland waterways of England. It is sometimes possible to see the characteristically craggy pair of towers of the church of St Anne, Limehouse, built early in the eighteenth century by Nicholas Hawksmoor, Wren's assistant. The river turns southwards at the picturesquely named Cuckold's Point which, according to an old legend, owes its name to a disreputable incident involving King John. It then flows through areas entirely devoted to docks and to shipping. The right-hand side (the Surrey side) is covered by the Surrey commercial docks and its many subsidiary docks and wharves, while the left-hand side houses the India and Milwall docks. It was from the Millwall docks that Isambard Brunel launched his enormous ship, the *Great Eastern*, and the side of the dock wall has marks painted on it, visible from the river, showing the ship's great length of 680 feet. On the right-hand side of the river at Deptford can be seen a splendid Baroque tower of St Paul's, Deptford, built by the architect, Thomas Archer, between 1712–30. This is an historic area of docks and wharves, for the Royal Naval victualling yards at Deptford are on the site of some of the earliest shipyards in the history of England. Henry VIII had his fleet fitted out there, and it is also the place where Sir Francis Drake was knighted by his grateful queen on 4 April 1581 after his voyage round the world. It was at Deptford that the Tsar, Peter the Great of Russia, learned about shipbuilding, but the earliest buildings to be seen there now date from the eighteenth century. As the boat swings round the curve of the Isle of Dogs on the left, the whole magnificent panorama of Greenwich comes into view – the hill of Greenwich Park crowned by Wren's observatory, and the water-meadows below wearing the Queen's House and the Naval Hospital like an architectural necklace. To the right of Greenwich Pier can be seen the masts of the *Cutty Sark*, a tea-clipper now in permanent dry dock, while beside it, looking absurdly tiny and fragile, lies another gallant little ship, *Gypsy Moth IV*, in which Sir Francis Chichester sailed round the world single-handed.

Before actually visiting the noble collection of buildings at Greenwich, it is rather pleasant to cross the river to the Isle of Dogs and survey the whole scene. This entails walking *under* the river, entering the little domed structure near the *Cutty Sark*, descending in a lift, walking through a tiled tunnel and finally emerging on the Isle of Dogs in a little park facing Greenwich Park, the Naval Hospital, the Queen's House, and the observatory on One Tree Hill. The Isle of Dogs seems to have received its

name because the Royal Kennels housing the hunting dogs were situated there as early as the reign of Henry VIII, who used to hunt over Greenwich Park and Blackheath when staying at the old Palace of Placentia.

Back on the south bank of the river, the first building to visit is the Queen's House, or the 'House of Delight', which Inigo Jones built as a hunting lodge for Anne of Denmark, who in fact died before she could use it. It stands on the same central axis as Wren's Naval Hospital, although Wren originally thought it too small a building to occupy such a position, and would have concealed it behind a central domed building had he not been prevented from doing so. It is deceptively simple – a trim box with a severe roofline; the colonnades on either side were not part of the original plan, but were added much later to commemorate the Battle of Trafalgar in 1805. The building was originally planned in the shape of the capital letter 'H', the crossbar of the letter running north–south, forming a bridge spanning the main road, and the long strokes of the letter, running east–west, more or less parallel with the river at this point. The side facing the river has a little double stairway by which to ascend to the main entrance on the terrace; there is also a squat little doorway in the centre below the terrace by which to enter the unimportant ground floor. The central section of the facade projects very slightly, but sufficiently far forward to emphasise the symmetry of the flanking sections, and a simple balustrade conceals the low roofline, broken only by four exactly placed chimneys, two at either end. The building is of brick, now entirely covered with stucco, but it is thought that when it was first built its upper part was left plain brick. The central

window has a semicircular head and a little dummy balcony below, deliberately breaking the pattern of the other twelve windows and the door, all of which have square-headed openings. The windows would originally have been mullioned, but sash windows were inserted later.

The side facing the park is very different for there is no stairway on this side, but an elegant loggia on the second floor, overlooking the park. The central section breaks forward ever so slightly and each of the upper windows flanking it has a dummy balustrade, echoing the practical balustrade of the loggia. The opening of the loggia has two pairs of slender Ionic columns, but the central space between them is very slightly wider than the spaces between the pairs of columns, thus again there is an emphasis on the central axis and an insistence on symmetry. Entry to the Queen's House is now through a later building on Park Row, linked to it by the eastern colonnade; this entails passing under a later bridge which was made by John Webb after the death of Inigo Jones to support a new room above, and finding a small and rather insignificant doorway on the right, under Jones's original bridge. The large stones forming the road after the descent from the colonnade are the ones which formed the original seventeenth-century highway.

The humble little door by which visitors enter the Queen's House in no way prepares them for the magnificence of the main hall – a perfect 40-foot cube. It is a light airy room, scantily furnished, with a symmetrical pattern on the floor complementing the panelling of the ceiling where paintings of the period have been placed. The smaller, minor rooms leading off the main hall are now used to display paintings and furniture, mostly of the seventeenth century or earlier, and they form an intimate setting for some of the fine paintings which belong to the Maritime Museum. The main access to the upper floors is by a singularly beautiful spiral staircase in the south-eastern corner of the main room; the decorative motif on the wrought iron stair rail is a curved tulip, and the staircase is therefore known as the Tulip Staircase and is one of the most delightful features of the Queen's House. The balustrade is supported by classical consoles (or brackets). From the upper balustrade there is a passage over the central bridge to the loggia, which commands a fine view of Greenwich Park and the observatory, but this is not now normally open to the public for security reasons.

From the Queen's House it is a stiffish climb up a winding path to the observatory built in 1675 in place of Duke Humphrey's tower in the Tower of London for Flamsteed, the Astronomer Royal. From this observatory, with its meridian set in the grounds, all the longitudes are calculated, and although the present Royal Observatory was moved to Herstmonceux in Sussex in 1950 because of the pollution of the atmosphere, the neat red brick and stone building with its central octagonal room is still very much an attraction, for it is now beautifully fitted as a museum and exhibits an extraordinary range of astronomical instruments from some of the very earliest to some of the more recent aids to the study of the stars. It is very interesting to read Wren's own assessment of what he thought might happen after he had built this observatory. 'A time would come', he declared, 'when men would be able to stretch out their eyes and extend them to fifty feet in length, by which means they should be able to discover ten thousand times as many stars as we can . . . and find the galaxy to be myriads of them, and every nebulous star appearing as if it were the firmament of some other world . . . buried in the vast abyss of intermundious vacuum.' The vision of this extraordinary seventeenth-century prophet and architect has since been confirmed by the radio telescope.

One conspicuous feature on the outside of the observatory is a bright orange ball, about five feet in diameter, which is hauled to the top of the mast at five minutes to one and then allowed to slide down at precisely one o'clock. Before the invention of a more precise means of registering Greenwich Mean Time for navigational purposes, every ship on the river would have had a spyglass focused on this ball in order to set right their own chronometers, and although this is no longer necessary, the ceremony is still performed every day to the delight of visitors.

From the top of the hill on which the observatory stands, it is possible to see the whole layout of the area below. In the centre stands the Queen's House, with its later colonnades on either side connecting it to the two wings of the Maritime Museum. Beyond that towards the river is the Royal Naval College, a building originally designed by Wren as the Royal Naval Hospital.

Of the Maritime Museum there is much which should be written – it deserves a chapter to itself. It is one of the finest museums in Europe and contains a magnificent series of paintings and portraits connected with the great naval history of these islands, as well as a unique collection of models of ships of many periods. It should be emphasised that every model was made *at the time when the ship was being commissioned*, and many of them are the shipwrights' models which were placed before the Admiralty for their consideration before the ship could be built. No matter how accurately or beautifully a modern man might make a model of an eighteenth-century ship, it would be rejected by the Museum, and the only exception to this rule are working models of engagements at sea during the last war. The museum cannot be too highly praised for its contents and for the way in which they are displayed.

The Royal Naval Hospital as Wren designed it consists of four blocks of buildings, although the one at the far north-western corner, known as King Charles's Block, was actually built by John Webb as the beginning of a new palace for Charles II. The building was never to be completed as a palace, and in the year of her death, 1694, Queen Mary made arrangements to have it converted into a hospital for superannuated or disabled seamen of her navy. The south-east wing was erected by Sir Christopher Wren from 1699 until 1716 when he resigned as Surveyor, the work being carried on by Sir John Vanbrugh, assisted by Nicholas Hawksmoor. This is now known as Queen Mary's Block. King William's Block, the corresponding wing to the west, containing the famous Painted Hall, was the work of Wren 1698–1716, with additional work by Sir John Vanbrugh. The last wing, in the north-eastern corner, is Queen Anne's Block and was largely the work of Nicholas

King Charles's Block

Hawksmoor. All the architects who worked at various times on this complex of buildings would, of course, have been aware of the overall design by Wren, even if they occasionally varied details to suit themselves. The blocks are all approximately the same size, although those nearest the river – King Charles's Block and Queen Anne's Block – are very slightly narrower and more widely spaced, so that the space between the remaining blocks form a tighter avenue along which to view the Queen's House in the distance. The first two blocks have neither that marvellous colonnade nor the domes which are such a feature of the Queen Mary and King William Blocks.

Queen Mary's Block contains the chapel, of which only the outside is Wren's work, for the interior was gutted by fire towards the end of the eighteenth century and was rebuilt by James ('Athenian') Stuart from 1779–89. It is an impressive interior with a large painting behind the altar by the eighteenth-century American artist, Benjamin West, of St Paul, shipwrecked on Malta. There is a most elegant restrained pulpit, a well proportioned cylindrical shape mounted on columns of the Corinthian order of architecture. James Stuart was one of the few eighteenth-century architects who visited Greece and made a detailed study of the classical architecture there (hence his nickname 'Athenian' Stuart), so that the feeling of the chapel is more Grecian than Roman.

The Painted Hall on the opposite side of the hospital occupies a similar position to that of the chapel. This also has a large lofty vestibule with *trompe l'œil* sculpture, and a large plaque on the right which records donations of various sizes by benefactors of the Naval Hospital. The Painted Hall, now the dining hall of the Royal Naval College, over 100 feet long, about 50 feet high and 50 feet wide, is a most impressive room, and the *trompe l'œil* paintings by Sir James Thornhill are probably the finest ever executed by the artist; whereas his painting in the dome of St Paul's Cathedral is carried out in monochrome, the ceiling here is full in colour and exuberant in design. Thornhill employed an almost monochromatic scheme for the painting of the walls and for the side of the great arch which pierces the main wall of the dining-room, and beyond this there is a secluded chamber reserved for the dining tables of the senior officers, which has its own mural in full colour.

A series of tall majestic windows occupies most of the wall space on either side of the dining hall, and Thornhill has availed himself of the cross lighting from these in such a way that the highlights and cast shadows of the sculpture and mouldings in the window recesses and walls give the impression that they are actually decorated in high relief. The whole scheme is in fact a brilliantly executed optical illusion. In the same way, the painted pilasters and carvings with which the top and the sides of the central arch are decorated are mixed so skilfully with real sculpture and real mouldings that it is difficult to tell the real from the painted illusion.

For the monochromatic paintings on the walls, the artist was paid at the rate of £1 per yard, but he received three times as much for the elaborately

The Painted Hall, decorated with *trompe l'oeil* paintings by Sir James Thornhill

decorated ceiling. The huge central panel is undoubtedly his masterpiece – a *trompe l'œil* work of great imaginative power: the effect is such that the roof of the building looks as though it has been slid back to reveal the heavens above, with a host of deities circling with admiration round William and Mary. It is an elaborate charade, a grand diplomatic gesture with flattering allusions to the patronage of the arts and sciences by a munificent and enlightened monarchy. It is the finest example of a baroque decoration in the Grand Manner in these islands and Sir James Thornhill spent about eighteen or nineteen years carrying it out. Another allegorical composition by the same artist covers the wall at the far end behind the archway – the newly completed St Paul's Cathedral is a major feature in the background, and a self-portrait of the artist in a full-bottomed wig and wide skirted coat is represented in the foreground.

There is a great deal more of seventeenth-century London to be seen in this area, both to the east and the west of the main Naval Hospital. Many of the buildings eastwards are either later alterations to seventeenth-century buildings, or built on seventeenth-century sites. On Crane Street, almost on the river, there are two taverns – Trafalgar Tavern, the present built in 1837, and The Yacht, both at one time famous for their whitebait dinners which were a feature of a river trip to Greenwich from the City. Still further east, almost next to the power station, is Trinity Hospital, more visible from the river than from the landward side. Formerly founded by the Earl of Northampton in 1613 as an almshouse for 'twenty old and decayed housekeepers, twelve of whom are to be chosen for Greenwich, the rest alternately from two parishes in Norfolk', it is still used as almshouses, but very little seventeenth-century work is to be seen. The best place in which to see buildings contemporary with the Naval Hospital is on the far side of the power station – Ballast Quay, reached by going eastwards along Old Woolwich Road and then turning left down Lassell Street and along the quay, past the nineteenth-century Cutty Sark tavern. The terrace of seventeenth-century houses on Ballast Quay has been altered somewhat, particularly in the eighteenth century. To the west of the Naval Hospital many of the buildings are a great deal later, and the *Cutty Sark*, magnificent as it is, was not built until 1869 when steam was already threatening the supremacy of the sailing vessel. Nevertheless, she was the fastest tea clipper on the high seas, and no one should go to Greenwich and fail to go on board. Below decks the whole ship has been arranged in such a way that the visitor has the impression that she might still be in service. The figure-head of the *Cutty Sark* is a carved effigy of a woman wearing a chemise, for it was a 'cutty sark' or chemise worn by the witch in 'Tam o' Shanter' by Robert Burns which gave the name to this tea clipper. The ship actually carried bales of wool from Australia as well as tea. There is a superb collection of figure-heads on permanent exhibition. *Gypsy Moth IV*, weighing only 11 tons and measuring 53 feet long, is tiny by comparison, but it is fitting that she should be laid up alongside the *Cutty Sark*.

West of the Dreadnought Seaman's Hospital is the church of St Alfege,

St Alfege, Greenwich

beautifully restored after having suffered heavy bomb damage during the St Alfege, Greenwich
Second World War. It was the work of Nicholas Hawksmoor and a minor
architect, John James (who completed the western towers of Westminster
Abbey), and it is still not clear which parts of this church were which
architect, although it seems likely that Hawksmoor was responsible for the
overall design, and James for the tower. The church registers go back to the
early seventeenth century and can be seen on request, but the fine
seventeenth-century fittings with carvings by Grinling Gibbons no longer
exist. St Alfege's Church was one of fifty new churches planned by Queen
Anne early in the eighteenth century, but only a fraction of that number
were actually built.

St Alfege's Church (where the great General Wolfe, victor at Quebec, lies
buried) is near to Croom's Hill, a steep road which forms the western
boundary of Greenwich Park and which contains a number of fine private
houses, some of them of the seventeenth century. Some small, rather
humble seventeenth-century houses are to be found at the bottom of
Croom's Hill with their backs to the park, with somewhat grander
eighteenth-century houses facing them. Further up the hill, just past
George Street, lying well back from the road on the right is The Grange, a
seventeenth-century house with eighteenth-century additions, with a little
gazebo, dated 1672, near to the road. A little further up the hill by a church is
a notable seventeenth-century house, The Presbytery, built about 1630 with
to large gables and dormer windows. Its neighbour on the other side of the

227

The Ranger's House,
Greenwich Park

church, The Manor or Manor House, although somewhat later retains much of the seventeenth-century appearance, despite the hooded porch which one associates with the reign of Queen Anne. Still further on is the house of the Earl of Chesterfield, which is now known as the Ranger's House and is open to the public all the year round. An early eighteenth-century house, it was extended by the 4th Earl of Chesterfield later in the century and is now used as a centre for art exhibitions. There is usually a permanent show of seventeenth-century portraits as well. The outside façade is beautifully balanced, but a hideous chimney to a boiler-house to the rear unfortunately ruins the whole appearance. There are remnants of more seventeenth-century buildings in the area, for John Evelyn describes how he went to visit a new tavern and bowling green opened by Snape, the king's farrier, in May 1683, and Macartney House, now a set of private apartments, is believed to have been part of an area of speculative building by the same sergeant farrier. Far more impressive is the mansion on the other side of the park, on Maze Hill, the road which acts as the eastern boundary of the park. This is Vanbrugh Castle, built by Sir John Vanbrugh shortly after he succeeded Wren as Surveyor in 1715. It is an extraordinary building – a mock castle in brick, with turrets and battlements and all the trappings of an eighteenth-century 'Gothick' folly. Vanbrugh actually lived there and had a fine library with windows looking out on to the Naval Hospital on which he was working at the time. For a time it was used as the RAF orphanage, but has now been converted into private apartments.

Crossing the park from west to east, it is quite apparent that the great central Blackheath Avenue with its rows of fine sweet chestnut trees was carefully and consciously designed, somewhat in the French manner, in the

reign of Charles II; from the air, the pattern of planting is far more formal than one would guess from ground level.

Vanbrugh Castle

There is only one more seventeenth-century building of importance in this area – Charlton House, about a mile or so to the east of the Queen's House, now owned by the Greenwich Borough Council and used as municipal offices. Built about 1607–12, it is so typical of the Jacobean houses that it makes one realise what a revolutionary building the Queen's House must have seemed to the contemporaries of Inigo Jones, for they would have been familiar with the little pepper-pot domes to the towers, and the strange muddled decoration – half medieval, half German Renaissance – with which the central door of Charlton House is embellished. The Queen's House with its severely mathematical shapes and untroubled roofline must have seemed exceedingly 'modern' by comparison with the Elizabethan–Jacobean tradition of Charlton House. However, the architectural revolution started by Jones was stifled by the Civil War, and it was not until the eighteenth century that the classical tradition was to be given full rein.

6

Eighteenth-Century London

Any great city such as London is a living organism. As the years pass, parts of this organism become obsolete, die and are replaced by new forms. Other parts prove themselves capable of modification in the face of changing circumstances and thus survive, but in an altered form, while yet another area survives almost unchanged until it becomes jealously preserved as an integral part of London's history. The growth of seventeenth-century London, to which the genius of Sir Christopher Wren contributed so magnificently, merged almost imperceptibly into the London of the eighteenth century – the London of William Hogarth, for one cannot think of the London of the first half of the eighteenth century without thinking of the engravings and paintings of that remarkable cockney artist. Seventeenth-century London belonged to the diarists, Samuel Pepys and John Evelyn, but they recorded their London in private journals which were not published until long after they were dead. Hogarth's London on the other hand was recorded by the artist and published in his own lifetime, and its follies and brutalities, its injustices and its stupidities thrust under the very noses of the Londoners as they went about the City.

William Hogarth was born in 1697 and he was baptised in the Norman church of St Bartholomew the Great in Smithfield at the very font which is still in use today. When he was ten or eleven years of age, he saw his father held for debt in the notorious Fleet Prison – a traumatic experience of the darker side of eighteenth-century London which was to have a profound effect on the stunted little boy. From the time when he emerged from his apprenticeship to Ellis Gamble, the engraver who had his workshop off Leicester Fields, until his death in 1764, Hogarth portrayed contemporary life in London with such a passionate sincerity and feeling that it not only colours our own vision of this period of London's history, but undoubtedly moved many of his fellow Londoners deeply, and stressed the urgent need for humanitarian reforms at that time. Hogarth's paintings and engravings are certainly a salutary antidote to the sickly sentimentality of the popular image of the London poor as seen in engravings of the street hawkers made from Francis Wheatley's paintings. They also contrast with the paintings of the refined patrons who thronged to the 'sitting-room' of Sir Joshua Reynolds – 'women who wished to be transmitted as angels, and with men who wished to appear as heroes and philosophers' – and were rarely disappointed when the portraits by Reynolds were hanging on the walls of their fine country homes.

opposite, The Egyptian Hall in the Mansion House

London had been spreading westwards since the middle of the seventeenth century, but after the great fire, many refugees who had sought temporary accommodation elsewhere – particularly in the areas north of London Wall – decided to settle there. The drift to the east was less pronounced, although little ribbons of houses began to appear on the Mile End Road as White Chapel (now Whitechapel) expanded, and along the Ratcliffe Highway towards Shadwell. By the first quarter of the eighteenth century there must have been a marked increase in the population of this area to justify the erection of St George's-in-the-East, Christ Church, Spitalfields, and St Anne's, Limehouse, three major parish churches erected by Nicholas Hawksmoor by 1725.

Nevertheless, Henry Chamberlain's map of 1769 shows huge tracts of open country between Shadwell and Mile End Road, with Bethnal Green little more than a country hamlet, and two large marshy fields just north of Wapping which were much later dug out to form the London Docks, the actual shape and dimensions of the fields corresponding exactly to the shape of the dock basins of Western Dock, East Dock, and Shadwell Basin.

Bishopsgate extended still further north to join Shoreditch, to enclose the almshouses of Sir Robert Geffrye, Bart., which must have been in a rural area when they were built in the first decade of the eighteenth century. This elegant and charming group, with a full-length statue of the benefactor, wearing a full-bottomed wig and holding his sword of office as Lord Mayor and Master of the Ironmongers Company, positioned in a niche over the centre doorway, lies back behind trees on the eastern side of Kingsland Road. It was built in 1714–15, but in 1914 it became the Geffrye Museum, a craft museum for all the furniture trades centred on Shoreditch. It later developed into one of the finest museums for children in the country and perhaps in Europe, its principal aim being to help children enjoy their visits to museums by ensuring that they participate actively in the exhibitions. The almshouse buildings have been skilfully adapted to their new role. The chapel has been converted and there is now a central hallway, reading room and library. The original cubicles have been turned into small period rooms tracing the evolution of domestic interior design from the Tudor period to the twentieth century, and the larger halls in the wings are now used as studio workshops for the children, and as rooms for art exhibitions and demonstrations.

When the original inhabitants of the almshouses were moved out to more congenial surroundings in the Kentish countryside, they took the statue of the founder with them, so that the one which is now to be seen over the central doorway is in fact a copy. The appearance of the buildings from the outside otherwise remains unchanged and is typical of the sober and dignified architecture of the opening years of the eighteenth century.

Good examples of eighteenth-century architecture are not easy to find in the areas which lie to the east of Bishopsgate and Kingsland Road, and the visitor will have to trudge through some sadly overbuilt and sometimes squalid streets to find them. Nevertheless, if one visits such areas as Whitechapel, Stepney Spitalfields and Bethnal Green, one can gain a much

The Geffrye Museum

better understanding of the richness and complexity of London.

Southwards from the Geffrye Museum, the first notable eighteenth-century building on Shoreditch High Street in St Leonard's Church, just south of the railway arch. This most elegant church, which stands on an island of grass and mature trees, was built by George Dance the Elder in 1740 on the site of a much earlier church which may well have been built shortly after the Norman Conquest. The 192-foot-high spire is placed over the west portico, like that of St Martin-in-the-Fields built by Dance's contemporary, James Gibbs, but it actually resembles much more closely the spire of St Mary Le Bow, Wren's graceful church on Cheapside. Dance the Elder also built St Botolph, Aldgate, but his best-known work is

St Leonard's Church, Shoreditch

undoubtedly the Mansion House, the residence of the Lord Mayor at the very heart of the City.

The interior of St Leonard's Church, Shoreditch, was probably inspired by Wren, and its beautifully maintained interior is far more light and airy than one might suspect from the drab red brick exterior and the darkened stone columns of the portico. The modern fluorescent lighting of the interior is so simple that the tubes do not jar on the appearance of this eighteenth-century church, but seem to harmonise with the Tuscan columns supporting the roof, and on sunlit days the church has a pearly classical quality that is very unexpected by anyone who has been trudging along the somewhat dilapidated Kingsland Road. The pulpit is well proportioned, the font a sturdy one of eighteenth-century design, and although the galleries which used to be on the side walls were removed in the middle of the nineteenth century, the one remaining at the west end which supports a fine organ with a carved case suggests that they must have been worthy of Shoreditch – the centre of the woodworking trade. The carved surround to the clock in the middle of the west gallery is of such superb workmanship that it must have been the work of one of the finest carvers in the whole area.

St Leonard's Church, however, is not known as the woodworkers' church, but as the actors' church, and a plaque on the north wall lists the actors who are known to have been buried in the churchyard. Erected by the London Shakespeare League in 1913, it mentions, among others, such famous theatrical figures as 'James Burbage (d. 1597) ... the head of Lord Leicester's Players, who in 1576 built in Shoreditch the first English Playhouse. This he called "the Theatre".' This first theatre was erected in Curtain Road*, a thoroughfare which runs parallel to Shoreditch High Street to the west. Also commemorated at St Leonard's Church are Cuthbert Burbage (d. 1636), the son of James Burbage, who following his father's profession built the famous Globe theatre in Southwark, and his brother, Richard (d. 1619), a great tragedian and the first to play the parts of Hamlet and Richard III. The court jester of Henry VIII, Will Somers, who died in 1569, also lies buried there, and Richard Tarlton, one of the Players of Queen Elizabeth I and the greatest comedian of his age. Not all players or actors were honoured by burial there – their reputation at times was little better than that of rogues and vagabonds, and many less fortunate than the Burbage family may have suffered punishment in the stocks or at the whipping-post now carefully preserved in the churchyard a little to the north of the main entrance. Even seen against the charming background of roses and other flowers, there is something very sinister about the heavy wooden struts and iron rings which held the unfortunate wretch while punishment was being inflicted.

The stocks and whipping-post in the churchyard at St Leonard's

John Wesley, 1703–91

From St Leonard's Church, it is best perhaps to cross the High Street – noting just outside the church a strangely isolated little house dated 1735 – and then turn westwards along Old Street. In the area of Hoxton (Hogsden Square – formerly Hogsden Fields, where Ben Jonson killed a player, Gabriel Spenser, in a duel – there are a few little Georgian houses. Walking still further westwards along Old Street, if one turns south down the City Road one comes to the house which belonged to John Wesley – a charming, unpretentious little house which the great preacher built for himself in 1777, just beside his chapel. The latter has been altered and restored considerably, but nothing has been done to spoil the sobriety and clarity of the interior, and many of the fittings are original.

Right opposite Wesley's chapel and his house is Bunhill ('Bone-hill') Fields burial ground, a tree-shaded haven of quiet, with little drifts of leaves softening the impact of the hard stones which mark the graves. There, in the cemetery reserved for Dissenters since the seventeenth century, lie Wesley's mother, Susannah; John Bunyan, the author of *Pilgrim's Progress* (interred in a newly erected sarcophagus in 1862, with a recumbent sculptured figure of the writer on the lid); William Blake, artist and mystic poet; and Daniel Defoe, best known for his *Robinson Crusoe*, but also for his imaginative (and imaginary) *A Journal of the Plague Year*.

A little to the south of the graveyard there is a very military building – a castellated and battlemented building which is somehow reminiscent of an enlarged toy fort. This is the City Road entrance to the premises and fields of the Honourable Artillery Company, and once inside the grounds, it is clear from the field guns and army vehicles that this is still a military establishment, even if one of great antiquity. Its foundation goes back to the reign of Henry VIII, and the Artillery Ground has been used in the past not only for proving weapons, but for training the men who used them. Indeed, so well trained were they during the seventeenth century that the army of Charles I suffered severe defeat at their hands when he attempted to take the City of London, and not even Prince Rupert's cavalry was able to dislodge them from their fortifications.

The central block is a fine eighteenth-century building of about 1735 with sculptures of exploding grenades or cannon-balls where one would expect to find classically shaped vases. The parade ground in front is bordered on one side by a fine row of mulberry trees which are perhaps descendants of those used by the Huguenot refugees who fed their silkworms in this area so near to Spitalfields. The toy-fort façade on the City Road is a Victorian addition to the older buildings – an example of Victorian 'Gothic' designed by Jennings in about 1857. The Honourable Artillery Company is the only volunteer body to take precedence over others, next to the regular army units, and it is the oldest military body in the United States: the Ancient and Honourable Artillery Company of Boston, Massachusetts, was founded by members of the original London company in 1638.

Walking due west across Bunhill Fields by the central footpath, the visitor reaches Bunhill Row. To the left is Artillery Walk, a neat row of Georgian terraced houses, each with the metal badge bearing the insignia of the City of London, and at the end of the walk there is a narrow warehouse with a block and tackle outside it. This last building is actually a converted chapel. The poet Milton lived in a house in this street, long since demolished, but a little to the north is Milton Street, originally Grub Street but renamed in 1830. Grub Street was defined by the great lexicographer, Dr Johnson, in his dictionary as follows: 'Grub Street, the name of a street in London much inhabited by writers of small histories, dictionaries, and temporary poems; whence any mean production is called Grub Street.' The derivation of the word is obscure, but it is thought that the bowmakers and the fletchers (who made arrows) worked in this area, and that as early as 1307 'grobbe strete' was associated with the flighting of arrows for use on the open practice fields of Moorfields and of 'Fensbury'. This area seems to have had military associations for a very long time, and it is fitting therefore that in part of the brewery of Messrs Whitbread, which was founded in the mid-eighteenth century, there is now a remarkable embroidery permanently on exhibition of 'Overlord, the story of the Normandy Landings, D. Day, June 6th 1944'. The buildings of the brewery and some eighteenth-century houses adjoining, situated near Artillery Lane, are also of interest. The room in which the Overlord Embroidery is exhibited is the 170 feet by 65 feet Porter Tun Room, built for Whitbread in 1784, with a massive unsupported king-post roof. The embroidery, commissioned by Lord Dulverton as a tribute to and a permanent record of the military action by Allied forces which liberated Europe from the Nazi oppression, was designed by Miss Sandra Lawrence, and was executed by a team of twenty embroideresses from the Royal School of Needlework. Consisting of thirty-four panels, each 8 feet wide and 3 feet high, the whole embroidery is about 272 feet in length and took five years to complete. It is permanently housed in an almost unique eighteenth-century room, beautifully adapted for its new role.

From Milton Street and Chiswell Street it is necessary to turn south down Moorgate and then eastwards along London Wall just south of Finsbury Circus to find another eighteenth-century church – the church of All Hallows, London Wall. This is the work of the son of George Dance the Elder, who built St Leonard's, Shoreditch. It is an unpretentious little church of brick with a tower of Portland stone, and has a light interior, dated 1765. The north wall actually incorporates part of the fabric of London Wall itself, and the stairs from the vestry by which the vicar reaches the pulpit are embedded in the much older fabric; to the west end of the church a stretch of the churchyard wall is largely composed of the medieval walls which used to encircle the City. The eighteenth-century interior is a remarkable accomplishment for Dance the Younger, who was only twenty-four years old when he designed this church. A large painting by his brother, Sir Nathaniel Dance-Holland, acts as a reredos behind the altar. The church has no aisles, the tunnel vault of the simple nave being supported by Ionic pilasters, and it was repaired after the Second World War. Its organ comes from an old chapel in Islington, and its font from St Paul's.

Still further eastwards on Bishopsgate is another, rather more impressive

A NEW and Correct PLAN of LONDON WESTMINSTER and SOUTHWARK with the Additional Buildings to the Year 1770.

London in 1770, the light grey area representing the City of London

eighteenth-century church – that of St Botolph without Bishopsgate, near to the site of the old City gate which was demolished about 1760. Gilded mitres from the old gate are embedded in the wall and a plaque on the corner of Wormwood Street states: 'Adjoining this spot Bishopsgate formerly stood.' That the church of St Botolph was just outside the City wall is acknowledged by the addition of 'without Bishopsgate' to its name, and this also helps to distinguish this church from others dedicated to this very popular saint about whom almost nothing is known, except that he seems sometimes to have been a patron saint of travellers. The church stands on part of the old protective ditch which once surrounded the City, and there seems to be some doubt as to its actual architect – it was possibly a little-known architect named James Gold (or Gould). It is a solid, unpretentious eighteenth-century church, – a building of red brick with stone dressings and a stone tower over the east end, above the chancel. It has retained its galleries on the north, south and western sides, but was altered somewhat during the nineteenth century when a glass dome was inserted in the roof over the nave, and later when bomb damage had to be repaired after the Second World War. The pulpit and the font (in which the poet Keats was baptised) are both eighteenth century, as is the altar-piece in the Lady Chapel. Outside the church there is a hall on which stand two of those rather endearing little figures of charity children in early nineteenth-century costume which one encounters in different places in the City. These are of Coade stone – a composite artificial stone first evolved by a Dorset man, and

left, St Botolph without Bishopsgate
below, Figures of charity children

239

then manufactured in large quantities for architectural ornament in Lambeth by his widow, Mrs Eleanor Coade, during the latter half of the eighteenth century and part of the nineteenth century.

On the opposite side of Bishopsgate is Artillery Lane (not to be confused with Artillery Walk which is to the rear of St Botolph's), and there one finds a quite unexpected pleasure for, among the warehouses and the other buildings which serve Spitalfields Market, there is an exquisite little eighteenth-century shop, with a central door flanked by bow windows and another classically ornamented door at the end giving access to the rooms above. To the east of the shop is the huge facade of Christ Church, Spitalfields, one of Nicholas Hawksmoor's most original designs – a wayward and imaginative frontage which combines a huge triumphal arch, surmounted by another somewhat similar series of arched forms, and then topped by a spire in the Gothic style which rises to a height of 234 feet, dominating the whole area. It was built in 1729, at a time when the area had a thriving silk industry, thanks to the influx of refugees from France – Huguenots who fled to England after Louis XIV revoked the Edict of Nantes which had previously protected their right to worship as they pleased. At one time the whole of Spitalfields as far north as Bethnal Green was a silk-weaving centre, and there are still a few houses in the area of Bethnal Green Museum which can be identified as those used by the weavers by the large windows on the upper storey by which their looms were lit. Their names, such as Maître, Le Brun and Leroy, became anglicised into Masters, Brown

A shop in Artillery Lane, 1757, which was owned by a mercer, Nicholas Jourdain

left, Christ Church, Spitalfields, designed by Nicholas Hawksmoor
right, Fournier Street, Spitalfields

and King, and it is interesting to see John Stow's comments on an earlier influx of refugees: 'God's blessing is surely not only brought upon the parish by receiving poor strangers but also a great advantage hath accrued to the whole nation by the rich manufacturers of weaving silks stuffs and camlet, which art they brought with them.' Among the second generation of this Huguenot group was Dolland, the inventor of a number of important optical devices.

The silk-weaving industry has disappeared and the Huguenots absorbed, and since then other wretched, frightened waves of refugees have arrived at the London Docks from Poland, Russia and other anti-Semitic regimes, the most recent of these being the refugees from Hitler's Germany in the 1930s. They all settled in this eastern area and formed their own virile communities in which they were free to preserve their own traditions until they were absorbed by London. One aspect of this change of population can be seen in Fournier Street, where an eighteenth-century Wesleyan Chapel has been converted into a synagogue.

Since the 1930s the whole area has been repopulated by refugees from places such as Uganda and the Indian sub-continent, all of whom have made homes for themselves there, trading, building shops, starting small businesses in the markets, working hard to establish for themselves and for their children a better life in every way than they could have hoped for in their own homelands.

Architecturally, Middlesex Street (better known by its old name of Petticoat Lane) and Houndsditch have little to offer, but at the southern end of Houndsditch at its junction with Aldgate there is yet another church dedicated to St Botolph – St Botolph, Aldgate, built 1741–4 by George Dance the Elder on the site of an earlier medieval church. As one might expect from so traditional an architect, it shows the restrained taste of the mid-eighteenth century rather than the more adventurous approach of Nicholas Hawksmoor's Christ Church, Spitalfields. St Botolph, Aldgate (not to be confused with St Botolph, *Aldersgate*, which is on the western side of the City), is not as attractively sited nor quite as impressive as St Leonard's Church, Shoreditch, by the same architect, for the tower tapers less and is almost dumpy. Inside the church, J. F. Bentley, the Victorian architect who built Westminster Cathedral in a pseudo-Byzantine style, converted the eighteenth-century classical interior to a strangely pompous 'classical' version of his own, adding a great deal of ornament which tends to destroy the clarity of the church as it was designed by George Dance the Elder. Yet churches are much more than objects of polite architectural interest, and the traditional role of an East End church has always been that of a missionary, bringing the Christian message to a population where the children are likely to receive little or no instruction in Christian matters in their homes or schools. St Botolph, Aldgate, is thus a church which is tackling with great energy the daunting task of bringing the Christian message to a poor and often alien population, and anyone visiting the church will fast become aware of the need for a very different approach from that of a church in the more affluent and educated parts of London.

There is still plenty in this church, however, to remind one of the past, including a monument to Thomas Lord Darcy and his companions, executed on Tower Hill, after a 'framed' trial held by Thomas Cromwell under the orders of Henry VIII. The monument takes the form of an emaciated carved figure under a canopy supported by classical Corinthian columns. More relevant to the East End is a memorial window to the great eighteenth-century philanthropist, Sir John Cass. Before he died in 1718, he endowed a school for the poor children of Aldgate and a trust for this purpose which, by skilful administration, has now become so profitable that it also sustains the Technical Institute by which his name is probably better known, the Sir John Cass College – an educational establishment from which a great many poor boys and girls and adults have benefited very considerably, entering careers which might have been denied to them under less happy circumstances. It is said that while he was signing the necessary deeds of gift for the original foundation, Sir John suffered a haemorrhage, staining the quill with blood, and the girls attending his school have always

Hertford House, the
home of the Wallace
Collection

by Richard, the fourth Marquis, who not only inherited the accumulated treasures of his ancestors, but also the family passion for collecting rich and beautiful things, and added to this collection that of his brother, Lord Henry Seymour, after the latter's death in 1860. The collection then passed into the hands of Sir Richard Wallace, Bart., another fastidious collector, thus the entire collection reflects the taste of generations of avid connoisseurs. With a collection of this diversity and richness, it is not easy to select any one aspect of art for which it is notable, except possibly the *objets d'art* of seventeenth-century France; nowhere in the British Isles can this particular aspect of European art be seen in such variety under one roof. Other important aspects of European art are also well represented: examples of seventeenth-century Dutch painting, some from eighteenth-century France and England, and the many precious works of craftsmanship from almost every period, from the Middle Ages (including armour and weapons) right into the nineteenth century. The Wallace Collection was opened as a national museum and art gallery by Edward VII (then Prince of Wales) on 22 June 1900, and it is open to the public every day but Sunday.

From Manchester Square it is a very short distance westwards to Portman Square, one of the most fashionable of all London's eighteenth-century squares, of which the north side was completed about 1768 and the rest of it some twenty years later. Portman Square was owned by William Henry Portman of Orchard-Portman in Somerset, and the whole London estate covered about 270 acres. He also possessed lands in Dorset, near Blandford, and Bryanston Square, built early in the nineteenth century, was named after his estates there. Baker Street was named after his friend Sir Edward Baker of Ramston in Dorset, and the church of St Paul, on the corner of Robert Adam Street and Baker Street, was intended as a chapel for the Portman estate. It suffered a drastic alteration in 1870, but a little of the

255

eighteenth-century work still survives inside, although the galleries have been removed.

The most notable house to survive in Portman Square is Home House, built and decorated throughout by Robert Adam and his remarkable team of craftsmen for Elizabeth, Countess of Home. The house is not usually open to the public, but it is now the Courtauld Institute of Art, the part of London University which has trained so many eminent and scholarly curators and art directors for museums and art galleries all over the world. It would be a dull student indeed who failed to benefit from working in such a superb environment. There are many other delightful eighteenth-century exteriors to be seen in the area, with their original ironwork and fenestration intact.

Built on open fields, the Portman estate occupied the sites of Great Gibbet Field and Little Gibbet Field, these names being particularly significant in view of the proximity of the gallows at Tyburn, which stood just north of the present Marble Arch. A plaque in the traffic island at the southern end of Edgware Road marks the spot where many hundreds of poor wretches were hanged, to the delight of the spectators who came from every part of eighteenth-century London to watch the ceremony. Tyburn or 'Tiburn' is a corruption of 'Aye-bourne' or 'T'Ayebourne', a bourne, burn, or stream which flowed through the area, and which also accounts for Brook Street just to the south of Oxford Street. The public hanging of such a notorious highwayman as James Maclean, an elegantly dressed 'gentleman of the road' who robbed Horace Walpole (among other notable eighteenth-century characters), would have attracted an audience of over 100,000 people. The road from Newgate Jail to Tyburn would have been lined with thousands of spectators – the less fortunate ones who were unable to obtain a grandstand view of the hanging. With over 150 offences punishable by death, there was a steady flow of ten to fifteen executions per month, despite the reluctance of some juries to convict, and it is perhaps significant that even during the hanging of a pickpocket on the gallows, nowhere were his fellow pickpockets more active than among the crowd attending the execution. A valedictory speech or gesture of defiance could be expected from some of the more famous criminals – the most noteworthy perhaps being from the notorious Jonathan Wild, a criminal who informed on many of his fellow criminals, but was finally brought to justice. He picked the pocket of the priest performing the last rites on the platform of the gallows and died clutching the corkscrew he had stolen in his hand. He was then taken to Surgeon's Hall for dissection.

More ordinary felons could hardly expect quite so ardent a following, and as the gallows was built on a tripod, nine executions could be carried out simultaneously – three to each side of the triangle. Death was by strangulation, friends of the convicted performing a last service by hanging grimly on the legs of the jerking body to shorten the death agonies. It is thought that the first man to be executed by the 'drop' method, whereby the weight of the body falling a calculated distance dislocated the spinal cord, causing a more merciful and instant death, was Earl Ferrers, who was

opposite: above,
Kensington Gardens
below, Interior view of
the Orangery at
Kensington Palace

left, Chester Terrace
below, Cumberland
Terrace

hanged for killing his steward. Even Sir Joshua Reynolds, the President of the Royal Academy, was persuaded to accompany James Boswell to an execution, and wrote him a charming letter of thanks for having given him the opportunity to witness it. It is clear that few eighteenth-century people could resist the lure of a public hanging. Many of these spectators came from the elegant houses to the south of Oxford Street and east of Tiburn Lane (now known as Park Lane).

The whole area round Grosvenor Square, Berkeley Square and Hanover Square is so rich in examples of eighteenth-century architecture that it would be quite impossible to list them all, but a gentle stroll along such streets as Bourdon Street, Charles Street, Curzon Street, and Brook Street, whose dignified houses are still furnished with wrought iron railings and link-snuffers, will give the observant visitor a great deal to enjoy. Just south of Grosvenor Square, Mount Street derives its name from Oliver's Mount – fortifications erected in 1643 during the Civil War by the Cromwellian forces.

Little of eighteenth-century Grosvenor Square remains, although there are a few early interiors concealed behind nineteenth-century façades. The character of the square, laid out by Sir Richard Grosvenor *c.* 1725, is entirely different now that it is dominated by the huge buildings of the United States Embassy by the Finnish architect, Eero Saarinen. The square

Tyburn Turnpike, 1820

opposite: above, The entrance to Hyde Park *below*, St Andrew's Place

257

Grosvenor Square in
1870

has many American associations, including the statue of Franklin Roosevelt.
In 1785–88 John Adams, Minister to Great Britain and later the second
President of the United States, lived at the corner of Duke Street and Brook
Street, and during the First World War, the American Ambassador, Walter
Hines Page, lived at No. 6, Grosvenor Square.

Grosvenor Chapel in South Audley Street has an oddly attractive naïve
quality, not unlike some of the early churches in the United States – Bruton
Church in colonial Williamsburg in Virginia, for example. It is not clear who
was responsible for its design, although it was apparently built by a little-
known builder, Benjamin Timbrell, about 1730. It is somewhat smaller in
scale than most estate churches, and it is built of yellowish brick, with a
porch of four columns and a small tower. Inside one can still see the original
galleries, but the interior was altered by Sir Ninian Comper in 1912 by the
addition of a large open screen which tends to obscure the original
eighteenth-century reredos. The pulpit is the original one, but the high altar
dates back only to 1912.

Berkeley Square, just south of Grosvenor Square, was started in about
1737 after the demolition of Berkeley House, a seventeenth-century
mansion built shortly after the Restoration. Of all the eighteenth-century
houses to survive, the most striking ones are on the west side: No. 44 has
been described as 'the finest terrace house in London' by Professor Pevsner,
who asserts that, 'there is no other eighteenth-century staircase in England
which can so convincingly be compared with those of the great German and
Austrian architects.' Unfortunately, most visitors must be content with
gazing at the house from the outside. It was built for Lady Isabella Finch by
William Kent, an enemy of Hogarth's who built the Horse Guards Parade in
Whitehall. The exterior is most impressive – it is one of a series of

eighteenth-century terrace houses, many of them with elaborate link-snuffers and all demonstrating the impeccable sense of proportion which is such a predominant feature of an eighteenth-century façade. The proportions of the windows to each other and to the whole façade of No. 44, Berkeley Square, is typical of this preoccupation with harmonious details. The size of the windows of the rooms on the ground floor indicates the fact that these rooms are less important than those on the first floor. The windows of the first floor, the *piano nobile*, show by their greater height and architectural surround that they light the most important rooms in the house. Smaller windows above these indicate more rooms of a lesser status, and those in the attic are more or less concealed by a fine brick cornice. No. 44 no longer has its wrought iron link-snuffers, but the houses north of the building can boast some very fine examples.

The house adjoining No. 44 was built somewhat later, and was decorated for its occupant, Clive of India – Sir Robert Clive, Bart., a brilliant soldier and administrator who laid the foundation of the British Empire in India. He committed suicide in this house while in a state of acute depression.

There are other fine eighteenth-century houses in Charles Street, south and west of Berkeley Square. This street was named after Charles, Earl of Falmouth, brother to the first Lord Berkeley of Stratton, who was formerly Sir John Berkeley of Bruton – sufficient material with which to name half the

No. 44 Berkeley Square, by William Kent, showing link-snuffers

259

streets in this area! Curzon Street, south of Charles Street and running parallel with it (named after George Augustus Curzon, third Viscount Howe, who was the ground landlord), also possesses some good eighteenth-century terrace houses and one superb free-standing one, Crewe House, built originally by Edward Shepherd about 1730, but altered a good deal later in the century. It is in a beautiful state of preservation, its stucco front painted, its mouldings fresh. Chesterfield Street, linking Charles Street and Curzon Street, also has some excellent examples of eighteenth-century terrace houses, almost intact.

The whole of this area from Bond Street westwards is known as Mayfair, for there was a fair held in Brook Field for many years from the reign of Charles II onwards. The riotous behaviour of some of its visitors caused it to be suspended for some years, and it was eventually suppressed at the end of the eighteenth century. Shepherd Market, however, still survives – one of those charming village-type communities with a sense of individuality which is characteristic of London. It was built by Edward Shepherd (or Sheppard), an architect who had built the elegant Crewe House as well as a row of houses on the north side of Grosvenor Square, and possibly others in South Audley Street.

Mayfair borders on Piccadilly, and a little to the east is Dover Street where there are some very well preserved houses of this period, including Ely House, a magnificent building erected as the town residence for the Bishops of Ely in 1772 when their former house built in the Hatton Garden area was found to be on property which had reverted to the Crown. The architect was Sir Robert Taylor, whose work will be mentioned later in connection with the Stone Buildings in Lincoln's Inn, and who also built much of the Bank of England. The façade of Ely House is particularly impressive, the stone facing on the ground floor round the door and windows being heavily rusticated, a form of carving derived from such Italian examples as the Pitti Palace in Florence, and intended to give the building a somewhat martial appearance. The windows on the first floor are enclosed in richly designed frames (or aedicules), each with a carved pediment and flanked by classical columns of the Corinthian order. Above them there are three circular plaques, the central one bearing a carved bishop's mitre. The street is unfortunately somewhat too narrow and often restricted even further with traffic for one to be able to appreciate fully the splendour of this house.

Grafton Street turns at right angles to Dover Street's northern end and contains several eighteenth-century houses, some of them possibly by Sir Robert Taylor, and some less ostentatious ones in red brick. Grafton Street emerges into Bond Street and this leads one northwards to Hanover Square, built 1716–20 and named after the new dynasty, when the old Stuart line died with Queen Anne and Georgian London proper began.

Much of eighteenth-century Hanover Square has disappeared, and even the statue of William Pitt by Sir Francis Chantrey was not executed until 1831, but some of the houses (Nos. 16 to 24) are original, built of red brick with finely worked stone dressings, and they give some idea of how very much more attractive the square must have looked before it suffered so much alteration. The most impressive eighteenth-century building in this area is the church of St George, Hanover Square, which is situated in St George's Street just south of the square. It was built between 1721 and 1724 by John James, an architect who had been one of a team working at Greenwich Hospital with Wren, and whose best-known work is probably the upper part of the western towers of Westminster Abbey, designed by Hawksmoor, but carried out by James. At St George's, Hanover Square, he used completely classical forms – the portico, the windows and all the details are very like those at St Martin-in-the-Fields, the parish from which the new parish of St George's, Hanover Square, was carved. It was, however, James who was the initiator, and James Gibbs who followed, for St George's anticipated St Martin-in-the-Fields in some respects. St George's also resembles Wren's St James's, Piccadilly, for its interior has a somewhat similar plan; James was, after all, Master Carpenter at St Paul's from 1711 onwards. St George's has retained its eighteenth-century galleries, and has a wide east window of the Venetian style, but it would not originally have contained stained glass, and the resultant darkening of the building makes it more difficult to see a reredos painted with 'The Last Supper' attributed to William Kent. The stained glass came from a church in Antwerp and is late medieval work – not very suitable for an eighteenth-century church which should look light and airy. The pulpit is rather an austere one for this period, but elegant and neat, and the whole church is very restrained decoratively by comparison with its near contemporaries, such as St George's, Bloomsbury, and St Martin-in-the-Fields.

Outside there are two iron dogs in the entrance, the work of one of the most distinguished painters of animals of the Victorian period – Sir Edwin

left, St George's,
Hanover Square
right, St Giles-in-the-
Fields

Landseer, R.A. – but there seems to be no record of how they became part of the portico or why, and one just accepts them gratefully as part of London's delightful eccentricities.

The area south of Tottenham Court Road underground station, which includes Soho, is not perhaps the most promising one in which to look for remnants of eighteenth-century London. It seems to have been a poor area for most of its history, and one to which foreigners flocked – particularly the Huguenot refugees who later built their own little chapel in West Street, near to Cambridge Circus. It is now a warehouse, although the exterior is still much as it was in 1700. It was later taken over by the Wesleyans, and John and Charles Wesley both preached there, but when it appeared in the Hogarth engraving of 'Noon', one of the four 'Times of Day' engraved in 1738, it was still in the possession of the French Protestants. The pulpit used later by John Wesley has been partially preserved, and the upper part, simply moulded and painted white, is still to be seen in the church of St Giles-in-the-Fields.

St Giles was the patron saint of the crippled and the poor, and three churches have occupied the site of the eighteenth-century church of St Giles-in-the-Fields since a hospital was first founded there as early as the twelfth century. The present church was built in 1733 by Henry Flitcroft, known as 'Burlington Harry' who was employed as a draughtsman by Lord Burlington, although he was a skilled joiner. He was also employed by the Duke of Bedford, both at Woburn Abbey in Bedfordshire, and on the Duke's Bloomsbury estate, but St Giles-in-the-Fields is the only one of his churches to survive. This church also bears some resemblance to St James, Piccadilly, by Wren, but the design of its steeple was very much more

influenced by James Gibbs, the architect of St Martin-in-the-Fields, and
the emphatic stone work which surrounds the door is of a pattern known as a
Gibbsian surround. The interior is comparatively simple; the pulpit is
preserved from the seventeenth-century church which this one replaced,
and the eighteenth-century reredos has a painting on either side – one of
Moses and the other of Aaron by a little known eighteenth-century artist,
Francisco Vieira the Younger. The church no longer has its eighteenth-
century galleries on either side, but is in most other respects fairly typical of
a church of this period and has very fortunately preserved the model of the
original design.

The district deteriorated sadly during the nineteenth century, especially
west and south, where it became one of the infamous 'rookeries' which
Charles Dickens knew only too well and described so vividly. In the
eighteenth century, however, condemned criminals on their way to Tyburn
from Newgate would stop at the church there for a drink called St Giles
Bowl, which probably lulled their fears somewhat. Many of them were
interred in the churchyard on the return journey, unless they had been
earmarked for dissection at the Surgeon's Hall. After the terrible
persecution of the Roman Catholics which resulted from the mendacity of
Titus Oates in the seventeenth century, many of those martyrs were also
buried in this churchyard, including the famous Archbishop of Armagh,
Oliver Plunkett.

Soho Square, on the west side of Charing Cross Road (which is a
comparatively recent addition to this neighbourhood, having been opened
in 1887), has few eighteenth-century buildings, although there is a fine
example on the corner of Greek Street, and a building in Manette Street
which was designed as a parish workhouse by James Paine in 1770. It is
south and west of Soho Square, tucked away between Wardour Street to the
west and Charing Cross Road to the east, that there is a great deal of
eighteenth-century London.

Greek Street, which derived its name from a Greek Church which was
once in the neighbourhood, and Dean Street, named after Bishop Compton,
the Dean of the Chapel Royal during the eighteenth century, both possess
fine examples of Georgian buildings, and even those which have had shop-
fronts added to them much later have in many instances retained their
eighteenth-century upper rooms and cornices. There are more examples to
be found in Frith Street (the street in which both William Hazlitt and
Charles Lamb died), including an eighteenth-century shop-front built
about 1791 and still in remarkably good condition. Meard Street or Meard's
Court, as it was once called, a small street running westwards off Dean
Street, is probably the most delightful surprise to be found in this area – a
virtually intact street of eighteenth-century houses of the humbler kind, but
still a remarkable unit. Nearby, lying back a little from Wardour Street, are
the tower and fragments of the walls of St Anne's church, Soho. The oddly
proportioned tower dominating the little green churchyard is not the one
originally built by Wren, but was erected by S. P. Cockerell at the turn of the
eighteenth century. There have been great efforts to turn the churchyard

St Anne's, Wardour
Street

into a little green oasis amid the squalor of Wardour Street, but all too often it is the refuge of alcoholics or other unfortunates snatching a rest before moving on.

A little further west is Berwick Street with its raucous colourful market, and it is difficult to imagine now that once, in 1708, it was 'a kind of a Row, the fronts of the houses resting on columns, make a small piazza'. At its northern end in D'Arblay Street there are still a few eighteenth-century houses to remind one of its former elegance, and even Wardour Street, now the centre of the film industry and of other less reputable sources of entertainment, can still boast some houses of the same period. There are more eighteenth-century houses in Broadwick Street leading westwards off Wardour Street; this street was the site of the birthplace of William Blake, the English artist, poet and mystic, but the blue plaque recording this fact is affixed to a modern building.

Golden Square was built at the end of the seventeenth century and during the opening years of the eighteenth century. It was at first called Gelding Square after a hostelry by that name in the area, but later renamed Golden Square by the indignant tenants. This square has also suffered considerable changes, although it is still the site of a statue of George II in the dress of a Roman emperor, crowned with a laurel wreath, and holding, for some entirely unexplained reason, a lizard in his left hand. It was the work of John Van Nost, who arrived in England from Malines in 1678, and it was originally made for the Duke of Chandos. Still further west, between Old Bond Street and Golden Square, a number of eighteenth-century houses still survive in Savile Row, Clifford Street and the Albany – a complex which is strictly neither a street nor a square, but something of both. It is a series of private chambers or bachelor apartments of the most exclusive kind, named after the house of Frederick, Duke of York and Albany, the second son of George III, and best remembered for the rhyme about 'the grand old Duke of York'. Built for him by Sir William Chambers, he was obliged to sell it to a builder to pay off some of his more pressing creditors, and the builder promptly converted it into apartments. It was later altered by Henry Holland, the Regency architect, so that the building is now 'H'-shaped, with a stuccoed frontage set back from a courtyard to the north, facing Vigo Street. The front faces Piccadilly but is set back in its own courtyard; it has a plain brick front with a central porch and pediment and is a house of considerable dignity and restraint.

Despite considerable alterations, Burlington House, now the Royal Academy of Arts, but formerly the town residence of Richard Boyle, third Earl of Burlington, is still clearly an eighteenth-century house, although it has lost the imposing gateway so savagely caricatured by Hogarth, and little of Colen Campbell's original design is visible after the remodelling of the house by Samuel Ware in 1815–18 and then again in the middle of the nineteenth century. It has a pseudo-Renaissance façade along Piccadilly, and after considerable alterations inside some attempts were made to give it a genuine eighteenth-century appearance by the insertion of some of the ceiling panels by Benjamin West, the American President of the Royal

Burlington House

Academy who succeeded Reynolds, and his gifted contemporary, Angelica Kauffmann, from Somerset House, the original premises of the Royal Academy in the eighteenth century. The Saloon is probably more nearly in the condition in which it was originally designed by Colen Campbell than any of the other rooms, although the Ballroom (now known as the Reynolds Room) is largely eighteenth century. This was in fact somewhat later than the Saloon; it was designed by Isaac Ware, a chimney-sweep's boy who was befriended by an eighteenth-century nobleman (possibly Burlington himself), educated, and became an extremely able writer on architecture as well as an architect. The ceilings of the other rooms were probably painted by William Kent and Sir James Thornhill (Hogarth's reluctant father-in-law), but experts disagree on the attributions. The rear of the building now houses the ethnographical galleries from the British Museum, known as the Museum of Mankind. This part of the building was the work of Sir James Pennethorne in 1866-9. The Piccadilly side is occupied by a number of distinguished bodies. In the west wing is the Society of Antiquaries, founded in 1707, the Royal Astronomical Society, and the Linnaean Society, the world-famous natural history society founded in 1788 and named after the great Swedish botanist, Carl Linnaeus, In the east wing are housed the Royal Society, the Geographical Society and the Chemical Society. It is not surprising that Dr Johnson could remark of eighteenth-century London: 'I will venture to say, there is more learning and science within the circumference of ten miles from where we now sit, than in the rest of the kingdom.'

There are two other major eighteenth-century buildings still to be seen in Piccadilly, but further west, facing Green Park. The first of these is the Naval and Military Club at No. 94, known as the 'In and Out Club', possibly because of the piers which flank the entrance. It was originally the residence of the Duke of Cambridge, another son of George III, and later the home of Lord Palmerston. It was badly damaged during the Second World War, but has since been restored. The other building is now St James's Club, a late eighteenth-century house with much of the decoration

left, Goodwin's Court, off St Martin's Lane
right, Interior of St Martin-in-the-Fields

by Robert Adam still intact. This is the full extent of eighteenth-century London in the Piccadilly area except for one small but very famous shop at the top of Haymarket – Messrs Fribourg and Treyer's, purveyors of snuff and tobacco since the middle of the eighteenth century.

Walking eastwards from Leicester Square underground station along Cranbourn Street to St Martin's Lane, it is easy to miss a little doorway with a kind of dog-leg entrance on the east side of St Martin's Lane. This leads directly into Goodwin's Court, the south side of which is lined with a row of eighteenth-century shop-fronts; most of them are now offices for architects or other professional bodies and have been beautifully preserved.

There are three or four little pairs of eighteenth-century buildings in St Martin's Lane south of Goodwin's Court, including one house (No. 31) which might well be late seventeenth century. However, it is the church of St Martin-in-the-Fields by James Gibbs which is the truly outstanding eighteenth-century building in this area, and its lovely spire (whose design was chosen from one of five produced by Gibbs) and columned front are probably as familiar a symbol of London as Tower Bridge or St Paul's Cathedral. It was a surprising innovation on Gibbs' part to place the steeple over the centre of the portico, for Wren, whom James Gibbs admired immensely, had always placed his steeples elsewhere, but it was a device which succeeded and was widely copied in the USA where Gibbs' books were well known – indeed, the Americans have since paid Gibbs the compliment of producing various versions of St Martin-in-the-Fields, adapted sometimes for different materials.

Gibbs was one of the few eighteenth-century architects who, early in his life, studied in Rome under an Italian architect. He was therefore used to churches with naves that were empty of pews and concentrated much of the accommodation for his worshippers in the galleries over the aisles. Nevertheless, he obviously considered Wren's definition of the differences between Roman Catholic services, where the worshippers were reduced to the role of passive spectators, and the services of the Protestant church, where there was a good deal of audience participation and the congregation needed both to see and to hear clearly. Thus, in St Martin-in-the-Fields, a royal church built on the site of a medieval church in open fields, he not only provided ample gallery space, but a royal box for George I as well. The church cost the vast sum of £70,000, of which the king contributed £29,000 towards the cost of the building and the installation of the organ, and the Royal Family are still technically parishioners. To many visitors, the interior of St Martin-in-the-Fields, with its richly ornamented roof and elaborate plaster decoration by two master Italian craftsmen, Guiseppe Artari and his partner Bagutti, might seem far too ornate and frivolous for a Christian church. But St Martin's is in fact extremely active in its Christian duty of acting as a refuge and a sanctuary to the human flotsam and jetsam washed up on its steps and into its crypt every night of the year.

St Martin-in-the-Fields

St James's Square

One side of Canada House on the west side of Trafalgar Square is also very much in the eighteenth-century tradition, for it was built as part of the Royal College of Physicians by Sir Robert Smirke early in the nineteenth century. Cockspur Street to the west has little to show except for a rather jolly equestrian statue of George III looking far more like 'Farmer George' than the demented tyrant he is alleged to have been by some students of the American revolutionary wars. Cockspur Street runs into Pall Mall, on the north side of which is one of London's most attractive squares – St James's Square, with some very fine eighteenth-century buildings. Although the square was first laid out shortly after the Restoration of 1660, none of the seventeenth-century buildings have survived and the earliest ones are of the eighteenth century. The square has examples of the work of a surprisingly wide range of eighteenth-century architects, the earliest being an Italian, Giacomo Leoni, the only Italian among the little group which gathered round the third Earl of Burlington, the leader of the followers of the theories of proportion propounded by the sixteenth-century Italian architect, Andrea Palladio. The house attributed to Leoni is No. 4, but since Edward Shepherd (who built Shepherd Market in Mayfair) received payment after the earlier house on the site had been severely damaged by fire, and since drawings for this house were found among the effects of Nicholas Hawksmoor, Wren's assistant, when he died in 1736, the identity of the actual architect is still something of a mystery. No. 10, a sober brick house with a balcony across the frontage below the first floor windows, was the home of the Earl of Chatham (Pitt the Elder) from 1759–1762, and was later occupied by two other British Prime Ministers, Lord Derby and Mr

Gladstone. This and No. 9 were built by Henry Flitcroft, who also built St Giles-in-the-Fields, Soho. Despite later intruders, much of the north part of St James's Square is eighteenth-century work, although the London Library in the north-western corner is considerably later, having been built in 1896. The west side of the square has some of the most engaging eighteenth-century houses, including Lichfield House built in 1764 by James 'Athenian' Stuart. Despite some alteration later in the century, this building, which is now the offices of an assurance company, has been beautifully maintained and adds grace to this side of St James's Square. Its only possible rival is a house by Robert Adam occupying the lower half of the western side of the square, which has most sensitively been partly reconstructed and partly restored. No. 20 was the original Robert Adam house, and its wrought iron railings and rusticated lower walls, with giant pilasters linking the *piano nobile* to the smaller upper storey, are all typical of an eighteenth-century stone façade, although the doorway is at the northern end. When the premises next door were taken over by the Distillers Company they decided that it should be worthy of its neighbour, and since 1922 it has been virtually impossible to tell which is the original and which the duplicate, so beautifully have the two houses been integrated. The original house had been built for a wealthy and fastidious Welsh baronet, Sir Watkin Williams-Wynn, and with characteristic thoroughness Robert Adam not only designed the house, but was also personally responsible for the details of the interior decoration and furniture – even the door-knocker, Sir Watkin's sedan chair, and Lady Watkin Williams-Wynn's watch-case! Many of the details of this house are described in the standard *Works of Robert and James Adam*, published in 1773-9.

There appear to have been two houses called Norfolk House in this square: the first is now called Chatham House and is on the north side of the square, and the second, where George III was born, built early in the eighteenth century, was in the south-eastern corner. This was replaced in 1939 by the present building which has the distinction of having been the headquarters of General Eisenhower and his staff of Allied forces during the preparations for the invasion of North Africa and later military successes.

The square still has a well-kept central garden with fine mature trees, and an equestrian statue of William III, in bronze, by John Bacon the Younger, placed there in 1808.

All the major buildings in Pall Mall, to the south of the square, were built in the next century, except Schomberg House which is basically a seventeenth-century building. Mention should be made of it here, for it has a very striking appearance and was for years the home of Thomas Gainsborough, the painter of a whole series of magnificent portraits of eighteenth-century men and women. It was in Schomberg House that a notorious quack doctor, Dr Graham, had what he called his 'Temple of Health' with magical baths of mud, electrical treatment, and attractive young women who wallowed in the nude and persuaded the gullible that they were endowed with such charms because of the treatment. (It is said that at one time Emmy Hamilton participated in this ritual.)

Pall Mall ends almost in a cul-de-sac, past St James's Palace and Marlborough House to the south, with Clarence House still further to the south and Lancaster House almost as far as Green Park. These latter two houses were both built in the next century.

St James's Street, which runs due north of St James's Palace, has a number of very well-preserved eighteenth-century buildings, with side turnings and courtyards revealing all kinds of charming glimpses of this period. Such a courtyard is Pickering Place, just beside the fine late eighteenth-century or early nineteenth-century shop-front of the wine merchants, Berry Bros and Rudd. Pickering's Place is on the east side of James's Street and is surrounded by demure little eighteenth-century houses, now shops and offices. It was apparently a secluded little court where 'affairs of honour' might be settled without interference – less public for duelling than the parks. Gambling for high stakes took place at No. 5, Pickering Place, as well as at many of the clubs in this area, so it was appropriate that Hogarth chose St James's Street when he was looking for a setting in which to stage the arrest of his anti-hero, the Rake, in his famous series 'The Rake's Progress'. Pickering Place derived its name from the owner of a coffee house on the site now occupied by Messrs. Berry Bros and Rudd, and in the courtyard there is a little sundial with the inscription, 'William Pickering Fundator 1710 Geo. B. Harvey Memorator 1919'. High up on the left-hand side of the passage leading out into St James's Street is a small modern inscription recording the fact that the house was in 1845 the official residence of the representative of the Republic of Texas to the Court of St James.

A little to the north is Loft's hat shop, a delightful example of the best of tradesman's architecture, when shop-fronts were designed with as much respect for proportion as the façades of the houses of the noblemen who patronised them. It was built about 1780.

The next important eighteenth-century building on this side of the street is Bootle's Club, built by John Crunden in 1765 and resembling closely the work of the Adam brothers. Although it started as a coffee house, it became renowned for its high stakes and deep drinking, and was known as the 'Savoir vivre'. Some alterations were made to the accommodation to the rear early in the nineteenth century, but the very elegant brick front facing St James's Street, with its central Venetian window on the first floor surmounted by a fan of stucco, its twin porches with columns exactly balanced on either side of the bow window on the ground floor, and its beautifully detailed brick pediment, is typical of the sophisticated town architecture of the period.

White's Club to the north is also an eighteenth-century building, erected in 1784–8, although the club itself is considerably older, having been established in a chocolate house which was burned down earlier in the eighteenth century; it was re-established as a club in 1736. Episode six of 'The Rake's Progress' shows the fire starting. The present building was erected by James Wyatt, a rival and to some extent an imitator of the Adam Brothers, but it was considerably altered in the middle of the last century.

left, Schomberg House,
Gainsborough's home
and studio
below, Messrs. Berry
Bros and Rudd, late
eighteenth-century
wine merchants, and
the entrance to
Pickering Place

Bootle's Club, St James's

(White's was notorious for the betting which took place there: members would make a bet on the most extraordinary pretext, such as the possibility that Sarah, the Duchess of Marlborough would outlive the aged Duchess of Cleveland!)

Some clubs had strong political affiliations – Brooks's Club, for example, on the opposite side of St James's Street, was the club to which many important Whigs belonged. The club began as 'Almacks' in Pall Mall in 1764, but moved to its present position in 1778 when Henry Holland built it for Brooks, a wine merchant, money-lender and the proprietor at that time. The betting records which have been preserved contain such famous names as Richard Brinsley Sheridan, playwright and Member of Parliament, who was at first debarred because his father had been an actor, but was later admitted by a ruse practised by George IV (then Prince of Wales). Of the same company were Charles George Fox, another politician, Sir Joshua Reynolds, David Garrick, Gibbon, the historian, and many other famous eighteenth-century people. The club stands on the corner of St James's Street and Park Place and is built of a white stone-like brick; there are Venetian windows on the side facing Park Place, and five square-headed windows on the side facing St James's Park, and the whole facade is bonded visually by pilasters with Corinthian capitals, the pilaster starting at the base of the *piano nobile* and ending at the cornice. There is a triangular pediment to the roof on the St

James's Street face, and a bold balustrade along the roofline in Park Place.   Brooks's Club

Park Place also has a few eighteenth-century houses, but none of any great distinction and there are better examples to be seen in Arlington Street, which can be reached through the extension of Jermyn Street across the west side of St James's Street. Still further south there are more remnants of the eighteenth-century London to be seen in St James's Place and Little St James's, where hotels have converted some of the earlier buildings with some skill. The finest building in this area is Spencer House; one side occupies the south-western end of St James's Place, but its main and very imposing façade faces the park and is best viewed from the little bandstand, for the hedges and walls screen it pretty effectively from the footpath bordering Green Park. A number of distinguished eighteenth-century architects have made alterations to the interior – James Stuart in the 1750s, Sir Robert Taylor in the 1770s, and Henry Holland about 1787, but the exterior is the work of John Vardy, William Kent's assistant, and was completed from 1752–4 for John Spencer, first Lord Spencer of Althorp, in Northamptonshire. Spencer House is said to have some of the finest interiors in London, but it is a private house and not open to the public. The view of Spencer House from Green Park shows what a traditional architect Vardy was, for the façade is most beautifully balanced, with a heavily rusticated ground floor and round-headed windows, and two narrow wings recessed slightly to give emphasis to the central masses. The *piano nobile* is marked by corresponding windows above, although these are square-headed and strongly framed; round half columns support a triangular pediment and cast emphatic shadows which impart a palatial aspect to the whole front. The whole building stands on a heavily rusticated plinth pierced with small grilled windows, but this is scarcely visible from the park.

St James's Place had a number of remarkable tenants during the eighteenth century: these included Joseph Addison, who lived there in

Spencer House, facing
Green Park

1710; the notorious John Wilkes; Warren Hastings (of Indian fame); and an
author, Samuel Rogers, a friend of Lord Byron and Thomas Moore, the
Irish writer who stayed with Rogers in secret to escape debtors.

Walking through Green Park towards St James's Park, one passes
Buckingham Palace which is of course an historic building, although the
façade it presents to the Mall is a twentieth-century veneer applied by Aston
Webb in 1913. The original building was erected by John Sheffield, the
newly created Duke of Buckingham, in 1703, on land given to him by Queen
Anne which had been one of the extensive grounds planted a century earlier
by James I to encourage the growth of the silk-weaving industry.
Buckingham House was a smallish red-brick mansion and was bought for
£28,000 by George III in 1762 as a present for Queen Charlotte, and then
renamed 'the Queen's House'. It was there that George IIIrd's remarkable
library was housed – this was later transferred to the British Museum – and
that the famous meeting between Dr Johnson and his monarch took place,
when the latter complimented Johnson on his writing. George IV put John
Nash to some trouble to make additional alterations, but he died before they
could be completed and was replaced by Edward Blore, although the marble
arch designed by John Nash was left in position. In 1851 this was transferred
to its present site near Tyburn Tree at the head of Park Lane.

Walking down the Mall from Buckingham Palace and turning right just
by the Duke of York steps, it is possible to see a number of important
eighteenth-century buildings from the rear, since they face Whitehall. On
the north side of Horse Guards Parade, somewhat heavily disguised by the
later addition of a dome and a network of radio masts, is the Admiralty

windows to be regarded as possible fire risks, and instead of the wooden window frames being virtually flush with the brick surround, it became illegal to have them set back less than four inches, so that they were provided with a depth or 'reveal' of brickwork between the wall surface and the wood of the window frame. All the houses at this end of Queen Anne's Gate must then have been erected before the passing of these statutes, for they all have cornices of wood and the window frames are almost flush with the wall surfaces. They are also of red brick – a material which became somewhat unfashionable in about 1730 when it was replaced by a greyish brick, a more gentle tint. Later in the century extensive use of stucco covered the surface so that less and less bricks were exposed, but this mainly applied to houses, for most architects and builders prescribed stone as the only possible building material for public buildings. Further south in Queen Anne's Gate the houses are clearly of a much later date, for the windows are set well back and the cornices are of stone or stuccoed brick. It was in the row backing on to Birdcage Walk that Lord Palmerston was born in 1784. The rather battered statue of Queen Anne on the corner opposite was intended to be erected outside St Mary-Le-Strand, a very fine Church by James Gibbs which will be introduced later in the chapter, but the Queen's death made certain rearrangements necessary.

Queen Anne's Gate

From Queen Anne's Gate the street turns south just by the eighteenth-century house which is now most appropriately the headquarters of the National Trust. It emerges into Broadway, close by the St James's Park underground station and Petty France, so called presumably because like its namesake in the City, it was the residence of a small French colony. Near the southward branch of Broadway there is another unexpected and delightful example of eighteenth-century architecture – the 'Blewcote School', erected in 1709 for a charity school founded in 1688, but not to be confused with the much more famous Christ's Hospital school which used to be in the City. This building is a rather naïve and appealing example of early eighteenth-century architecture; it attempts to emulate the houses of the more wealthy citizens with a *piano nobile* of sorts and a classical doorway. Squeezed in between the heavily pilastered surround there is a little charity boy in uniform in a niche over the door, and a curly little pediment over the centre, known as a broken pediment because of the contrived gap in the middle where an ordinary pediment would form a complete triangle. This building is also now the property of the National Trust. Moving across Victoria Street and eastwards into one of the little roads such as Great Peter Street, dominated by a most impressive Victorian church, one comes to Smith Square, which despite heavy bomb damage has much to offer the explorer of eighteenth-century London. The *pièce de résistance* is the church of St John the Evangelist – a rugged forceful design by Thomas Archer built in 1721–8, but which suffered grave damage from fire in the 1750s and was then reduced almost to a shell in the Second World War. It has always been a controversial church: its architecture was described by one writer as an example of a building so grand that 'hardly anywhere else in England has the Baroque manner been so dramatically and forcefully handled', while others have been far less complimentary. The giant shell with its twin towers has now been restored, and it is used most successfully as a concert hall. Some of the eighteenth-century houses in this square developed by Sir James Smith still survive, and Lord North Street, to the north of the square, has an almost perfect array of houses of the same period, with equally fine examples in Cowley Street, in Barton Street adjoining it, and in Little College Street.

From Westminster it is an easy walk due north up Whitehall, pausing perhaps to look at Downing Street, one side of which has a terrace of much restored eighteenth-century houses including the famous No. 10, and No. 11. Still further north, on the west side of Whitehall, is the Scottish Office of which the part facing Horse Guards Parade – the work of James Paine – has already been mentioned. The front on Whitehall was inserted in 1787 by Henry Holland for the Prince Regent, and it is certainly an elegant classical introduction to the interior. Almost directly opposite is Gwydyr House, named after Lord Gwydyr, erected about 1772 and built traditionally by John Marquand, a surveyor in the Office of Woods and Forests. (It is quite remarkable how many buildings were the work of men with little or no architectural training: Sir John Vanbrugh, who built Blenheim Palace, was a playwright; Lord Burlington an intelligent dilettante; William Kent a kind of painter; Thomas Ripley a carpenter; and Henry Flitcroft a

Gwydyr House, 1772

carpenter-joiner. Even Wren received no formal architectural training.) Gwydyr House is of brick, with all the hallmarks of a gentleman's town house, but in no way ostentatious. It has a fine Venetian window in the centre over the door, and has retained some excellent wrought ironwork and its link-snuffers. Although its material and its proportions are somewhat different from the adjoining Banqueting House, they complement each other quite well – which is more than can be said of the hideous out-of-scale modern buildings to the rear.

The front of the Horse Guards facing Whitehall conforms to all the Palladian rules of proportion, and if only the courtyard were not so small, it would not be difficult to imagine it as a country mansion. Its rigid symmetry, the beautifully balanced fenestration, the flanking turrets with little Inigo Jones-type pavilions on each and the cupola surmounting the whole composition make it one of the most delightful buildings in this part of London.

Further north, in front of Thomas Ripley's Admiralty building, there is a screen by Robert Adam – this fulfils a useful function by dividing the courtyard from the main highway of Whitehall, but it is also extremely attractive, the gateposts being decorated with sea-horses, their bodies as those of normal horses, but with webbed hooves and fish-like hindquarters. A little plaque on either side shows dolphins supported by cherub-like children. The screen, consisting of a series of beautifully spaced columns, is designed to cast deep shadows and to lighten the effect of a solid wall, but the

The Admiralty screen

ends of the screen and the centre are relieved only by three shallow niches positioned at either end and at the entrance in the centre. Apart from the absence of some wrought iron lamp-fittings, the screen today is exactly as it was when Robert Adam built it in 1760.

Before 1874 a large Jacobean mansion, Northumberland House, used to occupy much of the north-eastern corner of Whitehall almost opposite the statue of Charles I, but this was demolished to make way for the present Northumberland Avenue, and with it a number of rooms which had been installed there during the eighteenth century by Robert Adam.

Further east, Craven Street, which acts as a southern boundary to Charing Cross station, was named after another Jacobean house built near Drury Lane for the 1st Earl of Craven and now sadly destroyed. This has a number of solid unpretentious eighteenth-century houses, one of which, marked by a plaque, was occupied by Benjamin Franklin for eighteen years when he was agent for the House of Assembly, Philadelphia, and for other provinces. Benjamin Franklin left Craven Street in about 1773, but he had clearly not been very happy with his surroundings by the river side: 'The whole town is one great smoaky [sic] house', he wrote, 'and every street a chimney, the air full of floating sea-coal soot, and you never get a breath of what is pure, without riding some miles for it into the country.' The house he occupied is now the headquarters of the British Society for International Understanding and for various Anglo-American societies. During his stay in Craven Street, Franklin must have watched the erection by the Adam brothers of a huge building project, laid out between 1768–74, called the Adelphi – a name derived from the Greek *adelphoi* – the 'brothers' of the Heroic Epistle. It was a compact mass of buildings with apartments above

and stores and warehouses on river level, supported by a series of archways
from which goods could be offloaded from barges moored under them,
occupying much of the site of old Durham House. Virtually nothing of the
Adelphi remains – its destruction was probably one of the most
reprehensible acts of commercial vandalism perpetrated in the 1930s.

A number of eighteenth-century buildings still survive in Buckingham
Street, which runs parallel to Villiers Street and ends at the old York
watergate from which the Duke of Buckingham would have embarked on
his boat, the river at that time occupying the whole area now known as the
Victoria Embankment Gardens.

During the eighteeenth century the river was still the main and most
enjoyable thoroughfare between Westminster and the City, and there was
still only one bridge – London Bridge – spanning the river until
Westminster Bridge was built in 1750 after fierce opposition and sabotage
by the watermen who quite naturally saw it as a threat to their livelihood.
Westminster Bridge was followed by Blackfriars Bridge in 1760 and
Battersea Bridge 1771–3, but it should be emphasised that none of the
bridges now standing are the original eighteenth-century ones.

Among the eighteenth-century houses still to be seen and enjoyed in
Buckingham Street is one built on the site of a house occupied by Samuel
Pepys from 1679–88 and marked with a blue plaque to that effect. Charles
Dickens not only lived for some time at No. 15, but used the street as the
place in which the kindly Betsy Trotwood paid for rooms for her ward,
David Copperfield, and Dickens mentions the proximity of the river to the
street in his novel. Some of the houses towards the river have very fine link-
snuffers and beautifully proportioned doorways, their porches supported by
richly carved brackets of acanthus leaves.

John Adam Street

283

left, Eighteenth-century link-snuffers in Buckingham Street
right, The Royal Society of Arts

John Adam Street runs at right angles to Buckingham Street, following roughly the curve of the river at this point, and contains more good examples of buildings by the Adam brothers, one notable one being the headquarters of the Royal Society of Arts, designed especially for that distinguished institution, built 1772–4. It is built of brick with stone facings, and a noble Venetian window on the *piano nobile* is flanked by stone columns of the slender Ionic order, the central entrance porch being supported by somewhat sturdier columns of the Roman Corinthian order. It is a suitable impressive building for such a society, which should be known perhaps by its proper name, The Society for the Encouragement of Arts, Manufactures, and Commerce, founded in 1754. The interior is as imposing as the exterior, and the lecture hall still preserves a series of allegorical mural paintings by James Barry, the arch enemy of Sir Joshua Reynolds. To give some idea of the diversity of interests of members of this society, mention should be made of the leading role they played in the Great Exhibition of 1851, the encouragement they have given to such important training bodies as the City and Guilds, and the premiums they gave to promising young artists who later became world famous men such as J. M. W. Turner, Edwin Landseer and many others. The statue in the hall is that of Joshua Ward, whose invention Friars' Balsam is far more widely known for its medicinal properties than is the name of its creator.

The north-eastern end of John Adam Street is sealed off visually by another very fine example of a typical Adam façade; its thin pilasters are richly decorated with classical motifs such as the Greek honeysuckle pattern in stucco, and the richly worked iron balconies use the same motif, adapted for the different material. It is the ability that Robert Adam possessed to design, in very clear lively drawings, patterns which could then be interpreted by the craftsmen which gives such an overall harmony to his buildings. This also accounts for the harmony of his interiors, examples of which are to be seen in some of the lovely domestic interiors he designed in country houses in the London area, Kenwood House and Syon House, for example. The Sir John Soane Museum in Lincoln's Inn Fields contains literally thousands of drawings from this most remarkable Scot. This central façade is designed as a focal point at the end of John Adam Street, and the other buildings in the street were intended to play a subordinate role but to retain the balance by their similar proportions and fenestration. While some are more or less intact, others have unfortunately been altered, the proportions of the windows changed and the unity of the street destroyed.

The next few blocks eastwards along the Strand have nothing of significance for the eighteenth century until one comes to Somerset House, the work of Sir William Chambers, founder member of the Royal Academy in 1768, and an important writer on architecture. Only the great central block which stretches from the Strand to the Victoria Embankment and which originally stood on the very edge of the river, is the work of Sir William Chambers. The eastern unit was designed by Sir Robert Smirke

A view of Somerset House, showing the water gate

285

and built in 1829–35; it is now part of King's College, London, having had additional facilities built since. The western wing, which was the work of Sir James Pennethorne in 1853, was heavily damaged during the Second World War and has been largely rebuilt. It was in this wing that the Navy Board was accommodated in the original building, and some of the smaller brick buildings were used as houses for its members.

The central area is reached from the Strand through an impressive high arched entrance, which then opens out into a vast quadrangle measuring 329 × 224 feet, giving ample room from which to study the stone buildings which enclose it. Apart from the Navy Board and certain branches of the Admiralty – some of the decorative sculpture indicates which areas were devoted to them – the building was designed to house the Royal Academy and its students, the Royal Society (not to be confused with the Royal Society of Arts in John Adam Street, for the latter is a more recent organisation), and the Society of Antiquaries. The Royal Academy rooms have been beautifully restored and the mural paintings cleaned, and the room in which Sir Joshua Reynolds, as President of the Royal Academy, delivered his famous last discourse is still to be seen on the upper storey. A number of most impressive art exhibitions have been held in some of the best eighteenth-century rooms there, the surroundings being as much of an attraction as the contents of the exhibitions.

Imposing as Somerset House is from the courtyard and from the Strand, it is considerably more impressive from the Embankment, and its 800-foot frontage, viewed from Waterloo Bridge, especially when the trees which line

The courtyard of
Somerset House

the Embankment are leafless, make it one of the most spectacular parts of the whole river-front, possibly as far as Greenwich. It was designed to rival the Adelphi in splendour, for Sir William Chambers and the Adam brothers were at daggers drawn, Sir William sharing a certain anti-Scot feeling rife in a fashionable world which saw a great deal of favouritism being shown to Scottish immigrants by the Earl of Bute and his pro-Scottish Queen. Sir William had achieved fame by his study of Chinese gardens when he was in China as a young man, but this was by no means his only architectural experience. He studied for five years in Italy before returning to become architectural tutor to the Prince of Wales (later George III) and to build that charming folly, the Pagoda, in Kew Gardens. He published a book entitled *Designs of Chinese Buildings, Furniture, Dresses, etc.* in 1757, and a far more scholarly book, *Treatise on Civil Architecture*, in 1759. He became one of the two architects to the Crown, the other being Robert Adam, thus it was not surprising that they became deadly rivals, or that Somerset House should have been Chambers' answer to the Adelphi.

The building of so great a project as the frontage of Somerset House was not without its problems. The area chosen was largely mudflats, and one night a large portion of Somerset House slid quietly into the Thames while under course of construction. It was an opportunity for satire too good to be missed by the eighteenth-century lampoonists, and one of them, Peter

A view of Somerset House from the river

Pindar (his real name was John Wolcot) increased Sir William's chagrin by writing one of his notorious 'Odes' which began:

Sir William! cover'd with Chinese renown,
Whose houses are no sooner up than down,
Don't heed the discontented Nation's cry;
Thine are religious houses! – very humble;
Upon their faces much inclin'd to tumble;
So meek they cannot keep their heads on high . . .

This venomous little dart was discharged in 1785, but visitors today should be assured of the stability of the building. The central block on the embankment is eighteenth-century architecture at its most noble – forms massed as though built by one of the old gods of ancient Rome, yet of practical use, for rings by which the boats were tethered at the edge of the Thames are still to be found at intervals along the water-level. The entrances from the river are massively cut arches of large blocks of stone, flanked by rusticated Tuscan columns supporting a solidly built parapet with a heavy balustrade on either side, but unpierced in the centre. The central mass has a simply carved sway and is flanked by two stone lions. Beyond the main entrance, another columned portico arises on the first floor, a screen of Corinthian columns which is linked to the main range of buildings on either side by a Corinthian pilaster, and is crowned by a pediment which just interrupts the balustrading concealing the roof behind it. The whole looks like a splendid stage setting – except that instead of being made from wood and canvas, with painted shadows, every element here is of beautifully cut stone. The Strand entrance is impressive but somewhat crowded, and it is the entrance from the Embankment which displays the dramatic flair of the building's architect.

A little to the east of the Strand entrance, breasting the tide of traffic on either side, is the church of St Mary-Le-Strand, built by James Gibbs as the first of 'Queen Anne's fifty churches' in 1714–17. It cost about £16,000, and although desperately in need of funds for restoration, it is one of the most lovely churches outside the City, with a tower of five stages so beautifully proportioned that it rivals that of Gibbs' other church – St Martin-in-the-Fields. Two major considerations affected the design of St Mary-Le-Strand. The first was its site, for Gibbs realised that it would be impossible for church services to compete with the noises of the streets on either side if windows were put in the lower storey. He was also very aware of the fact that the church would be seen from every angle, unlike many City churches with their sides and east ends hemmed in and therefore almost invisible. It was initially designed without a steeple: instead there was to be an extremely high column outside the west end about 250 feet high (about 66 feet higher than Nelson's Column in Trafalgar Square), surmounted by a statue of Queen Anne, with a more humble campanile as part of the church. After the death of the queen, the scheme had to be modified considerably, and after Gibbs had submitted five or six different designs for the steeple at the west

left, St Mary-le-Strand
right, St Clement
Danes

end, the present one was selected and erected. Unlike the portico to his later church, St Martin-in-the-Fields, St Mary-Le-Strand has a delightful semicircular porch, derived no doubt from churches which he had studied in Rome under Carlo Fontana, but neither this church, nor any other by Gibbs is a lifeless copy of an Italian prototype, rather a virile and original design.

The interior of St-Mary-Le-Strand is surprisingly uncomplicated, but beautifully proportioned and uncluttered, and the fine plasterwork on the ceiling by two London craftsmen, John Wilkins and his partner Chrysostom, has been well restored. A fine Hanoverian coat of arms fills the central part of the pediment at the east end, where a great architectural feature not unlike a Roman triumphant arch introduces the curved apsidal end in which stands the altar. Unlike the pulpits to be found in so many Wren churches, the one at St Mary-Le-Strand is unobtrusive, and there are no galleries in which the congregation might be accommodated.

It would be a tragedy if this church were to collapse from neglect or lack of funds, but like so many City churches, it was built at a time when church-going was compulsory and today suffers from the absence of a congregation sufficiently large to maintain it.

Further eastwards, also on an island site in the Strand, is the church of St Clement Danes – almost certainly the church associated with the nursery rhyme that begins: 'Oranges and Lemons, say the bells of St Clement's'. Sadly the original bells were badly damaged during the blitz, but they were recast in 1957 from the old metal by the firm which cast the sanctus bell (this survived the blitz) in 1588. The association with oranges and lemons is obscure, but it may be that the church is connected with the delivery of these fruits to Clare Market – a delivery which entailed trespassing on Clement's Inn (then one of the Inns of Court) and for which the tenants demanded a toll. Frank Lockwood, a nineteenth-century writer, describes how he was presented on New Year's Day with an orange and a lemon by the porter of the Inn, who then demanded half a crown in payment.

A very much earlier church on the site of Wren's church may well have been used by a community of Danes who had been converted to Christianity, and a Danish flag hung in the chancel at one time. St Clement Danes was built by Edward Pierce under Wren's supervision, but the steeple remained unfinished until James Gibbs added the upper storeys in 1719. This steeple survived the blitz, but the church was gutted and remained derelict for over ten years until it was beautifully rebuilt, and in 1958 it was reconsecrated as the church of the Royal Air Force. There are 735 crests of RAF units carved in slate now inset into the floor of the nave. The church also contains a memorial to the Air Forces of the Commonwealth, and under the west gallery there is a shrine commemorating members of the United States Air Force who died during the Second World War in defence of our common freedom. The pulpit was pieced together from fragments of the original one (probably by Grinling Gibbons), but the painting by William Kent which, thanks to Hogarth's ridicule, made him the laughing stock of eighteenth-century London, was in fact removed even before Hogarth's engraving was published in 1725. Dr Johnson was a regular worshipper at the church, and a statue of the famous lexicographer and thinker, made by Percy Fitzgerald in 1910, now stands on the little triangle of turf immediately outside the east end.

From the statue of Dr Johnson it is a logic step to seek out his house in Gough Square, about 200 yards further east and reached by a well-signposted alley on the north side of Fleet Street. It is a solid, squarish eighteenth-century house with a minute garden, but a building which nobody interested in the eighteenth century should fail to visit. It was in this house that Johnson, with his team of secretaries, produced his famous Dictionary, published in 1755, and from which he wrote a devastating rebuke to his hitherto reluctant patron, the Earl of Chesterfield.

In this area there is a succession of little courts, such as Crane Court and Red Lion Court, which are worth investigating, for there are some surprisingly well-preserved late seventeenth- and early eighteenth-century houses tucked away just north of the frenetic Fleet Street. Johnson's Court is just east of Red Lion Court, and Dr Johnson actually lived there from approximately 1766–76, but oddly enough the name has no connection with him, and it is just a coincidence that he lived in a house which once stood there.

If one walks westwards from Gough Square, across New Fetter Lane and down Greystoke Place, one comes to Cursitor Street which leads into Chancery Lane. The 'Cursitors, or Coursetours, or Cgerici du Cursu', who gave their name to Cursitor Street, were originally twenty-four in number

Samuel Johnson

and were responsible for writing out and issuing writs in the name of the Court of Chancery.

A little gateway at the northern end of Chancery Lane on the western side leads into Stone Buildings – the next major example of eighteenth-century building in this part of London, and the work of Sir Robert Taylor in 1774–8. The west side is faced with beautifully cut stone – some of the best in Lincoln's Inn, but still badly scarred by shrapnel from bombs which, to judge by the pitting of the brickwork on the eastern side, must have exploded between the buildings. Still further westwards is the charming array of grass and tall plane trees of Lincoln's Inn Fields, with a number of eighteenth-century houses on the north side interspersed with houses of different periods, the most important being the Sir John Soane Museum. This was formerly the home of one of the most original English architects and now contains, among many other treasures, two of Hogarth's most famous series. The first of these, 'The Rake's Progress', painted in 1733, portrays many of the follies, stupidities and brutalities that were rife in London at that time. In 1754 the corruption of Parliament was the target of his series of four paintings of 'The Election'. Quite apart from the brilliant way in which Hogarth satirised the conduct of an eighteenth-century election campaign, these are most beautifully painted, and show what masterly control he could exercise over oil paint. The eighteenth-century houses in which Sir John Soane lived and in which his collection is now on display can be readily distinguished from other houses of the same date on the north side of Lincoln's Inn Fields by the presence of the stone-faced ground floor with semicircular arched windows. The *piano nobile* is enriched

left, Interior of St Clement Danes, with the RAF insignia carved into the floor
right, Dr Johnson's house in Gough Square

by low balustrades and topped by a pair of statues and is a neat architectural proclamation of the individuality of the owner. The museum is entered by a door on the west side, a narrow passage which is almost immediately met by a lovely winding stair with a niche at the turn of the stairs. To the right is one of the many surprises in store for the visitor – a spacious room which has been made to appear more spacious still by the insertion of mirrors, a device which this highly original architect uses elsewhere.

The contents of the museum are as original and as eccentric as the man himself – grimy plastercasts of architectural or sculptural details are to be found hanging in the same room as fragments of Parian marble statuary from Greece. The range of objects is bewildering: tiny exquisite objects in bronze and a huge granite sarcophagus of an Egyptian pharoah, Seti I (*c.* 1392 B.C.); paintings by J. M. W. Turner and engravings of more archaeological interest than beauty; and pictures, including the famous Hogarths, hinged so that they can be laid back like the door of a cupboard to reveal a second layer of paintings behind them, or to enable the visitor to look down a kind of lift shaft to a 'monk's parlour' tricked out with fragments of medieval interest.

Upstairs there are two beautifully lit rooms containing all kinds of treasures, arranged in a rather more orderly fashion. There is a collection of over eight thousand drawings by Robert Adam, and models of some of Soane's own buildings – whether actual or projected. It is one of the most fascinating museums in London, a very personal collection of a wealthy, successful and original architect whose work extended right into the nineteenth century, and whose influence still endures today, for this man, the son of a bricklayer, endowed a valuable travelling studentship at the Royal Institute of British Architects and a fund for architects less fortunate or successful than he.

Another eighteenth-century house of some interest is on the western side of Lincoln's Inn Fields, immediately south of the more famous Lindsey House, possibly by the great seventeenth-century architect, Inigo Jones. The eighteenth-century house in the Palladian style of 1730 was built by a little known architect, Henry Joynes, and since it is designed on the same principles of proportion as those employed by Inigo Jones, the two houses harmonise well with one another.

The next major eighteenth-century building to be seen is easily reached from St Paul's underground station – the church of St Botolph, Aldersgate, which stands north of St Paul's Cathedral, almost on London Wall, and is probably more easily seen from the overpass leading into the Museum of London than from the tree-shaded Postman's Park on the church's south side. The church which previously occupied the site escaped the great fire, but was nevertheless rebuilt in 1754; its interior was entirely redesigned in 1788 and additional changes were made to the east end in 1831, but in keeping with the rest of the church. There is some doubt as to its architect – it was possibly Nathaniel Wright who was responsible for the late eighteenth-century interior. The church has retained its Georgian galleries (although the box pews have gone), and after its rather drab exterior, the lightness and the elegance of the interior are a most joyful discovery. The high ceiling is lit with a series of semicircular windows and decorated by restrained plaster ornament. The east end contains a painting of 'The Agony in the Garden' on glass by James Pierson, carried out in 1788. The pulpit, its sounding-board and the organ-case are all of approximately the same period.

On the opposite side of London Wall in the Museum of London, there are many remarkably fine examples of the buildings of eighteenth-century London and their contents, from the most delightful shop-fronts (including a particularly lovely one from Cornhill, originally kept by Birch and Birch) to the grimmest of reminders of the prison conditions, including the heavy door of the condemned cell from Newgate Prison. There are complete rooms from houses of the period and many examples of the craftsmanship which adorned them, all most beautifully displayed, and one very favourite exhibit is the glittering golden Lord Mayor's coach which is used every year to make the annual journey through the City, drawn by the magnificent Whitbread horses, bearing the new Lord Mayor to the Guildhall. It is an elaborate carriage, almost the equal of the royal coach; it has panels on the side painted by Cipriani, an eighteenth-century Italian artist, and it is richly carved with symbolic figures emphasising London's splendour. The Museum of London was specially designed to display this lovely example of the coachmaker's art to its best advantage, and also to allow it to emerge into the thoroughfare of London Wall for the Lord Mayor's show.

Just west of the Bank underground station there is another major eighteenth-century building at the very heart of the City of London – the Mansion House, the official residence of the Lord Mayor during his term of office. It is not normally open to the public, although written permission can be obtained in advance. The Mansion House stands at the intersection of Poultry and Cornhill with Walbrook, Princes Street and King William Street, on the site of the old Stocks Market and part of a churchyard. It was designed by George Dance the Elder and first occupied in 1752. As there is no room for a forecourt, the steps and entrance porch look rather crushed against the facade, and it is really not as impressive as it should be for a building of such importance. During the eighteenth century it had two additional buildings on its roof: the one which the cockneys promptly dubbed 'Noah's Ark' was removed in 1795, but the other, known as 'The Mare's Nest', remained in position until 1842. The allegorical figures on the pediment which symbolise various aspects of London's great traditions were the work of an ambitious and able young mason-sculptor, Robert Taylor, who eventually became an architect and achieved a knighthood. He has already been mentioned in connection with his work on Stone Buildings Lincoln's Inn, and the Bank of England. The estimated cost of the Mansion House varies considerably, but Henry Chamberlain, who dedicated his great work, *A Compleat History and Survey of London*, to the Lord Mayor of London, Samuel Turner, in 1769 from his address in Hatton Garden, gave

The Mansion House

the cost as £42648 18s. 8d. and this included about £3900 compensation paid for the removal of houses on the site.

The interior of the Mansion House is as richly ornate as might be expected for the home of so important a citizen of London, and the first floor, from the main entrance southwards, has a succession of majestic rooms, culminating in the Egyptian Hall – a name derived from the books of Vitruvius, a Roman writer, whose knowledge of the real nature of Egyptian architecture was slight, but whose books were revered by all eighteenth-century students of Palladian architecture, including Lord Burlington, who built a similar Egyptian Hall in York. There is a large Ballroom on the second floor, reached by means of a noble stairway, and functions at the Mansion House, when the historic plate and insignia are in use, are some of the most impressive in the City of London.

Almost nothing remains of the eighteenth-century work at the Bank of England, for although Sir Robert Taylor built a great deal, and Sir John Soane added to this later, an almost complete rebuilding programme undertaken by Sir Herbert Baker in the 1930s destroyed most of the eighteenth-century rooms. All that remains is part of the screen wall by Sir John Soane on the south side – part of the Princes Street wall and some of that on Threadneedle Street – and a statue in Lothbury of Sir John Soane which is a somewhat belated acknowledgement of the architectural contribution he made to the building.

Eastwards, off the south side of Cornhill, there are some little courtyards containing eighteenth-century buildings squeezed in between the high walls

with James Gibbs early in his career. The interior is somewhat more ornate than the exterior might suggest.

There are a number of more ordinary eighteenth-century houses in this fashionable area – Montpelier Row between Marble Hill Park and Orleans Road has some charming examples, and there are others, more countrified in appearance, near to the river bank and almost opposite Eel Pie Island. It is a rewarding district in which to wander, and the only real disappointment is the parish church – St Mary's, a medieval church with a medieval western tower to which an eighteenth-century body was added by John James in 1714–15 as an economical rebuilding and part of Queen Anne's scheme for fifty churches. This church is more notable perhaps for its association with Alexander Pope, whose villa was in the neighbourhood but of which almost nothing remains. St George's, Hanover Square, which was also designed by John James, shows some originality and taste, but the classical addition to St Mary's Church seems to be a well meaning series of architectural clichés, with all the correct details but no conviction – a spiritless performance.

No one could apply this criticism to Strawberry Hill, Horace Walpole's 'Gothick' house, a mile or so south-west of Marble Hill. It is now occupied by St Mary's College, but is usually accessible to visitors if prior arrangements have been made in writing, especially during the college vacation.

Horace Walpole, fourth Earl of Orford and the youngest son of his famous father, Sir Robert Walpole, acquired a house on the site from a Mrs Chenevix who kept a famous toy shop and china shop near Charing Cross,

Strawberry Hill House with the Victorian wing on the left

305

and this association with toys appears from time to time in letters from Horace Walpole dealing with his activities at Strawberry Hill. There is no better way of getting the feel of eighteenth-century London than by reading the letters of this exceptionally witty, astute and interesting man, for they range over a very wide field and are the observations of a remarkably perceptive interpreter of the events which took place during his lifetime, including the American War of Independence and the French Revolution.

Strawberry Hill is probably the finest example of the 'Gothick' revival in the country, but in no way to be identified with the rather ponderous 'Gothic' of the next century which produced the Houses of Parliament, St Pancras Station and Hotel, and Tower Bridge. The decoration, derived from medieval sources, use recognisably Gothic forms and details in a wholly un-medieval way. The medieval shapes – the ogival arches and crockets of the tombs in Westminster Abbey (that of 'Crouchback', for example) – appear here in Strawberry Hill as fireplaces and overmantels, and the great stone fan vaults of Henry VII's Chapel are transformed into papier mâché and plaster roof decoration for a tiny Long Gallery. As the years passed, Walpole became more and more absorbed in the development of Strawberry Hill, and as he had both taste and was wealthy enough to be able to indulge himself, the result is delightful. While other eighteenth-century gentlemen contented themselves in the main with the erection of a few 'Gothick' ruins as eye-catchers in their spacious grounds, Horace Walpole was one of the few who built an entire house in this style. He possibly began on this project somewhat flippantly, for he had no intention, he wrote, of making his house 'so Gothick as to exclude convenience and modern refinements in luxury', but he did suggest that if the house was imprinted with 'the gloomth of abbeys and cathedrals', the garden was to be in contrast to this, and to reflect 'the gaiety of nature'.

The fact is that there was something of a reaction against the impeccable formality of eighteenth-century classical buildings, and, as a relief from their cold perfection, wealthy landowners turned to two very different forms of architectural decoration. As Mrs Montague admitted in 1749: 'sick of Georgian elegance and symmetry, or Gothic grandeur and magnificence, we must all seek out the barbarous gaudy gout of the Chinese.'

Thus, at Horace Walpole's 'little Gothick* castle at Strawberry Hill' even Robert Adam toyed with 'Gothick' forms in order to design a ceiling, while in Kew Gardens, about four miles north of Strawberry Hill, that most Palladian of architects, Sir William Chambers, indulged in a number of Oriental buildings of which only the Pagoda now survives. This interest in Oriental decoration was probably engendered by the numbers of eighteenth-century gentlemen who had spent some profitable years in the East, and who returned with curios and reminders of their 'bungalows' (the first time the word appears in the English language) and had Chinese wallpapers on their walls even in an otherwise classical suite of rooms.

It was not of course necessary to accept Palladian principles completely, or to adopt as the only alternatives the 'Gothick' or the 'Chinese'. A man as

*The various spellings of the word Gothic may cause some confusion. Gothic denotes medieval Gothic; Gothick refers to the Georgian version of this style; 'Gothic' is the Victorian version.

Strawberry Hill House
– the Long Gallery

creative as Robert Adam very soon devised a number of decorative schemes which, loosely based on classical motifs, escaped the pedantry of his contemporaries such as William Chambers. One of Adam's most beautiful houses is near Isleworth (or, as it was called in the eighteenth century, Thistleworth), a couple of miles due north of Marble Hill House and Strawberry Hill. This is Syon (or Sion) House, which is still in the hands of the original noble family, the Dukes of Northumberland, who commissioned Robert Adam to take a much older house, built on the site of a convent dispossessed after the Reformation of 1535, and to modernise it throughout.

The rather bald exterior of Syon House, with its entirely unconvincing battlements, giving no inkling of the splendours within. The Great Hall, two storeys high, is formed like a Roman basilica, but with curved recesses at either end, and it measures about 50 feet wide by 30 feet deep, the recesses adding length to the central block. The decoration is all derived from Imperial Rome, but without very much colour, only the stark geometry of the pavement giving relief from the icy grandeur of the walls and ceiling. It is all rather overwhelming despite the grace of the moulded plaster work by

307

The entrance to Syon House

Adam's craftsman, Joseph Rose, and the fluted columns which guard the openings of the doors and the ground-floor windows. Most of the sculpture is of clear white stone, except for a magnificent bronze, 'The Dying Gaul' at the foot of the stairs to the right, between the Roman Doric columns and the entablature defining the recess to the east.

From this glacial magnificence one enters the Ante-Room, surely one of the most richly ornate rooms ever designed by Robert Adam. It is not a large room – it has two columns at the east end which give the impression of a recess, but actually reduce the central floor space to a thirty-feet square. The columns are of a most beautiful greenish marble-antique stone or stone veneer – and great panels by Joseph Rose of trophies of arms in the Roman manner fill the spaces between doors and windows. In order to preserve the symmetry there is a door on either side of the richly ornate fireplace, but only the one leading to the Dining-Room on the right is a practical door, the one on the left being an identical dummy one. The whole room is rich in gold leaf, and even the statues which surmount the entablature over each column of green marble are gilded. Yet it is neither vulgar nor ostentatious.

Confronted with such decorative splendour, it is easy for visitors to be deceived into thinking that Robert Adam was wholly concerned with the appearances of his rooms, and not with the functions for which they were designed. This is quite untrue, and in a long passage, too long to be quoted here, he explained the considerations which obliged him to design the Dining-Room as he did. First, he argued that, unlike the French, the eighteenth-century Englishman of any standing was much concerned with the government of the country, and since many of the decisions were made by groups of parliamentarians over dinner, it was natural that the Dining-

public in the Hampstead area, but there are many more humble but still lovely examples of eighteenth-century architecture to be seen in Hampstead – in fact too many for much more than an indication of their whereabouts. When Henry Chamberlain wrote his *History and Survey* in 1769 he described how Hampstead 'used to be resorted to for its mineral waters', and it seemed at one time that it might have become a spa, such as that at Bath or Cheltenham, but it remained just a kind of oasis for the merchants and citizens of London. Thanks to a very active preservation society it has survived surprisingly well the inevitable sprawl of the city, and there are many areas in which the eighteenth-century atmosphere has been retained, long after the more popular pleasure gardens such as Vauxhall and Ranelagh have disappeared.

Hampstead still looks very much like a village, for despite a great deal of later building the very nature of the site, with its changes of level and little intersecting lanes, its small clapboarded houses with white palings overlooked by larger more sophisticated houses with important facades, pillared porches and other signs of a wealthier owner are all rural rather than urban. A number of writers and artists have lived in this area over the past 100 years, and many of their dwelling places are marked by blue plaques; particular mention must be made of John Keats, John Constable, John Galsworthy and Robert Louis Stevenson, but there are many others who found refuge in this village so near to London.

It is a place that invites wandering and is an unfailing source of discovery for the curious. Even the names of some of the lanes reflect its early history: it was in Well Walk, for example, that the eighteenth-century visitors sought the medicinal water, and in Flask Walk where they could buy bottles of it to take home. It was in Flask Walk that members of the famous Whig club, the Kit-Cat Club, foregathered for their summer meetings. The rest of the year they met near Temple Bar on the premises of a pastrycook named Christopher Kat, renowned for his pies, and it is thought that the name of this club, which counted in its membership such distinguished men as the Duke of Marlborough, Sir Robert Walpole, Sir John Vanbrugh, Sir Christopher Wren, Joseph Addison and Richard Steele, was either derived from the name of the proprietor, or from the sign of the 'Cat and Kit' outside.

Of the great variety of buildings which make up the original village, there are some clapboarded houses which would not look out of place in a Kentish village such as Tenterden – rural building such as that in the Vale of Health, or the one in the centre of the village at the corner of Hollybush Hill. This is the house built as a studio by George Romney in 1797, the artist best known perhaps for his portraits of Lady Hamilton, Lord Nelson's mistress. (Two of Romney's portraits of this lady hang in Kenwood House, but they are somewhat earlier in date than this house.)

There are many eighteenth-century terraced houses, the most unspoilt group being in Church Row to the south-west of the village, but these are by no means the only examples. Another row, just south-west of Whitestone Pond, called Lower Terrace, contains the house to which John Constable

left, Church Row,
Hampstead
right, Fenton House

brought his sickly tubercular wife in the hope that the clean air from the heath would cure her, but in vain. He painted a number of his finest pictures in this area – not only his windswept landscapes of Hampstead Heath, but the Admiral's House, a well-preserved eighteenth-century mansion quite near to Fenton House. Only two of these houses in Hampstead are open to the public – Fenton House, and the house which belonged to John Keats and is now a museum to his memory.

Out of the village on the north and north-eastern sides overlooking the heath, there are other large houses – one in which William Pitt the Elder, Earl of Chatham, lived – and two famous inns. The first, Jack Straw's Castle, seems to have had some connection with the notorious rebel, Jack Straw, who was second-in-command of the insurgents led by Wat Tyler in the Peasants' Revolt of 1381, and who presumably had some kind of a stronghold in this area. The present building, however, cannot be older than eighteenth-century; it had to be extensively repaired after the Second World War and was restored very much to its appearance as described by Washington Irving in *Tales of a Traveller* in 1824. Still further north is The Spaniards Inn with its little toll-house, famous for the part which its landlord, Giles Thomas, played in saving Kenwood House from the mob during the Gordon riots of 1780. It apparently derived its name from a house on the site which was at one time the residence of the Spanish ambassador to the court of James I. Between Jack Straw's Castle and Golders Green to the north-west there is another notable inn, made famous by the music-halls of the nineteenth century. This is The Old Bull and Bush, featured in the Victorian music-hall song – a reminder of the rumbustious parties of Londoners who came to the heath on high days and holidays. An unscrupulous lord of the manor tried to enclose parts of the heath and to build on it, but he lost the lawsuit which followed in 1816 and there is little chance now that the heath will ever be built over.

Three famous invalids sought relief in Hampstead: the first has already been mentioned – Mrs John Constable. The second was Robert Louis Stevenson, and the third, perhaps the best known of all, was John Keats. He came to Hampstead early in the nineteenth century by which time the tentacles of ribbon development were already stretching out towards the village and its district. John Keats lived in a house in what was then John Street, but is now named Keats Grove after its famous inhabitant. He lived there in a three-year-old house from December 1818 to September 1820, but died in Rome the next year. It was in his trim little Hampstead garden that he wrote some of his loveliest poems – notably his famous 'Ode to a Nightingale', and the Keats Museum has many relics of this unhappy young genius.

On the corner of Keats Grove is the church of St John, an early nineteenth-century church, not to be confused with the parish church of Hampstead, which is also dedicated to St John. The parish church was originally built by an architect named Sanderson in 1744–7, but possibly designed by Henry Flitcroft, whose work at St Giles-in-the-Fields, Soho, has already been mentioned. St John's is mainly of yellow brick, with a tall spired tower which is a landmark for miles around, but the interor was much altered in the nineteenth century, and it is now basically a Victorian church. John Constable's grave is in its churchyard.

The little church of St John on Downshire Hill is a neat chapel of the Regency period, about 1818, and seems to fit neatly in the area of Regency stucco and demure façades of the houses around it. Inside it is light, untroubled and serene, with high pews, and galleries supported by graceful slender pillars. The reredos is classical in design and shows that the Regency period inherited much of the taste and reticence of the eighteenth century.

George III reigned from 1760 to 1820, although the last years were badly disrupted not only by his own madness, but by the Napoleonic wars. Eventually the royal playboy, George, Prince of Wales, emerged from the wings and took the centre of the stage, and whatever his faults, he left London with some of the loveliest streets of houses to be seen anywhere in this great metropolis. It is the works executed under the direction of this royal patron that will be the subject of the next chapter – the London of *Vanity Fair* and *Sense and Sensibility*.

7

Regency London

———————❦·❧·❧·❦———————

The buildings of Regency London show logical developments from those of the eighteenth century, and although, technically, the Regency style may be said to date from 1811 when the Prince of Wales assumed the title of Prince Regent at the age of forty-nine, the style of art and architecture associated with his name had been evolving for many years.

The predominant interest in details derived from Greek art rather than from the art of the Romans was stimulated as early as 1762 by the publication of the writings of James 'Athenian' Stuart and his partner, Nicholas Revett. Such characteristic architectural details as the Ionic columns, with their easily distinguishable capitals with ram's horn volutes and their slender proportions, and the increasing frequency with which the Greek anthemion (the honeysuckle motif) appeared, not only in the delicate iron balconies but in the stucco panels which decorated much of the work of Robert Adam, all anticipated the decorative themes of the Regency style. Even the harmonious Regency terraces, squares and crescents were only in fact the logical development of the eighteenth-century idea that they could be designed as a unity.

The interest in Greek art was further stimulated by the arrival in London in about 1812 of a series of Greek sculptures bought from the indifferent Turkish rulers of Greece, and thereby saved from destruction either by carelessness, vandalism or the relentless effects of wind and weather. It should be emphasised that the acquisition of the famous Elgin Marbles was not, as is sometimes implied, the looting of a small nation's art treasures by a more powerful and more wealthy country. Thomas Bruce, the eighth Earl of Elgin, bought them from the Turks and sold them to the British Museum for £35,000, a fraction of the price he eventually had to pay for them. One has only to compare the condition of this magnificent collection, safely preserved in the British Museum, with that of those sculptures left behind on the Acropolis to see how much better it might have been had Lord Elgin been able to transport every piece of sculpture on the site to the safety of the British Museum.

The most important contribution to be made to London during the Regency period began with the reversion of Marylebone Park to the Crown in 1811, and with the possibilities which this presented to the Prince and his architect, John Nash, for planning a great architectural scheme which would link Buckingham Palace and the Mall to a most ambitious complex

opposite, Gloucester Gate

occupying the whole of the area now returned to the Crown. They had a vision of a great processional way stretching first from the Mall to Piccadilly Circus, then going northwards, demolishing a number of insignificant streets in its path to form a new royal road to be called Regent Street, which would link with the existing Portland Place and the southern rim of Marylebone Park. At this point there was to be an entirely new development with houses set in tree-planted open spaces, a new canal, and terraces linked in one great harmonious scheme at the centre of which would be a royal pleasure garden, pavilions, a *cour d'honneur* and a huge double circus. The cost of the scheme was, of course, astronomical, but the Prince Regent was unlikely to let such a sordid detail cloud his soaring imagination, and his architect was certainly unwilling to curb his royal patron's ambition.

The choice of John Nash as the architect to the Prince Regent was perhaps a strange one, for until Nash married a very beautiful woman somewhat late in life, his architectural career had not been entirely successful and he had been bankrupt once. Mrs Nash had apparently been involved in some secret liaison in the strangely raffish crowd which thronged the 'Vanity Fair' of Carlton House where the Prince set up his little court before becoming Regent. There is, however, no firm evidence that John Nash's marriage was a marriage of convenience and that he was husband in name only, nor that Mrs Nash had ever been the mistress of the Prince. Nevertheless it was strange that she should appear from time to time with an increasing little family of children from the Isle of Wight by the name of Pennethorne, to whom she was guardian, and gossip was not slow to suggest that they were her own children, fathered not by her husband, but by the Prince. Again, nothing was ever proved. Yet the success of John Nash as an architect does seem to have been connected in some way with his marriage.

Carlton House was built by Lord Carlton early in the eighteenth century; it was then bequeathed by him to Lord Burlington and later acquired by the Prince of Wales. In 1788 it was extensively redecorated and modernised for George Frederick Augustus, Prince of Wales, later the Prince Regent, and further alterations were made to its interior in about 1815. Despite its reputation, Jane Austen, whose sedate and perceptive novels portrayed a society very different from that which frequented Carlton House, was shown all round its gilded rooms by the Prince's personal chaplain, the Reverend James Stanier Clarke, who was most anxious that Jane Austen should undertake the writing of a historical novel on the House of Coburg. However, she declined to do so, and this was the last contact between the world mirrored in Thackeray's *Vanity Fair*, and that of *Pride and Prejudice*.

The work on the processional way which was to start at Buckingham Palace began in 1812, and it appears that John Nash relied considerably on his builders and his subordinates to interpret his somewhat loose sketch plans, although he made his intentions about the significance of Regent Street quite clear. 'It will be seen by the plan', he wrote, 'that the whole communication from Charing Cross to Oxford Street will be a boundary and a complete separation between the streets and squares occupied by the nobility and gentry, and the narrow streets and meaner houses occupied by

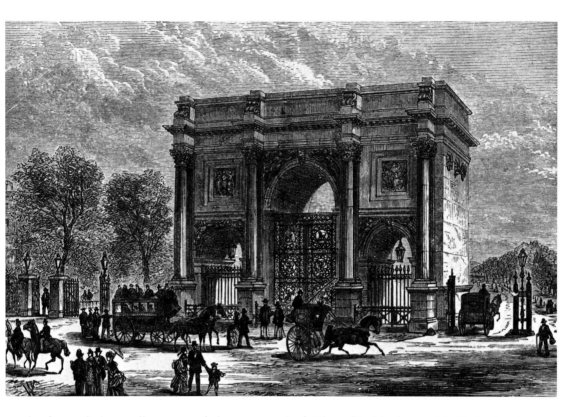

mechanics and the trading part of the community.' First, Buckingham Palace had to be altered and enlarged, and a triumphal arch erected outside in front of the main gate. This is the arch now known as Marble Arch, and it was originally intended that it should be surmounted by an equestrian statue of George IV. A somewhat fanciful contemporary print shows it in front of the palace, but the equestrian statue was at that time a figment of the engraver's imagination and is quite unlike the one eventually carried out by Sir Francis Chantrey, which depicts the king in semi-classical costume, riding without stirrups. The statue now stands in the north-eastern corner of Trafalgar Square, but the arch was removed from outside Buckingham Palace and placed in its present position in 1851. It is based on the Arch of Constantine in Rome, for the Greeks produced no triumphal arches of this kind. The low reliefs on the north side were carved by Richard Westmacott, and those on the south by Edward Bailey. The new processional way gave the Prince Regent an opportunity to have Carlton House demolished, but in the interests of economy, (a somewhat belated effort), the columns which had been such a feature of the old house were used in the construction of the new National Gallery, and the architect, William Wilkins, was not only ordered to use these columns, but forbidden to erect any buildings which might impair the splendid view of St Martin-in-the-Fields offered by the clearance of some less significant streets in the construction of Trafalgar Square.

Marble Arch as it was in the nineteenth century

above, An artist's
impression of Marble
Arch standing in front
of Buckingham Palace,
the position for which
it was originally
intended
right, A contemporary
picture of Marble Arch

It had been intended that, in addition to the processional way linking the Mall with Marylebone Park, another fine road would be made eastwards, joining Trafalgar Square to Bloomsbury. This was in fact never finished, although a few buildings of this scheme still remain and will be mentioned later.

The main approach eastwards down the Mall is marked by the two blocks of Carlton House Terrace, one on either side of the Duke of York Steps, and a short road joining the Mall to Waterloo Place. It is said that the two Carlton House blocks were inspired by the two stone-built ones which the French architect, J. A. Gabriel, built on either side of the end of the Place de la Concorde in Paris, but there are many differences between the scheme by Nash with its long range of stucco-covered brickwork and the ground floor with its short stumpy Doric columns of iron, and the severe stone buildings in Paris. Carlton House Terrace looks particularly lovely from between the trees of St James's Park, when the sunlight casts deep luminous shadows between the columns and the light sculptures are seen against a summer sky.

The Duke of York's Column is at the top of a flight of steps which would clearly have been something of an obstacle had the Prince Regent decided to use Lower Regent Street for a great triumphal procession. The statue of the Duke of York by Richard Westmacott stands on top of a 124-foot high column designed by Benjamin Wyatt, sufficiently high, some Regency wags said, for him to be out of reach of his creditors, but since the statue was paid for by a 'voluntary' contribution of one day's pay from every man in the British Army, there might have been other reasons for putting it so far out of reach.

The blocks of Carlton House Terrace which flank the Duke of York's steps are each thirty-one bays wide. The main building of each is enriched by Corinthian columns supporting an attic storey, the roofline is scarcely broken by a pediment, and the end of each block is stated quite firmly by a projecting pavilion. Together the two blocks constitute a street of apartments with a beginning, a middle and an end, and any addition or subtraction would ruin the overall classical balance.

At ground level, the service quarters and storage announce their more humble status both by being smaller in scale, and by having stumpy Doric columns instead of the more stately Corinithian ones above. These Doric columns are made of iron – this was one of the first examples of the constructional use of iron in an architectural scheme, although it had been used decoratively for centuries. Carlton House Terrace was erected after the demolition of Carlton House in 1827–9, and it was originally intended that in addition to the present blocks on the north side of the Mall, there should be an 'answering' one on the south side, but this was never carried out.

Once the upper level of the terrace has been reached at the top of the Duke of York Steps, a short walk to the right shows an entirely different aspect of the building; one house has been taken over by the National Portrait Gallery to enable them to stage a series of excellent exhibitions, so it is now possible not only to enjoy paintings which have hitherto been seen in somewhat congested rooms, but also to enjoy the lovely interiors of Carlton House Terrace, adapted for this purpose.

Immediately to the left, just past the trees and enclosed lawns of Carlton Gardens, stands the Athenaeum, a very famous club which, founded in 1824, numbers among its members some of the most eminent names in the worlds of science and the arts. The present club house, its classical portico surmounted by a gilded statue of Athena, the Greek goddess of wisdom, was designed by the most important of the pupils and assistants of John Nash, Decimus Burton, in 1829. Decimus Burton was the tenth son (hence his name) of James Burton, an indefatigable builder and land speculator, and in his design for the Athenaeum he was clearly influenced by his admiration for the Elgin Marbles, for a frieze based fairly closely on the Parthenon frieze is to be seen just below the original roofline; the uppermost storey is a later addition which somewhat spoils the proportions of the building. The little frieze of cantering horses by John Henning – rather more domesticated than the fierce chargers on the original Parthenon frieze – has now been restored to its original colours. The statue of Athena, resplendent with gold leaf, was sculptured by Edward Hodges Bailey, whose work is also to be seen on Marble Arch. He was the son of a Bristol carver of figure-heads for ships, but he worked with the great Regency sculptor, John Flaxman, and later in the Royal Academy schools.

Facing the Athenaeum on the opposite side of Waterloo Place is another building, the United Services Club, which was founded by surviving veteran officers after the Napoleonic Wars in 1813 and built by John Nash in 1827, although it was extensively altered by his pupil, Decimus Burton, in 1858. This also has a noble two-storey portico on Pall Mall, but its present

left, The Athenaeum
below, The United
Services Club

use seems in some doubt. One can easily distinguish the more flamboyant detailing of Decimus Burton from the more restrained work by John Nash.

The Crimean Memorial, designed by John Bells in 1859, which dominates the central space of Waterloo Place, is clearly of a much later date; it commemorates those members of the Guards Regiments who fell during the Crimean War. The figure of Florence Nightingale, that wonderful and indomitable woman who did so much for the nursing profession, was not erected until 1915.

There is almost nothing left of the buildings which used to be part of the grand design in Lower Regent Street, but the Haymarket Theatre, the Theatre Royal, founded in 1720, still preserves the classical portico designed for it in 1821 by John Nash, although most of the rest of the building is much later. Along Pall Mall to the west, however, a succession of buildings show the Regency style and the developments which emerged as the century progressed. Immediately west of the Athenaeum is the Travellers' Club, founded by Lord Castlereagh in 1819, the present club house being a very original design for the period in which it was built (1829–32) by Sir Charles Barry. To qualify for membership of the club the applicant had to prove that he had travelled out of London in a straight line for at least five hundred miles! It seems odd that so eminent a traveller as Cecil Rhodes should have been blackballed and denied admission.

The style of the Travellers' Club constitutes an architectural break with the Regency tradition of using ancient Greece as the inspiration for buildings at this time. Charles Barry, who had in fact travelled in Greece as a young man, turned for his inspiration to the magnificent palaces erected during the Italian Renaissance for such merchant princes as the Medicis, and, apart from the stucco surfaces of the Travellers' Club, the details are drawn from fifteenth-century Italy. The view from Carlton Gardens, where the red brick façade is only outlined in stucco, is rather more reminiscent of Venice than of Florence, with the round-headed windows on the upper floor and little balconies below each of them, and an overhanging cornice supported by Italianate brackets. The Mall façade is rather more Florentine, however.

It was also fifteenth-century Italy to which Barry was to turn for inspiration when he designed the adjoining Reform Club, founded in 1836, although his building was not completed until 1841. By this date he had competed successfully with a Gothic-Tudor design for the new Houses of Parliament, the old ones having been destroyed in a fire in October 1834. This ability to design a building in whatever architectural style happened to be popular at the time was an absolute necessity for any ambitious young architect during the opening years of the nineteenth century, and was to come to fruition as the reign of Queen Victoria produced an increasingly wealthy and self-confident Britain, although by then even the vestiges of classical disciplines, already eroded during the Regency period, had entirely disappeared.

Further along Pall Mall, past Schomberg House, there is one Regency building which still clings to the classical tradition. This is the building

housing the Oxford and Cambridge Club, designed in 1835 by Sir Robert Smirke, the son of an architect, and his brother, Sydney Smirke. It was completed about 1838, and with its adherence to such classical details as the honeysuckle frieze it must have seemed very old-fashioned to the newly-fledged Victorian architects who were ransacking books of historic ornament for some novel form of decoration with which to embellish the bare bones of their buildings, no matter how incongruous or unsuitable it was functionally.

The Travellers' and the Reform Clubs

Two other buildings of this period remain to be mentioned, although both of them have undergone considerable modification since they were planned. They were under construction at the same time, and the resultant confusion did not always make for good relations between the architects, nor their patrons.

York House, later Stafford House, and now better known as Lancaster House, was first designed for the Duke of York by Robert Smirke in about 1821, but this architect was replced by Benjamin Wyatt before the house was built, and the house as it stands is now largely the work of the latter. Its impressive Corinthian porticoes are now familiar to television viewers all over the world as they were shown as a background to the interviews granted – or not granted – by various members of the opposing sides at the Zimbabwe-Rhodesian conference held at Lancaster House in 1979. York House was acquired by the Stafford family, and the money which the Crown received from the sale was devoted to the purchase of Victoria Park as a recreational area for the children of the East End who were sadly deprived of light and air, trees and grass in that congested slum district. So impressive was Lancaster House when it was in the possession of the Stafford family

right, Admiralty Arch
below, Nelson's
Column, the National
Gallery and St Martin-
in-the-Fields

(and then known as Stafford House) that it was reported that when Queen Victoria accepted an invitation to visit it, she is supposed to have greeted her hostess with 'I have come from my *house* to your *palace*!'

Much of Clarence House was originally built by Sir John Soane, but the serene and dignified building one now sees is largely the work of John Nash and others. It was there that the newly crowned William IV lived with his wife, Queen Adelaide, preferring it to Buckingham Palace and the Palace of St James, where he usually conducted official business; at one time an overhead corridor existed which enabled him to leave his quarters in Clarence House to go to the Palace of St James for official purposes, and to return at the end of the day. Clarence House is now the home of Elizabeth,

the Queen Mother, widow of George VI, so there is always a mounted guard there – part of the Palace Guard – and when she is in residence her personal standard is flown at the masthead.

From Clarence House it is a very short step southwards back into the Mall, and so eastwards towards Trafalgar Square. The Admiralty Arch at the far eastern end is a comparatively modern addition to this part of London, for it was built there in 1911 by Sir Aston Webb as part of the national monument to Queen Victoria at the same time as Buckingham Palace received its present façade. Just north of it a short passage called Spring Gardens records the site of an eighteenth-century garden in which, by inadvertently standing on a certain stone slab, an unsuspecting visitor could be drenched by a spring of water thus released.

As its name implies, Trafalgar Square was designed to be a fitting memorial to the sea battle which finally freed Europe from the tyranny of Napoleon and left Great Britain mistress of the seas. A square was envisaged by John Nash in this area as early as 1812, and he intended that there should be a road leading westwards from it towards Pall Mall, (now called Pall Mall East) and eastwards to the Strand, clearing away a number of smaller streets and showing St Martin-in-the-Fields to best advantage. The square received its present name in 1830. By this time Sir Robert Smirke had built on the west side what is now known as Canada House, but was previously the Union Club and the Royal College of Physicians. This was completed by 1827, and in the meantime a magnificent art collection assembled by John Julius Angerstein, a friend of Sir Thomas Lawrence, the President of the Royal Academy, had been acquired by the nation for about £57,000, and was to form the nucleus of the National Gallery which now occupied the northern edge of Trafalgar Square.

The building was designed by William Wilkins, an architect who was perhaps best known for his work at the University of Cambridge. In his work on the National Gallery he was severely restricted by such considerations as the site on which it stood – formerly the Royal Mews and stables, with barracks to the rear which could not be built upon – and the incorporation into the design of the columns salvaged from the ruins of the demolished Carlton House. The design could thus only be a compromise, and the original building, which cost about £96,000, although it was to be

331

shared by the National Gallery and the Royal Academy, who vacated Somerset House, could only be one room deep at that time – a narrow drawn-out façade extending the whole width of the square but with little to the rear. Even today it is not a very imposing building, and certainly gives no idea of the treasures housed within. The National Gallery is by no means as large as many galleries on the mainland of Europe and contains only about 2000 paintings, but the quality of these paintings makes it second to none in the world. It contains numerous masterpieces painted by some of the world's greatest artists, and they have been freed from the disfiguring layers of dirty varnish which so often seem to be retained by Continental galleries as the hallmark of an 'Old Master', and are displayed, so far as possible, in the condition they were in when they left the master's hand. The contents of the National Gallery, moreover, give a much more balanced survey of European art as a whole than the Louvre, for example, where the emphasis is heavily weighted in favour of French painters. While certain British artists are well represented at the National Gallery, the bulk of this school of painting is to be seen at the Tate Gallery on Millbank, and their pictures at the National Gallery are there to show the place which painters from these islands have, by right, in the story of European art. Extensions to the west of the Gallery have now been completed, thus the boast that every picture possessed by the Gallery can be seen on exhibition (unless, of course, it has had to be withdrawn for attention by the Gallery's own conservation department) is not only still valid, but the collection can be displayed far more effectively. (Some continental galleries admit to having vaults full of paintings which are rarely seen by the public owing to inadequate space for display.)

The National Gallery has an extensive publications department, which produces a wide range of prints and slides of the contents of the Gallery and a series of catalogues compiled by the staff of art historians which display scholarship of the highest quality. It is also possible for any member of the public who possesses an oil painting to arrange to bring it to the National Gallery for the purposes of identification or any other kind of advice, although, in common with the other British galleries, no indication as to the value of the pictures brought will ever be made.

A little to the west of the National Gallery extension is Suffolk Street and Suffolk Place which still retain a few houses that were originally part of the ambitious scheme planned for the Prince Regent, but which never came to fruition. Other buildings east of the gallery, behind St Martin-in-the-Fields, include the impressive stuccoed St Martin's School designed by John Nash 1827–30, with its rusticated ground floor, round-headed windows, and fine Ionic pilasters dividing off the beautifully proportioned facade. It is noticeable how beautifully the inscription is designed as a part of the whole, so that the lettering – a bold Regency version of a Roman alphabet – is not something stuck on as an afterthought, but an integral part of the whole concept. Just to the east of St Martin's School is Adelaide Street, named after the queen of William IV who reigned only seven years, and the newly restored façades of a central block of buildings, originally part of the scheme which Nash had planned to link the St Martin-in-the-Fields area to Bloomsbury, are bounded by this short street, by King William IV Street, and by the Strand. This block has been virtually rebuilt, but the architects have contrived to preserve the main proportions of the Nash facades (although they have taken considerable liberties with the ground floors), and the rounded ends surmounted by elegant 'pepperpot' terminals have been most beautifully restored, so that the feeling of the original Regency building has been retained.

The abandoned Charing Cross Hospital on the north side of King William IV Street was clearly part of the original complex, although this was designed by Decimus Burton and built in 1831–4, with some heavy additions westwards very much later in the century, when storeys built above spoiled Decimus Burton's elegant building. The neglected and scabrous condition of this building makes a sad contrast with the clarity and cleanliness of the newly restored buildings opposite.

Before visiting the major Regency complexes in the north-west of London,

left, A corner of Adelaide Street and the Strand, built by John Nash
right, Charing Cross Hospital

one should return to Trafalgar Square for a final survey and look at its focal point, Nelson's Column. The plinth of this monument is usually the platform for the main organisers and speakers of many dissident groups and the point from which many political and similar rallies set out down Whitehall to lobby Parliament or to present petitions to the Prime Minister of the day in Downing Street. Estimations of the height of the granite column, with its bronze Corinthian capital and the statue of Lord Nelson, seem to vary considerably, but it seems generally agreed that the column itself is about 170 feet high, and the figure of Nelson 17 feet high. The pedestal is decorated with low reliefs, each commemorating naval victories for which Lord Nelson was responsible – namely the Battle of St Vincent, the Battle of Aboukir, the Battle of Copenhagen, and the one at which he met his death, the Battle of Trafalgar. The bronze from which the reliefs were cast came, appropriately enough, from melted down metal from captured French cannons. The relief depicting the Battle of St Vincent on the western face was sculpted by Watson, that of the Battle of Aboukir (or Nile) on the north side by Woodington, the Battle of Copenhagen on the east face by Ternouth, and the Battle of Trafalgar, portraying the death of Nelson on the south side facing down Whitehall, was by Carew. The four lions, each 20 feet long and 11 feet high, were added considerably later in 1868, and were the work of Sir Edwin Landseer, Queen Victoria's favourite animal painter, who was also her art master for a while. The fountains were redesigned in 1939 by Sir Edwin Lutyens, and the charming figures added at the same time. The merman is the work of Sir Charles Wheeler, and the statue of the mermaid by William McMillan.

Other statues in the square include one of General Sir Charles Napier, sculpted by G. G. Adams in 1855; the statue of Sir Henry Havelock by Behnes in the south-eastern corner was placed there in 1861; and there are busts of the famous First World War Admirals – Jellicoe and Beatty – on the north side. There are also standard measurements of one inch, one foot, one yard, one chain and 100 feet recorded on the north side.

The most recent additions to the square are the railings designed to control the crowds when meetings of various kinds take place there, and when the pedestal is used as a platform from which the main speakers can harangue the crowd. There are more festive occasions around Christmas when a magnificent Christmas tree – an annual gift from the people of Norway – is ceremoniously 'unveiled' and illuminated, and carols are sung, and on New Year's Eve, when the square is thronged with happily bibulous revellers, some of whom always find their way into the fountains.

From Trafalgar Square there is still a little more of John Nash's work to be seen before one reaches Piccadilly Circus. This is just off Pall Mall on the north side, tucked away behind the towering mass of New Zealand House at the bottom of Haymarket, and is known as the Royal Opera House Arcade, designed by John Nash with the assistance of G. S. Repton about 1816–18. It is a charming little backwater and often missed by visitors. Orange Street, a turning on the east side of Haymarket, is the only reminder of three streets in the area behind what used to be the King's Mews, the site of the present

National Gallery. The royal stables were divided into three areas – orange, blue and green – and at one time there were three little streets by the names of the colours. Only Orange Street survives.

Piccadilly Circus is best seen at night, when the illuminated advertisements cast a glamourous impression and divert the attention of the visitor from much of the squalor of every kind which laps the steps of Eros. By day the skeletal remains of the sky signs, attached to buildings which were never very distinguished at the best of times, do nothing to improve them, but at night it is an exciting and colourful sight, and when gaslights were first introduced into this area in 1814 it must have been a great attraction for visitors. The first gaslights had in fact appeared somewhat earlier outside Carlton House in 1807, and the south side of Pall Mall had also been provided with a few, although these were only lit on occasions of celebration. (A protest was launched by the many prostitutes frequenting the area of Piccadilly, as they claimed that well-lit streets endangered their business!)

Of the delightful appearance of Regent Street only the sweeping curve now remains, for the charming colonnade was demolished largely on the pretext that it was a rendezvous for those same 'ladies of the town' – a great loss. It is to be seen in drawings by such artists as Thomas Shotter Boys, the Pentonville-born artist who left some remarkably beautiful records of London of the 1840s, and it had a series of cast-iron columns supporting the roof which provided shelter for the leisurely shoppers using the lines of shops behind. Regent Street it still, of course, one of the major shopping centres in London, but nothing of the original scheme remains and all the shops are much later in date.

left, The royal mews
right, The Quadrant,
Piccadilly Circus

The next major Regency building is to be found in Langham Place, an extension of Regent Street north of Oxford Circus. The church of All Souls, Langham Place, was intended by John Nash to provide a visual 'stop' – an indication that there was going to be a change of direction so that Upper Regent Street, his own creation, could link quite naturally with the existing Portland Place. This function of the church was possible until the BBC placed Broadcasting House in its present position in 1931 – a building so different in scale from All Souls that it dwarfed the sharp emphatic spire and destroyed the effect that Nash had planned. Since then additional buildings erected by the BBC to the east of the original Broadcasting House have completely overwhelmed the little church porch and spire, and with buildings of such magnitude in the immediate vicinity there is no longer any opportunity for the church to assert itself as it should.

The design of All Souls, Langham Place, is most unusual, even for as original an architect as Nash, and it attracted a great deal of adverse criticism when it was first erected. One caricature shows the architect transfixed by his breeches and dangling from the top of the sharp spire, the caption being one of those dreadful schoolboy puns in which our nineteenth-century ancestors seemed to revel. It refers to the church as 'Nash-ional Taste'! The church has a giant circular portico on a shallow flight of steps. Above the portico is a kind of elongated drum, and then an acutely pointed spire, an entirely unclassical feature. The interior of the church, in contradiction to the prevailing fashion, has departed from the Greek style to one much nearer to that of Imperial Rome, and it has an ostentatious splendour very unlike the cool clarity of much of the architecture of this period. This church was one of the ones built in response to the Church Building Act of 1818, and was erected between 1822–25, but one suspects that its main function (for Nash) was as a superb piece of architectural scenery.

From All Souls, Langham Place, it is a short walk northwards to Portland Place, which, since it was originally intended to be a tree-lined thoroughfare, is 125 feet wide, the widest street in London apart from Parliament Street. Portland Place leads directly to Park Crescent, a semicircular road announcing the culmination of Nash's grand design. Park Crescent is crossed from east to west by Marylebone Road, and this forms Park Square immediately to the north.

The design of Park Crescent implies that it is on the central axis of the great park of 412 acres, but in fact it is very much nearer to the eastern perimeter of the park. The circumference of the park is about three miles, but it is crossed by a number of paths, the main one linking Hanover Gate on the west to Gloucester Gate in the north-east. The only way to appreciate fully the beauty of the park and its surrounding terraces is on foot – it is one of the most beautiful examples of townscape in Europe. On a fine summer's day, when the roses are in bloom in Queen Mary's Rose Garden, or in the evening when *Midsummer Night's Dream* is being performed in the open air theatre, a visit to Regent's Park can be a memorable occasion, and a visit to the zoological gardens established in the north of the Park in the 1830s can also be rewarding, especially for the younger generation.

All Souls, Langham Place

The buildings of the zoo not only include some of the original nineteenth-century ones, but some of the most inventive and most enterprising of the twentieth century. Among these are the penguin pool, one of the first buildings in the whole country in which the potential of reinforced concrete was realised; the gorilla house and the elephant house, both good examples of elegant functional architecture; and much later, Lord Snowdon's wonderful cat's-cradle of an aviary. It would have been more logical perhaps to have reserved the zoo for the final chapter on twentieth-century London, but it is such an integral part of the whole of the complex designed by Nash that it would be unfair to omit it at this point.

The park is almost encircled by a series of magnificent Regency terraces – some by John Nash, others by his assistants such as Decimus Burton, whose father, James Burton, was also responsible for the erection of some of the buildings. One of the villas in the park, just to the north-west of the Inner Circle, was designed for James Burton by Decimus.

337

The terraces on the west side of the park look at their best in the morning light, and those to the east are truly magnificent in the late evening sun, when the shadows are getting longer and the pale stucco has a kind of glow on it. On the west, the outer ring of terraces consists of York Terrace, Cornwall Terrace, Clarence Terrace, Sussex Place, Kent Terrace and Hanover Terrace, Regent's Canal acting as the northern boundary north of the zoo. On the east side are St Andrew's Place and Cambridge Terrace, between which Nash built a Colosseum which has since been demolished and replaced by a Victorian terrace, Chester Gate and Chester Terrace, Cumberland Place, Cumberland Terrace, and just to the north a new church and buildings of St Katharine's Hospital which was moved from its site east of the Tower of London to make way for St Katharine's Docks in 1826. The following year Decimus Burton planned the layout of the zoo, and by 1830 the entire menagerie which had been housed in the Tower of London for centuries was transferred to its new quarters in the north of the park. To the rear of St Katharine's Church is Park Village West, and on an outer road to the east, reached through Gloucester Gate, is Park Village East.

The centre of the park is known as the Inner Circle, and this contains the open air theatre, as well as delightfully arranged flower gardens, fountains and a restaurant, from which can be seen glimpses of the stucco terraces on the Outer Circle. To the west of the Inner Circle is a sheet of water – an irregular lake covering about 22 acres, and alive with waterfowl which forage among the varied waterplants fringing the lake. The Inner Circle is reached through York Gate to the south.

On the south side of Marylebone Road there is a fine church which forms a dramatic introduction to York Gate immediately opposite. This is St Mary's, the parish church of Marylebone, built on the site of a medieval church which was replaced by a Georgian church about 1741, the interior of which forms the background to the marriage of the Rake in Hogarth's series 'A Rake's Progress'. The present church is even later, and was designed by Thomas Hardwick between 1813–17, so that it was already in position when Nash decided upon the layout of this part of the Regent's Park scheme, a factor which perhaps determined his positioning of York Gate.

St Mary's has an imposing porch of Corinthian columns, with the tower consisting of a sturdy cubical base, a drum above surrounded by free-standing columns, and topped by a small dome which in turn supports a small cupola with carved classical figures as buttresses. The church was drastically altered by Thomas Harris in 1885 when the choir was entirely remodelled, but Hardwick's nave, with its flat ceiling and galleries on three sides, is much as he designed it, and a second storey to the western gallery forms a dignified end to the church.

From York Gate one enters York Terrace, the longest of the Nash terraces on the perimeter of the park, about 1080 feet in length, but so designed with a giant Corinthian order as the central block and pavilions announcing the ends of the terrace that the style never becomes monotonous despite its great length. The builder of this terrace was James Burton.

Immediately north-west of York Terrace is Cornwall Terrace, only about 560 feet long and with a more complex arrangement of masses, so that although the materials are the same as those from which York Terrace was built, the way in which the architect – possibly Decimus Burton – manipulated the façade, gives a very different effect of light and shade. Decimus Burton was probably also responsible for the next terrace to the north – Clarence Terrace – another small terrace built by James Burton in which the same architectural units were employed, but varied somewhat in scale and in detail, although not sufficiently to break the essential harmony between the sequence of separate terrace blocks. However, with so much emphasis placed on the façade, there was sometimes a lack of internal planning, and to approach some of the terraces from the rear can be a disappointing experience, especially if those aspects facing the park have been a little too persuasive.

The somewhat unusual appearance of the next terrace to the north – Sussex Place – certainly raises doubts as to the suitability of the houses as dwelling places, although externally it is one of the most original and most striking terraces on this side of the park. Sussex Place is about 650 feet in length and consists of a central section 47 bays long, with a curved wing of 8 bays on either side, and then a fairly substantial pavilion at either end of 7 bays. This is the only place in the whole scheme where domes were used to give a different and slightly less happy skyline, and the central section, set back behind a portico of columns, must consist of some very dark rooms, which must have been even darker when the terrace was designed, *c*. 1822. The use of the most unclassically-shaped domes was perhaps intended by Nash to provide an element of surprise after the reasonably 'correct' use of classical motifs in other areas, but it does seem a rather bizarre departure. Sussex Place is now occupied by the London Graduate School of Business Studies.

Hanover Terrace, immediately to the north of Sussex Place, is a very charming little terrace scarcely half the length of Sussex Place, with Roman Doric columns and an untroubled roofline which restores the feeling of classical harmony slightly interrupted by the eccentricity of its neighbour to the south. To the rear of Hanover Terrace is a rather more pedestrian project – Kent Terrace – built in 1827 by a man named Smith, who, while conforming to all the conventional requirements of a Regency architect, had little creative ability when compared with men such as John Nash or Decimus Burton. Hanover Lodge, a small elegant house set back from the road, is now part of London University – a joyous little composition with an enclosed entrance set back slightly behind Ionic columns, with a gently projecting block at either end, all beautifully proportioned but as unpretentious as possible. It is the prototype of many similar Regency houses to be seen in such spa towns as Cheltenham and is the kind of house from which it is easy to imagine a Jane Austen character emerging into her sedate and somewhat restricted neighbourhood, very different from that of Becky Sharp with her salon in one of the great Regency terraces.

One of the most enjoyable features of the eighteenth century and of the Regency period which followed was the attention paid to the minor details such as lodge gates, iron railings and balconies. The Regent's Park area has some delightful street furniture – bollards and lamp posts, for example – which adds its own particular ingredient to the overall charm of the district. It was most unfortunate that during the early years of the Second World War, much of this was torn down in an excess of misguided patriotism under the impression that no matter how precious the artefact, if it was of iron, it would be suitable for making munitions or guns. The sacrifice was in vain, for the iron was often quite useless for this purpose and merely rusted away in some forgotten scrapyard. This was particularly regrettable when the railings which surrounded some of the Regent's Park terraces were taken away; some of their replacements would be unworthy of a cattle market, let alone a district of such importance as this.

Hanover Terrace

The Outer Circle continues in a great eastward sweep, with the canal flowing parallel to it just to the south, but it would perhaps be more enjoyable at this point to enter the park by Hanover Gate and then to walk across eastwards to Gloucester Gate, just south of the zoo. It is by Gloucester Gate that one can see the skill with which a Regency architect could vary his details in such a way that a comparatively small house, such as Gloucester Lodge, would appear to be part of the same scheme of which the much grander Gloucester Gate is a more important unit. Gloucester Lodge is a detached house with its own rather fine portico of Ionic columns occupying two storeys of the front. Gloucester Gate is announced by an Ionic portico on the first floor, with a comparatively simple rusticated ground floor and clearly has more prestige than the detached house to the rear. These buildings were erected about 1827, certainly under the influence of John Nash and perhaps even by the great man himself, although he was often all too willing to leave a great deal to his subordinates who were not always worthy of the trust he placed in them. His builders sometimes took advantage of the stucco surfaces to conceal shoddy workmanship beneath.

The flow of classically inspired buildings is briefly interrupted by the insertion of an unashamedly Gothic church just south of Gloucester Gate. This is almost certainly modelled on an example of English Perpendicular Gothic – the chapel of King's College, Cambridge. It was the chapel of St Katharine's Hospital which was originally, in 1148, a royal hospital and a religious foundation founded by Matilda, the queen consort of King Stephen, just east of the Tower of London. But the site was required for the building of St Katharine's Docks in 1825, and the new building, designed in yellow brick, with the chapel, six residences for the pensioners and a separate house for the master, was designed and built just east of Regent's Park by Ambrose Poynter. The church was taken over by London's Danish community in 1950, whose own building in Limehouse had been bombed during the Second World War, and outside in the forecourt is a replica of the Jelling stone – the original being a remarkable example of tenth-century art commemorating the victory of King Harald Bluetooth who drove the Norwegians out of Denmark and made the Danes Christians. The interior of the church is modern, but it contains two carved figures by the seventeenth-century Danish sculptor, Caius Cibber, who also carved the famous phoenix group for Sir Christopher Wren on the north transept of St Paul's Cathedral.

To the east of the park there are two small groupings of houses designed by Nash and his assistants: Park Village West, immediately to the rear of St Katharine's, and Park Village East. The former group is virtually intact, but the latter is incomplete. These houses are entirely different in scale and very varied in style, with all kinds of motifs culled from the Gothic architecture of Europe, and details reminiscent of Italian villas and Swiss chalets. They are detached and owe little allegiance to each other, and charming though they are individually, there is a puckish romanticism about some of them which augured sadly for the future of London architecture, when less sensitive builders were to take them as exemplars

Cumberland Terrace

and produce street upon street of them in long ribbons leading far out into the disappearing countryside. If an eighteenth-century square or terrace could be compared with a carefully graduated rope of pearls, the streets which were derived from this rather charming little fantasy could be more readily likened to a string of beads composed of a glass marble, a wooden cotton-reel, a fragment of bone and a plastic disc – a heterogeneous thread of houses with neither the charm of a house in its own grounds, nor the companionship of a properly designed terrace conceived as a unity.

Immediately south of St Katharine's Church one encounters yet another great unified group – Cumberland Terrace, a noble composition about 800 feet long, designed in 1826. Its length is handled well, for it has a most impressive central block with giant Ionic columns topped by a great classical pediment filled with classical figures in various elaborate positions in the grand manner of Imperial Rome. On either side there is a kind of triumphal arch, and these link two other massive apartments to form one unified composition. The arches themselves, apart from being essential links between the central mass and the buildings on the flanks, provided the right of way for carriages through the central archway and for pedestrians through the smaller arches. Cumberland Terrace is set back from the road with a miniature park with lawns and trees acting as a screen from the traffic which flows southwards towards Park Crescent and the Marylebone Road. It is somewhat impressive when viewed from the rear, although the mews and stables have been converted into small houses or garages.

The last of the Nash terraces which has survived unaltered on this side of the park is Chester Terrace, immediately south of Cumberland Terrace, which is entered by its own triumphal arch from the north. Its lovely Regency 'Roman' lettering is still intact, and the central arch is high and imposing, with two smaller arches for the use of pedestrians. Chester

Terrace is in fact the longest uninterrupted composition of all the terraces, about 940 feet long, 99 bays wide, but its structure was so manipulated by the use of groups of columns of the Corinthian order superimposed at intervals, and with the windows on the first floor provided with iron balconies, that the eye never has a surfeit of long monotonous stretches of simple fenestration. The doors and windows on the ground floor have semicircular arched heads and those above are square-headed. The upper storeys are set back behind a fairly emphatic cornice, which continues the entablature supported by groups of Corinthian columns at certain intervals and at either end of the whole terrace. This terrace has its own grassy tree-shaded garden between its own road and the main road to the west. Cumberland Terrace and Chester Terrace together form a breathtaking backdrop to the park.

Before the middle of the nineteenth century there stood a huge domed building to the south of Chester Terrace called the Colosseum, decorated within with a vast painted panorama of London. The whole building was demolished about 1875–7, and the Victorian terrace which was built in its place was known as Cambridge Gate, taking its name from a smaller Nash terrace – Cambridge Terrace – just beside it. The architect of this flamboyantly Victorian building of Cambridge Gate was clearly inspired by French châteaux rather than by classical temples, and he made no kind of compromise to the buildings nearby but rather asserted himself with complete disregard to the earlier environment. It is not surprising then that the modern architect, Denys Lasdun, decided that frankness of statement was best and built the College of Physicians in a twentieth-century style.

South of the College of Physicians there remains almost the final phase of the Nash scheme, St Andrew's Place, which runs at right angles to the eastern arm of Park Square and is a lovely example of the way in which Nash

343

could manipulate the turning of a corner. From the north the facade of St Andrew's Place is perfectly balanced with two semicircular bays enclosing a doorway at either end, but with the western bay looking from Park Square as though it is in fact part of that street. Nash also echoed the presence of real windows with shaped recesses in his stucco fronts. The individual floor levels are defined with iron balconies at intervals and the length of the street is concealed by a periodic projection of part of the facade. It is in this area that some of the best of the Regency ironwork bollards and lamp-posts have been preserved.

At the junction of Marylebone Road and Park Square are some little Doric temples – scarcely twice the size of a modern phone booth, but just enough to remind the visitor that the park scheme is about to unfold.

East of Park Square on Marylebone Road there is a church by Sir John Soane which faces north–south so that the altar would be at the north end. This was the church of the Holy Trinity which is now no longer used as such, but is the headquarters of the Society for the Propagation of Christian Knowledge and a library. It has a curiously proportioned porch of Ionic pillars which extends from the ground almost to the roofline, and a somewhat elongated and narrow composite tower of two stages over the liturgical west end. It was built between 1824–28 and is best seen from Great Portland Street.

To complete this somewhat extensive tour of the park, it would be best to walk south along the eastern curve of Park Crescent, not only to admire the

The church of the Holy Trinity

considerably larger to be of any use for Christian worship. There was also one other disconcerting fact for the Regency architects, W. and H. W. Inwood, for although it was always understood that one of the essentials in classical architecture was the insistence on perfect symmetry, the Erechtheum was irregular in plan and had the famous Caryatid porch attached to the north-western corner. However, undaunted they built their 'Erechtheum' as large as necessary and then added *two* Caryatid porches, one on either side to preserve the 'classical' symmetry. The one solitary maiden taken from Athens and now in the British Museum provided the model for the classical maidens bearing on their heads the weight of the whole cornice and entablature on the two porches for St Pancras. One problem remained. Christian churches traditionally had at least one spire whereas a Greek temple had none, and the Inwoods were faced with the problem of designing the kind of spire that a Greek architect would have designed had he needed one. They solved this problem by searching in Athens for buildings of the kind which might be converted into the architectural feature they required, and they eventually found two. One of these was the Monument of Lysicrates, a small circular building erected in 334 BC. The other was a small octagonal tower – the Tower of the Winds – which was originally a sundial outside and a waterclock within and was built *c*. 48 BC. With some ingenuity W. and H. W. Inwood took these forms, adapted them most skilfully to a spire form acceptable to Regency London, and produced the spire which still dominates the south side of Euston Road.

(It is interesting that a somewhat similar solution was used by an American architect, W. Strickland, when he designed the Merchants' Exchange in Philadelphia in 1832.)

A delightful street of Regency shops is to be found on the east and south side of St Pancras Church. This is generally known as Woburn Place or Woburn Walk, although some maps show it as Duke's Road. It is an L-shaped street; the southern part is for pedestrians only, and the eastern pavement was built well above the road to protect the charming little shop-fronts from fast-moving carriages or gigs. Most of the shop-fronts are intact, and some of them have preserved the Regency lettering. St Pancras Church and Woburn Place are manifestations of the taste and charm of the Regency period.

The streets and squares in this area are of course natural developments of the great Bloomsbury estates, Fitzroy Square probably being the most varied, for although the east side was the work of the Adam brothers, the

Woburn Place

northern and western sides date from about 1827–35, and the square also suffered some bomb damage during the the Second World War. Nearer to Euston, Tavistock Square (clearly part of the Bedford Estate since Tavistock is one of the names used by the Dukes of Bedford) was built from 1826 onwards partly by James Burton and then by his successor, Thomas Cubitt. The grouping of houses into imposing terraces or squares attracted middle-class men who felt that they were living in a somewhat similar environment to that of the wealthier class who had houses standing in their own grounds. It is significant that Charles Dickens could afford to live in Tavistock Square when he was a successful author in 1851–60. There is a blue plaque fixed to the British Medical Association's premises which take up a great deal of the east side of the square, but it is poor consolation for any Dickens admirer who has made the pilgrimage to see the house in which Dickens wrote such masterpieces as *Bleak House* and *Hard Times*, although part of his little garden still survives behind the Mary Ward Settlement.

Bloomsbury Square and Russell Square were both designed by Humphry Repton, and the great plane trees with their dappled trunks and swinging tossibobs are always a pleasure to see, even if the layout has been considerably altered since the squares were first designed at the turn of the century. The plane trees which form such a feature of the London parks and squares were selected because of their natural ability to shed the bark – an advantage which enabled them to survive the polluted, smoky atmosphere of nineteenth-century London when other trees were choked by it. Humphry Repton is better known for the redesigning of many landscapes surrounding English country houses where he became the natural successor to 'Capability' Brown, often collaborating with John Nash who dealt with the house while Repton re-ordered the landscape. It was at this time that another tree, very evocative of this period, was first introduced. This is the 'monkey-puzzle' or Chile Pine from South America, a sharp-scaled intruder in many gardens in the outlying suburbs of London at this time, which still defeats the most intrepid climber.

Russell Square contains a statue by Richard Westmacott, RA, of Francis, Duke of Bedford, the proud owner of much of Bloomsbury, so that many of the streets and squares in the area are named after one branch or another of his family: Russell Square, laid out in 1800; Tavistock Square in 1806–26, but since much modified; Torrington Square, named after the family of the first wife of the sixth Duke of Bedford, in 1825; and the latest, Gordon Square, laid out in 1850, named after the Gordon family, of which his second wife was a member.

The one notable building in the area east of Gordon Square is at the northern end of Gower Street – University College, designed in 1827 by William Wilkins, the architect of the National Gallery. In this case, since he was subject to less restriction, he was able to produce a more imposing building. The foundation stone was laid in April 1827 by HRH the Duke of Sussex, and the institution, which later became part of the University of London, was founded for the purpose of providing 'literary and scientific education at a moderate expense', as distinct from the older universities

University College

which were still largely finishing schools for wealthy young men.

University College has a 400-foot-wide frontage and a great central flight of stairs leading to a portico consisting of ten great Corinthian columns behind the pediment of which arises a well-proportioned dome. The interior has been modified a great deal, partly because of the different modern academic requirements from those envisaged in the nineteenth century, and partly as the result of damage by incendiary bombs during the Second World War. It is now only one of several colleges which comprise London University, and although it has many departments it is probably best known for the Slade School of Art, a famous art school which is still a rival to the Royal Academy Schools and complementary to the later Royal College of Art. It has a well-known collection of the work of the eighteenth-century sculptor and designer, John Flaxman, one of the pioneers of the classical revival in England, who was made Professor of Sculpture to the Royal Academy in 1810, and whose sculptured memorial figures in St Paul's (Admiral Nelson, Admiral Howe and Sir Joshua Reynolds) and in Westminster Abbey are fine examples of Regency taste in sculpture. The Slade School of Art derives its name from Felix Slade, an art collector who left £35,000 in 1832 for the endowment of Slade professorships in art at the Universities of Oxford and Cambridge and at University College, and a very considerable collection of books, engravings, glass and pottery to the British Museum.

One somewhat macabre figure in the history of University College is that of one of its founder benefactors – Jeremy Bentham, the lawyer who wrote extensively on jurisprudence and the philosophy of legislation. He bequeathed his corpse to medical science and his skeleton was eventually cleaned and wired together, and an effigy of him in his original costume at one time presided over council meetings. It is now preserved in a glass case.

From University College southwards, Gower Street leads directly through Bedford Square to Bloomsbury Street and the British Museum is a few yards east of the junction of Bloomsbury Street and Great Russell Street.

The British Museum

The beginnings of the superb collection now housed in the British Museum were originally kept in Montague House in the same area, and the nucleus was a number of exhibits left to the nation in 1753 by Sir Hans Sloane, some of them very strange indeed to judge by the list published in Henry Chamberlain's survey of 1769. This included 'the skeleton of a unicorn fish', 'several large corals, a substance produced in the sea, but in what manner is not yet determined by the naturalist', as well as 'several Egyptian idols in bronze', an Egyptian mummy, fragments of others, rare stones, and so on.

Two other very important collections which formed the 'Foundation Collections' were the Cottonian, a remarkable array of early records of English literature preserved by the Elizabethan antiquary, Sir Robert Cotton, after the Reformation, and the Harleian Library, collected by Robert and Edward Harley, first and second Earls of Oxford. At the same time, the magnificent library assembled by a succession of monarchs which had been given to the British Museum by George II in 1757, could now be found a more permanent home.

The interest in antiquity shown by so many eighteenth-century noblemen had resulted in some very fine private collections being obtainable either by purchase or by bequest, and the defeat of Napoleon in his Egyptian campaign meant that many Egyptian antiquities collected by his team of archaeologists were ceded to this country under the Treaty of Alexandria. The salvaging of the sculptures of the Parthenon etc. by Lord Elgin also meant considerable additions to the original collection, so that new purpose-

351

built premises became essential. The part of the present building in Great Russell Street was designed by Sir Robert Smirke, and once again the inspiration for the entrance was the Erechtheum on the Acropolis at Athens. No normal stone blocks, however, could possibly span the spaces between such columns, so that the stone construction is really little more than a substantial front and steel girders concealed by the stonework are the major functional framework. Any sharp-eyed visitor who looks at the frieze over the columns will see that the intervals of stone are wrongly placed, for the joint between one stone and its fellows would actually have to be directly over the capitals of the column supporting it, not in between the columns, where it would have no support at all. The building was erected in 1842–7.

The British Museum was begun in 1823, and the east wing was originally intended to house the King's Library – some 22,000 documents and books, largely dealing with the Civil War given to the British Museum in 1762 by George III, together with the Angerstein collection of paintings, later to become the nucleus of the National Gallery. The west wing followed in 1831–4 and the north wing in 1833–8. Sir Robert Smirke's quadrangle within was filled with the library and the great circular reading room, surrounded by cast-iron bookstacks, designed by Sidney Smirke in 1852–7.

Additions have been made to the original accommodation provided during the nineteenth century, but even so it has been necessary to transfer some of the original departments elsewhere. The natural history exhibits were sent to South Kensington between 1880 and 1883. The ethnographical galleries were transferred to form the Museum of Mankind to the rear of Burlington House and the Royal Academy. The Elgin Marbles and other antiquities are now beautifully exhibited in galleries given by the late Lord Duveen and designed by an American architect, John Russell Pope, better known perhaps as the designer of the National Gallery, Washington, and the Jefferson Memorial nearby.

It is quite impossible to do more than to give an indication of the treasures to be seen in the British Museum, and although the exhibits are now beautifully displayed, it would be impossible for any visitor to try to see everything in one visit. Some visitors will be most impressed by the huge human-headed and winged bulls from Assyria, others by the massive fragments of Egyptian Pharaohs like the 'two vast and legless legs of stone' of Shelley's poem 'Ozymandias'. Some will find themselves fascinated by the beauty of the illuminated manuscripts from medieval Europe or of those painted for the Mughal courts, while others will remember the weakening scrawl and failing pencil of Captain Falcon Scott as he made the last entry in his diary and then died in the wastes of Antarctica. Some will pore over the superb collection of postage stamps, or the mystery of the Rosetta Stone, and some might even come from behind the Iron Curtain to pay homage to the building in which much of the work of Karl Marx was done before he wrote his famous 'Communist Manifesto' and other books on revolutionary activities. But it all began with the eighteenth-century connoisseurs and thinkers, and the building is largely the work of a Regency architect.

* * *

Examination of the 'Plan of London from Actual Survey, 1832', presented to the readers of *The United Kingdom Newspaper*, shows that from Edgware Road westwards there were still large areas of open fields with some projected streets and crescents sketched in tentatively, some of which have never actually been built. Just west of Edgware Road, opposite Nutford Place on the east, was a projected layout called 'The Polygon' in the area now defined by Cambridge Square to the north, Oxford Square to the south, Norfolk Crescent to the east and Hyde Park Terrace to the west. Just west of Connaught Square was a burial ground with a chapel (now part of Tyburn Convent), and this site is now the grounds of the Royal Toxophilite Society, with Connaught Place overlooking the site of the gallows of Tyburn where the last execution took palce in 1783.

To the north, Paddington Basin and Regent's Canal had already been dug, although the latter had necessitated the removal of Thomas Lord's cricket ground to its present site a few hundred yards to the north, at vast expense to the company financing the canal.

This whole area therefore was developed during the Regency period or shortly afterwards, and many of the little Regency houses still remain, somewhat more intimately grouped than those of the Regent's Park scheme. Many of them are stucco-fronted or have brick fronts with stucco embellishments, classical porticoes are to be seen in many streets, and the whole area, laid out to the designs of S. P. Cockerell for the Bishop of London has been described by Professor Pevsner as 'a scheme of tree-lined areas, squares and crescents, more spatially coherent than any known in London until then, and as leafy as the best'. Those houses facing the Bayswater Road are commonly five storeys high, but as a backdrop to Hyde Park the vista of the Bayswater Road cannot compare with the splendour of the Nash terraces which are such an asset to Regent's Park. Park Lane, which forms the eastern perimeter of Hyde Park, has been ruined by the demoliton of most of the Regency houses, and the skyline is a jumble of different levels quite unworthy of the area.

Hyde Park, that wonderful 360-acre 'lung of London', (according to William Pitt the Elder), is smaller than Regent's Park (which covers 410 acres), but it nevertheless appears to have wider open spaces. It derived its name 'Hyde' from a corruption of the manor of Eia owned by Westminster Abbey, which Henry VIII took possession of after the Reformation and converted into a deer park for hunting. Oliver Cromwell sold it to one of his followers, who promptly started charging a toll of a shilling for coaches (although it had been a public park before the Civil War), but it returned to freedom after the Restoration. Charles II used it for exercise and established a racecourse there, as well as holding military reviews in it.

It was Caroline of Ansbach, the queen of George II, who, looking across it from Kensington Palace, realised that it had great decorative potential; she arranged for the River Westbourne to be cleansed and the small string of little ponds converted into the Serpentine river which is now such a pleasure to Londoners and visitors alike. One major contribution to the park during the Regency period was the erection of the bridge over the Serpentine by Sir

John and George Rennie in 1826 – a fine stone bridge of five arches by the sons of famous engineer, John Rennie, who built the first Waterloo Bridge in 1810. Lansbury's Lido, where there are bathing facilities, is a twentieth-century addition to the Serpentine, named after the well-known pioneer of the Labour Party, George Lansbury, and there is also a very tastefully designed restaurant erected in 1963. Of the statues, the most popular is certainly that of Peter Pan by Sir George Frampton; one of the most puzzling is 'Rima', Sir Jacob Epstein's memorial to the great nature writer, W. H. Hudson; and one of the most prominent is that of 'Physical Energy' by G. F. Watts, really in Kensington Gardens, but still part of the many exhibits to be found in this great parkland.

A pretty little complex of building and pools standing at the north end of the Serpentine includes Queen Anne's Alcove, attributed to both Sir Christopher Wren and William Kent, the more probable executor. When Queen Caroline first set in motion the re-ordering of the river and this part of what had been a wild park, a new palace in this area was contemplated, but it never materialised. The Serpentine was also used by the Prince Regent for staging a great sea battle with miniature ships as part of the celebrations of the Battle of Waterloo and the defeat of Napoleon, and the Battle of the Nile was re-enacted there with fireships and plenty of fireworks.

A more permanent memorial of the defeat of Napoleon, however, stands in the south-eastern corner of the park – a colossal 18 foot-high metal statue

Bridge over the
Serpentine

by Sir Richard Westmacott, cast from the cannon captured from the French, of a naked warrior called 'Achilles', financed by subscriptions raised in 1822 by the women of England in honour of the Duke of Wellington. The inscription reads as follows: 'To Arthur, Duke of Wellington, and his brave companions in arms, this statue of Achilles, cast from cannon taken in the battles of Salamanca, Toulouse, and Waterloo, is inscribed by their countrywomen.' The statue was not a success, for apart from it having been derived from one of the antique statues on the Monte Cavallo in Rome, although without the horse which appears in the original, a naked figure of these giant proportions caused some embarrassment to susceptible ladies unused to seeing a male figure unclothed.

Just south of the statue is one of Decimus Burton's little masterpieces – the entrance to the park from the south – a screen in which delicately poised Ionic columns and arched entrances, topped by a little frieze of galloping horsemen clearly derived from the famous Parthenon frieze, makes a charming line of demarcation between the western end of Piccadilly and the park itself. Just east of this lovely screen is Apsley House, at one time known as No. 1, London, and for many years the home of the Duke of Wellington – the 'Iron Duke' who engineered the defeat of Napoleon. Apsley House belonged originally to Henry Bathurst, Baron Apsley, and was built for its first owner by the Adam brothers; it was acquired by Marquess Wellesley, the eldest brother of the Duke, in 1817. The Duke had the house considerably altered in 1829 by Benjamin Wyatt, although some of the original Adam rooms are still to be seen within. Benjamin Wyatt encased the original Adam house of brick in Portland stone, adding the imposing portico, rusticated stone on the ground floor with Corinthian pillars above, and a simple pediment. He also added the famous Waterloo Gallery to the western side – a somewhat ostentatious room, 90 feet in length, decorated perhaps somewhat inappropriately in the French taste of Louis XIV, in which the Duke held a banquet annually on Waterloo Day, 18 June, from

1830–1852. The guests were originally intended to be the twenty of the Duke's generals who had fought at Waterloo, but George IV (who thought that he had), died before the room was completed, so that it was William IV who was the first king to attend such a reunion.

The room is furnished with an extremely fine display of plate, the centre piece of which is 26 feet long. The whole service was presented to the Duke by the Prince Regent of Portugal (afterwards King John VI of Portugal) in 1816. It consists of over one thousand pieces in silver and silver-gilt and is a most astonishing *tour de force* of craftsmanship. It is only one of the many lavish presents given to the victorious Duke – some of them, to our modern taste, more expensive than beautiful, pehaps, and as the building is now the Wellington Museum they naturally attract a great many visitors.

The Waterloo Gallery also has a number of very fine paintings of various periods and by artists of many nations. They include a portrait of the Duke by Francisco José de Goya y Lucientes (no doubt better known as Goya), one of the truly great masters of the Spanish court, who, it is said, became so exasperated with his noble model that he seized a sword and actually put the Duke to flight – a feat not even performed by Napoleon and the *Grande Armée*. There are a number of exquisite paintings by Velázquez, another great Spanish master – these, along with paintings by Peter Paul Rubens, Van Dyck, Jan Steen, and other European masters, were captured by Wellington's troops at the Battle of Vittoria in 1813, for Joseph Bonaparte, Napoleon's brother, had fled, stealing 165 paintings from the Spanish Royal Collection. His baggage was captured, but he escaped, shielded by his escort, and the collection was held by the Duke for safe keeping as he had no intention of retaining them as spoils of war. The new King of Spain, however, insisted on his keeping them, and they are now part of the permanent collection in this museum. There are many paintings of great merit throughout the house bought by or given to the Duke, as well as a selection of all kinds of rich and splendid *objets d'art* commemorating his victories, or given to him by various distinguished bodies as a mark of their admiration. There are also several personal effects preserved here – the Duke's tablet on which he scribbled dispatches to his field officers, his swords, and even some little medical supplies he carried with him. Perhaps the most memorable work of art, however, is a giant marble statue of Napoleon at the bottom of the staircase by the Italian sculptor, Antonio Canova. He was summoned from Rome to Paris to undertake a portrait, and he made this 11-foot high statue from this and from his imagination, portraying Napoleon naked but with a classical garment of some kind over his left arm, and holding in his right hand a small winged Victory of metal, the goddess with outspread wings and her back towards the figure of Napoleon. Exhibited at first in the Louvre, it was so disliked by Napoleon, who is said to have taken exception to the way in which the figure of Victory was placed as though about to fly away from him, that it was hidden away out of sight. In 1816 it was bought by the British Government for less than £3000 and presented by the Prince Regent to the Duke of Wellington.

The Wellington Museum displays an enormous amount of interest from the Regency period and is administered by the Victoria and Albert Museum. A statue of the Duke on horseback stands on a high plinth directly opposite the main entrance on the far side of Piccadilly. This equestrian statue is a later addition to this part of London and replaces a much larger equestrian statue modelled by Matthew Wyatt and his son, and erected in 1846 on the top of a great triumphal arch, now on Constitution Hill, designed by Decimus Burton in 1828 to stand at Hyde Park Corner. Wyatt's statue was however removed when the triumphal arch was moved to its present position in 1882–3 because of the traffic congestion it caused; it was then taken to its present site in Aldershot. The Constitution Hill arch remained without any kind of statue on top until 1912, when the present group of Peace in a four-horse chariot or quadriga was modelled for it by Adrian Jones. The equestrian statue opposite the Wellington Museum was modelled by Sir J. E. Boehm, RA, and placed in its present position in 1888; it shows the Duke on his famous charger, Copenhagen.

Marble Arch was also originally intended as a memorial to the victories of Trafalgar and Waterloo, as well as the royal entrance to Buckingham Palace, but when Marble Arch was erected in front of the Palace, the sculptural decorations were included in the exterior of the Palace instead, so that when the arch was moved to its present position in 1851 it was no longer regarded as having any connection with the Napoleonic wars.

In the meantime, considerable developments were occurring still further west with the building of a whole new section of London – Belgravia. St George's Hospital at Hyde Park Corner stands on the site of an earlier eighteenth-century house, Lanesborough House, but the present building is the work of William Wilkins, designed about 1835, and built at that time on the edge of open fields, some of which were little better than water-meadows and marsh. The building of Belgravia was to change this completely. An Act of Parliament empowered Lord Grosvenor to drain the area and raise the site, and by 1831 Thomas Cubitt had built a whole new and desirable estate, with most of the houses grouped around squares which are still a great asset to this part of London.

During the reign of George III the fields to the rear of Buckingham Palace came up for sale, but the Government declined to buy them for £20,000 to secure more privacy for the king, and the land was leased to speculative builders who erected a row of houses overlooking the private grounds. It was round this time that a suicide was committed at Hobart Place. It had previously been the custom to bury a suicide at the crossroads nearest to where he had taken his life, with a stake through his heart, but in this case the king not unnaturally felt that this macabre event would be an unwarrantable intrusion. An Act was hastily passed through Parliament in 1823 forbidding the practice for ever.

The growing prestige of Buckingham Palace as the residence of the monarch gave impetus to the development to the west now known as Belgravia. Almost the whole of the area had been inherited by the Westminster family from the manor of Ebury before the Civil War, but had remained a virtually deserted rural swamp. The development started with the building of Belgrave Square in 1825, and nearly all the streets and squares bear some connection with the names of the same noble family – Eaton Square and Eccleston Square, for example, derive their names from country estates near Chester, and Grosvenor and Belgrave both appear in the full titles of the Dukes of Westminster. The swamps having been drained, the in-fill was brought from the areas just downstream from the Tower of London where St Katharine's Dock was being excavated, and with George Basevi as the architect and Thomas Cubitt the main builder, an overall design control ensured that there would be some kind of harmonious relationship between Belgrave Square and other squares in the area yet to be built. Wilton Place to the north, formerly a cow-yard off Knightsbridge, followed in 1827, and Eaton Square was started at about the same time.

The large area occupied by Belgrave Square, about 10 acres, gave Basevi and his companion architects problems, for terraces such as those round Regent's Park might have been monotonous. Nevertheless, the constant repetition of Greek-style porticoes gives a restless feeling to the streets which form the square, and as no two sides of the street are quite alike, and as detached houses are placed at the corners, despite the uniformity of material there is a lack of cohesion. The pretty house in the south-western corner, now the Spanish Embassy, was built for a very successful builder of the same period – Thomas Kemp – who made a fortune by building Kemp Town in Brighton at about the same period in which the Burtons were

The Spanish Embassy
in Belgrave Square

building other coastal resorts. This house has a predominant centre block with a portico of coupled Ionic columns, and two more simple wings, one on either side. Like the rest of the square it is entirely stuccoed, and its roofline is kept simple by the concealment of the roof behind an unobtrusive parapet-balustrading.

Another individual building well worth seeking out in this area is the Pantechnicon, just west of Belgrave Square in Motcombe Street, and although some of the original building was damaged by fire in 1874, the exterior of the building is very much in the style of the Greek revival of the 1830s. It was originally built as a market hall and bazaar and specialised in the sale of carriages, their equipment, furniture and other household goods, including even wines. It is now the property of the famous firm of auctioneers, Sotheby's. West Halkin Street and Halkin Arcade (named after Halkin Castle in Flintshire, a country seat of the Westminster family) are also largely devoted to the display of antiques – a charming little shopping centre. South-eastwards from Belgrave Square, along Upper Belgrave Street – all part of the original scheme, is the church of St Peter, and facing it Eaton Square. This would certainly have been placed symmetrically on the axis to the Square had it been possible, but the position of King's Road unfortunately prevented it and the square therefore not only lost an eastward focal point, but is bisected by a wide thoroughfare which means that it loses the compact character which should be the essential quality of such a unit. St Peter's, Eaton Square, is a very fashionable church for society weddings, but it is not the original one erected during the Regency period, being a 'classical' building of 1875 designed by the Victorian architect, Sir Arthur Blomfield. There are many Regency houses to be enjoyed in this area, and a great many famous people lived and died here; it is also the location of a number of foreign embassies.

King's Road leads directly to Chelsea, via Sloane Square, and although such Regency buildings as the Duke of York's regimental headquarters built early in the nineteenth century as the Duke of York's School, and the Royal Military Asylum are still impressive, if somewhat forbidding examples of the Regency period, too much has happened to spoil what little remains of the Regency development in this area, and one has to haunt small side roads to seek out the notable finds of the old Chelsea. Cheyne Walk however still has some fine buildings of all periods, from the seventeenth century to the end of the nineteenth century. The reputation of Chelsea, apart from some fine eighteenth-century remains and the superb buildings of the Royal Hospital, rests mainly on its association with famous poets and artists, writers and architects.

One Regency church should be mentioned – not for its beauty, but for the style in which it was built by James Savage in 1820–24, at almost exactly the same time as the Inwoods, father and son, were undergoing such heart-searching as to the best way to build their church of St Pancras in the most authentic 'Greek' style possible. In Chelsea Savage chose to build his church not in any 'classical' style, but in a new Gothic style – it was one of the first to be built in this way and anticipated a rash of 'medieval' churches,

St Luke's, Chelsea,
where Charles Dickens
was married

town halls, offices, hospitals, banks and even railway stations such as St Pancras. St Luke's Church, then, is prophetic, if unlovely, with its Gothic detailing, its flying buttresses and groined vaults, and all the other obvious characteristics of the ecclesiastical buildings of the Middle Ages. It represents in some ways the opening shots of a Battle of the Styles which was to rage for the rest of the century, and it was also symptomatic of great changes to come. The very numbers of churches being built at this time might also have been suggestive of a sense of unease of the ruling class, for the French Revolution less than fifty years old had shown an ugly tendency for others to call into question the established order, and if 'religion, the opium of the masses' would anaesthetise a working class already demanding reform, then the sooner many more churches were built for this purpose, the better.

Another conflict was also soon to appear, for the technology employed by engineers for the building of bridges and factories in the Industrial Revolution could as readily be applied in architecture – a fact scarcely acknowledged by the more academically trained architects, but certainly realised by John Nash, with his constructional use of iron both in Carlton House Terrace and in the Royal Brighton Pavilion, and somewhat later in the century by the versatile Decimus Burton in the Palm House in Kew Gardens.

Thus the Regency period was a period of change, and with hindsight one can see quite clearly the emergence of these changes – social, technical and stylistic – although at the time they must have been undetected by most people in England.

One great technical development, however, must have been apparent – the building of a succession of new bridges over the Thames, some to replace ones which had long outlived their usefulness, and others to provide essential links between the new areas developing on either side of the river, particularly to the south where estates of a meaner kind were springing up to house the hordes of people seeking work in the new docklands of the south bank of the Thames, as well as in the areas downstream from the Tower of London. Moving downstream from the Chelsea area, the first of these was Vauxhall Bridge, built between 1811–16 and therefore originally called Regent Bridge, a name which fell into disuse as revellers from the north bank sought the delights of Vauxhall pleasure gardens. (This bridge has since been replaced by the present one, built in 1906, and the first at the time to be crossed by tramcars.) There was also a new bridge at Hammersmith, built in 1827, but this was replaced late in the nineteenth century, in 1887.

The next bridge downstream from Vauxhall Bridge was Westminster Bridge, at that time nearly past its prime and to be replaced in 1862, and then Waterloo Bridge, built 1811–17, at first known as Strand Bridge but almost immediately renamed to commemorate the victory of Waterloo. (This, too, has been replaced by the present one built by the modern architect, Sir Giles Gilbert Scott, one of the finest additions to London's river this century.) Blackfriars Bridge was a familiar sight to the Regency Londoner, for it had been built in 1769, but a new one still further downstream was Southwark Bridge, built between 1815–19, and replaced in 1921. So to a man born in the reign of George III, making his way by boat from anywhere west of Buckingham Palace, it must have seemed that all was change, and that a new London was being born even as the boat was moving downstream, for even London Bridge itself was being rebuilt. The old houses on it had been coming down anyway, and the Lord Mayor of London laid the foundation stone of the new London Bridge on 15 June 1825, the tenth anniversary of the Battle of Waterloo. On 1 August 1831, all the fashionable world gathered there to see the fine new bridge, begun in 1824 by John Rennie and completed by his sons Sir John and George Rennie, officially opened by the new king, King William IV, and his queen, Queen Adelaide. This bridge lasted until 1967, when it was dismantled and shipped to the Arizona desert to entertain tourists.

By the time that Queen Victoria succeeded to the throne in 1837, the changes which had been emerging in London during the Regency period were happening with increasing momentum. Of these changes, perhaps one of the most profound was the coming of the railways and the incredible increase in the population of London in the area which Greater London was to cover.

8

Victorian London

———————————⚜———————————

If Regency London can be represented by the characters from Jane Austen's *Emma* and *Pride and Prejudice*, by Thackeray's *Vanity Fair*, the paintings of William Hogarth of the diaries of Samuel Johnson, it was Victorian London which produced the originals of such characters as those to be found in the novels of Charles Dickens – Fagin, Gradgrind, Oliver Twist and Sir Mulberry Hawk, Samuel Weller and Sergeant Buzfuz.

William Hogarth and Charles Dickens had much in common. Each spent a sadly deprived childhood in London, and each saw his father in a debtor's prison – a traumatic experience which had a profound effect on the nature of the work of both of them. Each was to harness his own particular genius to the exposure of the injustices, the brutalities and the follies of his time, and although both men have been accused of caricature, it is not mere exaggeration but an intensity of vision which makes their work so terribly truthful. Dickens' delineation of character is unerring, and equally true and vivid are his descriptions of the social evils of his own day: the appalling 'rookeries' round St Giles-in-the-Fields, the squalor of the neighbourhood round the docks, the dreadful conditions of deprivation created by the building of the railways when whole neighbourhoods were torn down and the people rendered homeless. He knew only too well the harshness of the penal systems and the callousness of the Poor Law systems which were created to control but did little to improve the human products of such man-made environments. His written descriptions are borne out by the drawings made by the great French book-illustrator, Gustav Doré, who, in collaboration with Blanchard Jerrold, the son of Douglas Jerrold, an old friend of Dickens, produced 'London – a pilgrimage' in 1872, in which many aspects of London life were depicted, from the sleazy markets and neighbourhoods of the East End to the smart clubs and salons of the wealthier parts of London.

Furnival's Inn, where the young Charles Dickens, as a solicitor's clerk, learned all about the devious ways of the legal profession so contemptuously portrayed in *Bleak House* and many other novels, no longer exists. On the same site in Holborn now stands the huge red block of the Prudential Assurance Company offices, built by Alfred Waterhouse in 1879, although a bust of the novelist is to be seen on the west side of the great archway.

Dickens' experience as a shorthand writer in the House of Commons was also to engender in the young novelist a contempt for the chicanery and political manoeuvres of the so-called 'representatives of the people' at that

opposite, The Clock Tower and the Palace of Westminster

The Houses of
Parliament and the
Victoria Tower

time. The building in which he worked was burned down in the fire of 1834, and the Houses of Parliament which now occupy the river bank and are a symbol of parliamentary democracy are wholly Victorian buildings. The fire was caused by the burning of a great pile of notched wooden 'tallies', an obsolete method of keeping the exchequer accounts, and these were later used in a bitter attack on Parliament by Charles Dickens as a symbol of much which, long out-of-date, was still preserved by the ruling classes and which, unless reformed, would 'like the worm-eaten old splints that caught fire and destroyed the Palace of Westminster – would one day break into flames and consume them in its burning'.

The open competition held for the design for a new Houses of Parliament was won by Charles Barry (later Sir Charles Barry) and his architectural draughtsman, Augustus Welby Pugin. Pugin was the son of a French emigré, Augustus Charles Pugin, who had collaborated with Thomas Rowlandson in the production of a series of most lovely drawings of various London institutions in 1808–10, called 'The Microcosm of London'. Both Pugins were very accomplished draughtsmen, and although Charles Barry was the architect who planned the new Parliament buildings, the exquisite 'medieval' details were the work of Augustus Welby Pugin. Thus the buildings one sees today are actually the result of a most successful Victorian architect, who was equally at home with any architectural style, and his architectural draughtsman, Augustus Welby Pugin, a convert to the Roman Catholic faith to whom classical forms and even Renaissance forms with their pagan associations were utterly repugnant. The only style which he deemed suitable for the building of churches was that of the Middle Ages.

Perhaps the most characteristic feature of the new Houses of Parliament, and certainly the one known all over the world, if only for its chimes, is the clock tower with its huge clock-faces, known quite wrongly as Big Ben. Big Ben is in fact the great bell which tolls the hour and was so named after Sir Benjamin Hall, Commissioner of Works, in 1858, when the clock was being made. The bell, which weighs about 13½ tons, was cast from the metal of an earlier one given by William III to the Dean of St Paul's. The clock tower is 316 feet high, each of the four clock-faces is 23 feet in diameter, each hour-hand is 9 feet long, and the large hands which mark the minutes are all 14 feet long. Adjoining the first floor of the clock tower is a small room in which recalcitrant Members of Parliament can be imprisoned – the last man to be so confined was Charles Bradlaugh, the free-thinker, who declined to take the oath in 1880.

Although the designs for the Houses of Parliament were accepted in 1835, the foundation stone was not actually laid until 27 April 1840, for the building had to be put on a bed of concrete ten feet thick, and about 775,000 cubic feet of stone had to be quarried. The House of Lords occupied its new chamber in 1847, but the entire building with its eleven hundred rooms was not fully in use until 1852. The stone chosen was unfortunately a magnesian limestone from Yorkshire – admirable for the carving of the hundreds of statues, gargoyles and so on, but dreadfully vulnerable to the industrial

left, The House of Commons
right, The House of Lords

pollution of the London atmosphere until fairly recent times. The blocks of Portland stone used on the west front of Palace Yard carved by H. Armstead, RA, in 1866 are in a rather better state. The river-front, including the terrace where MPs entertain their guests and constituents, is about 872 feet in length; it was the Duke of Wellington, fearful of an insurrection, who decided that one side of the eight-acre complex should be protected by the river which could act as a defensive moat.

The west front, which extends from the clock tower upstream to the 323-feet-high Victoria Tower, is divided roughly into two halves by the central tower and St Stephen's Entrance. The northern half is occupied by the House of Commons and includes the superb medieval Westminster Hall, some of the other buildings saved from the fire of 1834, and New Palace Yard, the entrance for the Members of Parliament. The 'New' Palace Yard derives its name from the early Palace of Westminster and was given this name in 1098 in the reign of William II to distinguish it from the 'Old' Palace Yard, already in existence.

The present appearance of the outside of the western side of Westminster Hall with its flying buttresses was achieved when the Law Courts were removed to the new site in the Strand in 1882, and a sunken garden was made with the Grand Committee Room extension added. The statue of Oliver Cromwell by Sir Hamo Thornycroft, the gift of Lord Rosebery, was added in 1894.

The buildings from St Stephen's Entrance southwards to the Victoria Tower form two sides of Old Palace Yard, and there stands the famous statue of Richard the Lionheart by Marochetti, opposite the early medieval Jewel Tower which now houses a small museum. The Peers' Entrance is in the centre of the main façade, but at the opening of Parliament the Queen arrives at the archway under the Victoria Tower and ascends the Sovereign's Staircase, passing through the Norman porch at the head of the stairs to the Robing Room beyond. The Norman porch is so called because it was originally intended by Charles Barry to be decorated with posthumous and fictitious statues of the Norman kings, but this scheme was never carried out and it now contains portrait busts of a number of Prime Ministers. The remarkably fine vault above the porch is typical of the meticulous Gothic detail designed by Pugin, but the royal monogram VR which appears here and throughout the building betrays its nineteenth-century origins.

Tours of the Royal Palace of Westminster are for security reasons somewhat restricted at the time of writing, so that the descriptions of the various buildings which follows does not necessarily mean that they are open to the public.

The Robing Room is a very large and impressive chamber, about 54 feet long, 37 feet wide and 25 feet high, and was sufficiently commodious to be used by the House of Lords when their own room was taken over by the House of Commons after the extensive damage inflicted by the air raids of the Second World War. On some occasions both houses met in Church House in nearby Great Smith Street, the Lords then meeting in the Convocation Hall, and the Commons in Hoare Memorial Hall. An inscription in the latter commemorates this and was unveiled by the Rt. Hon. Winston Churchill after the war.

The walls of the Robing Room are decorated with deeply carved panels by H. Armstead depicting the legends of King Arthur and the shields of the Knights of the Round Table. The floor is inlaid with heraldic symbols of the royal house – the portcullis, the rose and the lion. Even the fireplace, enriched with marble inlay from stones in various parts of Britain, has two sculptures in bronze – one of St George fighting the dragon, and the other with the saint triumphant over the body of the beast. Almost every part of the robing room has decorative elements derived from the Age of Chivalry – a Victorian preoccupation engendered largely by the romantic novels of Sir Walter Scott. A canopy of oak, carved with the symbols of the rose of England, the thistle of Scotland and the shamrock of Ireland and with Queen Victoria's own monogram, is fixed over a dais at the far end of the room, and at the back is a most beautifully embroidered hanging with the royal arms and the Queen's monogram, worked by the Royal School of Art Needlework in 1856. It was in this nobly decorated chamber that George VI opened Parliament from 1941 to 1944.

From the Robing Room, the sovereign progresses along the Royal Gallery to the House of Lords for the state opening of Parliament and the reading of the Sovereign's speech. The Royal Gallery, an even larger and perhaps more impressive room, is 110 feet long and 45 feet wide, with a lofty roof 45 feet high. Most of the wall space below the range of windows on either side is occupied by large murals, two of them by Daniel Maclise, RA, a close personal friend of Charles Dickens. These depict the meeting of the Duke of Wellington with the German General Blücher after the Battle of Waterloo in 1815, and the death of Nelson at the Battle of Trafalgar in 1805. The figures in these two paintings are life-sized. The other pictures in the gallery include a number of royal portraits, and the room has been used for various very important occasions connected with the British Empire and Commonwealth. On 14 March 1947, a delegation from the USSR was formally received there by the Lord Chancellor and Mr Speaker.

Between the Royal Gallery and the House of Lords there is a smaller room known as the Prince's Chamber – a name derived from a room which used to adjoin the House of Lords in the ancient Palace of Westminster. Here the decoration is largely concerned with motifs and with posthumous portraits of the Tudor dynasty, but the room is dominated by a giant marble statue of Queen Victoria seated on a throne and occupying a round-headed niche on one wall. There are two exits to this room, leading into the House of Lords on either side of the thrones used by our present Queen and the Duke of Edinburgh at the State Opening of Parliament. Pugin, who was responsible for all the Gothic detail and furnishing throughout the Houses of Parliament, produced his masterpiece in the House of Lords, for the whole room is resplendent with carved and painted decoration; there are benches of red leather, the ceiling is enriched with carved beams, and the whole appearance is of regal splendour. Although it is in fact only 12 feet longer than the House of Commons destroyed during the blitz, and the same height and width (45 feet), it is far more sumptuous.

The Woolsack in front of the throne has traditionally been the seat of the Lord Chancellor since the reign of Edward III (1327–77) when wool was the main source of the wealth of England. The Woolsack today is stuffed symbolically with specimens of wool from many parts of the British Isles, and from the countries of the Commonwealth.

The lofty ceiling of the House of Lords is divided into eighteen compartments, each with its heraldic decoration. Here can be seen the white hart of Richard II, the sun of the House of York, the crown in the bush of the Battle of Bosworth, used as a symbol by Henry VII, the lion rampant of Scotland, the rose and the lion of England and many other symbols. There are galleries above the benches on either side and to the rear of the thrones, and these are allocated to various groups such as ambassadors, the Press and so on.

Immediately to the north of the House of Lords is the Peers' Lobby, about 35 feet square and 33 feet high, in which there are four doorways. The south one leads to the Lords' Chamber, the north one to the Central Hall, while the one to the east leads to the library of the House of Lords and conference rooms, and the one to the west to the Moses Room. The last named derives its title from a fresco on its wall of Moses bringing down the Tables of the Law from Mount Sinai, which was painted in 1864 by J. R. Herbert, RA. The room is at the disposal of the Chairman of Committees, but from time to time it is also used as a robing room for the peers.

The House of Lords library is nearly all contained in four rooms which overlook the terrace and the river, and it is here that some extremely important documents are preserved, including the original death warrant of Charles I with the signatures of the regicides after the trial of 1648–9. There is also a letter from Charles I to the House of Lords on behalf of Strafford, written in 1641, a selection of the king's papers captured by the Cromwellians after the Battle of Naseby, and the Articles of Union between England and Scotland, signed in 1706, as well as many other historic records. There are stringent regulations controlling the admission of visitors to this library, so that application should be made in writing and arrangements made in advance.

The Peers' Corridor leads northwards to the most accessible part of the building – the Central Hall. The corridor is lined with paintings by C. W. Pope, RA, but as with so many of the paintings commissioned for the new Houses of Parliament, they are badly lit and of no great artistic merit. They have historical subjects connected with the Civil War, and many of them have appeared from time to time in illustrated history books, particularly that of 'Speaker Lenthall asserting the privileges of the House of Commons when Charles I came to arrest the Five Members'.

The octagonal Central Hall is 75 feet high and 60 feet across, and it is here that constituents wait for the MPs with whom they have an appointment. It is an imposing building that undoubtedly impresses the provincial visitor with the importance of the occasion. The high roof is furnished with 250 carved and painted bosses, and Venetian mosaics fill the spaces between the

ribs of the vault. There are four doorways into the hall, each with a great decorative panel containing one of the patron saints of the countries which make up Great Britain – St George, St David, St Andrew and St Patrick, and all are accompanied by symbolic figures relating to the history of each country. The south doorway leads to the House of Lords, the north doorway to the House of Commons, the western door leads to St Stephen's Hall, and the eastern one to the dining-rooms and libraries. Another corridor leads north to the Commons Lobby and has large murals of historic events in the Stuart period, the artist for these being E. M. Ward, RA.

The Commons Lobby suffered grievously during the bombing which destroyed the House of Commons, so that the present one is in the main a very skilful reconstruction of that designed by Charles Barry. With one of those inspired ideas for which Sir Winston Churchill was famous, he declared that the blackened and bomb-scarred archway into the House of Commons should be preserved exactly as it was, 'as a monument of the ordeal which Westminster has passed through in the Great War, and as a reminder to those who will come centuries after us that they may look back from time to time upon their forebears who "kept the bridge In the brave days of old".' (The whole speech is recorded in 'Hansard' of 25 January 1945, col. 1006.)

The destruction of the Victorian House of Commons provided an unprecedented opportunity for the design of a House more suitable for the conduct of modern business, but with some of the old Gothic fittings replaced to give a sense of continuity. The foundation stone was laid by Mr Speaker, Clifton Brown, in 1948, and certain items, such as the green hide which covers the benches, have been continued – a tradition which is said to have been started during the reign of Henry VIII. The floor of the House has exactly the same dimensions as the old one – 68 feet long and $25\frac{1}{2}$ feet wide – but the galleries have been increased in size so that it is possible to seat 939 persons if necessary, although not all members of the House of Commons are likely to be present at the same time. A certain Gothic flavour has been retained, and the strips of carpet in front of each Front Bench are a reminder of the tradition that no member must cross them, for in the more violent periods of history they were a precaution to keep members wearing swords from using them on each other in the heat of the debate. The Government of the day is seated to the right of the Speaker, with the Prime Minister opposite the dispatch box. Immediately in front of the Speaker's chair is the table of the House, with its clerks and the Mace, the symbol of the authority of the Speaker over the House, but actually lent to him by the sovereign, who takes possession of it when Parliament is prorogued. It is carried in front of the Speaker by the Sergeant at Arms in procession to the prayers with which each parliamentary day begins; it is carried out by the same official before the Speaker when the House rises each night. The Mace rests on the table of the House when the Speaker (or his deputy) is in the Chair, but when the House goes into Committee the Mace is then placed on two supports beneath the Table to indicate that the House is not then properly constituted. The Mace normally in use (there are two) is silver-gilt

St Clement's Tower by day and by night

369

and is 4 ft 10½ in. long, and it is almost certainly one of the two made after the Restoration of Charles II. It is not therefore the one referred to by Cromwell as 'that Fool's Bauble' when he ordered its removal.

The House of Lords has its own ceremonial maces – one made during the reign of Charles II, the other made by a London silversmith in the reign of William III. The one normally in use is 5 ft 1 in. long, and both of them represent the royal authority. On any official occasion when the sovereign is not present the Lord Chancellor is always accompanied by a mace – as at the opening of the Law Courts, for example. There are other historic maces in use all over the world, including one made of wood in Monserrrat.

On either side of the House of Commons are the lobbies to which the members move when registering a vote – the 'Ayes' go to the corridor on the west side of the chamber, and the 'Noes' to the east side. (The Lords do not vote 'Aye' or 'No' – they declare themselves 'Content' or 'Not content'.)

The library of the House of Commons is also on the eastern side of the complex, overlooking the terrace and the river, and adjoining such rooms as the smoking rooms and dining-rooms. There is a strangers' dining-room and lounge to which an MP may introduce his visitors. Preserved in the strangers' room is an interesting exhibit which shows how much the composition of the House of Commons has changed since the time of Charles Dickens. This is the mallet and chisels used in the construction of the new House of Commons by a mason named Henry Broadhurst, who not only became an MP from 1880–1906, but in 1886 was Under-Secretary of State for the Home Department.

The normal entrance for visitors to the Houses of Parliament is on the west side through St Stephen's Porch, one of the parts of the building which had to be rebuilt after the bombing of the Second World War. It leads into St Stephen's Hall, at the top of a series of short flights of steps, the hall being on the site of St Stephen's Chapel. Ranged on either side of the hall there are statues of famous statesmen and politicians, silenced at last – Lord Clarendon; John Hampden; Lord Falkland; John Selden, the Cromwellian jurist and writer; Lord Somers; Sir Robert Walpole, effectively the first English Prime Minister; Lord Mansfield; Lord Chatham (William Pitt the Elder); Charles George Fox and his great rival, William Pitt the Younger; Henry Grattan, the champion of Catholic emancipation and one of the greatest Irish orators; and Edmund Burke, a champion of liberty but a profound believer in parliamentary democracy, as opposed to revolution for the setting right of wrongs. Ironically, the statue of Burke stands on the spot where John Bellingham, a bankrupt who attributed his failure to the Government, shot dead Spencer Perceval, the Prime Minister of the day, in 1812.

St Stephen's Hall is 95 feet long and 30 feet wide, and stands on the site of St Stephen's Chapel, built in the middle of the fourteenth century after a fire had destroyed the earlier chapel built in 1141 by King Stephen. The chapel built by Edward III, however, was suppressed by Edward VI in 1547, and the room was then taken over as the House of Commons until the fire of 1834, so that all the great events of English parliamentary history were

St Stephen's Hall

enacted in this hall – the struggle against the Stuarts for constitutional government, the pleas by such MPs as Edmund Burke for a more liberal treatment of the American colonies, the abolition of slavery bills, and the bitterly opposed Reform Bill which changed the whole course of parliamentary history. On the walls are murals by twentieth-century painters depicting events in English history. The finely vaulted roof was designed by Pugin, and there is a series of notable panels of mosaic and newly restored stained glass windows.

St Stephen's Porch leads out into St Margaret Street, but it is still possible to visit the newly decorated crypt of St Stephen, now known as the Chapel of St Mary, built on two levels in the reign of Edward I about 1292, the upper level originally being reserved for the royal worshippers. It was all beautifully restored after the fire in 1834, and again after the Second World War, and it can still be used for the marriage of any Member of Parliament or for the christening of a Member's children. There are two entries into the chapel – one from Westminster Hall and the other from the cloisters. These have also been restored after bomb damage.

Thus from the Gothic of the Middle Ages, through to the 'Gothic' of the nineteenth century, the visitor passes out into St Margaret Street to face the church of St Margaret, Westminster, or the eastern end of the great abbey church. Westwards is the main abbey church, the upper parts of the twin western towers being eighteenth-century 'Gothick', and the north porch and north transept with its wheel window being almost entirely the work of Sir George Gilbert Scott. Scott, the son of a poor village parson, became the most prolific and the most famous of all Victorian architects, especially in the 'Gothic' style of the nineteenth century.

It is not always easy to distinguish the work of the Victorian restorer or craftsman from that of the original, especially if the stone has weathered, but there is often a strangeness of proportion and a certain mechanical and repetitive quality about the carved mouldings which betrays the nineteenth-century work. The mouldings are sometimes shallow, so that there is not the rich interplay of light and shade to be found in medieval work, and there is sometimes a general feeling of 'thinness' unlike the robust quality to be found in the earlier buildings. Nineteenth-century sculptured figures are easier to detect, for Victorian saints and other angelic characters have a blandness and a sentimentality and nothing of the intensity of the medieval figures. This is particularly apparent if the visitor has been studying such masterpieces of medieval sculpture as the tomb figures of Eleanor of Castile, Edward III or Henry III, or the carved figures held in the niches of Henry VII's Chapel, and then turns to the sculptures in the north porch.

In other buildings associated with the abbey, but not necessarily part of the main church, Victorian additions can often be detected by the abundant use of brickwork with so-called 'Gothic' decoration, for medieval brickwork was extremely rare until the opening years of the sixteenth century, and even then tended to be used exclusively on such important buildings as St James's Palace, where the small Tudor bricks can easily be compared with the larger Victorian ones used in the restoration. An example of the Victorian brickwork is to be seen in the entrance to Dean's Yard and in some of the nineteenth-century additions to the buildings surrounding it.

The elaborately decorated column of red granite immediately west of the west end of the abbey is also the work of Sir George Scott, and stands on the site of the old Gatehouse Prison from which Sir Walter Raleigh went to his execution. This is the Westminster Column, a memorial erected to commemorate the former scholars of Westminster School who died during the Crimean War of 1853–56 and the Indian Mutiny of 1857–9. The Westminster Column stands at the junction of three main streets – Storey's Gate, Victoria Street and Great Smith Street. Storey's Gate was named after Edward Storey who was the Keeper of the Volary (Aviary) which Charles II kept in St James's Park, and leads northwards to the park. The huge ostentatious building with the dome which dominates Storey's Gate is not strictly part of Victorian London, for it was built between 1905–11, but it can most conveniently be described at this point. Designed by Edwin Rickards and his partners for the Wesleyan church assembly hall, it is one of the best examples in London of *art nouveau*, a movement which is essentially French in origin, and it seems somewhat incongruous that a religious body which is usually associated with an austerity of outlook, should commission a building which externally, at least, is much more reminiscent of a continental opera house or *Kursaal* than a meeting place for Nonconformist bodies. It is, however, an excellent concert hall, and is used for a great many different meetings other than those organised by its sponsors. Its dome, 90 feet in diameter and some 220 feet high, is the third largest in London, being only slightly smaller than those of the reading room at the British Museum and St Paul's Cathedral.

Great Smith Street is of little interest to the visitor, although the public baths just south of Old Pye Street which were erected in 1892 are significant of the stirrings of the Victorian conscience about the plight of the London poor. Old Pye Street and many of the surrounding roads are new streets which were built to improve an area once occupied by another of the notorious 'rookeries' – a slum area so densely populated that it was a standing reproach to the abbey in the shadow of which it lay. Pye Street, Westminster, was about 300 yards long and contained 190 houses. In those houses lived no less than 700 families, together with their animals – a total of about 3000 people on one short road. It is no wonder that, with the river as their only source of water, many of them died of cholera or other waterborne diseases, especially in the dreadful year of 'the Great Stink' – 1858 – when the drought produced so limited a flow of water in the Thames that it became little better than concentrated sludge.

Some of the most nauseous slums were swept away in the making of Victoria street which, from about 1845 onwards, drove an 80-foot-wide swathe from the Broad Sanctuary to Shaftesbury Place, Pimlico, while at about the same time efforts were made to build decent lodging houses and accommodation for working men in the surrounding streets. Charles Dickens was an active supporter of such schemes for reform, and was a personal friend of Miss (later Baroness) Burdett-Coutts who worked tirelessly to provide decent dwelling places and other amenities for the poor of London, including schools for the droves of illiterate street children for whom there was otherwise so little escape. Another notable philanthropist, an American who put to shame the niggardly efforts of the British public, was George Peabody, whose tenement buildings for the London poor are to be found in several parts of London – including one in Old Pye Street nearby. Some harsh things have been said about some of these schemes, although many of them still provide accommodation for Londoners, but in the century in which they were erected they were infinitely better than the slums which their tenants had been obliged to live in previously. George Peabody, who gave immense sums for the alleviation of the London poor, died in 1869; he was temporarily buried with great ceremony in Westminster Abbey, before his body was taken on board HMS *Monarch*, a British warship, and, with an American ship as escort, returned to his native country. A statue to this great philanthropist now stands in a little courtyard to the rear of the Royal Exchange in the City.

In the middle of the nineteenth century, with industrial production

left, The Peabody
buildings in Old Pye
Street
right, The statue of
George Peabody

increasing rapidly, Victorian enterprise developed not only the rich natural resources of the United Kingdom but those of the ever-expanding empire overseas. This fact made it possible to abolish three taxes which had exercised restrictions on the development of building of all kinds: the tax on glass was abolished in 1845, the brick tax in 1850, and finally the obsolete and harmful window tax in 1851. The results became evident almost at once. Enormous deposits of clay for brick-making in Huntingdonshire and Bedfordshire could now be exploited, and 'flettons' – a brick which derived its name from a village in Huntingdonshire, near Peterborough – began to appear in increasing numbers. These variously coloured bricks enabled architects to produce buildings in a style advocated by the very persuasive writer, John Ruskin, known as constructional polychromy – i.e., buildings in which the actual materials used provided the colour contrasts rather than something added later.

Victoria Street has changed considerably since it was first built, and it has lost a great deal of its nineteenth-century character as aggressively twentieth-century buildings overshadow what remains of the earlier street. Even the Army and Navy Stores, originally designed as a distillery, was extensively altered in the 1920s, but Caxton Hall, once Westminster Town Hall, is still to be seen just north of Victoria Street.

On the south side of Victoria Street is the Roman Catholic Cathedral of Westminster, its 273-foot-high bell tower a landmark for miles around this area. The work of J. F. Bentley, its foundation stone was laid in 1895, and its style shows admirably the changes which had come over Victorian architecture as it developed. Bentley chose neither the 'Gothic' favoured by Sir George Scott, nor the 'classical' favoured by Sir William Tite, the designer of the Royal Exchange. Instead, it was to the early Christian churches of Byzantium that Bentley turned for inspiration, and with a persevering sincerity he sought to recreate a church of an era when Christianity was young and ardent. The cathedral dominates the whole area with its impressive west front, and St Edward's Tower, the campanile or bell tower, is only 30 feet lower than the clock tower which houses Big Ben. It was described by another Victorian architect, Norman Shaw, as 'beyond all doubt the finest church which has been built for centuries. Superb in its scale and character, and full of the most devouring interest, it is impossible to overrate the magnificence of the design'. It is a verdict endorsed every year by thousands of visitors, and since Shaw wrote those words, much which was mean and unworthy has been cleared away from the west front, so that it can be seen to even greater advantage by the modern visitor.

The main building is huge, for the interior is 342 feet long, and the overall width, which includes the nave, aisles and side chapels, is 148 feet wide. At the east end the floor of the beautifully furnished sanctuary is $4\frac{1}{2}$ feet higher than that of the body of the church, so that it is clearly visible for the whole length of the cathedral. The nave is 60 feet wide, and the three domes which span it, each 60 feet in diameter, are 112 feet high. The main material from which the cathedral is built is brick, in the Byzantine tradition, and between ten and twelve million 'flettons' from the London Brick Company's works near Peterborough and in Bedfordshire were used, with bands of stone and stone facings making the cathedral a triumphant vindication for Ruskin's claim for constructional polychromy. The vaults have been furnished with glittering mosaics during the past few years, but there are still many who preferred the plain brick vaults which used to span the nave.

The foundation stone was laid by Cardinal Vaughan on 29 June 1895, but the architect, J. F. Bentley, died in 1902 so he never saw his designs completed. The building was in use by 1902, but as it is a custom of the Roman Catholic Church not to consecrate a new church until the fabric is constructionally complete and paid for, the actual consecration ceremony could not take place until 28 June 1910.

The many-coloured marbles used throughout the church came from various sources – some from the same quarries from which those which decorate Sancta Sophia were dug, and others from Thessaly and Euboea. The yellow marble is Veronese, the red marble is from Languedoc, and the Byzantine-type fretted and carved capitals at the top of each column, each different in design, are cut from Carrara marble. The High Altar is fashioned from a ten-ton block of Cornish granite.

Impressive as the building is overall, this remarkable essay in the style of a past age does not always carry conviction, and the mosaics, in particular,

seem rather tame by comparison with those of Ravenna or St Mark's, Venice. Mosaic, like stained glass, should exercise a discipline over the designer, but as soon as either medium is used for picture-making of the more obvious kind, it loses much of its essential character. This is clearly stressed by a famous American art historian, Dr Helen Gardner, who, writing of true Byzantine mosaics said: 'The mosaics . . . do not pretend to picture on walls an illusion of nature, but to decorate the surface and at the same time carry a message symbolically.' A good craftsman always respects his medium and understands its essential qualities, and if one medium merely imitates a different one – if stained glass, mosaic or embroidery, begin to lose their own peculiar qualities and take on those of painting, for example – the final result is unnatural and unsatisfactory.

No such mistake is to be found in the stations of the cross, beautifully carved by one of the greatest artists of this century – Eric Gill. This is the work of a man who *thought* in terms of the stone he was cutting and the tools he employed. The incised figures have the kind of intensity one finds in medieval sculpture, although it is no imitation of a past style but a modern interpretation by a twentieth-century artist. Eric Gill's work is also to be seen on the St James's Park underground station and on Broadcasting House, as well as in the many beautiful typefaces he designed and the books he wrote or illustrated. The stations of the cross in Westminster Cathedral rank among some of the finest sculptures to be seen in London, and are the perfect fusion between the medium and the message it conveys. It is interesting to compare this sculpture by Eric Gill with some medieval work in the cathedral, and to see how each era expressed itself in stone. The carving of the Virgin and Child by the south transept is the work of a fifteenth-century Nottingham carver – one of the many created from the local alabaster. Much of this kind of work was exported to the Continent, and sadly, because of the destruction which took place during the Reformation and the Commonwealth, some of the finest examples are only to be found on the mainland of Europe.

The whole of Westminster Cathedral is rich in works of art of various kinds, but it is also notable for the splendour of the music which may be heard there.

A lift has been installed in the campanile, so that for a small charge a visitor can enjoy a breath-taking view of London. To the south-east, almost in the shadow of the tower, is St Stephen-the-Less, a church endowed by Baroness Burdett-Coutts. It was designed by Benjamin Ferrey in 1847-9 and, unlike the cathedral, is designed as closely as possible to look medieval, not Byzantine. The Victorian school associated with the church, was built at about the same time, also by the generosity of the Baroness. At least one of her pupils repaid her for her philanthropy, for after having received much of his education at this school, a Welsh lad named William Morris Hughes emigrated to Australia and eventually became Attorney-General and one of the most important statesmen in the Commonwealth.

From the top of the tower it is surprising to see how richly endowed London is with great open green spaces and mature trees, most of them accessible to the public. Almost due north are the expanses of St James's Park, Green Park and the grounds of Buckingham Palace, with Hyde Park to the north-west. Due east, by the river and the Palace of Westminster, is Victoria Tower Gardens, and on the other side of the river behind the modern buildings of St Thomas's Hospital and Medical School, and the red-brick buildings of Lambeth Palace, one can see Archbishop's Park, and still further east the grounds of the Imperial War Museum, known as Geraldine Mary Harmsworth Park, just south of the Lambeth Road. Further south is Kennington Park, and somewhat nearer, but still on the far side of the river, Vauxhall Park. South-west there is a huge play area – Battersea Park – and opposite, on the north side of the river, is Ranelagh Gardens, only a small part of the eighteenth-century pleasure gardens, and now largely occupied by the buildings and grounds of Wren's Chelsea Military Hospital.

From this vantage point it is possible to detect the pattern of development of Victorian London in every direction. At first many Victorian houses continued the Regency tradition with stucco fronts, decorative motifs derived loosely from classical sources, and a certain unity imposed on the overall design of streets and squares. Their names often give some clue as to their dates – Alma Terrace, Sebastopol Place, Albert Road, Gladstone Street, Canning Street, and so on. Later in the century, as the suburbs sprawled further and further afield, and more and more City clerks took advantage of the new railway or omnibus routes, the houses lost their stucco, and architects and builders ransacked textbooks of historic ornament in order to make houses more and more aggressively individual. The street deteriorated into a string of detached houses, and the skyline became a jumble of turrets, minarets, battlements and spires. (Charles Dickens pokes gentle fun at Mr Wemmick's little Gothic house in Walworth in *Great Expectations*, but the joke was to turn sour as Walworth, too, disappeared beneath the rising tide of new buildings.)

Nevertheless there was nearly always a site left for the building of a church to serve the new neighbourhood – such churches, for example, as St James-the-Less, just west of Vauxhall Bridge Road and within easy reach of Westminster Cathedral. This church in polychrome brick is the work of G. E. Street and was built in 1858–61. Street, a pupil of Sir George Gilbert Scott, was to become famous for his Law Courts in the Strand later in the century. At roughly the same time Sir George Gilbert Scott also built a church in Westminster in Great Peter Street, but this is in stone, and the lack of a spire on its massive tower makes it difficult to see from the campanile of Westminster Cathedral. It is worth visiting, however, if only to see the characteristically rich furnishings designed for it by another of Scott's pupils, George Bodley. Apart from Westminster Abbey, which Scott restored, and the Foreign Office, there is little of his work to be seen in this area, but Battersea Power Station was built by his grandson, Sir Giles Gilbert Scott. Sir George Gilbert Scott is perhaps best known for his mighty St Pancras Hotel, the facade to St Pancras station.

Any chapter on Victorian London would be incomplete without some mention at least of the railway stations built during this century. There may well be a great deal of interest for the railway enthusiast in both Victoria stations, but very little of the old buildings survive apart from the Grosvenor Hotel and the walls which screen the railway from Buckingham Palace Road. The stations were originally built for the London, Chatham and Dover Railway and the Great Western Railway, and the two glass halls with semicircular arches over Platforms 1 to 8 are still largely the work of the Victorian engineer, John Fowler. A great many alterations and additions have occurred since 1862, however, and the Grosvenor Hotel, originally built as part of the scheme by J. T. Knowles about the same time, exhibits the strange mixture of styles which is characteristic of the Victorian public building, with details from St Mark's, Venice, the châteaux of the Loire and other historic buildings, adapted for 1860s travellers. It is regrettable that Victoria stations are often the first contact with London for visitors from the Continent, for it is unworthy of a great modern city.

The next important Victorian building in this area is the Tate Gallery on Millbank, a little north of Vauxhall Bridge. The Tate Gallery stands on the site of the old Millbank Penitentiary, and the name 'Millbank' is derived from the watermills which used to be in this area, owned by the Abbots of Westminster before the Reformation. The main Victorian part of the building is clearly recognisable by its flight of steps leading through a portico of Corinthian columns into the vestibule. This original building owes its inception to the increasing demand for greater representation of British art at the beginning of the Victorian period, but it was not until Mr (later Sir) Henry Tate offered not only sixty-five works of art by British artists, but sufficient money to build a gallery worthy of them that this was possible. The Tate was formally opened by the Prince of Wales (later Edward VII) on 21 July 1897, Sir Henry Tate's original gift being considerably augmented by works from other collectors and from the overcrowded National Gallery in Trafalgar Square. A number of extensions were added during the next few years, and in 1910 the superb collection of works by J. M. W. Turner were hung in a gallery financed by the famous art dealer and connoisseur, Lord Duveen.

The history of the growth of the Tate is too complicated to be dealt with

The Tate Gallery

at any length, but in 1917 it was constituted by an Act of Parliament not only as a general gallery of British art, with particular responsibility for modern British art, but also as a National Gallery of modern foreign art. Thus, a number of later architects have made notable additions to the original gallery by Sidney Smith, especially after the heavy damage it suffered in the Second World War.

The Tate is now completely independent of the National Gallery in Trafalgar Square, but both galleries interchange works of art and works acquired as modern by the Tate – works by Van Gogh, Renoir and other Impressionist painters, for example – can take their place rightfully in the National Gallery as acknowledged Old Masters.

Only at the Tate Gallery can one study Victorian painting and sculpture in detail, for apart from the works of Turner and Constable, it also has a fine collection of work by such Pre-Raphaelites as Sir John Everett Millais (whose statue stands outside), Holman-Hunt and Dante Gabriel Rossetti, as well as works by those other popular nineteenth-century artists such as W. P. Frith, whose 'Derby Day' is still a great favourite with the thousands of visitors to the gallery. The Tate, however, is best known for its collection of modern art, although some of the more bizarre examples acquired recently have attracted a great deal of adverse comment. But it must be remembered that, unlike a private collector who acquires only what he likes, the director of a museum or art gallery must try to present a properly co-ordinated representative survey of every important development of the period, so that art historians of the future are properly informed of the range and quality of the art of this century.

In addition to the permanent collection of over 4000 examples of work by British artists, over 300 of modern foreign works, and nearly 400 pieces of modern sculpture, the Tate Gallery also arranges temporary exhibitions, with loans from art galleries from all over the world.

It is not only at the Tate Gallery that one can study the development of British twentieth-century art, for it is shown most vividly in a partly Victorian building across the river, just off Lambeth Road – the Imperial War Museum. During the First World War many young artists actually involved in the tragedy of Flanders and other theatres of war sought to find adequate means of expressing what they knew and felt about the obscenity of war, for the old conventions depicting battle were false, debased and wholly unacceptable.

The premises now occupied by the Imperial War Museum are actually part of those originally used for the Bethlem Hospital – the hospital for the mentally ill. This was initially housed in premises vacated at the Reformation by the monks of the Priory of St Mary of Bethlehem or Bethlem, near Bishopsgate. The asylum subsequently moved to other buildings in Moorfields and then later crossed the river to this site where it remained until its final move to its present home in Beckenham in 1931. The buildings now occupied by the Imperial War Museum were part of the administrative block of the hospital, to which the portico and dome were added by Sydney Smirke in 1846. Thus, the coat of arms of the House of

Hanover in Coade stone and the Latin inscription referring to Henry VIII under it have no connection with the museum, but with its predecessor.

In addition to the truly remarkable series of armament, equipment, relics, models and dioramas of two World Wars on show, the museum has over 10,000 drawings and paintings by famous British artists such as Augustus John, for example, who worked in both wars. There are works by such men as Stanley Spencer, C. R. Nevinson, Wyndham Lewis, Paul and John Nash, Eric Kennington, as well as some of the best work of John Piper, Graham Sutherland, Jacob Epstein, Edward Bawden, Eric Ravilious, Henry Moore and other British artists who have achieved international fame.

While the Imperial War Museum in no way glorifies or condones war, it does pay tribute to the gallantry, the endurance and the sacrifice not only of the fighting men and women of the British, Commonwealth and Allied armies, but also to those qualities displayed by civilians who, caught up in the holocaust of the Second World War, displayed such courage and resourcefulness in the face of appalling dangers.

The obelisk outside the museum has no connection with it, but was originally erected at St George's Circus, just north-east of the museum, to commemorate the courage of Brass Crosby, a Lord Mayor of London who refused to convict a printer in 1771 for having published parliamentary debates. Crosby was imprisoned in the Tower of London, but so great was public indignation that he was released, and Press reporting of debates in the House of Commons has been continued ever since.

Walking from the Tate Gallery to the Imperial War Museum one crosses Lambeth Bridge, which was originally a Victorian suspension bridge, built in 1862. This was taken down in 1929 and the present bridge dates from 1932. Near Lambeth Bridge is Victoria Tower Gardens – a public park which borders the Thames and is notable for two sculptures with nineteenth-century connections. The first is a replica of Rodin's famous 'Burghers of Calais' in which the unfortunate Frenchmen, prisoners of Edward III, are roped together and confront an invisible king in various attitudes of defiance and of despair. Nearby is a statue of Emmeline Pankhurst, who was born in Manchester in 1858 and became one of the most important women in the nineteenth century. Although her courage and determination to secure Women's Suffrage did not bear fruit until the twentieth century, it must be very largely due to the indomitable courage with which she faced even imprisonment that there are now women sitting both in the House of Lords and the House of Commons.

Not far from the statue of Emmeline Pankhurst is the statue of another famous woman – that of Boudicca (or Boadicea), Queen of the Iceni, who is somewhat inaccurately portrayed by Thomas Thornycroft as a full-bosomed Roman matriarchal figure restraining her horses with some difficulty from breaking loose from the plinth anchored firmly at the north-western end of Westminster Bridge. It was sculptured in the 1850s, but not unveiled there until 1902.

In Whitehall there is another major work by Sir George Gilbert Scott.

The statue of Boudicca
by Thomas
Thornycroft

When he won an open competition organised by the Tory government for the new government offices in Whitehall, he intended to produce 'Gothic' buildings which would rival those designed by Sir Charles Barry for the Houses of Parliament. But when the Tory government was defeated, the new government under the Prime Ministership of Lord Palmerston had very different views as to the kind of designs they would accept. The result of this change of government and its impact on the work of Sir George Gilbert Scott is told in a hilarious passage by Philip Guedalla in his biography of Palmerston. The new Prime Minister firmly declined the new 'Gothic' designs, and told the hapless architect to redesign the buildings 'in the Italian manner'. The unfortunate man struggled to eradicate the 'Gothic' and to produce something which the Prime Minister would accept, but these new designs did not satisfy him either. Palmerston called the result 'neither one thing nor t'other – a regular mongrel affair'. The final result of Sir George Gilbert Scott's painful rethinking can be seen in the area bounded by Downing Street to the south, by Great George Street and Parliament Square to the north, and includes King Charles Street as a central dividing line. The exterior views are almost entirely the work of Sir George Gilbert Scott, although the courtyard on what was then the India Office is the work of Sir Matthew Digby Wyatt, a fact admitted by Scott. The work is sumptuous with a strong Italian Renaissance flavour, the facades faced with

The Foreign Office buildings, with the statue of Robert Clive in the foreground

Portland stone and with granite columns, but it created a great deal of controversy in the House of Commons when Palmerston was called upon to defend its appearance. It was in fact dubbed not 'Gothic' or 'Renaissance', but 'Palmerstonian'. The buildings are further complicated stylistically by the additional work on Great George Street by a less well-known Scots architect, John McKean Brydon, a former pupil of Norman Shaw. Brydon also designed Chelsea Town Hall (1885–7) and Chelsea Polytechnic (1891–5).

The development of the Treasury buildings just north of Sir George Gilbert Scott's government buildings scheme is even more complex, for both William Kent and Sir John Soane worked on it before Sir Charles Barry added its Whitehall facade during the 1850s. They were built on the site originally occupied by part of Cardinal Wolsey's palace which was annexed by Henry VIII.

Still further north on the east side of Whitehall, near the statue of Charles I, there used to be a palace of the Scottish kings in the area later known as Scotland Yard. It was there that the Metropolitan Police Force had their first offices, after their formation by Sir Robert Peel in 1829. To allay fears that this was a para-military organisation, the men were dressed in civilian-type top hats and blue frock-coats, and they carried only a truncheon for their own protection. The original police manual laid down certain rules for

383

the conduct of the police, which despite changing circumstances are still an integral part of the police training. It also stated that each police officer 'must remember that there is no qualification so indispensible to a police officer as a perfect command of temper'.

The original police office was in Whitehall Place and has long since disappeared, but the separate detective branch, formed in 1842, first had offices in Scotland Yard and then transferred to a large building designed for it by Norman Shaw in the 1890s, almost opposite Downing Street. Both parts were built by Norman Shaw, the ground floor being of granite and the upper floors of brick, banded with stone, with château-like turrets on each corner. New premises were built for Scotland Yard in Victoria Street in 1967, and the building in Whitehall is now called Norman Shaw Buildings, north and south.

The formation of a special police force to deal with the crime on the river had preceded the Metropolitan Police by several years, for there was a police office at Wapping New Stairs as early as 1789. The City of London was to form its own separate police force, and it is still possible to distinguish the City of London policeman from the Metropolitan policeman by the different colour of his armband and the ridged crest on his helmet.

The Victoria Embankment, a magnificent engineering feat carried out from 1864–70, was the work of Sir Joseph Bazalgette for which he was awarded his knighthood. It is 100 feet wide and over a mile long, extending from Westminster Bridge downstream to Blackfriars Bridge. The building of it reclaimed 37 acres of wasteland and provided public gardens as well as a broad highway, opened in 1870 by Edward VII (then Prince of Wales). There is a memorial to Joseph Bazalgette in the wall of the Victoria Embankment opposite the east end of Northumberland Avenue, but his real memorial is the Embankment itself and the immense benefits which have accrued since its construction.

The Albert Embankment on the opposite bank of the river from Westminster and extending upstream is a somewhat less ambitious scheme, but it provided among other advantages accommodation for St Thomas's Hospital, which had sold its land to the Southern Railway for the building of London Bridge station and other facilities in 1863. The Albert Embankment is the broad road which extends downstream from Vauxhall Bridge to Lambeth Bridge. Most of the Victorian buildings of St Thomas's Hospital were heavily damaged in the Second World War and have been rebuilt.

The Victoria Embankment narrowed the river by draining the mudflats and then enclosing the Thames between massive brick walls, faced with granite. The wall on the west bank extends $32\frac{1}{2}$ feet above high water mark and 14 feet below low water mark. The first of the public gardens formed by the Embankment are the Victoria Embankment Gardens, interrupted briefly by Horse Guards Avenue, and bordered on the west by Whitehall Court, a lively and assertive series of buildings housing a number of clubs.

Unlike its dour companion, the Ministry of Defence, Whitehall Court has an almost over-exuberant skyline, with spires and turrets, pinnacles and roofs, and the whole building is supplied with balconies and loggias as though Thomas Archer and his partner, A. Green, felt obliged to show just what could be done in 1884. This building is in fact much more acceptable than the one they produced at Cambridge Gate, among Nash's stucco terraces, which jars very badly.

Adjoining Whitehall Court is another virtuoso performance, this time by Sir Alfred Waterhouse, the building which is now the National Liberal Club. Designed in 1885–7, the interior was modified at the beginning of the twentieth century.

Northumberland Avenue joins Whitehall to the Victoria Embankment just south of Charing Cross station, but none of its buildings justifies the sacrifice of a great Jacobean mansion, Northumberland House, which was destroyed in order to build this connecting road. There is, however, an amusing little public house which a student of Victoriana should certainly visit. Originally The Northumberland Arms, it has been renamed The Sherlock Holmes, and the brewers, Whitbreads, have produced a delightful reconstruction of the study used by the most famous detective in the world of fiction so that his admirers, frustrated in their search for the chambers in Baker Street, can go there to enjoy the meticulous care with which this room is designed. The public house is also hung with genuine theatrical posters and with the photographs of famous actors who have interpreted the role of Sherlock Holmes in a number of stage versions of his exploits.

The Avenue theatre, which stood at the eastern end of Northumberland Avenue, was opened in 1882, but during repairs to the roof of Charing Cross station a tie-rod gave way, and the whole roof slid sideways and crashed on to the theatre, which was fortunately empty at the time. The present Playhouse theatre was built on the site of the old Avenue theatre ruins in 1905, and is now used exclusively by the BBC as a theatrical studio.

The building of Charing Cross railway bridge necessitated the demolition of the old Hungerford Market, and the footbridge still retains the name of the seventeenth-century nobleman, Hungerford, who built the first market on this site by Hungerford Stairs, leading down to the river at the place where there once stood the blacking factory and warehouse in which Charles Dickens worked. The footbridge is now a first-rate vantage point from which to look downstream and enjoy the remarkable improvements which have been made to the South Bank since 1951.

Charing Cross Hotel on the Strand, in front of John Hawkshaw's station and railway bridge, is the work of E. M. Barry, who also assisted his father with the Houses of Parliament and completed them after his father's death in 1860. Charing Cross Hotel is not in the 'Gothic' style, but a rather nondescript kind of Renaissance style, with odd additions of Flemish strapwork decoration over the windows. It is in no way remarkable. The station to the rear is a jumble of re-adjustments, repairs and improvisations. The 75-foot-high cross in the forecourt is a sincere attempt by Barry to reproduce one of the original crosses which marked the funeral cortège of Queen Eleanor, and which had been erected at the head of Whitehall in 1294 on the site now occupied by the equestrian statue of Charles I. The medieval

The Victorian version of Charing Cross

385

cross was destroyed by Cromwellians sometime between 1643 and 1647 as a
symbol of both royalty and popery, and the present cross was carved by
Thomas Earp and designed by E. M. Barry in 1863.

The former Charing Cross underground station has been renamed
'Embankment', and immediately north of this station is one of the largest
tracts of land reclaimed by Sir Joseph Bazalgette – Victoria Embankment
Gardens, which, with its neat lawns, mature plane trees and bright
flowerbeds, is one of the pleasantest parts of this area. The extent of the land
reclaimed can most easily be recognised by the position of the York
watergate which, when it was built in the opening years of the seventeenth
century, was at the very edge of the Thames.

To the west the land rises sharply, and modern Adelphi buildings have
now taken the place of the great eighteenth-century complex erected there
by the Adam Brothers, but demolished in the 1930s.

Still further north is Shell-Mex House, its massive bulk looming 201 feet
above the gardens, and its clock-face the largest in London. This building
erected by Messrs Joseph in 1933, stands on the site of a famous Victorian
hotel, Hotel Cecil, which failed after a financial scandal and was
subsequently pulled down. The Hotel Cecil in its turn had been built on the
site of the town house of Sir Robert Cecil, the Elizabethan statesman, this
having occupied the site of the town house of the Archbishop of York in the
Middle Ages. The whole area is typical of the accretion of historical
associations in so many parts of London.

Almost opposite Shell-Mex House, but on the very balustrade of the Embankment, is Cleopatra's Needle, a sixty-eight-foot-high obelisk of reddish granite weighing 180 tons which was transported with much difficulty and loss of life from Egypt and erected there in 1878. It actually has no association with Cleopatra, but stood with its companion (now in Central Park, New York) in front of a great temple at Heliopolis, having been erected there by the Pharoah, Thothmes III, *c.* 1500 BC. Rameses II, the Pharoah of the notorious oppression of the Israelites, later added an inscription of his own to one side, but considerably later still the victorious Augustus Caesar had both obelisks taken down and moved to Alexandria, and it is apparently at this point that it became associated with Cleopatra. After the defeat of Napoleon, Cleopatra's Needle was offered as a tribute to George IV by the Egyptian viceroy, Mohammed Ali, but this was declined as was another offer made to William IV. It was after many such overtures that the generosity of a famous Victorian surgeon, Erasmus Wilson, eventually saw that the obelisk was brought to this country. Some idea of the problems encountered in bringing so unwieldy an object to England may be gained by the terse inscription which reads: 'Through the patriotic zeal of Erasmus Wilson, FRS, this obelisk was brought from Alexandria in an iron cylinder; it was abandoned in the Bay of Biscay, recovered, and erected on this spot by John Dixon, CE, in the 42nd year of the reign of Queen Victoria.' Buried beneath Cleopatra's Needle is the most extraordinary collection of objects for the benefit of historians of the future: a complete set of coinage of the period, including an Empress of India rupee, Bibles in various languages, Bradshaw's railway guide, a box of hairpins and ladies' ornaments, a feeding bottle and children's toys, pipes and cigars, and other strange items, including a translation of the hieroglyphics on the obelisk. The large bronze sphinxes which flank the obelisk are the work of a man named Vulliamy, but unfortunately the building contractor positioned them the wrong way round, for they should face outwards. The seats which are provided on the Embankment have Egyptian motifs in their supports – sphinxes and squatting camels in iron, for example – and some of them were the gift of W. H. Smith, the son of the original W. H. Smith who founded the famous firm of booksellers. W. H. Smith Jun., went into politics and became First Lord of the Admiralty in 1874: he was the original of the character portrayed by Gilbert and Sullivan in *H.M.S. Pinafore*. A memorial to Sir Arthur Sullivan is also to be found in this area, in the Embankment Gardens, just a little to the east of the Savoy theatre where so many thousands of Savoyards have rejoiced at the wit of his partner Sir William Gilbert and the beauty of his own music. The Savoy theatre has been subject to considerable alterations since it was first built for Richard D'Oyly Carte to house the Gilbert and Sullivan Opera Company, but the performances of the operas are still very similar to those which enchanted the first audiences during the halcyon days of D'Oyly Carte.

Almost nothing remains of the Savoy Chapel in which Chaucer may have been married, and the present building is entirely Victorian – partly the work of Sir Robert Smirke and partly that of his younger brother, Sydney

Cleopatra's Needle

Smirke, in 1841–3. The damage sustained during the Second World War has been most beautifully repaired and the whole chapel is now the chapel of the youngest Order of Chivalry, the Royal Victorian Order. Unlike some Victorian churches, this one is quiet and has a reticence of decoration – it is a little haven away from the turmoil of the busy newspaper offices nearby. As the original chapel was once part of the Hospital of St John (1510–16), it still has some medieval stained glass, and although the calligrapher is modern, the list of members of the Order is written with a quill and worthy of the great medieval tradition. The vestibule is decorated with an attractive heraldic plaque in high relief which, on examination, proves to be not metal, but gilded marrow seeds tightly packed into the writing shapes of the leopards of England. One of the Victorian windows commemorates Richard D'Oyly Carte, whose only failure seems to have been the launching of the English Opera House in 1891. This had been built in Cambridge Circus, and later became the Palace theatre under different managements, and then a music-hall.

Savoy Street runs parallel to the approaches of Waterloo Bridge and Lancaster Place; considerable reorganisation of this area has resulted from the erection of the new Waterloo Bridge, designed by Sir Giles Scott before the Second World War, but not completed until 1945, even though it was the successor to Rennie's nineteenth-century bridge. With five low graceful arches, it was the only concrete bridge crossing the Thames until the new London Bridge was built in 1973. The iron spans of the temporary Waterloo Bridge played their part in securing victory, for when it was dismantled, the whole complex ironwork was carefully preserved and finally adapted to provide a bridge for troops to cross the Rhine after D-Day, after the enemy had destroyed all the others.

A British achievement of quite a different kind is commemorated by the little ship moored off the embankment, just downstream from Westminster Bridge. This is HMS *Discovery*, the ship in which Captain Robert Falcon Scott, an officer born in 1868 and trained in the finest traditions of the Royal Navy, explored the Antarctic wastes in 1900–4. The leader of a later ill-fated expedition, he died there in 1912.

To the rear of the Embankment is the 800-foot-long mass of Somerset House. The major part is the work of Sir William Chambers, the eighteenth-century architect, but the western wing was added by Sir James Pennethorne in 1856, and the eastern end, housing King's College, was built by Sir Robert Smirke from 1829–35. Both of the later architects have tailored their designs to match that of the earlier building.

Moored downstream from the *Discovery* are two sloops of the First World War I – HMS *Wellington*, the headquarters of the London division of the RNVR, and HMS *Chrysanthemum*, the headquarters of the RNR – and HMS *President*, a frigate of the Second World War and the Livery Hall of the Honourable Company of Master Mariners, one of the most recent City companies, formed in 1926. The latter lies just off Temple stairs, almost on the boundary of the City with the City of Westminster – a boundary marked by two dragons, each mounted on a high plinth, flanking the Embankment.

One of the dragons
dividing the City of
London from the City
of Westminster. They
were taken from
outside the Old Coal
Exchange.

Walking further east towards Blackfriars Bridge, there are various Victorian
buildings between the Temple Gardens and the bridge, including the City
of London School (for boys), a somewhat over-emphatic building built in
1881–2, with a wealth of coupled classical columns supporting a façade of
arches, and statues of such worthies as Shakespeare, Milton, Sir Isaac
Newton, Sir Francis Bacon and Sir Thomas More. The school was
originally in Milk Street, but it now occupies part of the site of one of the
first gasworks ever built in London in 1814 and rebuilt later in Barking.
Another part of the same Whitefriars site is occupied by a lighter, more
'Gothic' building – Sion College Library, which was built as a reference
library and social centre for the clergy of London by Sir Arthur Blomfield in
1886. It is of a somewhat harsh red brick, with delicate, well-manipulated
Gothic forms. Some of it was unfortunately destroyed to allow the new
underpass for Blackfriars to be built.

An important Victorian building lies to the north on the far side of Middle
Temple Lane, at the point where Fleet Street changes its name to the Strand
on another boundary between the City of London and the City of
Westminster. This dividing line is also marked by a rampant dragon
struggling to free itself from the plinth which holds it fast on the site of old
Temple Bar. The building in question is that of the Royal Courts of Justice,
known more familiarly as the Law Courts, perhaps to distinguish them from
the Central Criminal Courts in Old Bailey, well to the east on the far side of

389

Farringdon Road. For centuries the Royal Courts of Justice had been at Westminster, at one time in Westminster Hall, but by the middle of the nineteenth century the premises there were quite hopelessly inadequate for the demands made upon them. An open competition was held for the design of new premises in 1866, and won by G. E. Street, a former pupil of Sir George Gilbert Scott. The foundation stone was laid in 1874, and the whole complex of buildings, covering about 5½ acres, was completed in 1882, one year after Street's death, by Street's son, A. E. Street, and his assistant, Arthur Blomfield.

G. E. Street's Royal Courts of Justice dominates this part of the Strand, a vast building enriched with details drawn from the buildings of the Middle Ages – particularly from French Gothic – with deep pointed archways holding deep shadows and round turrets corbelled out over the pavement. The clock tower, some 160 feet high, has a roof clearly derived from a French château, but the huge central hall is crowned by a needle-like spire not unlike that on Notre-Dame in Paris. The Strand frontage of stone is 483 feet long, skilfully broken up by arcading, windows and deeply recessed doors, with the main entrance leading into the central hall. The walls facing the courtyard and Bell Yard are a mixture of brick and stone, the whole complex takes into account the fact that the Carey Street front is actually 15 feet higher than that of the Strand. Bomb damage inflicted during the

Second World War has been made good, and some additional building absorbed into the huge complex, but Street's original idea of having a wing to the west to balance that to the east was never carried out.

The most impressive part of the interior is the central hall, which is 230 feet long, 42 feet wide and 82 feet high, with a great rose window at the far end. On the walls are several portraits of judges and a statue of G. E. Street. Only people actively concerned with cases being heard in the courts are allowed into the hall, but anyone may go to the public galleries.

The Public Records Office in Chancery Lane, a little to the east of the Royal Courts of Justice, is another impressive Victorian building, but here a different style of Gothic was chosen by Sir James Pennethorne for the part he built on Fetter Lane in 1851–66, as well as by his successor, Sir John Taylor, in 1891–6 for the part on Chancery Lane. Instead of looking to French architecture for their inspiration, they went to the last phase of English Gothic – the Perpendicular period in which certain Tudor buildings such as Henry VII's Chapel in Westminster Abbey were produced – and they used such details as the wide window with the flattened arch, the shallow mouldings, and the diminutive octagonal capitals at the end of thin linear columns to convey the impression of the Tudor age. There are still traces of medieval buildings which formerly occupied the site, in particular a large arch which was originally part of an early medieval chapel for the use of Jews converted to Christianity, but this can only be seen with previous permission. The Records Office is open to the general public on weekdays and has some unique exhibits of general interest. These include the original volumes of the *Domesday Book*, that most remarkable survey of England made for William the Conqueror, which was begun in 1085 and completed in 1087 and recorded the owners of every part of the land, the nature of crops cultivated upon it, and the number of inhabitants and their respective classes, whether freemen, villeins or serfs. It enabled the new king to levy taxes and was in effect a census of the population and a record of the value of each estate in the country. There are also letters from many of the most famous people in England's history – from Cardinal Wolsey, Anne Boleyn and Catherine of Aragon; documents concerning the famous Gunpowder Plot; a letter from George Washington to his 'great and good friend', George III; and 'The Olive Branch Petition' to that same monarch, dated 1775, from representatives of twelve of the states of the American colony telling him how they 'ardently desire a restoration of the former harmony between Great Britain and her colonies.' It is a most enthralling collection, even if the writing on these documents is faded and the hand almost illegible, for it provides a tangible record of British history.

A little further north on the opposite side of Chancery Lane is the medieval entrance to Lincoln's Inn, and to the west of this there is another most imposing building, also in the Tudor style, although this is actually by a Victorian architect. A smallish, pleasant square just west of Lincoln's Inn Chapel (which has a partly Victorian undercroft) has an unpretentious group of buildings designed by Sir George Gilbert Scott, built in the 1970s with a somewhat Elizabethan appearance.

The really outstanding building in this area is still further to the west – the new library and hall which takes in much of the western side of Lincoln's Inn and forms the eastern boundary of Lincoln's Inn Fields. This was the work of Philip Hardwick, and with its impressive staircase leading to the spacious hall with a timber hammerbeam roof, it could almost be the Tudor hall of some Oxford or Cambridge college. Hardwick designed it very much in the Tudor style and even enlivened any large blank areas of brick with a pattern of parti-coloured bricks – the kind of diapering which appears on such original Tudor buildings as Lambeth Palace and St James's Palace. The first stone of this building was laid on 20 April 1843, and the date of the building also appears in a darker coloured brick. The library was ready to receive its immense numbers of books on jurisprudence by 1845; the original collection was started in 1497 in the reign of Henry VII and is of great antiquity – it can claim to be the oldest library in the metropolis. Originally 80 feet in length, the building was extended in 1873 and it is now 130 feet long, 40 feet wide, and 44 feet high. The additions to the library, carried out after the death of Philip Hardwick, were made by Sir George Gilbert Scott, with some unwelcome interference under the guise of help by the amateur architect, horologist and QC, Lord Grimthorpe. It was Grimthorpe who was responsible for the clock in the clock tower of the Houses of Parliament, and the escapement mechanism known as the Grimthorpe three-legged gravity which is still used there today was for many years the standard mechanism in most public clocks. His architectural work unfortunately produced less happy results, particularly in the west end of St Albans Cathedral.

Walking westwards from the library through the original Tudor gate, which was also partially restored in the Victorian period, one arrives in Lincoln's Inn Fields where the most important Victorian building is the Royal College of Surgeons. Its impressive and dignified façade on the south side was built by Sir Charles Barry, the architect of the Houses of

The hall at Lincoln's Inn, by Philip Hardwick

392

Parliament, and is another excellent example of the versatility of such a Victorian architect who could turn from the unremitting 'Gothic-Tudor' of the Parliament buildings to produce a most elegant façade in the classical style with a great porch of Ionic columns. Despite alterations in 1888 by another architect, it still retains much of the sweetness of proportion which one hopes to find in any classical building.

There are several Victorian houses on the perimeter of Lincoln's Inn Fields, notably on the same side as the Sir John Soane Museum, but No. 58, the home of John Forster, the friend and biographer of Charles Dickens, and the original of Mr Tulkinghorn's house in *Bleak House*, is a good deal earlier, probably early eighteenth century with some later additions.

One of the most important and most impressive groups of Victorian buildings and institutions in the London area is to be found in South Kensington, with its remarkable collection of museums and other educational and cultural centres, so typical of one of the more endearing aspects of Victorian life. The whole development in this area was largely the result of two very important exhibitions – the famous 1851 Crystal Palace exhibition, and a less widely known one in 1862, both of which were to leave an indelible imprint on South Kensington and on London. The 1851 exhibition was not initially the concept of Albert, the Prince Consort, but of Henry Cole, an energetic and far-seeing writer and editor of a number of journals concerned with the development of British industrial design. Under his direction the Society of Arts held a series of exhibitions of art manufactures in 1847, 1848 and 1849 in an effort to raise the standard of design of goods which, hitherto produced by hand, were now being mass-produced by machines to an extent hardly thought possible at the beginning of the reign of Queen Victoria. As nothing of the old Crystal Palace remains – it was re-erected in Sydenham but burned down in 1936 – there is little point in describing it in detail, but it must be stressed that the structure of the building erected in Hyde Park for the Great Exhibition of the Works of Industry of All Nations

The two faces of the commemorative medal produced for the Great Exhibition in 1851

was to anticipate techniques which are now typical of modern architecture. Using pre-fabricated, standardised and interchangeable units of iron and glass designed by Joseph Paxton (no architect, but a highly intelligent and creative gardener formerly employed by the Duke of Devonshire at Chatsworth), the whole building, covering 18 acres, was erected in twenty-two weeks by Messrs Fox and Henderson, the builders. It was 1851 feet long (slightly enlarged from the original plan to fit the date) with a vaulted transept 408 feet long and 108 feet high, and the whole structure was so entirely novel that there were many who foretold its collapse. Nevertheless, after carts loaded with 8 tons of cannon-balls had been trundled up and down its galleries, and a whole corps of the Royal Sappers and Miners had marched, countermarched, and even marked time without bringing the whole structure down about their ears, the critics were confounded, and the Exhibition, which opened on 1 May 1851 and closed in October, attracted no less than 6,000,000 visitors and made a profit of £86,000.

Much of its success must be attributed to the Prince Consort, who threw himself into the planning with tremendous enthusiasm and became more popular with the nation than ever before. Half of the exhibitors were British, but forty other countries, including the United States, exhibited their products – a total of 15,000 firms. There was inevitably much disagreement about the artistic qualities of the exhibits, and William Morris, then an impressionable youngster of seventeen, 'stood aghast at the appalling ugliness of the objects exhibited, the heaviness, tastelessness, and rococo banality of the entire display'. There were also critics who deplored the imitative quality of the designs, the use of ornament applied for the sake of ornament alone, and the employment of such 'non materials' as papier mâché for architectural details and for furniture of various kinds, including a squat armchair described as the 'dreamer's chair'. More significant was the erection in Hyde Park, but outside the Crystal Palace, of a 'group of model dwellings for the poor', designed on the advice of Prince Albert, to house four families. It was built of hollow brick, and the walls and the floors inside were of glazed brick for easy cleaning. From the outside the group had a vaguely Elizabethan look, with a large central 'Flemish' gable, balanced by a slightly smaller one on either side, and an open verandah on the first floor over the main entrance. The estimated cost was £500, and the estimated rent was 5 shillings a week, the accommodation offered being infinitely superior to most working men's houses, especially those in such areas as Bethnal Green. After the 1851 Exhibition the houses were dismantled and re-erected in Lambeth, where, much modified, they were until quite recently the entrance lodge to Kennington Park.

The Great Exhibition of 1851 started a trend: there was a second exhibition in South Kensington in 1862, shortly after the death of the Prince Consort, and another in 1871, and although none was as popular nor so innovatory as the first, it meant that little by little, as some parts of the exhibition buildings were left to be adapted for a more permanent museum, South Kensington became established as a cultural and educational centre. It was natural that the opening of the Royal Albert Hall of Arts and Sciences

The Natural History Museum

in 1871 as a memorial to Prince Albert should act to some extent as a focal point around which other museums and buildings began to form, especially as the site on which it was built was acquired by the proceeds of the first Great Exhibition.

Thus, by the end of the century, South Kensington could boast a magnificent Natural History Museum (originally a branch of the British Museum); a school of arts and crafts; the Royal College of Music, opened in 1894; the Imperial Institute, which opened in 1893 and a few years later became part of the University of London; the City and Guilds of London Central Technical College; and, although it took nearly ten years to build and to furnish, the Victoria and Albert Museum, the foundation stone of which was laid in May 1899.

Although Thurloe Place and other streets in the immediate vicinity of South Kensington underground station are clearly of the nineteenth century – composed of houses with stucco fronts and pillared porticoes somewhat like the 'classical' Regency houses – the first major building in this new cultural centre was the Natural History Museum. It was built in 1873–8 by Alfred Waterhouse, RA, in brick on a steel structure, and richly endowed with terracotta cladding, with an impressive façade over 650 feet long and twin towers each 190 feet high. Waterhouse went to early medieval France for his inspiration – French Romanesque – and the vast portico with its recessed semicircular arches is perhaps reminiscent of an early French cathedral such as that at Poitiers rather than a building with serious scientific uses. The entrance hall is lofty and even dwarfs the little family of elephants which is there to greet the visitor. Everywhere, even on the staircases, there are terracotta low reliefs of every aspect of natural history, and before the Second World War, to all except the specialist, it was one of the dullest museums in London, with its lumpily stuffed corpses and glass-eyed creatures. It has since changed considerably and was in fact one of the first of the museums to set out to interest and to entertain its young visitors. Building on the foundations of the pioneer work which took place at such museums as the Geffrye Museum in Shoreditch, it is now one of the most attractive places to which to take a youngster, the whale room and the British bird pavilion being just two of the areas which exemplify the new approach to museum display.

The modern extension to the Natural History Museum on the western side of the Cromwell Road resembles its older neighbour in no respect, except perhaps by having its windows on a corresponding level, although those of the modern building are considerably larger and made of tinted glass. The proportions, the scale of the building and the materials are all typical of this century. Yet it is easy to see that the wing which projects into the grounds of the Natural History Museum is a natural descendent of the apse of a real medieval building, although there is no attempt whatever to imitate such a detail.

Immediately to the north of the modern wing of the Geological Museum building, and linked to it by a bridging corridor, is the part of the headquarters of the Geological Survey building which was erected beside the Science Museum in 1933, having been re-housed after its initial foundation in 1835. At that time it was based in Craig's Court, Charing Cross – a small courtyard tucked away almost opposite the statue of Charles I. The new Geological building has a gaunt skeleton of steel disguised by pseudo-classical details; the columns, which now look so convincingly structural, were swung in position, drum after drum, to fit *under* the capitals they now appear to support, and then firmly clamped in position on the steel girders. The architect of this structural deceit was J. H. Markham, and he was careful to make the façade of the Geological building match that of its neighbour to the north, the Science Museum, designed by Sir Richard Allison in 1913. Both buildings still bear the scars of the bombing of the Second World War.

The Institute of Geological Sciences contains exhibits of the 'the useful minerals of the world, coal, petroleum, metallic ores, refractories, marble, building stone, slate, precious and decorative stones, and actual and synthetic gems'. This is another museum in which the dioramas, the photographs and the displays are arranged with great artistic skill. It is a fascinating collection, setting forth with the minimum of scientific language such themes as the 'Story of the Earth', the 'Treasures of the Earth', and other brilliantly displayed aspects of the planet we inhabit and the universe around us.

It is very difficult to describe the treasures and the pleasures of the Science Museum next door, for the range and richness of the contents is so overwhelming that it would be wise for any visitor to be selective. One of the

most fascinating exhibits is the model of Foucault's pendulum near the entrance to the museum on Exhibition Road. The great brass ball, suspended on an almost invisible wire, swings slowly to and fro so that any visitor, making a note of the position of the swing at the beginning of his visit, can return much later to see that although the pendulum is still swinging in the same great arc, the world has demonstratively turned during that period of time. Foucault, a great nineteenth-century French scientist and philosopher, also invented the gyroscope, and before he died in 1868 he was one of the pioneers of the camera. Thus, to examine the work of just this one scientist, there are at least two departments in the museum to be visited. Multiply this a thousand times at least, and a visit to the Science Museum can be a daunting prospect! Nevertheless, as early as the 1920s, the authorities designed a fascinating children's gallery on the lower ground floor where generations of children have enjoyed the beautifully designed models and devices demonstrating scientific principles. On the ground floor there are vast and substantial exhibits such as Watts' beam pumping engine, rotative engines and a great variety of machines for making power, as well as an eighteenth-century fire engine.

The first floor is largely occupied by displays of both hand and machine tools, some of them invented and displayed at the Great Exhibition of 1851, and some earlier ones, such as those produced by Arkwright in the eighteenth century – labour-saving devices which, by causing unemployment, caused a great deal of industrial unrest and deprivation. Other machines manufactured to produce goods previously made by hand caused the famous Luddite riots. On the same floor there are machines for printing

Exhibition Road with the Geological and the Science Museums

397

and for paper-making, machines for the farm and the fields, and innumerable other uses.

The second floor displays a great many devices showing the development of photography, from the earliest experiments of such pioneers as Fox Talbot, to the first tentative attempts in the making of moving pictures, with many examples of apparatus used by Thomas Edison. There is also a modern display of the development of nuclear power, including some of the early work of Sir John Cockcroft, who blazed the trail into the uncharted lands of atomic research and was appointed Director of the Atomic Research Establishment in 1946. One can trace the story of navigation on land, on sea and in the air, and the development of the design of docks and harbours. The complicated apparatus for investigating the secrets of the continents beneath the seas of the world is also to be seen on this floor.

The third floor has many historic examples of man's probing of the mysteries of electricity and magnetism, and on display there is a fine collection of the early scientific instruments which belonged to George II. The exploration of outer space and the science of aeronautics are also on show in this area, as well as the crude apparatus by which John Lodie Baird transmitted the image of a little dummy head and crowned his efforts to invent television. There are displays of optical instruments, devices for measuring heat and its effects, instruments used in the investigation of acoustics, and so on. The list of subjects presented and explained here in this museum is endless. The museum is open daily to the public and has a magnificent reference library. Although many of the early exhibits are Victorian, the tendency is clearly for the museum to concentrate on the more recent developments in science, and the building itself is obviously of this century.

The Victoria and Albert Museum is a great nineteenth-century collection, composed entirely of works of art and craft. It is largely a Victorian building, especially those parts which face the Exhibition Road, some of which remained after the series of international exhibitions which succeeded the first Great Exhibition of 1851. The story of the accretion of buildings is rather complicated and not particularly relevant, but the most obviously early Victorian parts of this complex are those of red brick with terracotta enrichments, with motifs derived more or less from Early Italian Renaissance sources. The whole of the inner courtyard was designed by Captain Francis Fowke of the Royal Engineers. The later Victorian work is the main entrance on Cromwell Road, near to the Brompton Oratory. It was built about 1899–1909 and was the work of Aston Webb, who topped his main building with a tall cupola consisting of a two-staged octagon ringed about with classical columns but crowned with a lantern with open flying buttresses, not unlike that built by Wren for St Dunstan's-in-the-East, near the Tower of London.

The plan of the buildings is a complex one, for the museum covers an area of about twelve acres and includes premises taken over by the Royal College of Science, the South Kensington School of Art for the training of designers for industry – later the Royal College of Art – and the National Art Training School for the production of art teachers.

The Victoria and
Albert Museum

The collections within are extremely rich and contain some of the most
superb examples of art and craft to be found in Europe, many of them
unique. Like its opposite neighbour, the Science Museum, the Victoria and
Albert Museum houses a collection so varied and exciting that it is
impossible to give more than a general idea of the wealth to be found there,
and any visitor must be warned that they should not try to see all the
contents during the first visit. The museum also stages a number of very fine
temporary exhibitions. There is a superb reference library on art and a great
many catalogues on sale which not only have a world-wide reputation for
scholarship, but have frequently been exhibited at European book-fairs as
outstanding examples of beautiful publications.

For the lover of fine painting the museum can offer a wide range of
pictures and has on permanent display some of the finest examples, both in
oils and in watercolour, of the work of John Constable. These include not
only spirited sketches and studies for some of his most famous pictures to be
seen in major galleries throughout the world, but completed works of an
equally high standard.

There is a superb collection of examples of that peculiarly British art of
water-colour painting, with works by such famous British masters as Paul
Sandby, William Blake, J. M. W. Turner, John Sell Cotman, and others
including Richard Parkes Bonington, an English painter who had a profound

effect on the development of nineteenth-century French painting. There is a small but select collection of the work of continental artists as well as an extensive library of drawings and prints, including etchings and various types of engravings by most of the major European masters. One room contains a collection of cartoons by the Italian Renaissance master, Raphael: cartoons (full-sized working designs painted on sized paper) acquired by Charles I for use in the tapestry works at Mortlake, and now the property of H.M. the Queen, but on permanent loan to the museum. They are huge drawings averaging 11 feet high by 17 feet wide, and are the surviving seven from a set of ten originally commissioned by Pope Leo X in 1515. The cartoons form an extraordinary contrast with the miniatures in a nearby room by Nicholas Hilliard, 'master limnour' to Elizabeth I, whose tiny portraits could lie in the palm of a woman's hand.

The museum has many period rooms with examples of furniture from many periods of British and continental history, one somewhat curious exhibit being the famous (or notorious) 'Bed of Ware' – a vast Elizabethan bed mentioned in Shakespeare's play, *Twelfth Night*. Some of the rooms are those saved from destruction during the demolition of an historic house, while others are composed from various fine examples of the cabinet-maker's craft. Among the Victorian furniture in the museum are the desk of Charles Dickens, a number of Dickensian relics, and the original manuscript of *The Tale of Two Cities* bequeathed by John Forster, Dickens's friend and biographer.

There are also extensive costume galleries, a gallery of arms and armour, an important collection of musical instruments, and an overwhelming collection of the work of ironsmiths, silversmiths, goldsmiths and jewellers, carvers in stone, in ivory, and work in bronze from many periods of European history. There are collections of stained and painted glass, of porcelain and pottery, fine objects in glass and crystal, and other rare and beautiful objects.

There is even a wax anatomical model by Michelangelo, as well as work by other Renaissance sculptors such as Pietro Torrigiano, Michelangelo's rival and assailant, whose terracotta bust of Henry VII is clearly a study for the great tomb in Westminster Abbey.

In addition to the tapestries, embroideries and illuminated manuscripts from Europe, the museum displays an equally fine collection of many crafts from the Far East – from China, Japan, the Indian sub-continent, Persia and countries in the Middle East, including a ewer of rock crystal dated *c.* AD 1000, and many other exquisite objects of even greater antiquity.

One department is exclusively devoted to the many crafts concerned with fine book production, there is a huge architectural gallery, and another gallery containing plastercasts and replicas of many of the major European sculptures.

The list could be endless – the Victoria and Albert Museum is a quite remarkable example of the zeal of our Victorian ancestors, not only for collecting, but for making available to the general public treasures of arts and crafts which at that time were often only to be found in the private homes of wealthy people. It was all part of their desire that everyone should have an opportunity of self-education and a chance to better themselves.

The expansion of the collection was so rapid that additional buildings had to be constructed to keep pace with the flood of acquisitions and bequests. The north and south courts were finished by 1862, and the lecture theatre, the old refreshment room and the galleries above followed in 1868. By 1872 the huge Cast Court containing a full-sized cast of the Trajan Column in Rome, as well as many other architectural and sculptural details, was complete, and the library and east and west courts by 1872.

The laying of the foundation stone for the Cromwell Road entrance and its galleries in 1899 was the last major public ceremony performed by the aging queen, and it was by her direction that the name of the building was changed from the South Kensington Museum to the Victoria and Albert Museum. This extension was officially opened in 1909 by Edward VII.

The Victoria and Albert Museum also has a number of 'out-stations'. Mention has been made of the Bethnal Green Museum, the roof structure of which was derived from girders removed from the old south part of the V. and A. Museum in 1867, but there is also the Wellington Museum at Apsley House, Ham House – a lovely seventeenth-century mansion near Richmond, Surrey, and Osterley Park House.

Immediately east of the Cromwell buildings of the Victoria and Albert Museum is a sumptuous church built so emphatically in the style of the High Renaissance that it could easily deceive the casual visitor into thinking that this was sixteenth-century Rome, not Victorian London. This is the Oratory Church of St Philip Neri, designed by Herbert Gribble in 1878, and formally opened by Cardinal Manning in 1884. With the exception of Westminster Cathedral and York Minster, this church has the widest nave in England. The fine dome, which is such a dominant feature of this part of London, was a later addition.

Inside there are a number of chapels all enriched by carvings and mosaics, and various Italian features. Giant marble statues of the Apostles, carved for Siena Cathedral towards the end of the seventeenth century by Mazzuli, and a seventeenth-century altar originally in the Dominican church at Brescia, have now found their place here, together with a number of paintings of the life of St Philip Neri, the founder of the Oratorians. The church has a magnificent organ, which contributes much to its reputation for fine music.

Outside the church is an elaborate monument to the famous Cardinal Newman, an Anglican theologian who was converted to the Roman Catholic faith in 1845; this is the work of two former pupils of Sir George Gilbert Scott, George Bodley and Thomas Garner. Buildings for the Oratorians to the rear are somewhat earlier, having also been designed in the style of the Italian Renaissance in 1853 by J. J. Scoles. Further north, a number of streets including Ennismore Gardens are very typical of the rather more restrained aspects of Victorian middle-class housing, with All Saints Church a strange mixture of several periods of nineteenth-century decor.

Before the Second World War, there were many important Victorian buildings to be seen between Prince Consort Road and Imperial Institute

Road, but the latter is now almost entirely used as a car park, and the greater part of this area is covered by the clinically anonymous laboratories and offices of the Imperial College of Science and its companions. The 280-foot-high tower standing in isolation among these buildings, which was once the crescendo of a vigorous array of the Imperial Institute, is now an anachronism – a pathetic relic of a failed campaign to preserve the whole complex.

The contents of the old Imperial Institute, later the Commonwealth Institute, are now housed in a somewhat controversial modern building at the far west end of Kensington High Street.

Some of Victorian London, however, survives in Prince Consort Road, with the almost aggressively Victorian red brick of the Royal College of Music built by Sir Arthur Blomfield in 1883 quarrelling fiercely with the pseudo-classical buildings of what is now the Imperial College of Science, stone-faced, with ponderous sculpture groups, the whole designed by Sir Aston Webb.

Princes Gate to the west of Prince Consort Road is clearly derived from classical sources: most houses not only boast a pillared portico, but a second portico perched on top of the first for good measure, somewhat reminiscent of the home of the Veneerings so beautifully caricatured by Charles Dickens in *Our Mutual Friend*. The streets of stucco-fronted houses stretch westwards, but some have now fallen on their own hard times and are badly in need of repair.

In Prince Consort Road is the Victorian 'Gothic' church of the Holy Trinity, and outside is an ecstatic placard declaring it to be 'the masterpiece of G. F. Bodley's architectural career'. It has a fine west window (facing the geographical south) with curvilinear tracery, and the façade is enlivened with empty niches and other 'Gothic' details. It is placed somewhat unhappily beside a 1920s 'classical' building with details derived from Roman sources.

Immediately in front of the north entrance to the Royal College of Music is an imposing flight of steps leading to the rear of the Royal Albert Hall, at the top of which is James Durham's Memorial to the 1851 Exhibition.

The Royal Albert Hall must be almost as familiar a landmark to foreign visitors as the Tower of London, particularly as the famous promenade concerts have taken place there since the destruction of Queen's Hall in the Second World War. This was also designed by Captain Francis Fowke, but was completed by his successor, Col. H. G. D. Scott, also of the Royal Engineers. Roofed by a great glass and metal dome, about 700 feet in diameter and 140 feet high, this remarkable multi-purpose hall can accommodate about 8000 to 9000 people. Queen Victoria formally laid the foundation stone of this monumental building on 20 May 1867, and returned to open it on 29 March 1871. Students of the South Kensington School of Art assisted in the decoration of mosaics manufactured by Messrs Minton, and the whole building is a remarkable tribute to the engineering skill and sometimes misplaced decorative additions of our Victorian forefathers.

Immediately opposite in Kensington Gardens stands the Albert Memorial, a Victorian *tour de force* which, designed by Sir George Gilbert Scott, took twenty years to complete. Unlike the Royal Albert Hall, the Albert Memorial performs no practical function other than to provide a reminder of Prince Albert's importance to the nation. He was not only an important factor in the education and development of his young queen, but he eventually won grudging admiration from the alien people among whom he came to live. To many, his real memorial is the complex of educational and cultural buildings which occupies so much of South Kensington. Less tangible but perhaps even more important was his devotion to the cause of peace which drove him, a dying man, to prevent a disastrous war between Great Britain and the USA in 1861.

The Albert Memorial is an astonishing example of Victorian decorative art, a rich mixture of gilding, mosaics, multi-coloured stones and marbles, of carving in high and low relief – as confident an assertion of nineteenth-century wealth and talent as anything in London. The top of the memorial stands some 175 feet above the road on a great flight of granite steps 121 feet in width. These are anchored at each corner by great marble groups symbolising the four continents; their sculptors are now so obscure that only two, J. H. Foley, who designed 'Asia', and J. Bell, who designed 'America', merit the inclusion of their initials in reference books, the others being listed as Theed, responsible for 'Africa', and Macdowell, responsible for 'Europe'. In addition to these groups the memorial is embellished with about 175 other figures, many of them on the low reliefs, and most of them

The Royal Albert Hall

403

The Albert Memorial — either posthumous or fictitious portraits of prominent people whose work is part of our cultural heritage. The groups symbolising the continents are particularly well composed and can be examined with pleasure from any viewpoint; they were clearly designed in the round. J. H. Foley also designed the larger-than-life figure of the Prince Consort, which was completed in 1876. He is shown seated, studying a large book representing the catalogue of the Great Exhibition.

Despite the wealth of decoration and fine craftsmanship, the 'Gothic' canopy under which the statue of the Prince is seated is not well-proportioned, but like so many Victorian productions the Albert Memorial is such an essential part of London that one can forgive its blemishes.

The Albert Hall occupies a great deal of the site originally occupied by Gore House, formerly the residence of Lady Blessington, in whose salon many young and promising writers such as Charles Dickens and William Makepeace Thackeray were given encouragement and introductions to influential people. Lady Blessington, herself an authoress, was an acquaintance of many distinguished writers including Lord Byron, and her book, *Conversations with Byron*, went some way towards changing the attitude of the reading public to this controversial character. Gore House derived its name from Kensington Gore, the word gore meaning a wedge-shaped piece – a term still used in dressmaking, but in this case referring to the shape of the plot.

Just to the east of the Albert Hall is Lowther Lodge, built by Norman Shaw in the 1870s as a private house, but now the premises of the Royal

Geographical Society, with a later eastwards extension bearing statues of Sir Ernest Shackleton and Dr Livingstone. The building is of red brick and was built in a style now known as Queen Anne, but Norman Shaw's version of this period is by no means a copy of early eighteenth-century architecture, although it employs some characteristic details, such as the Dutch-flavoured gables.

To the west of the Albert Hall is a rather intriguing building, now the premises of the Royal College of Organists. It has a pretty design with bands of decorative children bearing musical instruments incised in the strips which define the floor levels of the rooms, and the panels into which the façade is divided. It was designed by Lt. H. H. Cole of the Royal Engineers in 1875 and is now almost dwarfed by the new buildings designed in 1961 for the Royal College of Art, by H. T. Cadbury-Brown, although the painting departments are still in their old premises adjoining the Victoria and Albert Museum, and the sculpture school in scruffy corrugated iron sheds to the rear of the Natural History Museum on Queen's Gate.

Some indication of the importance of the new extensions of London to the west, the north and the south can perhaps be gleaned from the large number of blue plaques commemorating famous Victorians to be found in this area. There is a little cluster in the Kensington Square area where the famous musician and composer, Sir Charles Hubert Parry, lived when he was Director of the Royal College of Music, before becoming the Professor of Music at Oxford in 1904. He was not only a brilliant composer, but a well-known writer on musical theory; his best-known work is undoubtedly his

The Royal College of Organists on the left, and the Royal College of Art on the right

setting for William Blake's poem 'Jerusalem', now the signature tune of the Women's Institutes.

Near Sir Charles Hubert Parry lived John Stuart Mill, the Victorian economist and reformer, and it was at No. 18, Kensington Square that he wrote his influential book on political economy. A little to the east are De Vere Gardens where lived two very important writers, though very different in outlook and technique: one was Robert Browning, one of the greatest and most flamboyant of Victorian poets, and the other was Henry James, the American-born writer who became a British subject in 1915. Another famous Victorian novelist, William Makepeace Thackeray, lived in Young Street – he only took up writing seriously after he had been rejected by Charles Dickens as a possible draughtsman for the illustrations for *The Pickwick Papers*. As his success grew he moved to No. 36, Onslow Gardens, an area to the west between Fulham Road and Brompton Road. James Froude, the historian and friend, executor and biographer of Thomas Carlyle, also lived in Onslow Gardens at No. 5, and later, an English Prime Minister, Bonar Law, was at No. 24. Thackeray later built himself a splendid mansion in Palace Green, overlooking Kensington Palace, not far from the residence of Sir John Everett Millais, Bart., PRA; he died there in 1863. Millais was an infant prodigy, but one of his first, most famous pictures, which is now in the Tate Gallery, 'Christ in the House of his Parents' or 'The Carpenter's Shop', was most viciously attacked by Charles Dickens and adversely criticised by John Ruskin. Yet he survived to become one of the wealthiest and most popular artists of the Victorian period and his magnificent house at No. 2, Palace Gate, now the premises of an international bank, was bought with the proceeds of such famous pictures as 'Ophelia', 'The North-West Passage', and 'The Boyhood of Raleigh', as well as portraits of such important contemporaries as Disraeli, Henry Irving, Alfred Lord Tennyson and Thomas Carlyle. The portraits were actually painted in the studio in this house. Millais was eventually reconciled to Charles Dickens and not only painted scenery for the amateur theatricals in which the novelist revelled, but was sufficiently intimate with the family to make a drawing of the bandaged head of the corpse of the famous novelist shortly after his death.

The spread of Victorian London from this area, south to Chelsea, north towards Paddington and St John's Wood, and still further west from Kensington, was so extensive that it would be tedious to try to enumerate each development, but mention must be made of the Holland Park area, of an important Victorian museum in Holland Park Road, and also of the exhibition buildings of Olympia which, although considerably extended and modernised, were begun in the 1880s.

The first area is grouped around a great Jacobean house built for Sir Walter Cope, once Chamberlain of the Exchequer and Keeper of Hyde Park in 1605. It later became the home of the indomitable Lady Holland and a meeting place for all sorts of powerful and influential Victorian figures, more political perhaps than literary, although Lord Macaulay was a frequent

visitor. And as soon as Lady Holland had ascertained that the author of *Nicholas Nickleby* – a book which she had enjoyed – was presentable, Charles Dickens was invited to take part in one of her many soirées.

Sadly the great house was heavily damaged during the Second World War, and the great Golden Gallery along which so many famous Victorians paraded no longer exists, but on the site now is a building which Dickens, with his great interest in the welfare of young people, would undoubtedly have admired – the King George VI memorial youth hostel. Parts of the older building are still to be found, however, and it is still a remarkably rural spot where, strolling in the grounds at dusk, a visitor might be startled by the sight of peacocks roosting in branches high above, or at almost any time of day catch a glimpse of a blue jay as it scolds from a nearby shrub. It is an area little known to many London visitors, even if they penetrate as far west as the Albert Hall, but one which has much to offer, with open air theatre in the summer, and other recreational facilities.

This area was also much frequented by Victorian artists – not the down-at-heel bohemians of Chelsea, or the revolutionary James McNeill Whistler, but the accomplished commercial painters who gave the Victorian patrons what they wanted – pictures painted with much detail but with craftsmanship of a high order, with themes which sometimes held a deep moral message, or with nudes so lacking in fleshly qualities that they were acceptable in the most refined of Victorian drawing-rooms. The area is embellished with a great many commemorative plaques – some of them the familiar blue ones, these being belated accolades awarded by the London County Council when their recipients had already been interred for some

Holland House as it was before extensive bombing in the Second World War time. One such plaque commemorating the stay of Thomas Babington Macaulay, the historian, is to be found in Camden Hill just to the north of Holland Park (the location of Queen Elizabeth College), while there are others to be found in Melbury Road to the south where lived William Holman-Hunt, whose painting of 'The Light of the World' is to be seen in St Paul's Cathedral, with other works by him in the Tate Gallery, and G. F. Watts, whose statue 'Physical Energy' is one of the most important sculptures in Kensington Gardens. Watts was also a very successful painter, some of his best work being the portraits of such famous Victorians as Gladstone and Lord Tennyson which are now to be seen in the National Portrait Gallery, and he was for a short time married to one of the most famous of all British actresses, Ellen Terry. In Melbury Road Norman Shaw built a house (No. 8) for another British painter, Marcus Stone RA, whose work is displayed at the Guildhall Art Gallery in the City as well as in the Tate Gallery, and another (No. 11) for a very popular Victorian painter, Sir Luke Fildes, whose paintings such as 'The Doctor' were reproduced as engravings and to be found in most Victorian homes. Fildes also executed a number of illustrations for *The Mystery of Edwin Drood*, and it is suggested that the main subject of his painting. 'The Empty Chair', was that of Charles

Tower House by
William Burge

408

Dickens now to be seen in the house at Broadstairs. A blue plaque marks the house of Sir Luke Fildes, and also that of another famous Victorian artist, Sir William Hamo Thornycroft, whose portrait statue of General Gordon stands in Trafalgar Square, whose statue of Queen Victoria is outside the Royal Exchange, and whose posthumous and imaginary statue of Oliver Cromwell is outside the Houses of Parliament a little to the south of his father's equally imaginative sculpture of Queen Boudicca in her chariot.

Another characteristically individual house in Melbury Road is that designed for himself by William Burges, an enthusiastic admirer of the Middle Ages and an imaginative furniture designer, whose house (not open to the public, and minus a blue plaque) is richly endowed with so-called medieval features – 'Gothic' windows, and a tall cylindrical turret topped by a sharply pointed conical tower. William Burges is best known for his work at Cardiff Castle and at Castle Coch in Wales, but visitors from the United States may be familiar with his partly executed design for Trinity College in Hartford, Connecticut.

A more important house built for a more widely known artist is to be seen and visited at No. 12, Holland Park Road – Leighton House. This has been most beautifully preserved as a museum which, in a surprisingly small area, seems to have everything which is summed up in the word 'Victoriana'. From the time that his work, 'Cimabue's Madonna carried in procession', was bought by Queen Victoria, Frederic Leighton's success was meteoric and assured. An ARA in 1864, an RA in 1868, and President of the Royal Academy in 1878, he was made a baronet in 1886 and a peer in 1896. Having studied in Europe both as a sculptor and as a painter, his remarkable versatility and his skill as a draughtsman made him one of the most successful of all the artists of the Victorian period, and the wan, carefully draped nude of 'The Bath of Psyche' was reproduced for a million Victorian homes, where anything more truthful to physical appearances would have been rejected as highly improper. The museum, originally Lord Leighton's house and studio, is richly furnished not only with nineteenth-century artefacts produced in Britain and in Europe, but with some brought back from his travels in the Middle East, which later were apparently used as props for his biblical illustrations, carried out for the Dalziel brothers.

William De Morgan, an equally versatile man, decorated much of the house with his unusual tiles, before he became a writer and created a reputation for himself as a novelist. But the Arab hall, which is such a striking feature of this museum, is decorated with tiles and pottery from the Middle East, some of it collected personally by Lord Leighton, while others were contributed by his friends, including the famous British explorer, Sir Richard Burton. There are many drawings and studies for Lord Leighton's completed works, as well as oil paintings which were in his possession at the time of his death in 1896. Apart from the works of art to be seen in this museum, there is a vast mural painting by Leighton in the Victoria and Albert Museum entitled, 'Industrial Arts of War and Peace', executed in 1872–3, as well as many works in the Tate Gallery, including two of his most famous sculptures, 'The Sluggard' and 'Athlete struggling with a Python'.

The house itself is not without architectural interest, for although Lord Leighton clearly designed much of it for himself, the architect was George Aitchison Jun., who, as a pupil of William Burges, travelled extensively with him, but seems to have been sufficiently strong an individual to create his own style, for his Founders Hall in St Swithin's Lane in the City owes little to the 'Gothic' extravagances of his master.

To many visitors to exhibitions at Olympia it may come as a surprise to know that this, too, is a Victorian building, erected in 1886 by the National Agricultural Hall Company. Most of the major events, such as the Royal Tournament and the Horse of the Year Show, are held in the grand hall, a building over ninety years old – a remarkable tribute to the durability of the buildings erected by Victorian engineers. The hall is 450 feet long and 250 feet wide, a total area of about $2\frac{1}{2}$ acres – half as much again as the Agricultural Hall in Islington which it superseded – and it is spanned by a huge roof of iron and glass. Olympia has, of course, been modernised and extended since 1886.

Another remarkable building of the same period was somewhat to the south of Olympia. Built on land formerly held by the De Vere family, the Earls of Oxford – hence its name, Earl's Court – the exhibition grounds were opened in 1887 to hold the first of the American exhibitions, held annually after that until the outbreak of the First World War in 1914. Between 1894 and 1907 one of the most sensational landmarks in this area was the great wheel, an attraction which was a larger version of the wheel built for the World's Columbian exhibition held in Chicago in 1893. The great wheel was demolished in 1907. The exhibition suffered a decline after the First World War, and the whole site was redesigned and rebuilt in 1935.

Earl's Court underground station is a Victorian building, opened in 1871 as the converging point of the Wimbledon, Ealing and Piccadilly lines, with direct links with Paddington; the extensions to Hammersmith followed in 1874 and to Walham Green and Putney in 1880. The earlier lines can usually be detected by odd areas of tiling, and the station names in Victorian lettering are sometimes partly intact despite the rebuilding or the graffiti. These lines are by no means underground for much of their routes, nor are the station platforms so deep that lifts or escalators are required for access.

The Victorians were responsible for the first underground line in the world, linking the metropolitan station at Smithfield with Paddington, Euston and King's Cross. It was opened in 1862 and was an immediate success, with over 26,000 people using it daily in the first six months. The fare for the Paddington–City journey was threepence, and the amenity not only reduced the road traffic considerably, but also encouraged the sprawl of London even further. As the new neighbourhoods appeared there was a considerable increase in the number of churches, most of them built in some 'Gothic' style, for writers such as Pugin deplored the use of such pagan forms as classical porticoes and coffered ceilings in buildings designed for Christian worship. The periods of Gothic architecture to which architects went for their inspiration differed widely, although the late period known as the 'Perpendicular' period was often rejected because of its associations with the Tudors and with the traumatic effect of the Reformation initiated by Henry VIII and continued by his son, Edward VI. Thus, in the Kensington area, St Barnabas in Addison Road, designed by Lewis Vulliamy in 1828, favours the Tudor style of Henry VII's Chapel in Westminster Abbey, while some forty years later the parish church of St Mary Abbots, designed by Sir George Gilbert Scott, was built in the earlier medieval style known as 'Early English'.

The underground from Earl's Court or High Street, Kensington goes through Paddington via Notting Hill Gate and Bayswater Road. Notting Hill Gate – now a somewhat unhappy area – like Shepherd's Bush derives its name from its earlier rural history. Owned by the De Veres, it was originally 'Nutting Barns', a manor on the hill later owned by Sir William Talbot. Bayswater owes its name to a tenant of the Abbot of Westminster, described in *The Domesday Book* as Bainiardus and later as Baynard, so that Baynard's well-watered land, known as 'Baynard's Watering', eventually became Bayswater.

The so-called underground railway – the metropolitan railway – driven by steam and therefore emitting clouds of smoke as it passed through a residential area, was something of an intrusion, so that it was found necessary in Leinster Gardens, Bayswater, to continue a short terrace with dummy house-fronts to screen the railway line, a subterfuge typically Victorian in its anxiety to cover up almost anything rather than frankly to admit its presence. It was this need to conceal certain functional facts which led to a great deal of wholly unsuitable architectural camouflage being applied to such buildings as the Tower Bridge.

The derivation of the name Paddington is somewhat obscure, for although a Padendene in Surrey is recorded in *The Domesday Book*, there is no mention of such a name in this area. The Surrey one was the 'dene' or 'den' of a family known as the Poedings, so that perhaps the 'Poedingsden' in this part of London was the home of an offshoot of the Surrey tribe. According to a map of 1815, Paddington was very little more than a hamlet, and apart from the canals in the area was very rural, with a church standing on the site of the older one in which William Hogarth and his wife, Jane Thornhill, were married after their elopement in March 1729. The parish church of St Mary now occupying this site was built in 1788–91 by an obscure architect named Plaw, but it has some interesting monuments, including a statue of Mrs Siddons on the green outside, and the tomb of Nollekens the sculptor who made a number of portrait busts of eighteenth-century notabilities.

The coming of the railway was the death blow to Mr Shillibeer's first omnibus service which plied its trade from Paddington Green to the Bank in the centre of the City, starting in 1829, but its fares were expensive (one shilling) by comparison with the railway fare of threepence, and the 'iron horse' faster and less liable to traffic jams than those driven by Shillibeer.

The new Paddington station built by Isambard Kingdom Brunel and Matthew Digby Wyatt was the inspiration for W. P. Frith's meticulously detailed painting of 1862 entitled 'The Railway Station', but the whole building has now been altered (and repaired after the Second World War) so extensively that there is not a great deal remaining of the original Victorian masterpiece. The Great Western Hotel, also somewhat altered, is still an excellent example of the opulence of Victorian hospitality. Designed by Philip Hardwick the Younger in 1852, it represents the facility with which the Victorian architects could ransack the textbooks of historic architectural ornament, heavily borrowing details from French Renaissance buildings and Baroque examples elsewhere to impress the travelling public, regardless of cost, and adding heavy architectural sculpture symbolising Peace and Plenty, Science and Industry to a classical portico.

The building of a great railway terminus and the canals ensured development of the whole area, and the extent by which the population increased can perhaps be gauged by the fact that between the early 1840s and the end of the century, no less than twenty-six churches sprang up in various forms of near-Gothic styles, one only being faithful to the early 'classical' style – that of St Peter in Kensington Park Road, built by T. Allom in 1852. The remainder, including two by the famous architect G. E. Street – St Mary Magdalene, Woodchester Street, dated 1868–78, and St James, Sussex Gardens, dated 1881 – all displayed a preference for some kind of 'Gothic'. At the church of St Augustine in Kilburn Park Road, John L. Pearson sought inspiration from French Gothic, even as late as 1881, while Norman Shaw, working in his favourite brick, built Holy Trinity (Harrow Mission) in Latimer Road with some acknowledgement to the Decorated period of English Gothic. Sir Gilbert George Scott's son, Oldrid Scott, went to Byzantium for appropriate details for the church of St Sophia in Moscow Road (the Orthodox Cathedral of Western Europe since 1932), built in 1877, and there is a distinctly Romanesque or Byzantine appearance to the synagogue in St Petersburgh Place, built by Audesley and Joseph in 1877 in red brick, with an oddly Oriental feeling about some of the details. In 1888 the Talbot Tabernacle was built for the Independent Evangelical movement, also in red brick in another near-Romanesque style, and in addition to building the Roman Catholic church of Our Lady of the Holy Souls in Kensal New Town in 1882, John Bentley, the designer of the Westminster Cathedral already described earlier in the chapter, designed a Lady Chapel and baptistery for the church of St Francis of Assisi in Pottery Lane. For anyone wishing to gain some idea of the extraordinary variety of styles used by the Victorians in church architecture, Paddington certainly has a great deal of material for study.

For many years the graveyards attached to the City churches had been a scandal and Charles Dickens was only one of the writers who exposed the disgraceful overcrowding and looting of the graves. To guard against such ghouls as Jeremy Cruncher (in *A Tale of Two Cities*) transferring the freshly interred corpses to medical schools, guard-houses were built. One such still survives in the churchyard of St Matthias, Bethnal Green. It was eventually decided that new sites for the overflowing churchyards would have to be found, and Kensal Green in Paddington was one of the first to be opened for this purpose. Kensal Green (formerly 'King's-field Green') is an area of about

left, The watch house at St Matthias, Bethnal Green
below, St Matthias

fifty-six acres and was first opened in 1833. It presents an extraordinary survey of funeral art and design for the last 150 years and contains the mortal remains of a host of important Victorians, including the two Brunels, Leigh Hunt, Thomas Hood, Robert Owen, Sir Robert Smirke, Francis Thompson and Alice Meynell, the poet and poetess, as well as Thackeray and other writers. There are also two tombs of members of the royal family – that of the Duke of Sussex, the son of George III, and of Princess Sophia, his daughter.

It is the network of canals in Paddington which gives this part of London a unique quality and has earned for it the nickname of Little Venice. The Paddington canal was a pre-Victorian development, having been opened for traffic with great celebrations – bells ringing, flags flying and gun salutes – in June 1801. Nineteen years later the opening of the Regent's canal extended the range of waterways, and although they had been designed primarily for commercial transport, the facilities offered very soon became available for pleasure trips between Paddington and Uxbridge. For those who could afford it they provide a welcome break for weary Londoners at weekends, and were a rival attraction to the pleasure steamers which plied from Westminster down the Thames to Rosherville Gardens near Gravesend.

Today the whole canal area is an exciting and enjoyable resort, and there are an increasing number of people who find living on a boat a pleasant and comparatively inexpensive form of accommodation. Commercial barges still use these waterways, and with the increase in the price of petrol and the congestion on the roads, it seems likely that this traffic will increase.

East of Paddington in the parish of St Marylebone, the building of a number of independent railway lines which eventually converged in this area necessitated the erection of Marylebone station to accommodate the newly named Great Central Railway, although there was fierce opposition from the members of Lord's Cricket Club in St John's Wood, and some from the gentler artists living in the same area. The cricketers were finally placated and the terminus of the Great Central Railway built, but not before some four thousand or more people had been rendered homeless as their miserable houses and tenements were demolished to make way for the railway and its buildings. The railway erected tenements in Wharncliffe Gardens for about half of them, while a gesture was made for others whose livelihood had been threatened by having to move further away from their work, by the provision of special workmens' fares.

Much of the parish of St Marylebone had been developed before the Grand Central Line was built towards the end of the century, but some of the new Victorian buildings are still to be seen there. One notable example, now the headquarters of the British Railways Board, was the former Hotel Grand Central, designed for Sir Blundell Maple by Robert William Edis, who also built three London clubs and the Inner Temple Library. The style is Jacobean, reminiscent of Charlton House or Hatfield House; the original frontage of the building was 215 feet, but there have since been modern extensions. There were 700 bedrooms and a cycle track on the roof, presumably for the guests. It has now been reduced to the anonymity of

No. 222, Marylebone Road – a sad fate for a building originally designed to impress the traveller with the prestige of the Grand Central Railway.

Little Venice

With a number of churches already existing in the St Marylebone area, there was not quite such an urgency to supply the expanding suburb as there had been in Paddington, and the new churches built – about a dozen – were all in the Gothic style, although this still gave the Victorian architect quite a lot of latitude. One outstanding example of Victorian church architecture is still to be seen well to the south of Marylebone Road in Margaret Street. This is the church of All Saints, erected by William Butterfield in 1849–59, a church so lavish in its decoration and vigorously Gothic in its detail that it can still engender both adulation and condemnation where many other Victorian buildings scarcely raise an eyebrow. Encouraged by a powerful society of churchmen and involved laymen, William Butterfield indulged his love of multi-coloured materials for both structural and decorative purposes. The church is built of dark red brick enlivened with bands of vitrified brick burned to a bluish-black intensity, and it is aggressively Gothic in inspiration. Inside, the latest and most durable materials, Minton tiles, coloured and glazed brick, are used for their permanent and unfading qualities. Butterfield approached the task with an unswerving sincerity – an Anglican who made sure that even the workmen were conscious of how privileged they were to be building such a sacred shrine. Sir John Betjeman declares that this church of All Saints, Margaret Street, 'is the pioneer church of the phase of the Gothic Revival which ceased to copy medieval

415

but went on with new materials like cast iron and stock brick from where the medievals left off. For the smallness and confined nature of the site the effect of space, richness, mystery and size is amazing. . . .' It is the durability of the colours which strike a somewhat strident note when this church is seen for the first time. Medieval colours tend to fade and to blend, but here the glazed brick, the incised stone filled with patterns of coloured mastic which covers much of the wall, the mosaics and so on are as brilliant as they were on the day they were executed, as is the enormous reredos with its flanking mural paintings by William Dyce, the artist who painted the Arthurian series in the House of Lords. Other eminent authorities have not been as complimentary as Betjeman about the work of William Butterfield, and phrases such as, 'He was a Gothic functionalist. He delighted in that kind of ugliness – the ugliness of ruthless realism and of the rejection of sentiment', written by no less a critic than Professor Robert Furneaux Jordan, suggests that All Saints, Margaret Street and its architect are matters for controversy.

The increase in population in these new regions of London naturally necessitated the building of more schools, some as part of the new churches, other sponsored by the local authority. The English public schools, many of them wards of one of the great City companies, were also enlarged to accept the sons of the wealthy industrialists and these new buildings tended to follow the prevailing 'Gothic' fashion. Thus, when St Paul's School, largely financed by the Mercers Company, moved out to more expansive premises at Hammersmith, the architect, Alfred Waterhouse, produced a building as aggressively 'Gothic' as his Prudential Assurance offices in Holborn. It would have been natural for church schools to have a somewhat ecclesiastical flavour, but not so obvious for the Board schools tamely to follow suit, even if they were more utilitarian 'Gothic'. The walls were thick, conserving the heat from the great 'tortoise' stoves which warmed the rooms. Windows were usually set high in the walls, so that the children would not be distracted by activities outside, and the wall areas provided admirable spaces for glazed maps of the world with the British Empire spreading its red further and further afield, for large placards of copperplate handwriting, and for pious extracts from the best authors or from the Bible. There is an admirable display of the corner of just such a classroom in the Museum of London, and some of these buildings are still in use in the London area.

The new underground continued eastwards, linking three important terminal stations – Euston, St Pancras and King's Cross. Very little of the original Euston station has survived the rebuilding which, despite protests, resulted in the demolition of Philip Hardwick's imposing Doric entrance, but St Pancras station with Sir George Gilbert Scott's enormous hotel front is still to be seen. This highlights the sharp division between the engineer responsible for the function of the railway buildings and the architect. It was a situation deplored by such Victorian architects as James Fergusson, a Fellow of the Royal Institute of British Architects (established in 1835), who complained that even if the basic, functional requirements of the railway stations had been already defined by the engineers, the professors of

architecture, 'if called in, would insist on the station being either Grecianised or Gothicised, or at all events, carried out in some incongruous style; and not one man in ten would have the courage to content himself with the ornamental arrangement of parts and ornamental accentuation of the construction'.

Sir George Gilbert Scott had no doubt as to where his loyalties lay when he designed St Pancras Midland Grand Hotel, a gesture of defiance in a way to Lord Palmerston who had humiliated him by insisting that he change the design for the government offices in Whitehall for a non-Gothic one. Scott would certainly have referred back to the many studies of medieval detail which he had made for the government buildings. Shortly after the opening of the station in 1868 he wrote of this masterpiece of Victorian Gothic: 'It is often spoken of to me as the finest building in London; my own belief is that it is possibly too good for its purpose, but having been disappointed, through Lord Palmerston, of my ardent hope of carrying out my style in the government offices . . . I was glad to erect one building in that style in London.' The station and the hotel are in fact so separate that they must be considered as different buildings, with little in common. Work on the preparation of the site for the whole complex began in 1866 and involved the clearance of huge areas of squalid tenements and houses largely owned by an eccentric and miserly lawyer named Agar (hence Agar Town). It was also an area which was used as a dump for London's rubbish, with mountains of ashes and refuse of every kind, so that although seven streets were swept away and over 10,000 people made homeless, the loss of what

417

St Pancras Hotel and station

Charles Dickens called 'our English Connemara' was an advantage. Some of Somers Town (named after a Tudor nobleman who acquired the lands of the Carthusian monks in that area after the Reformation) also disappeared in the digging of tunnels and preparation.

The engineer for the project was William Barlow, and the formation of the land with a change in level from the upper parts to the Euston Road gave him an opportunity to utilise the cavities to be made under the station as storage space for a brewery. It was this consideration which determined that St Pancras station should have a huge roof, unsupported by any columns which would interfere with the storage areas under the platforms; this also allowed a great flexibility for the allocation of space for rails, points, platforms and passenger accommodation. Thus the module (a favourite unit of measurement with modern architects) in this case was the width of a beer barrel. The construction of the roof, which contains $2\frac{1}{2}$ acres of glass, was left to Barlow's partner, R. M. Ordish. It is 689 feet in length, 245 feet across, and at the apex, 100 feet above the tracks.

The hotel, which is still such a prominent feature of London, gave full rein to Scott's romantic and imaginative draughtsmanship, for this 565-foot frontage, with its huge *porte-cochère* at the west end, the enormously high archway to the western entrance, and the 270-foot clock tower at the east end, is really like a vast theatrical backdrop. Edward Walford, one of the authors of *Old and New London* published in 1897, spent some time tracking down Scott's decorative motifs on the brick, terracotta and stone façade, and detected 'Lombardic and Venetian brick Gothic, or Gothic-Italian types

Postman's Park

The premises across the road are not particularly distinguished, although there are some fine remnants of the Roman London Wall in the grounds, and a statue of Sir Rowland Hill, the originator of the penny postal system in 1840, by the Victorian sculptor, Edward Onslow Ford. This provides an interesting contrast to the highly imaginative sculpture entitled 'Minotaur' by Michael Ayrton, the modern sculptor, in Postman's Park. On the wall of the General Post Office building there is a plaque commemorating the first successful transmission of a message by wireless telegraphy by Marconi from this very building in the last years of the reign of Queen Victoria.

After the Reformation Edward VI founded a school in this area, Christ's Hospital, which later became known as 'the Bluecoat School'. It moved to its present premises out at Horsham in 1902, but the street is still called King Edward Street, although it changes its name to Little Britain as it curves westwards to Smithfield. This new name is derived from a former residence of the Earls of Brittany who, according to John Snow, used to live in this area. The huge buildings which now house Smithfield meat market are mainly Victorian, although modern additions have replaced the meat, fish and poultry areas which were demolished during the bombing of the Second World War. The designer of the main body of the market was Sir Horace Jones and the building was finished by 1866–7. The old cattle market described so vividly by Charles Dickens in *Oliver Twist* was moved to the Caledonian Market in north London about 1852. Although it was the work of the man who built Leadenhall Market, Smithfield is far more specialised, far more spacious, and far less interesting.

The route southwards down Giltspur Street takes a visitor past the Victorian extension of the hospital of St Bartholomew – the library of 1878–9, and additions made early in the twentieth century – to Newgate

Smithfield

Street and the Old Bailey. Many famous trials took place in the buildings formerly on this spot, including that of the Mannings, murderers whose public execution moved Charles Dickens to demand the abolition of such spectacles. It was not in fact until 1868, about twenty years after his campaign, that public hangings were stopped. Mr and Mrs Manning, whose execution Dickens attended, were hanged outside the old jail in what was then Horsemonger's Lane – later Union Street – south of the river, and their gravestones are preserved in the Cuming Museum in Walworth Road, together with many relics with Dickensian associations including the old pump from the Marshalsea prison, mentioned in *Little Dorrit*. The present Old Bailey, which probably derives its name from the *baillium* or outer space beyond a fortified wall, was rebuilt in 1903–1906 by E. E. Mountford; the side of the building in Newgate Street was rebuilt in 1940 after heavy bombing.

The most important contribution made by the Victorian builders in this area was the construction of Holborn viaduct and bridge over the Fleet valley – a project which not only swept away from the north side some of the most villainous criminal haunts in London, but also made a much more humane route for the unfortunate horses who had been flogged mercilessly to get them and their loads up the steep slopes leading down to the valley which is now Farringdon Street.

The whole viaduct is 1400 feet long and 80 feet wide, but the cast-iron bridge crossing Farringdon Street is only 107 feet long. Field Lane and Chick Lane – notorious for the 'schools' for pickpockets which were so

graphically described in *Oliver Twist* – were destroyed, and three new roads, St Andrew Street, St Bride Street and Charterhouse Street, were designed to converge on the new Holborn Circus. The bridge is an excellent example of Victorian ornament, with bronze statues symbolising Commerce and Agriculture on the south side, and Science and the Fine Arts to the north. The viaduct was officially opened by Queen Victoria with great ceremony on 6 November 1869, the day on which a little earlier she had opened the new Blackfriars Bridge. The engineer/architect of the viaduct and bridge was William Haywood, and the river 'Hole Bourne' which gives its name to this area was tributary of the river Fleet.

Holborn Viaduct and Farringdon Street

The equestrian statue at the centre of Holborn Circus is that of the Prince Consort in the uniform of a field marshal, placed there some years after his death. It is unique in one respect at least, for although field marshals may salute on horseback, they never raise their hats. It was carried out by an obscure sculptor named Bacon in 1874, although William Haywood assisted him with the design of the pedestal.

The next important aspect of Victorian London are the theatres, which were well to the west of the City. One of the most significant was that at Covent Garden – now the Royal Opera House, the headquarters not only of the Royal Opera Company, but of the Royal Ballet, the Sadler's Wells Royal Ballet and the English Music Theatre Company. The first theatre on this site was managed by John Rich, who moved his theatrical company from Lincoln's Inn Fields in 1731, his first production in the new theatre being

Congreve's *Way of the World*. This theatre was burned down in 1808 and rebuilt by Robert Smirke, only to be so heavily damaged by fire in 1856 that it had to be rebuilt once again, this time by E. M. Barry. It opened with Meyerbeer's opera *Les Huguenots* in May 1858. E. M. Barry's portico has an orthodox classical appearance, and he also managed to incorporate in his design sculptures and low reliefs from the previous theatre by John Flaxman, the first Professor of Sculpture of the Royal Academy and a staunch classicist. Frederick Gye, the manager, whose renovated statue now stands in the theatre, was largely responsible for the Floral Hall next to the theatre. The Floral Hall and the other buildings which were formerly part of Covent Garden Market are all in the process of being adapted or removed as a new role is found for the site, now that the market itself has been moved to Nine Elms.

About a score of original Victorian theatres have survived, although the only one in the City at that time, called City of London, where a dramatised version of *The Cricket on the Hearth* was produced in 1846 was demolished when a Great Eastern Railway line was pushed through from Shoreditch to Liverpool Street. The Olympic Theatre was destroyed in the construction of Aldwych and Kingsway in the 1890s.

Using Piccadilly Circus as a focal point, it seems that most of the Victorian theatres, with the exception of the Old Vic and the Royal Court Theatre, are within easy walking distance. The Criterion Theatre on the south side of Piccadilly was built on the site of the old St James's Market in 1874 by Thomas Verity, who designed the Criterion restaurant in the same French Renaissance style at the same time. The first production was a dual bill – the play by J. H. Byron called *An American Lady* and W. S. Gilbert's *Topsyturveydom* appearing on the same night. The theatre was enlarged in 1883 and equipped with electric light in 1884, a remarkable feature at that time.

The statue of Eros in the centre of Piccadilly Circus is in fact a memorial to the great philanthropist and social worker, the seventh Earl of Shaftesbury, a champion in Parliament for better social conditions, particularly for educational facilities for poor children. His Lodging House Act to provide better housing was described by Charles Dickens as the best piece of legislation ever issued by Parliament. The statue was modelled by Sir Alfred Gilbert and cast in aluminium, and it was at that time the largest figure in that material in the world.

The Prince of Wales Theatre in Coventry Street to the east was originally a Victorian theatre called just 'the Prince's', and had the distinction of presenting the first production of *A Doll's House* by Ibsen in England. The theatre was entirely rebuilt in 1937.

The Comedy Theatre in Panton Street, Haymarket, was another theatre designed by Thomas Verity; it opened in 1881 with a comic opera in English, translated from an opera, *La Mascotte*, by the French writer Audran. The theatre is best known perhaps for its association with the great actor-manager, Beerbohm Tree.

Of the theatres built in London during the Victorian period, only three or

four have managed to retain the dignity of the original façades, the others
having been obliged to conform to the habit of covering the front of the
theatre with neon lights. The most obvious and admirable exceptions are the
frontages of such theatres as the famous Covent Garden Theatre, already
mentioned, Drury Lane Theatre, the original by Benjamin Wyatt was
added to by two Victorian architects, Samuel Beazley and James Spiller),
and the Old Vic in Waterloo Road.

Shaftesbury Avenue was thrust through towards Bloomsbury in 1886,
and about the same time as Cambridge Circus was made, Charing Cross
Road was opened and Piccadilly Circus enlarged. The tall buildings on the
south and the north sides of Cambridge Circus and Charing Cross Road –

most of them now with shop-fronts – were originally tenements built to accommodate those unfortunates whose homes had been demolished to make way for Shaftesbury Avenue.

The first theatre on the east side of Charing Cross Road is the Garrick, built by Charles Phipps and Walter Emden. Phipps was also the architect of the Savoy Theatre, the Lyric Theatre in Shaftesbury Avenue, Her Majesty's Theatre in the Haymarket, and Queen's Hall – the latter a casualty of the Second World War. The Garrick opened with *The Profligate* by Arthur Pinero in April 1889 and has an immensely successful record. Wyndham's Theatre, also in Charing Cross Road, is another Victorian theatre; it opened in November 1899 with *David Garrick*, with Sir Charles Wyndham in the title role. The architect was W. G. R. Sprague.

Cambridge Circus, where Charing Cross Road crosses Shaftesbury Avenue, is dominated by the Palace Theatre, which was originally designed by T. E. Collcutt for Richard D'Oyly Carte as the Royal English Opera House. It opened in January 1891 with the production of a little known grand opera by Sir Arthur Sullivan entitled *Ivanhoe*. The Royal English Opera House was not a success, however, and the Palace later turned to more popular entertainment.

The London Coliseum in St Martin's Lane, built in 1904 by Frank Matcham with the first revolving stage in the world, is now the home of the English National Opera Company (not to be confused with the Royal Opera Company) and is also leased by the New Opera Company Ltd. This theatre has also had a very varied career and at one time was even a cinema. Its great revolving dome, floodlit at night, is one of the most delightful features of the skyline of this part of London, especially when seen from Trafalgar Square. Another Victorian theatre in St Martin's Lane – the Duke of York's – has recently undergone considerable alterations and now contains recording studios. There are other studios and offices of film companies in the same area. The legitimate theatres in the western part of the Strand include the Adelphi, which first appeared in 1806 as the 'Sans Pareil', and the Vaudeville designed by C. J. Phipps in 1870. Both theatres have been so altered and modernised that neither of them is now typical of the Victorian period. A better example is the Savoy Theatre on the south side of the Strand, a little further to the east. Built by C. J. Phipps for Richard D'Oyly Carte for the staging of Gilbert and Sullivan operas, it opened in 1881 with a performance of *Patience*, followed the next year by *Iolanthe*. For many years only Gilbert and Sullivan operas were performed there, but the break-up of the famous partnership and the demand for a variety of plays eventually led to performances of the works of other such famous playwrights as Sir James Barrie. A few years after the opening of the theatre, Richard D'Oyly Carte commissioned T. E. Collcutt to design the Savoy Hotel as part of the whole complex, and after the building by the same architect of Savoy Court in 1903–4, the theatre was given a new façade to match.

Of all the Victorian theatres, it is probably the Old Vic which has exerted the greatest influence on drama, and which has made the British theatre the envy of the English-speaking world. It is to be found on the other side of

the river in Waterloo Road, in the shadow of Waterloo station. Built in 1818   The Old Vic
as the Royal Coburg Theatre, it derived its first name from the title of
Princess Charlotte, the only daughter of George IV, who married Prince
Leopold of Saxe-Coburg, and became the Victoria a little later. At first it
attracted a number of eminent actors – Edmund Kean, for example, was
paid the enormous sum of £100 for appearing there for two nights in 1830 –
but as the years passed, the roughness of the neighbourhood and the lurid
quality of the melodramas performed there resulted in its being closed in
1871–2. In 1873, altered and enlarged, it re-opened as the Royal Victoria
Palace theatre, only to run into financial trouble once again. It was finally
taken over by the redoubtable Emma Cons, an inspired philanthropist and a
pupil of John Ruskin, who gave up her career as an artist to devote herself to
good works. She had previously been involved in educational and housing
reform, but her greatest contribution to society was undoubtedly her
direction of the Royal Victoria Palace theatre where she organised the
production of good plays and operas at prices within the reach of many of
the working men and women who were normally denied such pleasures.
The magnificent tradition she established for such productions at the Old
Vic was not only continued after her death in 1912 by her niece, Lilian
Baylis, but was extended and reinforced by this remarkable woman, who
established a permanent Shakespearean company there in 1914 – a company
which was to prove to be the training ground for almost every famous actor
and actress performing in serious drama today. A drab, shy woman with a
speech impediment, Lilian Baylis was one of the most passionate and
practical idealists of this century – a woman who believed so profoundly in

the Old Vic and the work it was doing that she simply would not accept that there might be financial or other difficulties. In the 1930s, despite the recession and financial crisis, the Old Vic continued to produce magnificent drama on a shoestring, and she attracted to her side some of the finest producers, stage designers, musicians and young actors in what was at that time a fight for the Old Vic's survival.

An accomplished musician (she had toured as a child violinist in Great Britain and in South Africa), Lilian Baylis next turned her atttention to the need for a ballet company and an opera company which would provide entertainment as good as that provided by her Shakespearean company. For this purpose she leased the newly opened Sadler's Wells theatre near the Angel Islington, alternating the productions there with those at the Old Vic. Once again she attracted to her side some of the most creative and exciting musicians, conductors, choreographers, dancers and singers in Great Britain, and in a few years produced a national opera and a national ballet company with as high an international reputation as that enjoyed by her Shakespearean company. The results of the pioneering efforts which took place under the direction and inspiration of Lilian Baylis can now be seen at the Royal Opera House, Covent Garden, and at the newly built National Theatre, a few hundred yards away from the Old Vic, and it was natural that, when the National theatre was first formed in 1963, it should use the premises of the Old Vic until its own buildings were ready. The Old Vic is now perhaps somewhat overshadowed by the achievements of the National Theatre; it is used for performances of famous visiting companies and excellent repertory players. The teaching role which it discharged so effectively has now been taken over by the Young Vic in premises not far away in The Cut, Lambeth. It seems a shame that none of the three theatres forming the National Theatre was named after Lilian Baylis or Emma Cons as a permanent memorial to the work they did towards the establishment of a great drama tradition.

Waterloo station lies just to the west of the Old Vic and is a great sprawling complex which, like most Victorian railway termini, began in a modest way but accumulated more and more improvised platforms and services as the years passed, one of the most bizarre perhaps being that built in 1854 by the London Necropolis and National Mausoleum Company with a line to the cemetery at Brookwood. This particular platform survived until a landmine fell on it during the last war. Some later developments came about long after the reign of Queen Victoria but will still be mentioned at this point, especially as the most obvious of these features – the great entrance arch from York Road – sadly masked by a railway line high above the street, was erected as a war memorial shortly after the end of the First World War. Over the archway an assembly of gesticulating declamatory figures celebrates the end of the 'war to end all wars'. They include Bellona, the goddess of war, and her offspring, a serene and triumphant Peace with her offspring, and various symbols of peace and victory presided over by an omnipotent Britannia surrounded by her children and guaranteeing peace on earth.

A major alteration to London's network of roads, planned during the Victorian period, was begun in 1892 on the north side of Waterloo Bridge. This was the construction of Aldwych and Kingsway and the scheme was not completed until 1905, by which time a number of smaller streets, including Clare Market, Holywell Street and Wych Street, had been swept away to make room for the new thoroughfares. Wych Street was once a continuation of Drury Lane, known as 'Via de Aldwych'. The Royal Shakespeare Company at present leases the Aldwych Theatre, but there will clearly be changes when the new Barbican project is completed with its arts centre as it will provide new homes for the Royal Shakespeare Company, the Guildhall School of Music and Drama and the London Symphony Orchestra.

The Aldwych Theatre and its twin, the Strand Theatre, both suffer somewhat from the superimposition of lettering and posters on façades which really made no provision for these essentials. The Aldwych Theatre was built especially for Sir Seymour Hicks and opened in 1905 with *Bluebell in Fairyland*. The Strand Theatre, which occupies the site of an earlier theatre, Punch's Playhouse, was designed to combine architecturally with the Waldorf Hotel of the same time. Its first production was *Il Maestro de Capella*.

The Waldorf Hotel was designed by A. Marshall Mackenzie at the same time as the Strand Theatre in 1905–7, but in a style more reminiscent of a French château, with the kind of roofline and detailing that one associates more with the river Loire than the Thames. By the end of the century, the style displayed so triumphantly by Scott with his St Pancras Hotel had been eclipsed by the introduction to London's streets of elements derived from entirely different periods of European architectural history. The interiors of some of the Victorian hotels of London have changed considerably, but the exteriors still retain much of their original appearance.

The Russell Hotel in Russell Square, for example, modernised within, was built as early as 1898 with a distinctly French château flavour, although its architect, C. FitzRoy Doll, introduced elements in brick and terracotta which were as individual as his name, and an even more bizarre elevation to his Imperial Hotel nearby. The Hotel Cecil no longer exists, but much further to the west on Piccadilly, the Ritz Hotel, designed in 1906 by Mewes and Davis, owes its appearance entirely to French inspiration, to the period of Louis XVI, and it has the added advantage of a superb view over Green Park. Its arcading is very similar to that of the Rue de Rivoli in Paris, and is also rather like that which used to be enjoyed by the shoppers in the original Regent Street before it was modernised out of all recognition. Piccadilly Hotel, the creation of another Victorian architect of considerable originality, was not built until 1905–8. It has a Baroque quality which is not particularly characteristic of the work of its architect, Norman Shaw, who usually preferred his own, somewhat individual version of the Queen Anne style with Flemish or Dutch-style details. Claridge's, in Mayfair, another famous hotel of this period, was rebuilt in the 1890s by Sir Ernest George and his partner, Yates, but was modernised in 1931 by Oswald Milne. The Carlton, an equally noted hotel, survived until the 1960s when it was demolished to make way for New Zealand House on the corner of Haymarket and Pall Mall.

There were of course a great many little Victorian hotels and boarding houses, most of which have since been converted into private dwellings, but neither they nor the Victorian public houses come within the scope of this book. Nevertheless, it should perhaps be said that the best of the Victorian pubs are those which are still 'locals' – social centres for specific neighbourhoods. They can often be identified by the elaborately engraved glass panels on doors and on windows, and by the nature of their fittings within, polished brass instead of chromium plate, for example.

By the outbreak of the First World War in 1914, the emphasis on different types of architecture for certain buildings had been more or less resolved. For churches or for any other buildings associated with them – their schools, for example – a form of Gothic was still thought to be acceptable. For most public buildings such as post offices, banks, insurance offices and grammar schools, a pseudo-Georgian appearance was almost compulsory. The exciting new technical methods which had begun with such buildings as Decimus Burton's great Palm House at Kew and exploited so remarkably in the Crystal Palace, were speedily submerged under pointed arches and mass-produced 'medieval' ornament, but eventually this was also abandoned in favour of a kind of classical-cum-Renaissance façade, and it was only on the mainland of Europe and in the USA that the new techniques were not only accepted but developed.

There was a comparatively static pattern in both the Cities of London and of Westminster, for although individual buildings could be pulled down and rebuilt, in the main there was so little room for manoeuvre that the only developments possible were in the suburbs and along the new trunk roads.

In the City the old trade areas remained much the same – they had been established for so long that nothing short of another great fire could possibly move Billingsgate, Smithfield, or any of the other traditional wholesale market areas to another part of London. Dockland was inevitably tied to the river, and it was very much later that the dockers, conservative to the core, resisted the introduction of more modern container methods with a series of disastrous strikes and lost their jobs.

On the south bank of the river there seemed a little more room for change, and it was to Lambeth that St Thomas's Hospital moved when the new London Bridge station required more room in 1870–71. (Little of the hospital's original building of this hospital survived the Second World War.) In 1908 the south bank received another important building: the new County Hall, built by Ralph Knott, with arches and façades almost Piranesi-like in their bold masses and frankly Renaissance detail. It is still one of the few buildings of the reign of Edward VII which retains a certain majesty and dignity despite the considerable improvements which have taken place in what was at that time a very run-down area.

On the other side of St James's Park in 1913, Buckingham Palace lost most of its historic appearance under a façade of pseudo-Georgian

rustication and details built under the direction of Sir Aston Webb who, two years before, had designed the architectural surround for the imposing memorial to Queen Victoria which now dominates the traffic flow past the front of the Palace. The main memorial was the work of Sir Thomas Brock, RA, and was executed in 1911. The central pillar, surmounted by a gilded figure of Victory, has at its eastern base a colossal figure of the great queen, seated with regal dignity, and carved from one single block of white marble. This 13-foot figure is supplemented by a number of symbolic groups suggesting the virtues and achievements of her reign. There is one of Charity to the west, with Truth and Justice on the north and south sides. There are also a number of finely modelled bronzes, symbolising Progress and Peace, Manufacture and Agriculture, Architecture and Painting, and Shipbuilding and Mining – displaying an acceptable face of the period which might not have been wholly appreciated by those such as Charles Dickens who had lived through it. At the same time Sir Aston Webb closed off the entrance to the Mall from the east with the Admiralty Arch, another part of the same memorial by which the reign of Victoria was celebrated. But shortly afterwards in 1914, the complacence of such a memorial was rudely shattered by the outbreak of the First World War, and a new chapter of London's history was to begin, the effects of which are still with us today.

Buckingham Palace, showing the alterations that were made at the beginning of the twentieth century

9

Twentieth-Century London

A s the City of London was a strictly defined and confined area from the eighteenth century onwards, it is clear that additional buildings could only be erected at the expense of those already there. The erection of more modern, more efficient business premises to replace obsolete ones should not be condemned, however, for although the City is no longer a workshop and market combined, its traditional role is still as a financial centre and market of world importance – it is not a museum piece to be preserved at all cost – and although much of historic value has been lost, the changes have not been without advantages.

What remains of the rebuilding carried out in the City between the end of the reign of Queen Victoria and the outbreak of the First World War is just as accurate a reflection of the history of this period as any of the buildings which survive from the more remote past. On the whole, the impression given of this particular period is one of quite extraordinary smugness and complacency, with very little regard for the far-reaching and exciting experiments being carried out on the mainland of Europe and in the USA. The revolutionary building techniques evolved during the nineteenth century in England, which resulted in the Palm House at Kew, the Crystal Palace, and the developments of the 1862 exhibition in South Kensington, were seized upon and explored on the mainland of Europe and in the United States, but were almost ignored by architects in this country as being little more than engineering and quite beneath the consideration of their profession. Thus, although the new additions to the headquarters of the Post Office in King Edward Street designed by Sir Henry Tanner *c.* 1910 did in fact incorporate constructional techniques from France which were, for that time, the most modern in London, they were in the main carefully concealed under a convincing and conventional façade of all the old architectural clichés associated with pseudo-Renaissance buildings. Yet this group of buildings is nevertheless quite an impressive sight, and the interior, although modernised so that it is suitable for twentieth-century commercial demands on the postal system, is surely the most opulent Post Office in the country, with deeply coffered ceilings and an air of Edwardian luxury contrasting strangely with the more utilitarian counters. This building also houses the National Postal Museum where, beautifully displayed in discreet lighting, are some of the treasures of the philatelic world, including a particularly fine collection of British postage stamps. A large portion of the

opposite, Millbank Tower

445

The Bank of England

Roman and medieval walls of London occupies an inner courtyard, and this can be seen by any member of the public who has made written application; security reasons forbid too easy an access to the centre of this complex.

Much further eastwards, at the very heart of the financial centre of the City, the same preoccupation with obsolete historic forms permeates much of the twentieth-century building. When additions are being made to an existing building, especially if the latter is of some antiquity, an architect clearly faces a dilemma. If he builds quite frankly in a new style, he can be accused of being arrogant and of vandalising the earlier building, but if his additions are designed to match the existing building he will invite criticism by being architecturally dishonest to his period. However, although, Sir Herbert Baker used 'classical' forms when he added significantly to the Bank of England between 1925 and 1929, the scale and the crushing weight of such additional building reduced the screen wall which had been erected by Sir John Soane about one hundred years before to insignificance and resulted in severe criticism from such eminent critics as Sir John Summerson and Professor Pevsner. His additions proved inadequate after the Second World War, so that some of the Bank's activities had to be carried out in an annexe in New Change, just east of St Paul's Cathedral.

At the very beginning of Cornhill, just to the south-east of the Bank of England, there is another early twentieth-century building, erected in 1905 on the site formerly occupied by the business premises of Thomas Guy, bookseller and stationer, who devoted much of his fortune to the foundation of Guy's Hospital in 1722. This was designed by John Macvicar Anderson, a Scots architect, for the Liverpool, London and Globe Insurance Company. It is now occupied by the Allied Bank International and Royal Insurance Group. The façade is curved to fit the angular site, with a Wren-like dome and one central cyclopean clock-face, and is decked out with 'classical' mouldings and pilasters. It has been said that the horizontal banding of the first and second storeys are intended to harmonise with those on the façade of Hawksmoor's St Mary Woolnoth, but whereas the latter has a vigorous and convincing personality – one of Nicholas Hawksmoor's masterpieces – Anderson's building has little more than an aldermanic pomposity.

An earlier and much more satisfactory building by John Macvicar Anderson stands in Lombard Street beside the Wren church of St Edmund, King and Martyr. This was built in 1889 as the London offices of the Commercial Bank of Scotland and is now part of the Royal Bank of Scotland. Its façade is much enriched with its native granite in red, grey and black, and it is altogether a more unified and more dignified building than the one at the corner of Cornhill. It has well-proportioned windows with semicircular heads set back between robust columns on the first two floors, each storey being well defined by a bold frieze and entablature which adds a rich interplay of light and shade to the façade on sunlit days. The signs which hang on the outside of the building are interesting remnants of a period in London's history when nearly every business could be identified by its shop signs. Today very few exist, except for inn signs, but the one of the 'Cat a Fiddling' hanging from Nos. 60–62, Lombard Street originally belonged to a haberdasher named Andrew Dansie whose shop once occupied this site. During the middle of the 1740s a man named John Bland, whose sign was that of a black horse, occupied No. 62, and when Lloyds Bank took over these premises much later they adopted his black horse symbol and have retained it as their own to this day.

Further westwards in Poultry, such buildings as that designed for the Midland Bank by Sir Edwin Lutyens in 1924, but not completed until 1939, still retained forms of architecture long since obsolete, but this was clearly not because such an eminent architect lacked inventiveness, nor his clients enterprise. Their reticence even with new buildings of much more recent foundation than that of the Midland Bank, for example, was intended to imply at least that however new the business, it had a sound and reliable link with tradition. They imagined that this would be far more reassuring to would-be investors than a building with more obvious signs of modern architecture.

Newspaper offices, on the other hand, must give the impression of being very much up-to-date, and further west in Fleet Street, the headquarters of famous newspapers tended to be far less conservative in their choice of buildings than banks, for example. This is very obvious in the offices of the

Fleet Street, with the
Express offices on the
left

Daily Express, designed clearly in the idiom of the 1930s by the famous architect, Sir Owen Williams, and his partners in 1931. This is still an important example of a building designed for 'fitness for purpose and pleasantness in use' – a popular slogan at that time.

Just outside the City boundary to the west, the architects of the Aldwych complex were still absorbed with historic details, producing some fairly convincing versions of the more pompous eighteenth-century architecture by means of 'classical' columns and a cladding of cut and rusticated stone, although they included some of the first steel-framed structures in London. It was this timidity to reveal the essential construction of buildings in London which contrasted so strongly with the fearless acceptance of the new techniques to be seen on the mainland of Europe and in the United States.

The buildings at the east end of Aldwych were built by Sir John Burnet, and Australia House by A. Marshal Mackenzie, who was also responsible for the design of the Waldorf Hotel on the opposite side of the road. Australia House was formally opened by George V in 1918 although he had laid the foundation stone before the First World War. It has a modern steel-framed construction, but this is disguised by an exterior which somewhat resembles a Renaissance palace, with a huge gesticulating sculpture group on either side of the main entrance symbolising Exploration on one side and Agriculture on the other. More sculpture in bronze is positioned on the cornice immediately above the large central window, representing the Horses of the Sun. It seems a singularly conventional building for such a race of rugged individualists as the Australians, and the decorative forms owe more to antiquity than to the Antipodes, although the ten floors within are richly furnished with Australian woods and marbles.

Bush House, named after an American businessman, Irving T. Bush, is by far the most impressive building in the whole complex, not only because it occupies the central position facing the 100-foot boulevard of Kingsway, but because of the fearless handling of the massive façade by the architectural firm of Helmle, Corbett and Harrison of New York. Built in 1931, it has an impressive main entrance with a pair of colossal statues by Malvinia Hoffmann, carved in 1925, portraying two youthful figures holding a torch aloft, and dedicated 'to the friendship of English-speaking peoples'. It is significant that this building now houses the External Services of the BBC, whose motto is 'Nation shall speak Peace unto Nation'.

Another steel-framed building which conceals its construction, this time behind a screen of Norwegian granite, is Inveresk House on the western side of Kingsway. Of greater interest is India House, the office of the High Commissioner for the Republic of India, built by Sir Herbert Baker, joint architect with Sir Edwin Lutyens, for the new capital of India, Delhi. India House has a number of decorative motifs derived somewhat from Indian sources, but it still remains a doggedly European building, built in 1928–30.

Kingsway unfortunately never realised its potential and demonstrates all too clearly that whoever was responsible for this 100-foot-wide thorough-

Bush House

449

India House

fare was hampered from the start by being denied the free hand allowed to such great architects as the Adam Brothers, who designed streets so magnificently as a unified pattern, or John Nash with his genius for grouping what were virtually blocks of flats into a noble array surrounding Regent's Park. In spite of their virtues, the architects of many of the earlier buildings which formed the original Kingsway hardly came into this category, and Imperial House, Regent House and Windsor House, all built in 1913, to be followed in quick succession by York House in 1914, Alexandra House in 1916, Victory and Ingersoll Houses in 1919–20, Princes' House in 1920–21 and Africa House in 1921, are all buildings which are unimpressive and visually boring.

The large building on the south-eastern corner, like many of the original buildings, has changed hands since 1955. It was originally designed as the principal offices of the Royal Air Force in 1919, but it is now occupied by the headquarters of commercial television. Kingsway House, designed in 1916 by Sir Henry Tanner as the Public Trustee Offices, is only one of the buildings designed by this very prolific architect, who varied his style a good deal according to his clients. The building he designed in Lincoln's Inn Fields, for example, is in a neo-Jacobean style and was produced for the Land Registry department.

Three somewhat different church buildings are to be found in Kingsway: Kingsway Hall, the headquarters of the Methodist West London Mission, best known perhaps for its splendid concerts, but also a focal point for evangelical meetings and discussions; on the opposite side of the street is the

Roman Catholic church of SS Anselm and Cecilia, built in 1909 by Frederick Walters and repaired after some damage during the Second World War; and at the north-western corner the Protestant church of Holy Trinity, built in 1910 in a somewhat timid, rather clichéd ecclesiastical style. The Roman Catholic church stands on the site of a much earlier building – The Sardinian Chapel – which was put to the flames by the mobs in the notorious Lord George Gordon Riots of 1780. Fortunately the *Luftwaffe* were less successful than the eighteenth-century mob.

Of the other buildings in Kingsway, two should perhaps be mentioned. Kodak House was designed in 1911 by Sir John Burnet but, unlike its contemporaries, it makes no concessions to obsolete conventions. Sir John Burnet designed a refreshingly straightforward building which states quite clearly the way in which it was constructed and the purpose for which it was built. There is another example of his work in Kingsway, this time within another building, for although the architects of No. 22, Kingsway belonged to another firm (Lewis Soloman, Kaye and Partners), which built on the site of the old Stoll Theatre in 1959–60, inside is Sir John Burnet's Royalty theatre, entered not from Kingsway but from Portugal Street at the rear.

Magnet house, a huge post-Second World War building on the west side of Kingsway, is the most recent addition to this area, having been erected in 1964–8 by R. Seifert and Partners, who used pre-cast concrete members in its construction. Set back a little from the normal building line, it creates a little island of its own just off the broad sweep of Kingsway.

Along the Strand there are not many buildings of note, other than those already mentioned during the study of other periods, and although the general appearance of the Strand is not unattractive, and its association with such famous theatres as the Savoy and the Adelphi still suggests the gaiety of the West End, much of it is changed, and many of its buildings have been converted from their original purpose and altered accordingly. In the days when the music-hall song issued the invitation of 'Let's all go down the Strand', it was clearly much more of a centre of gaiety and revelry than it is now. Even the Strand Palace Hotel, built in 1925–30 by F. J. Wills, had a good deal of its original façade remodelled in 1967, and although it is possible that the present entrance is preferable to the original one, the latter was so characteristic of the 1930s that it should perhaps have been retained.

A building of the same period which has survived is Shell-Mex House on the opposite side of the Strand, but this is best viewed from the Embankment. Built on the site of the town house of the famous Elizabethan family, the Cecils, and replacing the Hotel Cecil, Shell-Mex House, when it was erected in 1931, was considered the very last word in 'modern' architecture with its uncompromising cubist appearance and its huge clock-face, still one of the dominant features of the river frontage. It has inevitably dated, for architects have learned to manipulate such structures with a much lighter touch since the 1930s, and although the constructional principles have not changed very much, the final results today would be far less ponderous. But whatever different opinions may be held by critics of Shell-Mex House, they are unanimous in their condemnation of the destruction of

above and right, Views
from Shell-Mex House

the famous eighteenth-century Adelphi and in their dislike of the new Adelphi which replaced it in the 1930s, a huge building entirely out of scale with the delicacy of the eighteenth-century houses which were part of the old scheme. It is indeed something of a shock to find it there, for the glimpses from the Strand down Adam Street suggest that there is much more of eighteenth-century London to be seen, and the enchanting facade of the rear of Robert Adam's Royal Society of Arts just behind some of the modern shops does little to prepare one for the brutality of the 1930s building.

A great deal of skilful restoration and adaptation has recently taken place to the north of the Strand opposite Charing Cross station and hotel. This area, which was originally part of a plan for an extension of the Pall Mall development planned by John Nash in the 1820s, has been very largely rebuilt, but the curved end features designed by Nash have been beautifully preserved, the stucco renewed throughout, and a large central feature which does not pretend to be anything but a functional twentieth-century addition inserted. If Charing Cross Hospital to the rear can be equally well restored this area will be a welcome addition to the Strand.

Villiers Street has undergone considerable alterations in the past few years, the latest being a new underground railway station of the most bizarre colouring which has reduced the entrance to the street by half its width. Further down on the west side, the great arches, which, before the Second World War were the refuge of the wretched outcasts sleeping rough, have had a new lease of life; they now house a market of lock-up shops and a centre for collectors of militaria, coins, stamps and other somewhat specialised items. A notable addition to the gaiety of this street is a skilful and enchanting reconstruction of the music-hall of the Victorian or Edwardian period, built into the spaces of the arches beneath what was once the South-Eastern and Chatham Railway. This is the Players' theatre where they have recreated the atmosphere of a more robust theatrical tradition, normally only to be found today in the annual pantomimes. In this theatre, fortified by refreshments placed on tables in the auditorium, the audience is cajoled or even bullied by a chairman or Master of Ceremonies into participating in the singing of choruses of songs patriotic or maudlin. The theatre is a valuable addition to an area once threatened with decline.

In Trafalgar Square, the most notable building facing The Strand on the east side is Sir Herbert Baker's South Africa House, built in 1935, with columns and other 'classical' features which can perhaps be defended on the grounds that these help the building to harmonise with its neighbour, the eighteenth-century church of St Martin-in-the-Fields, and with the National Gallery on the north side. Trafalgar Square has already been mentioned in the chapter on the London of the Regency period, and the twentieth-century additions have mostly been beneficial. Even the railings which are used to control demonstrations are not sufficiently obtrusive to mar the general effect of space and freedom which is an essential aspect of this area.

Westwards along Cockspur Street is a strange conglomeration of

New Zealand House

twentieth-century buildings: travel agents, banks, the quaint offices of the French Line, built in 1901 by W. Woodward, Aston Webb's Canadian National Railways building added about six years later, and the offices of the P and O Shipping Line of the same year. Behind them stands the delicately proportioned but towering office block of New Zealand House, another modern building in which the bones enhance the appearance of the structure as well as sustaining it. This building, the work of Robert Matthew, Johnson-Marshall and Partners, was completed in 1963: it not only has a refreshing candour which distinguishes it from many other buildings added to this part of London during the twentieth century, but also provides at roof level the most delightful observation galleries normally open to the public which give superb views of St James's Park, the Mall, Whitehall, Trafalgar Square and other areas usually only seen from ground level.

From New Zealand House at the junction of Pall Mall and Haymarket, it is but a short walk to Piccadilly Circus and so northwards to Regent Street, which is virtually a twentieth-century creation, for the present Regent Street owes all too little to the genius of John Nash, and only the ground plan can be said to be his. His colonnade of iron columns which provided shelter for shoppers was taken down in 1848 and the whole street rebuilt so many times – the last by Sir Reginald Blomfield in the 1920s – that nothing of Nash remains. Sir Reginald Blomfield's rebuilding at least unified the whole street, for he not only rebuilt much of the Piccadilly Circus and the whole of the important quadrant, but continued northwards. The famous Café Royal, the haunt of such bohemian artists as the young Augustus John, the 'Beggarstaff Brothers' and their associates, was also largely rebuilt about 1928 by Sir Henry Tanner, but some of the sumptuous internal fittings and decor were fortunately preserved. Perhaps the most striking building built between the two World Wars is not the Regent street façade of Liberty's, but that which extends along the south side of Great Marlborough Street – a building which, using the wooden structure of the Elizabethan age, gives a fairly convincing impression of a range of shops of that period, although the huge panes of glass would of course have been quite impossible in the sixteenth century. The timber-framing was fashioned as a structural necessity from the timber salvaged from old sailing ships. On the bridge spanning the entrance to Kingly Street there is a large clock, over which a little recess shows a knight which at intervals during the day celebrates the passing of time by attacking and defeating a fiercesome dragon. This bears some resemblance to the joust performed over the clock in Wells Cathedral, built in the Middle Ages.

Of approximately the same date but very different in feeling from Liberty's is a stark black granite building on the opposite side of Great Marlborough Street. This is now known as Palladium House but was formerly Ideal House and was the work of Raymond Hood, an American architect, whose approach is vastly different from the nostalgia of the past which prompted the design of Liberty's. Palladium House stands on the corner of Argyll Street which contains the famous music-hall, the Palladium, which since it was built in 1910 has been the Mecca of every aspiring vaudeville performer, not only in this country, but from across the Atlantic as well.

One of the most characteristic examples of the architecture of the period between the wars is Broadcasting House, the headquarters of the BBC at the northern end of Upper Regent Street on the corner of Portland Place. Designed by George Van Myer and F. J. Watson Hart, it has a charming, if a rather low entrance hall containing a delightful sculpture of Orpheus by Eric Gill, and the studios are given additional insulation from noise by being built as a central core, surrounded by the offices which form an outer ring. The exterior, however, is graceless, and the mean entrance overwhelmed by a large dual statue of Prospero and Ariel, also by Eric Gill. The scale of the niche in which the statues stand is far from happy in relation to the door beneath, but it is the impact of this whole building on its neighbour, the Church of All Souls, Langham Place, which is so deplorable. When John Nash designed his church with its acutely pointed spire, he devised it so that it would act as a 'visual stop', allowing the traveller to make the necessary adjustment as he moves from Upper Regent Street to the new axis of Portland Place. The BBC building, especially since its later additions, now defeats this intention of John Nash and dwarfs what should have been a notable landmark.

Of the rest of Portland Place little more need be said, for bombing destroyed many of the Adam buildings and ruthless commercialism, which thrust its way into what must have been a charming Adam group on the west side, took over when the *Luftwaffe* finished. The last act of commercial

vandalism took place directly opposite the headquarters of the Royal
Institute of British Architects, on the corner of Portland Place and
Weymouth Street, and is one of the few distinguished buildings erected in
1934 and designed by Grey Wornum. It has some gentle low reliefs on the
façade by Bainbridge Copnall, and the two pillars flanking the main
entrance are decorated with sculpture by James Woodford.

Oxford Street to the south is a historic thoroughfare, but again, many of
its most notable buildings have been replaced by modern commercial ones,
far less distinguished although no doubt more suitable for the display of the
goods they sell. One landmark in the design of a modern store is
undoubtedly Selfridges, well to the west of Oxford Circus on the north side
of the hill which reaches its climax at Marble Arch. This was started in 1908
by a highly successful and energetic American businessman who had
already amassed a considerable fortune in the USA as a partner in the
Marshall Field store in Chicago. Having sold out his interest in the Chicago
firm, Mr Harry Gordon Selfridge came to London and, seeing the potential
of the more westerly part of Oxford Street, he began to build the store which
now bears his name. As it became more and more successful he enlarged it to
at least twice its original size. It set out to attract the public, not only by the
range and quality of goods offered for sale, but by displaying them in the
most luxurious business premises to be seen in London at that time. The
great central feature with its ornate clock, the window displays, and the
impressive figure of 'The Queen of Time', the work of the English sculptor,
Gilbert Bayes, made the shop a great attraction and a landmark in

commercial design; and many other shops followed suit. But the aggrandisement of one part of the street at the expense of existing buildings naturally triggered off a kind of commercial one-upmanship which destroyed the street as a unified design.

Away in Kensington High Street, with Sir Reginald Blomfield's design for John Barker, the same kind of rivalry was to develop, although not quite to the same extent. The results, however acceptable in a shopping area, were less pleasant in one which was primarily residential.

Park Lane, which could have been as lovely as the Nash terraces surrounding Regent's Park, was subsequently subjected to the same process of exploitation as a series of hotels and other buildings, by their very diversity of scale and widely different materials, reduced the street into a series of disconnected and unrelated buildings. The most notable buildings of the 1930s in Park Lane were Brook House, built in 1932 by W. B. Simpson, but with a façade designed by Sir Edwin Lutyens, and then Grosvenor House, a hotel with flats, also largely the work of Sir Edwin Lutyens, which replaced the town house of the Dukes of Westminster. The Dorchester Hotel was built by Curtis Green in 1930 and replaced a

The Dorchester Hotel

luxurious Victorian mansion designed by Lewis Vulliamy for the multi-millionaire, R. S. Holford, and most sumptuously decorated within with mural paintings and marble fireplaces carried out by Alfred Stevens, the English artist. Fortunately some of this work was salvaged and is preserved in the Victoria and Albert Museum and the Tate Gallery. Park Lane ends in a crescendo of post-Second World War buildings, the peak being the controversial Hilton Hotel, a 20-storey building reaching a height of over 300 feet, designed by Lewis Soloman, Kaye and Partners, and dwarfing every building in its vicinity. It is also said to threaten the privacy of the royal gardens to the rear of Buckingham Palace.

A building of the 1930s which at that time was criticised with equal severity, but which has now been accepted quite happily, is to be found on the far side of St James's Park in Broadway, Westminster. This building, designed by Charles Holden in 1929, combines the headquarters of the London Transport Board with the St James's underground station; it was one of a series of underground stations to be built at that time which have since proved to be some of the most admirable examples of architecture from a period which was not notable for fine building. An austerely-shaped building with wings and a high central block, the features which probably excited most criticism were the sculptures commissioned by Charles Holden from a number of almost unknown young carvers. The work of Sir Jacob Epstein was well known, if not actually notorious, in the 1930s, for his low relief entitled 'Rima', designed as a memorial to W. H. Hudson in Hyde Park, made him the centre of a raging controversy when it was first exhibited in 1925. The work of Eric Gill and Henry Moore was not so well known, but both men were to make very important contributions to British art, and the latter, who is still alive and working, has been responsible for enhancing the status of England in the international world of art to a position hitherto unknown. At the same time as the work on the underground stations was being undertaken, Frank Pick, the directing genius behind the London Transport Board, commissioned the great calligrapher, Edward Johnston (a teacher of Eric Gill), to design a new type for the entire system, and it is this type, a model of clarity and efficient beauty, which is not only still in use but has had a profound influence on modern typography. None of the other young artists whose carving is to be seen on this building ever achieved such fame as that enjoyed by Henry Moore, Eric Gill and the older Jacob Epstein, the latter being responsible for the symbolic figures, 'Night' and 'Day', on the frieze of the lower storey of the building. The artists whose work is to be seen high up on the wings and the main building are as follows: E. Aumonier, A. G. Gerrard, Eric Gill, Henry Moore, F. Rabinovitch and A. Wyon.

Unfortunately no sculpture, however well carved or cunningly sited, could have improved the insensitive brutality of a building by the same architect which still dominates Bloomsbury. This is the Senate House, designed by Charles Holden for London University, and it is a towering graceless mass which, however persuasively photographed in the 1930s as a symbol of the 'New Age of Architecture', is still an affront to the whole Russell Square area.

Arnos Grove
underground station

More typical of the best buildings of the 1930s, however, and indeed almost the only happy outcome of the sad story of commercial exploitation and vandalism of the land so brilliantly denounced in *England and the Octupus* by Clough Williams-Ellis, were the underground buildings serving the inhabitants of the far-flung suburbs. Of these, one of the most brilliantly designed was that at Arnos Grove on the Piccadilly Line, on the northern perimeter of London. The designer of an underground station faces very different problems from those encountered by the architect designing a main-line railway station, but in this case Charles Holden and his partners solved the difficulties by using modern constructional techniques quite frankly, and they produced a building which is still an admirable example of functional beauty today.

The same can be said of the 1930s building designed in Greycoat Street, Westminster, as the Royal Horticultural Hall; by a Scots architect, J. Murray Easton, and his partner Sir Howard Robertson. Taking full advantage of the lightness and grace made possible by the right use of reinforced concrete construction, they produced a series of parabolic arches which not only allowed ample light through the glazed walls freed from sustaining the weight of the roof, but left the whole floor space free for exhibition purposes, uncluttered by supporting columns. The heating of the hall was also incorporated into the roof – one of the first examples of his technique in this country.

An equally elegant building of approximately the same period is to be seen just opposite the Sloane Square underground station. This is the store designed for Peter Jones by the firm of Crabtree, Slater and Moberly, with the great architect/teacher, Sir Charles Reilly, acting as consultant. Erected in 1935, it is still an astonishingly fresh 'modern' building. As with the Royal Horticultural Hall the walls have been almost entirely relieved of the necessity of acting as supports for the roof and are thus liberated spaces filled with glass, curved gracefully to accommodate the shape of the corner site.

459

However no such innovations are to be seen at Thames House, near the western end of Lambeth Bridge, a building as reactionary as possible in its rejection of the principles of construction which have contributed so much to the success of such buildings as the Peter Jones store or the Royal Horticultural Hall. Although it is in fact almost exactly the same date as the latter, it is at least fifty years older in thought and in execution and adheres to all the old architectural clichés which were current at the turn of the century.

Although the Vickers building designed by Ronald Ward and Partners a little upstream from Thames House is admittedly a post-Second World War creation, it is interesting to see how it is a natural outcome of the daring innovations which took place during the 1930s. It is an elegant building, although doubts have been expressed as to whether it should have been built in this particular site, i.e., so near to the Houses of Parliament, on the Thames.

Still further upstream on the same side of the river is Dolphin Square, built in 1937, and at that time said to be the largest self-contained block of flats in Europe. Designed by Gordon Jeeves, it covers $7\frac{1}{2}$ acres and has over 1000 luxuriously appointed flats, although by comparison with some of the buildings already mentioned it has a rather ponderous appearance.

Dolphin Square faces an equally characteristic building of the 1930s – Battersea power station, designed by Sir Giles Gilbert Scott. Unlike some of its contemporaries it has become far more attractive and acceptable as the years have passed and produced a growing interest in industrial architecture and archaeology. This particular building is worth studying if only for its impeccable brickwork, visible from almost any railway carriage passing the huge complex. Its location does little harm to the views of the river at this point, unlike the other power station on Bankside in Southwark by the same architect, which is most unfortunately situated opposite St Paul's Cathedral.

Little of note of this period is to be found between Dolphin Square and the Palace of Westminster, but in Whitehall, almost opposite the east end of Downing Street stands the Cenotaph, originally designed by Sir Edwin Lutyens to commemorate the fallen of the First World War. It is a dignified and well-proportioned memorial, with subtly tapered surfaces, and it has no indication of any specific religious associations since members of all creeds paid the supreme sacrifice. It used to merit the removal of hats by passers-by as a mark of respect, but is now almost entirely ignored, and even the two minutes' silence on 11 November is no longer observed although a service is still held there on Remembrance Sunday.

Nearby, on the east side of Whitehall, set back beyond a large grassy area where there is a small (imaginary) statue of Sir Walter Raleigh and a much larger-than-life-size statue of Field-Marshal Montgomery, stands the Ministry of Defence – probably the ugliest building in this part of London. Preserved beneath it is the wine cellar that belonged to Henry VIII. Public access to this remarkable relic of Whitehall Palace, which has been moved to its present site from the ground floor of Cadogan House, is now restricted for security reasons, but permission can usually be obtained by written

application well before the proposed visit.

On the same side of Whitehall but further to the north is the old War Office, designed in 1898 by William Young, but completed after the architect's death by his son in 1907. It uses all the pseudo-classical motifs, and its domes unfortunately break the skyline of the more elegant Horse Guards building when seen from St James's Park. Still further up Whitehall, but on the opposite side of the road, is one of the few theatres to be built in London during the 1930s. This is the Whitehall Theatre, designed by E. A. Stone and now famous for its comedy plays of a particularly English type. The same year, 1930, also saw the opening of the Cambridge Theatre in Upper St Martin's Lane, designed by the firm of Wimperis, Simpson and Guthrie.

But the gaiety of London was overshadowed by the growing threat of Nazi Germany, and although there was a brief respite after the meeting at Munich in 1938, in September 1939 the lights went out all over London and its inhabitants sent their children off to safer zones, bracing themselves for the most ruthless attacks from the air the country had ever experienced. There is little in the Whitehall area to remind us of that dark period, apart from the scars from bomb splinters on the Guards Memorial, and a craggy building known as the Citadel at the west end of the admiralty building facing Horse Guards Parade and St James's Park. This remarkable building – a cliff-like fortress and air-raid shelter designed by W. A. Forsyth, and fashioned from compressed pebble and flint – was the heavily fortified entrance to a subterranean shelter which enabled those entrusted with the conduct of the fight for freedom to work undisturbed and in safety, despite

461

the air-raids raging above the beleaguered city. The damage inflicted on London during the war years was widespread and terrible, and the short account which follows cannot possibly list all the casualties.

In the City itself, one great building which survived almost undamaged was St Paul's Cathedral. Although it sustained two direct hits, one on the choir and one in the north transept, and its courageous fire-watchers dealt with hundreds of incendiary bombs, its mighty dome stood inviolate high above the stricken city and became almost a symbol of the certainty of victory for the Londoners. It was still undamaged at the end of the war, amid over sixteen acres of devastation which surrounded it.

The City churches were less fortunate. Many were destroyed, or the body of the church gutted, although the blast from the bombs which destroyed the naves often left the towers intact, so that they now stand as landmarks beside the ruins of their churches. Among the most notable towers still to be seen in the City is that of Christ Church, Newgate Street, Wren's exquisite 'Gothic' spire of St Dunstan's-in-the-East near Billingsgate, and St Alban, Wood Street, while the restored tower of St Augustine with St Faith just east of St Paul's has been incorporated into the new choir school of the cathedral, a strange modern building with upper rooms reminiscent of water cisterns overhanging the main building. Today, many of the ruined City churches have been skilfully and lovingly rebuilt, although their exquisite fittings were destroyed and irreplaceable.

The halls of the City Companies suffered grievously from the air-raids, nineteen of them being heavily damaged or entirely destroyed. Goldsmiths Hall, Fishmongers Hall, Skinners Hall and that of the Apothecaries seem to have suffered the least, although none of them escaped unscathed. The Guildhall was also heavily damaged, although its walls and the medieval undercroft survived and the whole building now has little to indicate how badly it was damaged during the air-raids.

Despite its proximity to the docks which were under constant attack, very little damage was inflicted on the Tower of London, the most serious area to be affected being some nineteenth-century building on the north side.

The Inns of Court suffered considerably, so that the hall, the library and the chapel of Gray's Inn had to be rebuilt. Lincoln's Inn was more fortunate, although the Georgian area containing Sir Robert Taylor's Stone Buildings was hit, and the walls still show the scars inflicted during the raids.

Further south, the Temple area was also heavily damaged. The circular west end of the Temple church was gutted, and in addition to a number of buildings destroyed in this area, including Inner Temple Hall, which had to be entirely rebuilt, Middle Temple Hall was badly damaged. It has since been restored with some of the original materials and now looks very little the worse for its ordeal.

Considering the fact that the City was under air attack for nearly six years, culminating in appalling damage inflicted by the indiscriminate use of V1s and V2s when the *Luftwaffe* was no longer able to sustain the losses inflicted upon it by the Allied air forces, it is remarkable how much survived.

Westwards towards Westminster there were more casualties among some of the churches. St Clement Danes was gutted, and St Mary-Le-Strand, its neighbour, fared little better. St James's, Piccadilly, Wren's favourite church, was almost destroyed, as well as St John the Evangelist in Smith Square, but St Martin-in-the-Fields survived almost intact.

Buckingham Palace had its chapel destroyed and sustained some damage elsewhere, and there was some less serious damage inflicted on Kensington Palace, but in the main, attacks on these buildings were less effective than might have been expected. The Houses of Parliament were naturally a target and were attacked many times; the House of Commons was burned out and the Commons had to sit in the relatively undamaged House of Lords, while their Lordships transferred to the Queen's Robing Room to continue their debates. Fortunately the historic Westminster Hall was only slightly damaged. Westminster Abbey sustained damage when a bomb destroyed the crossing, but suffered less than some of the surrounding buildings.

Most of the devastation however occurred in the area of the docks and the railway termini, although no part of London escaped unscathed. The destruction caused in the thickly populated East End was not without some advantages for those fortunate enough to survive, for huge areas of slums were reduced to rubble and the spaces thus liberated presented a challenge to architects and builders to replace those depressed areas with homes more worthy of the people who had endured so much in the nation's fight for survival. Little need be said of the prefabs – temporary houses which, to our shame, are still inhabited over thirty years after the end of the Second World War. Nevertheless, many new rehousing schemes were undertaken, particularly in the north and the east, and many others are still under way and will probably be a source of exciting controversy until the end of this century.

One important development which affected London profoundly was the movement of its population to the new satellite towns, denuding the centre of the city of all but those who were either too poor to move or too reluctant to be uprooted at their age, so that a kind of vacuum was created, reducing London to an empty shell of silent offices and closed shops after office hours and at weekends. The New Towns Act of 1946 made provision for a number of new towns, most of them extensions of small existing villages, and planning the residential areas and industry so that although they were integrated, they were part of a series of communities, with shops, schools, churches and recreational facilities all being built at the same time. Such towns were not 'dormitory' towns with the breadwinners returning home from offices or factories after a long and expensive train journey, but communities closely linked to their work, yet at the same time segregated from the industrial areas. New towns such as Harlow in Essex accelerated the migration of large bodies of families out of the London area so successfully that it has recently been necessary to try and reverse the process by attracting people back into the heart of the city. However, the cost of land in London is prohibitively high and it is almost impossible to build small family homes with gardens. High-rise flats with common gardens have not been a success where the housing of families with young children is

The South Bank
complex

concerned. Nevertheless, if properly planned, a mixture of different forms
of housing can be used in the development of a neighbourhood, especially if
the schools form a nucleus for social activities, with the playing field acting
as an open green space and the school buildings being used after school
hours as a social centre, clinic and so on. Anyone passing from the misery
and squalor of the existing Brick Lane area in Spitalfields to Tower Hamlets
– once little more than a bomb-shattered wilderness – can see just what
should and must be done in the City.

The rejuvenation of one particularly derelict London area on the South
Bank, where it was necessary to reclaim four and a half acres of mudflats
from the river before preparing the site of the Festival of Britain in 1951,
demonstrates what could still be done with similar areas in other parts of
London. The Festival of Britain, despite the difficult economic climate in
which it was planned and the gloomy forebodings of its failure, was as great a
success as its predecessor, the Great Exhibition of 1851. Of all the buildings
erected for the Festival, the most important, which was intended to be
permanent, was the Royal Festival Hall, now a focal point for music-lovers
from all over the world and the first of a series of magnificent additions to
London's cultural life, culminating with the National Theatre.

The Royal Festival Hall, designed by Robert Matthew and Dr (now Sir)
Leslie Martin, provides accommodation for an audience of 3300 as well as
being able to hold a symphony orchestra of over 100 players and a choir of
250. It was so well designed that despite the nearness of the railway line and
the traffic on the roads to the rear, the interior is entirely free from external
noise and the acoustics are as perfect as modern science can achieve. Apart
from its function as a concert hall, the Royal Festival Hall provides
restaurant facilities and some of the finest views of London's river and

landscape, especially towards Westminster and the Victoria Embankment. Now that the whole river frontage from Westminster Bridge to Waterloo Bridge and beyond has been redesigned, with spacious paved areas on which to walk and ample facilities with which to enjoy the panorama of the river, it is difficult to recall how derelict and dangerous this district was before it was transformed by the designers of the Festival of Britain.

The Royal Festival Hall is particularly light and airy in design and neat in execution, with balconies and huge windows looking out over the river. Although it is constructed of reinforced concrete, it is clad on the upper storeys in Portland stone and Derbydene marble, with a surface of grey vitreous mosaic on the lower storey beneath the pedestrian levels.

The neighbouring buildings downstream are built almost entirely in exposed reinforced concrete cast *in situ*, and although some areas have been enriched with upright panels of Cornish granite aggregate, and great efforts have been made to use shuttering which would provide a texture of splintery wood with rivet holes to mitigate the monotony of great areas of concrete, the complex of buildings looks dour and forbidding by comparison with the Royal Festival Hall. This is a pity, for the Architects Department of the London County Council has succeeded in designing buildings which perform their various functions most admirably once the visitor is actually inside them, but their exteriors do little to entice the passers-by and give scant idea of the attractions awaiting them within.

Three buildings were designed as an integral unit – the Queen Elizabeth Hall, the Purcell Room and the Hayward Gallery. The Queen Elizabeth Hall is a concert hall which, while it cannot offer such large-scale entertainments as the Royal Festival Hall (it only seats 1106 people), is rather more flexible and has permanent built-in facilities for the televising of

The Royal Festival Hall

465

County Hall

the entertainments offered there which in no way distract the attention of the live audience. It is skilfully designed to take advantage of the most recent research into acoustical problems and satisfies the most fastidious audiences. The Architects Department of the London County Council was not only responsible for the structure of the building, but for the design of such details as the seats in the auditorium which are carefully sited so that there is an unobstructed view of the performers from every part of the hall. Afrormosia wood has been used for the floors, the railings, the doors, and for the case of the permanent chamber organ. This instrument, designed by D. A. Flenthrop, occupies a single section of the adjustable platform, but when it is not required it can be lowered and stored in a specially designed bay beneath the hall.

The Purcell Room, named after the great seventeenth-century musician, Henry Purcell (once the organist of Westminster Abbey), is by comparison with the Queen Elizabeth Hall, quite tiny. An intimate little concert hall which can accommodate an audience of about 370, this is also sufficiently flexible in design to enable it to be readily adapted for use as a small conference centre or lecture hall, in addition to its proper role as a hall for chamber music or recitals.

To the rear of the Queen Elizabeth Hall is a complex of art galleries known as the Hayward Gallery, It is named after Isaac Hayward, the leader of the London County Council from 1947–1965 – he was the last leader before the London County Council became the Greater London Council.

The Hayward Gallery is built almost entirely in reinforced concrete, cast *in situ*, with the exception of the welded steel framework which supports the roof of the upper galleries. The series of glass pyramids which form the roof

and are such an easily recognisable feature of this building, are largely self-cleansing and light the two upper art galleries. They have built-in devices with baffles operated by photo-electric cells controlling the amount of light admitted to the building. There are two upper galleries and three open air sculpture courts, and beneath these, three other galleries, lit artificially, with facilities for demountable display racks in addition to the wall spaces available for the presentation of exhibitions.

The Hayward Tower is surmounted by a rectangular construction of argon tubes in different colours which change according to the direction and speed of the wind. This kinetic sculpture is by Philip Vaughan and Roger Dainton and is fairly typical of some of the exhibits – some temporary, some permanent – to be seen in the South Bank area. To the uninitiated, whose conception of sculpture is the definition to be found in the *Oxford Dictionary* ('the art of forming representations in the round or in relief by chiselling, carving, casting or modelling'), some of the exhibits may well be somewhat puzzling. A stainless steel composition beside the Queen Elizabeth Hall by William Pye has the magnificently resonant title of 'Zemran', while a memorial to Chopin by Marian Kubica, in cast bronze, a gift of the Polish nation, is to be seen between the Royal Festival Hall and the Queen Elizabeth Hall. On the west side of the Royal Festival Hall, facing Hungerford Bridge, is a sculptured figure entitled 'The Cellist', fashioned by Siegfried Charoux from cement powdered iron bound with polyester resin, and a charming little wooden sculpture (rather like a small totem-pole surmounted by birds) has recently been placed near the entrance to the Royal Festival Hall.

On the far side of Belvedere Road to the rear of the Hayward Gallery stands the Shell Centre, a twenty-five-storey building designed between 1957 and 1962 by Sir Howard Robertson. It has attracted a certain amount of adverse criticism from architectural critics, largely because of its siting rather than for any lack of architectural merit, for looked at in isolation and in its immediate surroundings, the Shell Centre is far more elegant and proportionate than some of its neighbours. The viewing gallery under the roof is at present closed for reasons of security, so that the belvedere or fine view from which the road on which it stands derives its name is not at present available, but there is normally a superb view from the gallery extending over Westminster and the whole of St James's Park.

During the Festival of Britain, the site on which the Shell Centre now stands was occupied by a cinema, so that when the new National Film Theatre was designed by the Architects Department of the LCC they had to find an alternative site and tucked their theatre under one of the spacious arches of Waterloo Bridge. Since then the National Film Theatre has been considerably enlarged and developed by the GLC Architects Department; it now has one auditorium capable of seating 500 people and another seating about 150. It also has a riverside restaurant and an exhibition hall. The National Film Theatre is managed by the British Film Institute and not only shows films by all the great classical film directors, but also many foreign films unfortunately ignored by the commercial distributors and therefore rarely seen in this country.

Waterloo Bridge, designed by Sir Giles Gilbert Scott and the engineer, H. F. Nolans, in 1939 was not completed until 1945, and is the most perfect fusion of architecture and engineering. It crosses the river in five great

Waterloo Bridge

bounds like some sleek animal and offers a triumphant finale to the rejuvenation of the South Bank area. Immediately to the east of the bridge is the National Theatre, a complex building containing three different theatres, as well as all the services required for the production of plays selected from an immensely varied range and acted by one of the finest repertory companies in the world. With its widely projecting balconies and its spacious courtyards at different levels, the National Theatre is not an easy building to come to terms with, at first. Its forms have a certain aggression and the surface treatment of the walls, treated in much the same way as those of the Hayward building and the Queen Elizabeth Hall, does little, particularly on sunless days, to dispel this fortress-like impression. But this is a superficial judgement.

Denis Lasdun's design is very much dependent on people to make it come alive, and visitors to the National certainly take full advantage of all the facilities he has provided for their use, especially in the afternoons and evenings. Its contemporary, the Georges Pompidou Centre in Paris, has a vast barrack square in front which Parisians use for all kinds of sideshows and entertainments, but they seem to have little to do with the main building. The National Theatre, by comparison, is so designed that the various activities seem to be an integral part of the whole complex, both in the open air and inside the building. On a fine day one might find Morris Men dancing, children of all ages flying kites, or perhaps a puppet show, a rock or jazz group, or even an open air rehearsal by members of the repertory companies of the plays about to be seen on one of the stages within. The National Theatre is thus not just a series of buildings for the

The National Theatre

469

production of plays, but an exhilarating centre for all kinds of experiences.

There are three theatres operating inside this vast building. The largest is the Olivier Theatre, which seats 1160 people. It derives its name from that of the great actor, Sir Laurence Olivier, the first director of the National Theatre when it was housed at the Old Vic, from 1963 to 1976. The Lyttleton Theatre is somewhat smaller, providing seats for 890 people; it is named after Oliver Lyttleton, Lord Chandos, the first chairman of the theatre from 1962 to 1971, whose parents were also ardent campaigners for the formation of a national theatre for many years. The smallest of the three theatres is the Cottesloe Theatre, which seats only about 400 people, but is probably the most flexible of all three – a real workshop theatre. Lord Cottesloe is a former chairman of the Arts Council and a chairman of the South Bank Board, the body responsible for the building of the National Theatre.

Unlike so many theatres which have their scenery, costumes, props, etc. made away from the actual premises, and whose actors and actresses have to rehearse in draughty, grubby church halls, sheds and warehouses, the National Theatre has all its facilities under one roof, and one has only to undertake one of the excellent guided tours of the building to see how much these admirably designed ancillary buildings add to the efficiency and the convenience of the productions. In addition to the rehearsal rooms and workshops behind the stage, there are also excellent facilities for the general public, whether they are attending any of the plays or merely coming to enjoy the building and all it has to offer. There are restaurants, eight bars, bookstalls and cloakrooms, as well as ample wall-space and permanent display cases for the art exhibitions which are such a feature of the extra activities. There are also superb views of London and its river to be enjoyed from the balconies which lead off the floors at different levels.

The Olivier Theatre is built over the main entrance foyer on the ground floor. It has a fan-shaped auditorium but no proscenium arch, nor a safety curtain. By omitting these features it is not being outrageously modern but merely returning to a much older theatrical tradition, for the proscenium arch convention is only 300 years old. Its stage is very flexible and its shape and size can be changed as required. The walls of the auditorium are made of shuttered concrete – an ungracious medium, but acoustically good – and the exposure of the lighting racks and acoustic panels is a modern convention which might be something of a distraction if the settings and the acting were not so compelling.

The Lyttleton Theatre, on the other hand, appears to be much more conventional, with the familiar pattern of seating found in many theatres, although there are no obstructing pillars supporting balconies. A proscenium arch is in use, but it is one which can be readily adjusted so that it can be reduced in width and in height if required. Backstage and in the wings, there are large areas, concealed behind sound-proof doors, where complete stage sets can be built before being slid noiselessly into place when a scene change is required between the acts.

The smaller Cottesloe Theatre is a gloomy rectangular room with spaces which are extremely adaptable for even the most experimental kinds of theatrical productions. Many theatrical experts believe that the secret of the future success of the National Theatre might lie in this galleried garage, for without such a building and the experiments it makes possible, this or any other theatre could easily decline through complacency born of continued success. It is good that an official National Theatre has made room for such a workshop theatre as an integral part of its composition, and it is one characteristic of this complex which makes it one of the most exciting places in London.

One building which does not fit easily into any category can be seen from any of the viewpoints provided by the National Theatre. This is the Post Office Tower near Fitzroy Square, with its entrance in Maple Street. Erected in 1965, this 620-foot-high column, with its great paraboloid saucer-like aerials, is really one vast aerial mast. It provides vital services for the Post Office, for television and for radio, and it also has two viewing galleries – one 475 feet high, the other 10 feet higher – as well as a revolving restaurant which is normally open to the public. It is said that on clear days, Windsor Castle, the Chilterns, the North Downs and a great many other landmarks can be seen from the Post Office Tower. On the edge of Regent's Park there has recently been another remarkable addition to London's skyline – a mosque, which gives a very cosmopolitan aspect to this part of London. To the west one can see the BBC's TV Centre at White City, which can be visited if written permission is obtained first.

To the east, on the northern boundary of the City on London Wall, is another important aspect of modern London – the Barbican. This complex of modern buildings derives its name from the fortified gatehouse which

above, The Post Office Tower
below, The Barbican

used to defend the gate of the medieval City of London in the Cripplegate area. This part of London was very heavily damaged during the Second World War, yet the extent of the devastation was not without some advantages, for not only did the rebuilding present a challenge to a team of young architects, but it exposed much of London's history, hitherto buried beneath a sprawl of run-down and out-of-date buildings. The first area to be rebuilt was to the north – the Golden Lane scheme, named after the family called Goldyng who lived in the area in the thirteenth century. The architects who undertook the whole scheme were the newly formed firm of Chamberlin, Powell and Bon. They accepted the challenge that such an enterprise offered with elation, and something of their verve and freshness still survives in the buildings despite their having been in use since 1962. The scheme included not only various forms of housing, but a school, shops, a pub, and various kinds of recreational facilities, all intended to engender a community feeling. This was so successful that members of the area resented becoming part of the larger Barbican scheme. The original Golden Lane buildings – some twenty years older than the more recent additions – certainly look far lighter and more appealing thean the dour saw-toothed tower blocks which glower over the area. But the overall design of the Barbican is pleasant enough, with open areas of grass and trees and a charming paved piazza just outside the City of London School for Girls which gives value to the restored church of St Giles, Cripplegate, and there is a really splendid view of the newly revealed stretches of the Roman and medieval City Wall. Other fragments are to be found in Noble Street, just beside the modern building designed by Ronald Ward and Partners for the Plaisterers Company, with another substantial stretch just in front of the new hall of the Salters Company – an airy modern building which has a large block of amber-coloured rock salt in the entrance hall, looking remarkably like a piece of abstract sculpture. There is also one other City Company's halls in this area – that of the Ironmongers, built originally in 1924 by S. Tachell, and now tucked neatly into an angle of the Museum of London.

The Barbican scheme is not yet complete – but already there is the nucleus of a great centre of the arts. The new premises of the Guildhall School of Music and Drama have been in use for some time, and there is a great deal of work being directed into the construction of an art gallery, a permanent home for the London Symphony Orchestra, and a special theatre and headquarters for the Royal Shakespeare Company. It is particularly suitable that the latter should find a home in this area, for not only has the Cripplegate Institute offered facilities for the study of drama for many years, but it was a few hundred yards to the north-west of this site in Curtain Road that London had its first theatres, in 1575–6.

The most important building to be erected in this area as part of the Barbican scheme is the new Museum of London – a splendid amalgamation of the contents of the old museum which used to be temporarily housed in Kensington Palace, and those of the Guildhall Museum, now closed. In the new museum, most beautifully and imaginatively displayed, are an incredible range of objects demonstrating the growth of London from a

The Museum of
London

primitive settlement on the banks of the river to the modern city. It is an entrancing museum – a remarkable combination of scholarship and display craftsmanship which produces a vivid survey of London life through the ages, and it would be futile to attempt to do more than indicate the immense range of objects displayed here. There are flint arrow-heads painfully chipped out by some primitive Londoner long before the Roman Conquest brought a sophistication hitherto unseen in this island. There is a dazzling array of Elizabethan jewellery, the famous 'Cheapside Hoard', the stock-in-trade of a Jacobean goldsmith which was found buried beneath the cellar floor of a shop in Cheapside in perfect condition. One of the most popular exhibits of Restoration London, is the working model and panorama of the great fire. In a little darkened room visitors can watch the inexorable progress of the flames as they sweep from Pudding Lane to the east unchecked, destroying more than three-quarters of the city. There is an excellent sound track on which, amid the crackle of the flames and the cries of the fleeing Londoners, the voice of Michael Hordern can be heard reading the account of the fire written in the diary of Samuel Pepys. And one is reminded that on the very site upon which the Barbican is built, there was a great camp of the refugees from that fire, living in makeshift huts and being fed from emergency food kitchens. Another popular exhibit is the Lord Mayor's Coach, resplendent in carving and gold leaf – a huge eighteenth-century vehicle which is brought out of a special exit in the London Museum for the annual Lord Mayor's Show. Exhibits of other aspects of eighteenth-century London include not just the charm of Chippendale furniture, but the grim reality of the condemned cell from Newgate Jail, and so on, through the Victorian period with its little school room, posters of the industrial unrest of what George Bernard Shaw called 'the most villainous page in English history' to the death of Queen Victoria, the emergence of the suffragettes, exhibits from the First World War, and even an air-raid shelter of the Second World War. There is scarcely any aspect of London life which is not represented in the museum, and it makes an admirable starting point for any study of London. It must be remembered, however, that this great city is still a vital and developing organism, and will continue to develop as long as European civilisation lasts.

APPENDIX I *Historical Maps*

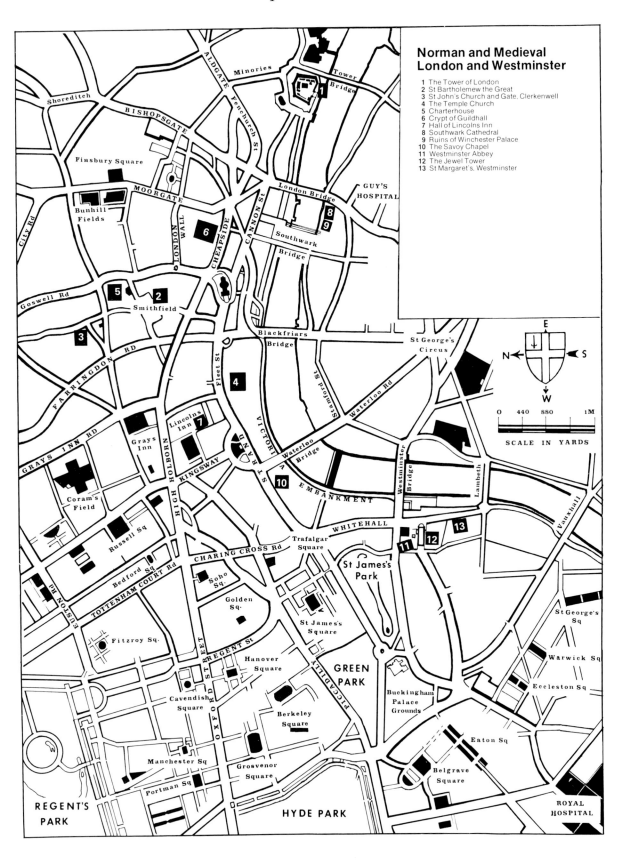

Norman and Medieval London and Westminster

1 The Tower of London
2 St Bartholemew the Great
3 St John's Church and Gate, Clerkenwell
4 The Temple Church
5 Charterhouse
6 Crypt of Guildhall
7 Hall of Lincolns Inn
8 Southwark Cathedral
9 Ruins of Winchester Palace
10 The Savoy Chapel
11 Westminster Abbey
12 The Jewel Tower
13 St Margaret's, Westminster

SCALE IN YARDS
0   440   880   1M

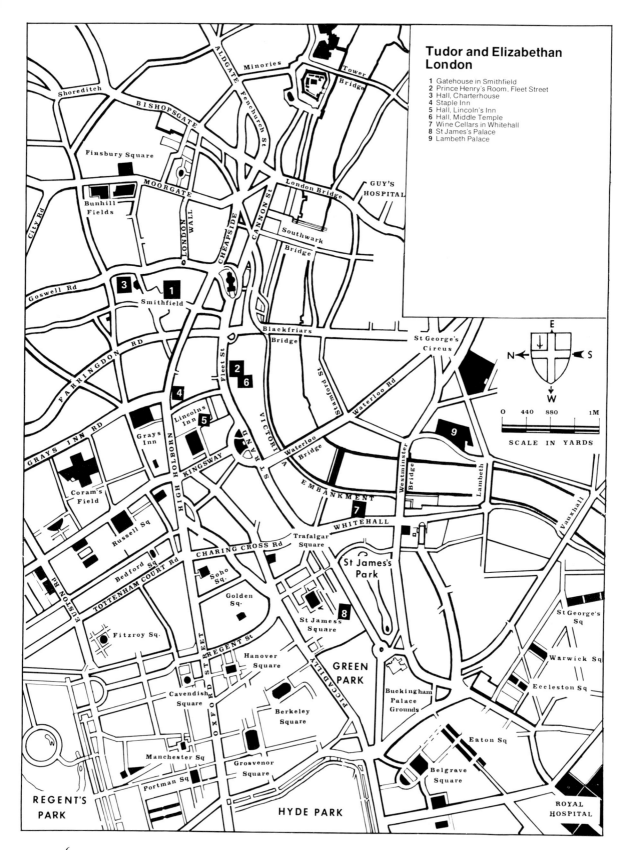

Tudor and Elizabethan London

1 Gatehouse in Smithfield
2 Prince Henry's Room, Fleet Street
3 Hall, Charterhouse
4 Staple Inn
5 Hall, Lincoln's Inn
6 Hall, Middle Temple
7 Wine Cellars in Whitehall
8 St James's Palace
9 Lambeth Palace

SCALE IN YARDS

0   440   880   1M

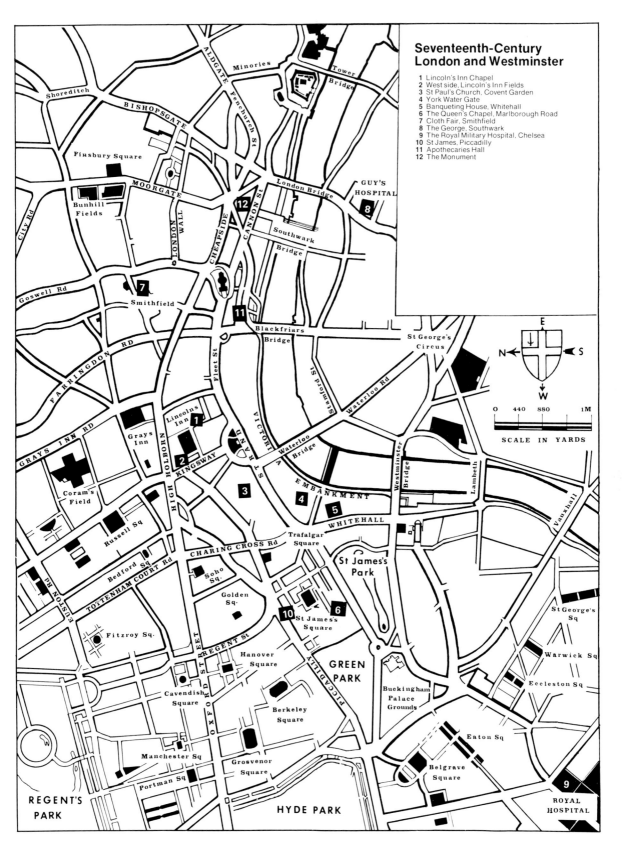

**Seventeenth-Century
London and Westminster**

1 Lincoln's Inn Chapel
2 West side, Lincoln's Inn Fields
3 St Paul's Church, Covent Garden
4 York Water Gate
5 Banqueting House, Whitehall
6 The Queen's Chapel, Marlborough Road
7 Cloth Fair, Smithfield
8 The George, Southwark
9 The Royal Military Hospital, Chelsea
10 St James, Piccadilly
11 Apothecaries Hall
12 The Monument

SCALE IN YARDS

0   440   880   1M

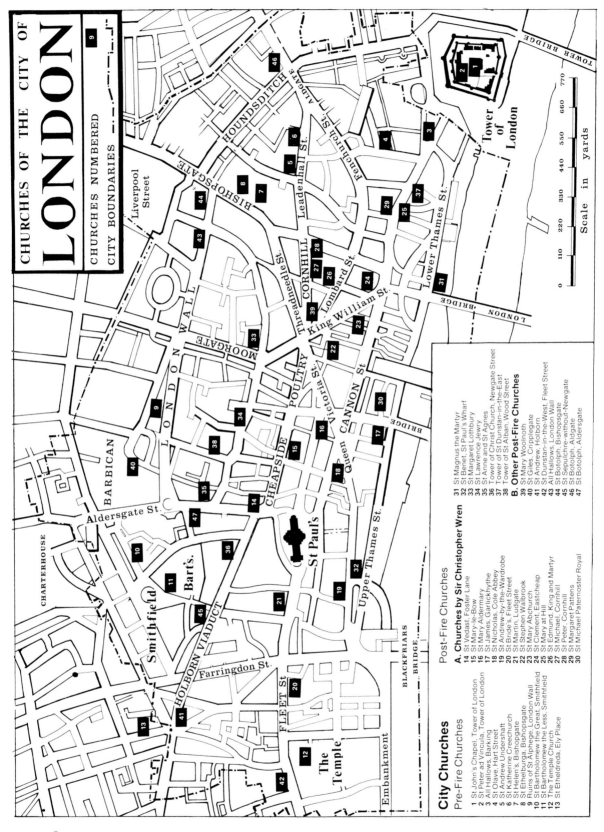

CHURCHES OF THE CITY OF LONDON

LONDON

☐ 9

CHURCHES NUMBERED ■
CITY BOUNDARIES ━·━·━

TOWER BRIDGE

Tower of London

Scale in yards

0 110 220 330 440 550 660 770

City Churches

Pre-Fire Churches

1 St John's Chapel, Tower of London
2 St Peter ad Vincula, Tower of London
3 All Hallows, Barking
4 St Olave, Hart Street
5 St Andrew Undershaft
6 St Katherine Creechurch
7 St Helen's, Bishopsgate
8 St Ethelburga, Bishopsgate
9 Ruins of St Alphege, London Wall
10 St Bartholomew the Great, Smithfield
11 St Bartholomew the Less, Smithfield
12 The Temple Church
13 St Etheldreda, Ely Place

Post-Fire Churches

A. Churches by Sir Christopher Wren

14 St Vedast, Foster Lane
15 St Mary-le-Bow
16 St Mary Aldermary
17 St James, Garlickhythe
18 St Nicholas, Cole Abbey
19 St Andrew-by-the-Wardrobe
20 St Bride's, Fleet Street
21 St Martin, Ludgate
22 St Stephen Walbrook
23 St Mary Abchurch
24 St Clement, Eastcheap
25 St Mary at Hill
26 St Edmund, King and Martyr
27 St Michael, Cornhill
28 St Peter, Cornhill
29 St Margaret Pattens
30 St Michael Paternoster Royal

31 St Magnus the Martyr
32 St Benet, St Paul's Wharf
33 St Margaret Lothbury
34 St Lawrence Jewry
35 St Anne and St Agnes
36 Tower of Christ Church, Newgate Street
37 Tower of St Dunstan-in-the-East
38 Tower of St Alban, Wood Street

B. Other Post-Fire Churches

39 St Mary Woolnoth
40 St Giles, Cripplegate
41 St Andrew, Holborn
42 St Dunstan-in-the-West, Fleet Street
43 All Hallows, London Wall
44 St Botolph, Bishopsgate
45 St Sepulchre-without-Newgate
46 St Botolph, Aldgate
47 St Botolph, Aldersgate

478

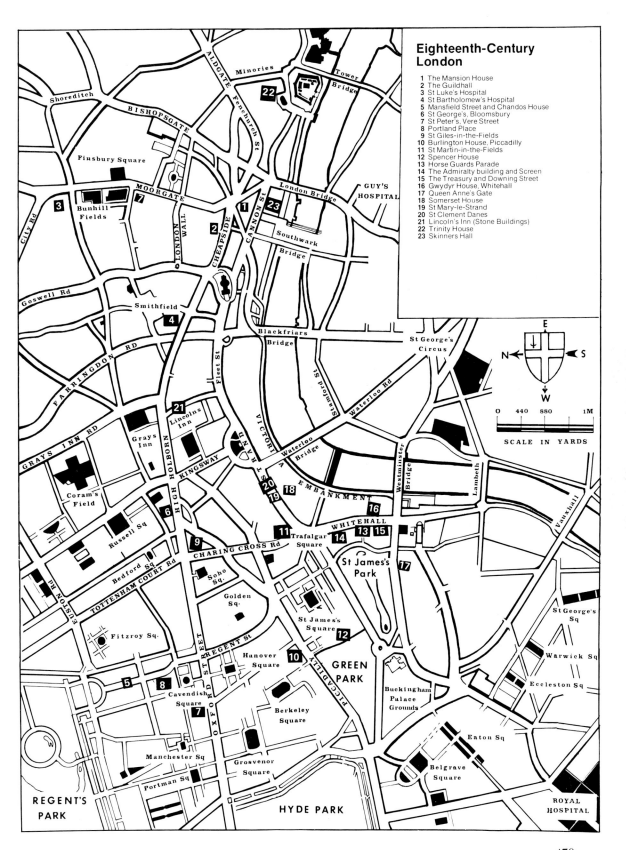

Eighteenth-Century London

1 The Mansion House
2 The Guildhall
3 St Luke's Hospital
4 St Bartholomew's Hospital
5 Mansfield Street and Chandos House
6 St George's, Bloomsbury
7 St Peter's, Vere Street
8 Portland Place
9 St Giles-in-the-Fields
10 Burlington House, Piccadilly
11 St Martin-in-the-Fields
12 Spencer House
13 Horse Guards Parade
14 The Admiralty building and Screen
15 The Treasury and Downing Street
16 Gwydyr House, Whitehall
17 Queen Anne's Gate
18 Somerset House
19 St Mary-le-Strand
20 St Clement Danes
21 Lincoln's Inn (Stone Buildings)
22 Trinity House
23 Skinners Hall

SCALE IN YARDS

0   440   880   1M

479

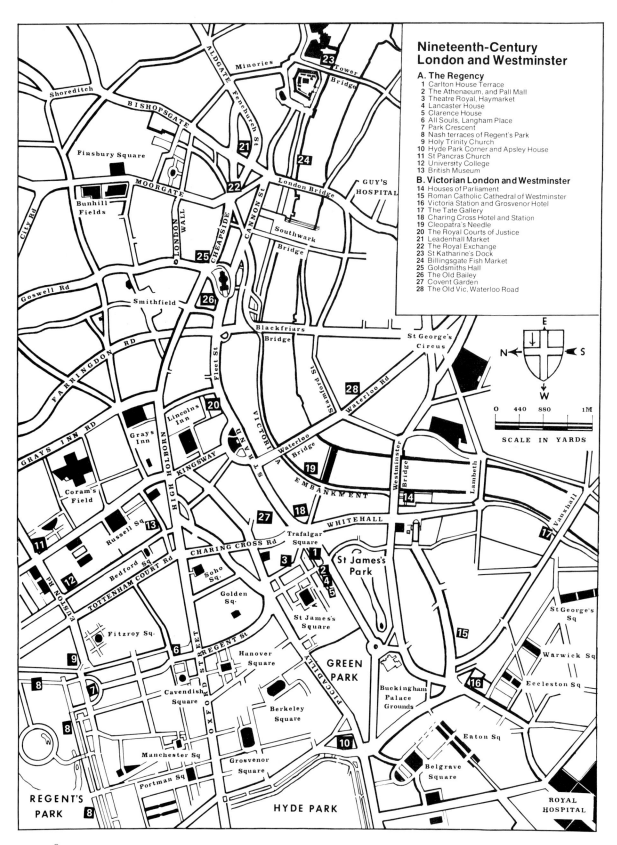

Nineteenth-Century London and Westminster

A. The Regency
1 Carlton House Terrace
2 The Athenaeum, and Pall Mall
3 Theatre Royal, Haymarket
4 Lancaster House
5 Clarence House
6 All Souls, Langham Place
7 Park Crescent
8 Nash terraces of Regent's Park
9 Holy Trinity Church
10 Hyde Park Corner and Apsley House
11 St Pancras Church
12 University College
13 British Museum

B. Victorian London and Westminster
14 Houses of Parliament
15 Roman Catholic Cathedral of Westminster
16 Victoria Station and Grosvenor Hotel
17 The Tate Gallery
18 Charing Cross Hotel and Station
19 Cleopatra's Needle
20 The Royal Courts of Justice
21 Leadenhall Market
22 The Royal Exchange
23 St Katharine's Dock
24 Billingsgate Fish Market
25 Goldsmiths Hall
26 The Old Bailey
27 Covent Garden
28 The Old Vic, Waterloo Road

SCALE IN YARDS
0 440 880 1M

APPENDIX II

The Origins of some Street Names

Aldersgate   Now a street, it was originally the name of a gate built by a Saxon named Aldred – hence Aldredsgate, and later Aldrichgate. The gate was demolished in 1761.

Aldgate   One of the four original city gates. The name is derived from the Saxon word 'aelgate', meaning 'free gate' or open to all.

Barbican   The Barbican was one of the outer defences of Roman London, and was built slightly north of the modern street which bears its name. 'Barbicana' means a watchtower, but it also implies a well fortified entrance to a castle or city.

Bath House   Formerly the town residence of the Bishops of Bath, and later confiscated and acquired by the Earl of Arundel who renamed it Arundel House.

Bevis Marks   The name is a corruption of 'Buries Marks', being the mark or site of a mansion which belonged to the abbots of Bury St Edmunds.

Billingsgate   The name is derived from that of a mythical king, Belin. This area has been associated with the sale of fish for hundreds of years, and in the Middle Ages it was a general wharf for small trading vessels. It is notable for its fresh fish and foul language.

Billiter Street   The medieval word for bell-founder was 'belzeter'. Bell-founders were known to have been concentrated in this street at one time.

Bishopsgate   It is suggested that this derives its name from a Saxon bishop named Erkenwald who levied a toll of one piece of wood from each cartload using the gate. Signs of other gates have been found on this site; the last Bishopsgate was demolished in 1760.

Bow Lane   Formerly called 'Hosier Lane' after the trade carried on there, its present name comes from the 'bow' of St Mary-le-Bow church (so named because of its arches or 'bows').

Bread Street   A decree issued by Edward I in 1302 forbade bakers to sell bread from their houses, but only from a bread market held in this street.

Bucklesbury   This street derives its name from that of an Italian family, Buckerel, who settled in this area during the thirteenth century. During the sixteenth and seventeenth centuries it became the centre of trade for druggists, grocers and herbalists.

Camomile Street   During the Middle Ages there was a camomile-covered piece of wasteland here where the herb was gathered to be sold in the Fenchurch and Gracechurch markets.

Candlewick Ward   The ward named after candle-makers – these tradesmen gave their name to the street known as *Cannon Street* since 1666.

(Candle-making was then an important trade due to the enormous demand for home and church use.)

Cannon Street   This has nothing to do with weapons. It appears in twelfth-century records as 'Candelwrichstrete', a little later as 'Candelwrit-estrate', in the reign of Henry VII as 'Canwikstrete', in Queen Elizabeth's reign as 'Canninge Street', and finally in Leake's map of 1666 as 'Cannon Street'.

Carlisle House   The town residence of the Bishops of Carlisle, later taken over to become Bedford House and then Worcester House.

Charterhouse Street   The Carthusian Priory or Charterhouse was built here in 1371 over the burial site of some 50,000 victims of the Black Death of 1348. The Carthusians, who defied Henry VIII at the time of the Reformation, were treated with appalling cruelty before execution, and their confiscated lands were taken over by Sir Edward North. In 1611 his house was acquired by Thomas Sutton, who founded Charterhouse School. It stood here until 1872, when it moved to its present site in Surrey.

Cheapside   A derivation of the Saxon world 'ceap' – to sell or barter. This street has been the main market of the City from its earliest history, but was once called 'Westcheap' to distinguish it from 'Eastcheap', a market near London Bridge. *Poultry* was the area of the market in Cheapside in which poultry was sold.

Clerkenwell   This means 'the well of the clerks', the clerks being those of the priory of St John of Jerusalem. As late as 1720, the water from this well was prized for its quality by John Strype, the historian.

Clink Street   Although 'being in clink' is a common colloquialism for being in prison, the derivation of the word 'clink' is obscure. One reasonable explanation may be its association with the Scottish 'to clink up', meaning 'to seize forcibly'.

Cordwainers Ward   The Cordwainers were workers in Spanish leather from Cordoba, but later the term was particularly applied to shoemakers.

Covent Garden   Originally 'Convent Garden' – land owned by the abbots of Westminster where produce for the monastery was grown. After the Reformation it passed into the hands of the Bedford family.

Cripplegate   Oddly enough, this gate has no connection with cripples. The Saxons called any tunnel-like entrance a 'crepful'.

Crutched Friars   The name is derived from the 'crutched' or 'crossed' friars, who were distinguished by the cross they wore on the back of their robes. This convent, founded by Ralph Hosier and William Sabernes, was just within the City walls.

Dowgate   Possibly a corruption of 'Downgate', as it was here that the main stream of the river Walbrook flowed into the Thames.

Duke's Place   The Duke in question is Thomas Howard, Duke of Norfolk, whose house was on this site.

Durham House   The town house of the bishops of Durham was on the site later occupied by the eighteenth-century Adelphi.

Ely Place   Named after John de Kirby, Bishop of Ely in 1286, who built a town house in this area, which remained part of the inheritance of the

Bishops of Ely until the end of the sixteenth century when much of the land was taken over by Sir Christopher Hatton. (There is still a Kirby Street in this area.)

Exeter House   Formerly the town house of the Bishops of Exeter, the estate was taken over the Earl of Essex and named Essex House.

Fenchurch Street   Originally 'Faenum Street', after the Latin word for hay, as a haymarket used to be held here.

Fetter Lane   A misleading name, since it has no connection with either manacles or fetters. It is derived from the French word '*fewtor*', meaning a layabout, and this is apparently where many congregated.

Giltspur Street   One of the streets along which, during the Middle Ages, knights, splendidly equipped and mounted, rode to the tournaments held in Smithfield.

Godliman Street   This could originally have been Godalming Street, so named by City shoemakers in honour of the colony of leather-workers occupying the Surrey town in the sixteenth century.

Gracechurch Street   A corruption of 'Grasschurch Street' after the grass or herb market which was held here during the Middle Ages.

Gresham Street   Named after Sir Thomas Gresham, one of Queen Elizabeth's most influential financial advisers, and the builder of the first Royal Exchange.

Hart Street   Fragments of church plate from an earlier church on this site were engraved with decorations consisting of tiny hearts. From this decoration it was concluded that the heart was the original emblem of the church, and that the street derived its name from this.

Hatton Garden   Named after Sir Christopher Hatton, Lord Chancellor to Queen Elizabeth I, who had orchards and other land in this area. (Hence Vine Street, Plum Tree Court and Saffron Hill.)

Holborn Circus   The original name of a tributary of the River Fleet was 'Hol-burne'. Holborn Circus is a Victorian production – hence the statue of Prince Albert in the centre of the road.

Houndsditch   The name is probably derived from the ditch which encircled the City walls, into which dead dogs and other filth found its way.

Jewry   The area previously occupied by the medieval Jewish community.

Leadenhall Market   A mansion with a lead-covered roof was erected in this area in 1309 by Sir Hugh Neville, and nicknamed 'Leaden Hall'.

Liverpool Street   Originally the site of the famous hospital for the insane, Bethlehem Hospital or 'Bedlam', the street was name after Lord Liverpool, Prime Minister in 1829. Later, Bedlam was moved to Moorgate, then, in 1812, to Southwark (on a site now occupied by the Imperial War Museum).

Lock Hospital   'Lock' is a corruption of the word 'loque', meaning rag.

Lombard Street   Named after the Italian family of Lombard or Longoboards who took over the rôle of financiers after the expulsion of the Jews by Edward I in 1290.

Ludgate   A gate at the base of the most westerly hill guarding the bridge over the River Fleet. The name is derived from that of King Lud – a monarch of very doubtful authenticity.

Mansion House   The residence of the Lord Mayor of London during his year of office. This imposing building was designed by George Dance the Elder and erected between 1739–53 on the site of the former Stocks Market and the churchyard of St Mary Woolchurch. (The church was destroyed in the great fire.)

Mark Lane   Actually 'Mart' or 'Market' Lane. Edward IV granted this area to the basketmakers for their marketplace.

Queenhithe   This apparently derives its name from Queen Adelaide of Louvain, wife of Henry I, in whose possession it was during the twelfth century. Later it was leased to the citizens of London at a farm rent of £50. It is also associated with Henry II's queen, Eleanor of Aquitaine.

Shoreditch   This was known as 'Shoreditch' in 1148, and 'Schoreditch' in 1236, so the name may come from the 'shore' or 'sor' – a sewer which existed in this area, near Hackney.

Sloane Street   Named after the great Irish physician and scientist, Sir Hans Sloane, who bought the manor of Chelsea in 1712, and founded the Botanical Gardens in 1721.

Smithfield   Literally, 'smooth field'.

Vintry Ward   The ward or district peculiar to vintners or those connected with the preparation or selling of wine. Because of the importing of wine, it was conveniently situated by the riverside, just west of the Customs House and quays.

Walbrook   Now a street, but originally the name of a small river which rose in Finsbury Marsh and later joined the River Thames. The Wallbrook was the main water supply for the first Roman settlement, entering the City by iron culverts in the foundations of the Roman Wall just to the west of All Hallows Church.

Watling Street   Originally the Saxon 'Atheling' Street, meaning noble. There is still a short stretch of Watling Street just south of St Paul's Cathedral, and a Watling Avenue in the Edgware district. Outside London, Watling Street is one of the major trunk roads.

Bibliography

Austen, Jane, *Northanger Abbey*
BBC Publications, *The Spirit of the Age*, 1975
Besant, Walter, *London*, Chatto & Windus, 1904
Boswell, J., *Life of Johnson*, Everyman
Briggs, A., *Victorian People: A Reassessment of Persons and Themes, 1851–67*, Penguin, 1970
Bryant, A., *The Age of Elegance, 1812–1822*, Collins, 1975
Burne, R. V. H., *The Monks of Chester*, S.P.C.K.
Byrne, M. S. and C., *Elizabethan Life in Town & Country*, University Paperbacks
Clark, K., *Gothic Revival*, John Murray, 1974
Clunn, H., *The Face of London*, Spring Books
Coghill, N., *The Canterbury Tales*, Penguin Classics
Crossley, F. H., *The English Abbey*, Batsford
Dalzell, W. R., *Architecture the Indispensable Art*, Michael Joseph
Dalzell, W. R., *Architecture – a little Colour Guide*, P. Hamlyn
Dutton, R., *The English Country House*
Evelyn, J., *The Diaries of J. Evelyn*, Everyman
Hammond, J. L. and B., *The Black Age*, Pelican
Hardwick, M. and M., *Dickens's England*, J. M. Dent
Harvey, J., *Gothic England*, Batsford
Hennessey, John Pope, *Charles Dickens*, Book Club
Hitchcock, H. R., *Architecture, 19th and 20th centuries*, Pelican History of Art
Irving, Washington, *Sketchbook of Geoffrey Crayon, Gent.*, Everyman, 1968
Jackson, Alan A., *London's Local Railways*, David and Charles, 1978
Jarrett, D., *England in the Age of Hogarth*, Hart Davis, 1974
Jordan-Furneaux, *Victorian Architecture*, Pelican
Kidson, Murray and Thompson, *History of English Architecture*, Pelican
Lees, Milne J., *Tudor Renaissance*, Batsford
Lees, Milne J., *The Age of Adam*, Batsford
Lloyd, N., *History of the English House*, Architectural Press, 1975
Massingham, H. and P., *The London Anthology*, Spey Books
Merrifield, R., *The Roman City of London*, Edward Benn, 1965
Mitchell, R. J. and Leys, M. D. R., *A History of London Life*, Pelican
Perkin, Harold, *The Age of the Railway*, Panther History, 1970
Pepys, Samuel, *The Diary of Samuel Pepys*, Everyman
Pevsner, N., *Buildings of England*, Pelican
Pilcher, D., *The Regency Style*, Batsford
Plumb, J. H., *The First Four Georges*, Collins
Power, E., *Medieval People*, Pelican
Quennell, P., *Hogarths Progress*
Sitwell, S., *British Craftsmen and Designers*, Batsford
Summerson, J., *Architecture in Britain, 1530–1830*, Pelican, 1970
Summerson, J., *Georgian London*, Barrie and Jenkins, 1978
Thackeray, W. M., *Vanity Fair*
Trevelyan, G. M, *English Social History*, Penguin, 1970
Turnor, R., *19th Century Architecture in Britain*, Batsford
Thornburg, Walter, *Old and New London*, Cassell, 1897
Thornburg, Walter, *Haunted London* (Edited by Edward Watford), Chatto & Windus, 1880
Webb, G., *Architecture in Britain in the Middle Ages*, Pelican
Wheatley, H. B., *London Past and Present*, 1891
Whinney, M., *Wren*, Thames & Hudson

Index